Hispanic American Religious Cultures

Selected titles in ABC-CLIO's **American Religious Cultures** series

African American Religious Cultures
Anthony B. Pinn, Editor

Asian American Religious Cultures
Fumitaka Matsuoka and Jane Naomi Iwamura, Editors

Hispanic American Religious Cultures
Miguel A. De La Torre, Editor

Hispanic American Religious Cultures

VOLUME 2: N–Y, ESSAYS

Miguel A. De La Torre, Editor

A B C CLIO

Santa Barbara, California • Denver, Colorado • Oxford, England

Library of Congress Cataloging-in-Publication Data

Hispanic American religious cultures /
  Miguel A. De La Torre, editor.
    p. cm. – (American religious cultures)
  Includes bibliographical references and index.
  ISBN 978–1–59884–139–8 (hardcopy : alk. paper) – ISBN 978–1–59884–140–4 (ebook)
1. Hispanic Americans–Religion–Encyclopedias. I. De La Torre, Miguel A.
BL2525.H57   2009
200.89'68073—dc22   2009012661

13 12 11 10 9   1 2 3 4 5

This book is also available on the World Wide Web as an eBook.
Visit www.abc-clio.com for details.

ABC-CLIO, LLC
130 Cremona Drive, P.O. Box 1911
Santa Barbara, California 93116-1911

This book is printed on acid-free paper ∞

Manufactured in the United States of America

To the millions of Hispanic congregations throughout the United States, accept this encyclopedia as our way of worshipping the Creator with all of our minds.

Contents

VOLUME 2

PART 2 ESSAYS

NATIVE AMERICANS

While the term "Native Americans" commonly refers to the numerous indigenous communities located in the United States, here it also refers to the various indigenous peoples in Central and South America. Many of these groups display a diverse array of cultural and religious practices that preserve direct continuity with the primal religions and cultures of their ancestors. For five centuries, these groups have been in direct contact, clash, and interaction with the dominant *mestizo* culture and local versions of Christianity. These are not dead religious traditions, but in many places represent dynamic thriving communities in which their religious activities, customs, rituals, and traditions are part of the very life of their communities.

The nations of Native Americans are not one homogeneous large group dispersed throughout the continent. Although no consensus exists as to how many ethnic and cultural groups presently populate the Americas, Alcide Dessalines D'Orbigny, in his *El hombre americano: Atlas e índice alfabético* listed over 250 different ethnocultural and religious groups. While Aztecs, Maya, and Inca, along with their descendants, have dominated the landscape, a greater diversity of indigenous communities exists, which cannot be reduced to just these three ancient civilizations. Native American nations are identified by their ethnocultural and religious composition, as well as by the regions they inhabit. When these indigenous nations encountered Europeans, they influenced, impacted, and contributed to the transformation of European versions of Christianity. These influences can be found throughout Latin America and among U.S. Latina/os.

Prior to the Encounter

Marked ethnic, cultural, territorial, and religious differences among some of the indigenous nations have historically led to violent encounters. For example, the Inca Garcilaso de la Vega writes that the

PEYOTE

Peyote (from Nahuatl *peyotl*) is a cactus native to southern Texas and northern Mexico, which many U.S. and Mexican Indians ritually consume as sacred medicine. Peyote contains mescaline, a chemical producing altered states of consciousness that can include visions. Although peyote is a controlled substance under U.S. and Mexican law, the state of Texas allows it to be harvested and sold to American Indians, a carefully regulated business historically led by Spanish-surnamed families. Mexican Indians have used peyote for thousands of years; the Huichols still make an annual 300-mile pilgrimage to peyote grounds near San Luis Potosí. Ritual peyote use, sometimes syncretized with Christian symbols, became established on U.S. Indian reservations beginning in the 1880s and was incorporated in 1918 as the Native American Church. Peruvian American Carlos Castaneda helped popularize peyote among the spiritual counterculture of the 1960s–1970s. In a widely criticized 1990 ruling, *Oregon v. Smith*, the U.S. Supreme Court denied First Amendment protection to peyotists, but subsequent legislation and court rulings in both the United States and Mexico have expanded protection for religious peyote use. While the Mexican government safeguards Huichol peyote grounds, peyote supplies in Texas are threatened by overharvesting and expanded ranching and mining.

—JCD

Inca people tended to function like an empire, invading the neighboring tribes, and assimilating them under the assumption that they were improving their existence. For different reasons, the Mexica people of the plains of central Mexico were also characterized as a military people, warring with neighboring tribes. Eventually, these tribes helped the Spaniards defeat the Mexica. While war was a part of some of these indigenous communities, it was considered a way for tribe members to demonstrate their bravery. In some cases, like the Arauca people of Chile, the purpose was not to destroy the opponent's warriors or village but to improve one's military skills. In the same way, there were other tribes, like the Taínos of the Caribbean, who promoted peace.

For indigenous peoples, religion is considered integral to their lives and cultures. Discussions of religious practices, customs, or beliefs are interconnected with all other aspects of life. According to their worldview (cosmovision), the entire universe originated from and is permeated by sacred energies that appear in many forms, as diverse natural beings, and through determining events. They conceive life holistically rather than the Western European individualistic worldview.

One commonality among indigenous peoples is their understanding of a unique powerful force that sustains all of life. This is identified by various names by different groups: *Kukulkan* (Quiche), *Pachacamac* and *Quollana Amo* (Quechua, Aymara), and more generally *The Great Mysterious*. These names are not equivalent to the Christian notion of God. The use of the contemporary *The Great Spirit* already displays a

Felipe Martinez uses an eagle feather to fan copal smoke at a banner with an image of the Virgin of Guadalupe, the patron saint of Mexico, during a Native American cleansing ceremony on March 6, 2006. Martinez is one of twelve day laborers on a 3,000-mile, two-month run from Santa Monica, California, to New York City to raise awareness of discrimination faced by undocumented immigrants. (Getty Images)

Christian influence attempting to reduce the reality of the sacred force into a being. For indigenous communities there is no radical dichotomy between the spiritual and material worlds. *The Great Mysterious* is not understood as an entity separate from the rest of creation, but as one with the totality of all that is, permeating all of life and reality. Indeed, for the indigenous communities the spiritual world and the material world are so interconnected that one's lifestyle and experiences reach out to both dimensions.

The Encounter

In 1492 the Spanish (and Portuguese) arrived at what today we call the Americas. According to Columbus's diary they first landed in the islands of the Caribbean (Cuba and Santo Domingo). On the continent, their invasion was systematic. They targeted the places with the largest concentration of natives: Hernán Cortéz in México, Francisco Pizarro in Perú, Diego de Alvarado among the Mayas of Guatemala, and Pedro Arias de Ávila in Nicaragua. Their goals were to ensure the submission of the indigenous peoples to the Spanish crown, the collection of gold and riches, and the Christianization of the inhabitants.

Clashes between the Spanish and the Natives ensued. In his *Short Account of the Destruction of the Indies* Bartolomé

POPOL VUH

The Popol Vuh (or *Popol Wuj*, "Council Book") is a collection of Maya myths, one of the few indigenous religious texts not destroyed during the Spanish Conquest. The surviving text was composed in Guatemala in the K'iche' language, written in Roman script during the 1550s, based on a hieroglyphic version that has not survived. The book recounts the creation of the world and of human beings, the exploits of the twin gods Hunahpu and Xbalanque, and the early migrations and wars of the K'iche'. Genealogies of their rulers down to the Spanish Conquest are also recorded. Since the 1990s, Maya Christians influenced by inculturation theology have reclaimed the Popol Vuh as scripture, reading it alongside the Bible in settings such as the Mass. Theosophists have claimed that the Popol Vuh contains parallels to their own doctrines; Mormons have made analogous claims (among them Allen J. Christenson, who has published academic translations of the Popol Vuh). More loosely, Maya cosmology has inspired New Age authors Daniel Pinchbeck and Mexican American José Argüelles.

—JCD

de Las Casas records how the Caribbean natives were decimated. With the superior weaponry and horses of the Spanish the various indigenous tribes of the continent did not fair better. Millions of indigenous peoples died in battle, thousands of others were tortured and forced to accept Christianity, and countless others died because of diseases brought by the Europeans for which the natives did not have the immunity.

As the clashes intensified, the worst victims of the Spanish invasion became the indigenous women. Thousands were violently abused and raped, and thousands of others, as spoils of war, were taken as concubines by the Spanish. As a result many mixed children were born. Labeled mestizo/as, these children were rejected by the Spanish people, the Catholic Church, and the indigenous. Spanish colonial society rejected them because of their mixed background. They were considered contaminated because of their indigenous blood. Among the Christian missionaries, many abhorred their presence because they thought that

mestizos embodied the libertine ways of the Spanish males and the sexual insatiability of indigenous women. Originally the Spanish crown encouraged marriages between noble Spanish and indigenous royal families, but most mestizo/as carried the stigma of illegitimacy because they were born out of wedlock. The indigenous peoples saw the mestizo/as as a reminder of their experience of rape and despoliation. This was exacerbated as many mestizos adopted their Spanish fathers' behavior by raping indigenous women, as narrated by Guamán Poma de Ayala.

Over time, the mestizo/as grew in number, and those who were children of noble Spaniards integrated Spanish colonial societies. Most mestizo/as, however, remained in an ambiguous existence from which they carved their own social space and identity as mixed people. The colonial caste societies started to crumble and turned into *pigmentocracies*, so many light skin mestizo/as claimed to be Spanish and denied their indigenous ancestry. By the time of the wars of independence, at the beginning of the nineteenth century, mestizo/as had become the dominant ethnocultural group. They, along with the few *criollos* remaining, were the protagonist in constructing the postindependence societies and nations imitating the European-Spanish cultural and religious world. In these new societies, indigenous and African peoples were sentenced to the margins. Through policies of Spanish literacy programs, systematic military invasions, and dispossession of lands, as well as economic pressures, the indigenous peoples were persecuted and condemned to assimilate the mestizo cultures and to remain on the fringes of the mestizo social fabric.

A Continuous Struggle

For five centuries the indigenous peoples of the Americas have struggled to survive and preserve their cultural and religious heritage. Their efforts received a new impetus as new movements emerged at the beginning of the twentieth century. Also, with the birth of liberation theologies and the impact of the Second Vatican Council in the 1960s, the attitude of the Catholic Church has changed toward indigenous religious traditions and practices. They were once considered an expression of devil worship, but now there are movements attempting to reclaim indigenous traditions as legitimate expressions of faith. This is also the case among some mainline denominations, i.e., the Anglicans and Presbyterians.

Reclaiming their cultures and religious practices are complemented with civil activism by which the indigenous peoples struggle for their rights as citizens, for the preservation of their lands and territories, and for their place within the social fabric of the Americas. The mobilization and creation of numerous indigenous movements, alliances, and coalitions resist the forces of global capitalism while proposing alternative ways to construct a better world. One example of the collective effort of these communities is the recent *Encuentro de Pueblos Indigenas de las Americas* (Encounter of the Indigenous Peoples of the Americas), which took place in Sonora, Mexico, October 11–14, 2007. Many indigenous communities continue their struggle to preserve their cultures and religions after migrating. They reconstruct their communities in new geographical regions. This is exemplified by the *Quiche* communities in Los Angeles, the Jacaltenango Maya in Jupiter, Florida, or the various indigenous seasonal workers that migrate into the United States to work the fields.

Influencing Latino/a Religiosity

The clash between indigenous peoples and the European conquistadors changed both the indigenous religions and European version of Christianity in fundamental ways. The result of these changes is seen today in various ways among Hispanics. The imposition of Christianity upon indigenous peoples gave birth to extraordinarily creative new religious expressions and symbols that incorporated both indigenous and Christian elements. European versions of Christianity and its cultures were transformed in profound and irreversible ways as demonstrated in the religious symbols and practices of Latina/os.

Negatively understood as syncretistic, these new expressions are specific ways in which the indigenous peoples adopted,

CORN

Corn has historically been the lifeblood of all the Americas. Almost every country in Latin America has its own unique national dish based on corn. Even in the United States, tortillas are the second highest selling packaged bread product—selling at a rate of one tortilla a day for every American. It is estimated that 98 percent of Hispanics eat either corn tamales or corn tortillas every day. The indigenous people who first grew corn regarded it as a sacred crop, as illustrated by ancient rock paintings. It was believed by the Mayan that the deities created humanity out of corn; hence, they came to be known as the "people of corn." They honored corn in its various forms of maturation—as a seed, as a sprouting plant, and as a full-grown plant. Corn served as an appropriate sacrifice to several of the Aztecs' agricultural deities. To this day, Hispanic farmers throughout the Americas sprinkle cornmeal on their fields during the planting season while chanting and praying for a successful crop so that it can provide health to the family and unity for the community.

—MAD

adapted, and reinterpreted Christian elements without fully abandoning their primal inherited religions and practices. The claims that many indigenous peoples have "converted" to Christianity should not be understood as a rejection of their primal religious worldview.

The interweaving of indigenous religious and Christian elements and Christian ones relates very closely to the nonexclusive cumulative quality of indigenous religions. This is what Joseph Epes Brown has termed "Polysynthesis," by which he identifies the ways in which more deities can be added to the indigenous pantheon without disturbing their religious world. This religious openness and the complementary dualistic character of the indigenous religions proves a fertile ground for new religious expression in which Christian symbols are reinterpreted in terms of the indigenous religious world. For example, in Mexico the interconnection between indigenous religious and Christian results partly from the Spanish missionaries' mistranslation of the Nahuatl word

teótl as "god," "saint," or "demon." But the Aztec *teótl* signified a sacred power manifested in natural forms—a rainstorm, a tree, a mountain, or persons of high distinction such as a king, an ancestor, a warrior—or in mysterious or chaotic places. What the Spaniards translated as "god" really referred to a spectrum of hierophanies, which animated their world.

Many of these symbols found their way into the cultural and religious context of Hispanics, pointing to the profound impact of indigenous religious and cultural traditions. What is defined as Hispanic cultural / religious ethos cannot be fully understood apart from the tapestry of indigenous and Spanish (European) religious and cultural elements. This is particularly true of architecture. The legacy of indigenous religions is found in the many basilicas that were built beginning in the sixteenth century in the various regions of the Americas. According to Sergei Gruzinski, as the Spaniards promoted the building of great cathedrals their intention was to build them in the Baroque style. Since they used the labor of the indigenous peoples as the builders, craftsmen, artists, and painters, the style was changed, displaying indigenous religious images and motifs. All of these, he argues, gave birth to what is commonly labeled the "American Baroque" architectural style. Indeed, Otto Morales Benítez, among others, insists that the American Baroque represents a unique way the indigenous and Spanish cultural and religious influences coalesce. The best interpretation of the Baroque is a unique expression of indigenous artistic creativity combined with resistance; refusing to be erased from history, the indigenous peoples left a rich religious and cultural legacy in the creation of sacred spaces.

Because the indigenous religions displayed an operative dualism, it is not surprising to find religious groups applying such dualism to Christianity. For example, for the Poluca and Nahua people of Veracruz, Mexico, God and the Devil are not enemies but brothers. In the lowlands of Chiapas, people have saints aligned with God and with the Devil. Among other groups, the solar god has been replaced by Jesus and the Devil for the master of the animals and of the subterranean world. Among the Mayans, Jesus is frequently depicted as crosseyed. And by the Txotxile and Mixe-Poluca Jesus is described as cross-eyed, with acne, bad body odor, pustules, and covered with flies, which is how the sun god is usually described. More specifically, sites that were traditionally part of the indigenous pantheon have now been reinterpreted as Christian shrines and popular expressions of the Christian faith. We can see this in *El Señor de Quyllur Rit'i* (*Quispicanchi*) located in

Peru, or *El Cristo negro de Esquipulas*, in Guatemala, which continue to attract large numbers of pilgrims throughout Latin America and Latina/os in the United States.

Another aspect of the indigenous religious legacy upon Hispanic religion and culture is the cult to Mary. The strong feminine spirituality in most of the indigenous religious traditions helps explain and understand this rich and complex aspect of Latina/o religious faith expression. In many places, the Earth Mother or the *Pachamama* has been replaced with devotion to Mary. In other places the *Pachamama* is portrayed with Marian overtones. As Diego Irarrázabal states, "Mary has been *Pachamamaized* and the *Pachamama* and its communities have been Marianized."

It would be a mistake to conclude that these are simply contextual expression and appropriations of devotion to Mary the mother of Jesus. Although there are Christian elements in each of the various Marys venerated by the people, a careful analysis of their origins and development reveals that these are the amalgam of indigenous and European religious elements. The various versions of Mary among Latina/o peoples are something entirely new and unique. This helps explain why Virgilio Elizondo refers to Guadalupe as a truly American expression of Mary. To him, the site of her apparition, the mention of flowers and songs, the printed image of Guadalupe on Juan Diego's tilma, and the various indigenous religious elements incorporated in her image demonstrate that she is not a mere contextual adaptation of European Marian devotion.

Guadalupe is not the only unique expression of Mary that has emerged from among the indigenous communities

LA LLORONA

La Llorona, Weeping Woman, is an ancient tale from the indigenous religions of ancient Mexico. *Cihuacoalt*, the earth goddess, wept and cried in the night, while haunting the countryside. A later Mexican oral tradition tells of an indigenous woman, *La Llorona*, who was courted and seduced by a rich Spanish *hidalgo*, nobleman. Together they had two sons, but after several years together he decided to return to Spain and planned to take his sons, while leaving her behind. She became mad with grief, shrieking and wailing and attacking her lover over her loss. In her mania, she took her two sons to the river and drowned them. She then died of grief at the side of the river. When she went to the gates of heaven, she was told she could enter if she brought the souls of her two lost sons. Unable to enter heaven, *La Llorona* continues to roam the countryside weeping and wailing as she frantically looks for her lost children. This tragic legend is sometimes tied with the story of *La Malinche*, the mistress of Cortez, who is considered a traitor to her people since she translated for him aiding his conquest of the Mexican people.

—*TLT*

and that today pervades the Hispanic religious world. Because of migration to the United States, many of these interpretations of Mary have become central to Latina/o religiosity. For example, among Cubans in the United States, *La Virgen de la caridad del cobre* remains a central part of people's devotion to Mary. Other Marian expressions are *María Candelaria, María de la concepción, La Virgen de Cancuc, La Virgen del Carmen*, and *La Virgen del Rosario*. According to Irarrázabal, these and many other Marian expressions exemplify some of the ways in which the Virgin of the Conquest was transformed into an autochthonous symbol as a result of the clash between the Spanish and the indigenous. Many of these various Marian expressions are displayed over the celebration of Easter, as people participate in the religious processions in their local communities. This is another clear example of the ways in which "indigenous Marianism" contributes to Hispanic manifestations of Mary.

Similar to these indigenous Marian expressions, there are also manifestations of Mary containing African religious overtones. Many of these Marian expressions are found in various ways among the Latino/as.

One final element of the indigenous religious impact on Hispanic culture is in the form of festivals or *fiestas*. Aside from their intrinsic cultural value and their tremendous community building power, festivals among Latina/os have deep religious roots, many of which can be connected to indigenous religions and traditions that have now become part of the Hispanic cultural-religious fabric. Festivals are often intrinsically related to the celebration of Patron Saints, many of which originated with the earlier indigenous practices of revering regional deities. These Patron Saint feasts (*Fiestas patronales*) play a central role in entire communities among Hispanics.

Although still containing religious overtones, numerous other festivals reveal the pervasive indigenous influence among Hispanics. The *Baile* (dance) of the *Toro-Venado* among Nicaragüans, and the *Baile de las máscaras* among Guatemalans represent a parody of the Spanish conquistadors. Similarly the festival of *Las Cruces* in New Mexico chronicles the struggles of the indigenous peoples as they confronted the Catholic Spanish conquistadors. The celebration of *la Piñata*, reminds us of the object lessons by which Spanish missionaries instructed the indigenous peoples on how to deal with the Devil. All of these festivals and Patron Saint's Day are colored by autochthonous dances, dishes, customs, and religious practices, many of which are characteristically indigenous in origin.

There are many other popular customs and traditions that Latina/os celebrate, which help them understand the indigenous impact. One of the most popular of these is the *Día de los muertos* (the Day of the Dead), which has intimate connections with indigenous beliefs concerning the afterlife. Other myths worth mentioning are the story of *La Llorona*, *El Cadejo*, and *La Sihuamonta*.

It is in these and many other ways that indigenous religious traditions remain present in Hispanic cultural practices and customs. They continue to shape Hispanic religious experiences with and notions of the divine, their identity as people, and their particular understanding of Land and Church.

Néstor Medina

References and Further Reading

Brown, Joseph Epes. *The Spiritual Legacy of the American Indian* (New York: Crossroads, 1982).

de la Torre López, Arturo E. " 'La más rigurosa secta de nuestra religión': La asociación evangélica de la misión israelita del nuevo pacto universal." *Religiones Andinas*, ed. Manuel M. Marzal (Madrid: Editorial Trotta, 2005).

Espín, Orlando O., and Miguel H. Díaz, eds. *From the Heart of Our People: Latino/a Explorations in Catholic Systematic Theology* (Maryknoll, NY: Orbis Books, 1999).

Irarrázaval, Diego. *Cultura y fe latinoamericanas* (Santiago de Chile: Ediciones Rehue Ltda.; Instituto de Estudios Aymaras, 1994).

López Austin, Alfredo. "Indigenous Mythology from Present-Day Mexico." *Native Religions and Cultures of Central and South America: Anthropology of the Sacred*, ed. Lawrence Eugene Sullivan (New York: Continuum, 2002).

Marzal, Manuel M., ed. "La Religión Quechua actual." *Religiones Andinas*, vol. 4, *Enciclopedia Iberoamericana de Religiones* (Madrid: Editorial Trotta, 2005).

Sullivan, Lawrence Eugene, ed. *Native Religions and Cultures of Central and South America: Anthropology of the Sacred* (New York: Continuum, 2002).

Vecsey, Christopher, ed. *Religion in North America* (Moscow, ID: University of Idaho Press, 1990).

Yujra Mamani, Carlos. *Nuestra cultura nativa es impresionante = Jiwasanakana nayra jakawinakasaxa sarnaqawinakasaxa uraqisanxa musparkañawa* (La Paz, Bolivia: Ediciones Gráficas E.G., 1996).

NEPANTLA

"Nepantla" is a Nahuatl term meaning in the middle, or the middle place. Nahuatl is the language of the Nahuas, the largest indigenous ethnic/cultural group in the central valley of Mexico during the 1500s. It is a living language and is

FLOR Y CANTO

The Spanish phrase "flor y canto" is literally "flower and song," a common Nahuatl diphrasism. A diphrasism is a compound expression like "bread and butter." It is a metaphor expressing an idea or concept by using two words that are adjacent to or complement each other. This diphrasism (in xóchitl in cuícatl) was used by Nahuatl philosophers (Tlamatinime) to refer to poetry, art, and symbolism as getting at the truth of human existence or as speaking truth. It is through flor y canto that humans can encounter the Giver of Life, and at the same time it is the fruit of this encounter. For this reason, the artist is the true theologian. Flor y canto may have been another way of speaking of Quetzalcoatl (feathered serpent). Flor being symbolic of the snake that crawls on the earth from which flowers come and feathers coming from the birds in heaven whose songs we hear. Flowers take the energy of the earth and transform it into beauty; songs lift the listener into heaven. Flor y canto are symbolic of the union of earth and heaven. Flor y canto were also the awaited signs of Quetzalcoatl's return, signs that accompanied the appearances of Coatlaxopeuh (Guadalupe).

—GCG

presently spoken in this region of Mexico. The word "nepantla" is usually attached to nouns in the Nahuatl language. For example, "tlalli" means land, so tlalnepantla means middle of the earth. Translated into the English language, to be "in nepantla" implies to be at the center.

The Dominican missionary, Diego Durán, recorded the use of the term in a sixteenth-century conversation between himself and an Aztec elder. The elder used the term to explain the psychological space that he and his people occupied as a result of the violent imposition of Christianity upon the native peoples of "New Spain." Upon further questioning about his use of the term, the elder explained, "Do not be frightened . . . they believed in God and at the same time keep their ancient customs." In essence, the elder attempted to explain the native's unwillingness to take sides in the religious conquest and their epistemological ability to provide space for

both religions to coexist in harmony, in a middle space, in nepantla, in a neutral space where one does not have power over the other. The elder's worldview was large enough to encompass multiple manifestations of the divine and reveals the tremendous agency at work when one occupies the middle space, nepantla.

Contemporary usage of the term by Latina/o writers, artists, and theologians is often employed to describe the middle space that non-White and mixed-raced persons inhabit on a daily basis. The writings of Chicana cultural theorist, Gloria Anzaldúa, initiated a reexamination of the term in her groundbreaking publication *Borderlands/ La Frontera: The New Mestiza* (1987). For Anzaldúa, straddling borders or spaces occurs "wherever two or more cultures edge each other, where people of different races occupy the same territory, where under, lower, middle and upper classes touch, where the pace between two individuals shrink with intimacy"

(1987, vii). Through her examination of the great tensions confronted by border inhabitants (mestizas and mestizos) who do not meet the standards of White America, Anzaldúa exposed the tensions and confusion of nepantla, but also the great creativity and joy experienced by "neplanteras" who are participating in "the further evolution of humankind" (1987). For Anzaldúa and those she inspired, nepantla is the middle space that, if not understood from a historical, cultural, psychological, physical, and spiritual perspective, can be confusing. But once the forces of colonization and domination are understood, and one's own integrity as a "person of color" is constantly nurtured, then nepantla becomes a site of meaning making and transformation. To be in the middle moves us toward a more whole perspective, one that includes rather than excludes. As Miguel A. De La Torre and Gastón Espinosa write, "Being in the middle does not imply a running away —from or to another place—but rather it describes an attitude, an outlook, a worldview, a state of being in its own right" (2006, 1).

Nepantla differs from the concept of syncretism that refers to the blending of diverse beliefs and practices into new and distinct forms. The term "syncretism" is often used to describe Latin American religions resulting from the European imposition of Christianity upon native religions. Scholars are realizing the limitations of this term as it can easily silence complex historical contexts, power relations, and the "phenomenological distress" (Carrasco 1995, 69) in which syncretic traditions evolved. According to Davíd Carrasco, syncretism "can be useful when viewed as a 'tool for interpretation' rather than a description of social patterns" (1995, 71). As such, he suggests the redesigning of the tool to better understand the dynamics of Latino/a cultures and religions. Redefining syncretism as shared culture, Carrasco illuminates what took place throughout colonial Latin America, in the "contact zone of incomplete and developing forms where the social and symbolic relations were permeated by conflict and loss, coercion and indigenous urging more than adherence" (1995, 78). Syncretism, when understood as shared culture, reveals the agency and ingenuity of the indigenous to transform Christianity for their benefit. For example, a crucifix made of corn husks conjoins the sacrifice of Christ with the sacredness of maize and "the cosmomagical powers stemming from the earth" (1995, 76). Syncretism as shared culture also exemplifies a middle space, and as such holds a place within nepantla, but as Klor de Alva points out, "Nepantlaism should never be confused with syncretism, which is, in both a historical and a psychological sense, the consequence of nepantalism" (cited in León 2004, 27). Nepantla, as a multifaceted psychological and spiritual space, provides for pre-Christian indigenous traditions and syncretic Christianity to coexist, side by side, in mutual harmony and respect. In nepantla, there is room for all. Nepantla provides a place where the indigenous elders and their descendants can survive, rest, and prosper. In the transparency of nepantla, there are no power struggles regarding who holds "the truth."

"Nepantla spirituality" attempts to bridge Christian and "pagan" worldviews for persons seeking to maintain ties to both. For practitioners of Nepantla spirituality, rather then being limited by confusion or ambiguity, they act as subjects in deciding how diverse religious and cultural forces can or cannot work together. Like the native elder of the sixteenth century, they creatively maneuver the boundaries and borders and consciously make choices about what aspects of diverse worldviews nurture the complexity of their spiritual and biological mestizaje, and what for them enables communication with spiritual forces. Within nepantla, Chicana/os and other Latina/os can have the wisdom of both the indigenous and the Christian. For "persons of color" who are products of cultural and biological mestizaje within a legacy of colonization, reconciling the differences and discovering the similarities between Christian and indigenous traditions offers healing. Healing in this context is about bringing forth self-knowledge and historical consciousness so that one may claim religious agency, or the ability to determine for oneself what is morally and ethically just, and what enables communication with the divine. As one practitioner of nepantla spirituality writes, "Nepantla spirituality is a useful concept because many people feel that the Catholicism alone will not satisfy their spiritual needs. Nepantla is the common ground, where both Indigenous and Christian religions can meet" (Medina 2006, 265).

To exist in nepantla is to live on the border, on the boundaries of cultures and social structures, where life is in constant motion, in constant fluidity. To be in nepantla also means to be in the center of things, to exist in the middle places where all things come together. Nepantla, the center place, is a place of balance, a place of equilibrium, or as discussed earlier a place of chaos and confusion.

Border people, *las mestizas y los mestizos*, constantly live in nepantla. We can never leave the middle space as that is where we were created, in "the contact zone." As Anzaldúa stated, "As you make your way through life, nepantla itself becomes the place you live in most of the time—home." How we choose to occupy our home is crucial. Nepantla offers a choice, a choice to exclude or to include.

Dieties

Ometeotl

Ometeotl is a composite of *ome* (two) and *teotl* (god/lord/divine energy). The oldest of the old gods, s/he is the one benevolent dual god/dess also known as Ometecutli (dual lord) and Omecihuatl (dual lady). S/he is the father/mother of the gods in Nahuatl mythology. S/he is also Totahtzin/Tonantzin our father/mother even though humanity was actually created by Ometeotl's children the four Tezcatlipoca (god of smoking mirrors) and not Ometeotl her/himself. The Tezcatlipoca are four manifestations of the one god. Ometeotl seems to have been a relatively unknown god/dess to the majority of the Nahuatl peoples. There were no images or temples erected to him/her. S/he was primarily referred to only in the poetry of the Tlamatinime (philosophers/knowers). From this poetry we find that Ometeotl is a god/dess of duality. Duality is not the same as dualism. Rather than being at odds with each other, in duality things like male and female, life and death, spirit and matter, stillness and movement are in harmony with each other. What seem to be opposites come together in Ometeotl to form one harmonic whole. Ometeotl can be found in all things and reveals his/her presence through flor y canto, the inspiration of art and poetry.

—GCG

Quetzalcóatl

Quetzalcóatl is a Toltec and Nahua deity with equivalents among other Mesoamerican peoples. Often depicted as a feathered serpent, Quetzalcóatl is a creator god associated with rain, wind, fertility, and the morning star. As Topiltzin Quetzalcóatl, he is a Toltec culture hero, possibly an actual tenth-century ruler, credited with abolishing human sacrifice and disappearing with a promise to return. Post-Conquest sources described Quetzalcóatl as a bearded White man, whom Spanish writers equated with Saint Thomas the Apostle. As a symbol, Quetzalcóatl has attracted twentieth-century Mexican or Mexican American artists and writers, among them Diego Rivera, José Clemente Orozco, Carlos Fuentes, and Alurista. Protestant liberation theologian Elsa Tamez reads stories about Quetzalcóatl alongside the Christian scriptures, seeing Quetzalcóatl as a revelation of God who, with Jesus, stands against war and injustice. Mormons have equated the bearded White god with an ancient American visitation by Jesus, as recounted in the Book of Mormon, while Mexican American José Argüelles and other New Age authors anticipate Quetzalcóatl's return in the form of a global spiritual transformation. A sculpture of Quetzalcóatl erected in San Jose, California, in 1994 led to an unsuccessful lawsuit alleging violation of church-state separation.

—JCD

Tonantzin

The Shrine to our Lady of Guadalupe is built on Tepeyac, which was considered the holy ground of the Nahuatl mother goddess Tonantzin. Tonantzin is known as Cihuacoatl (snake woman) and Coatlicue (she with a snake skirt). She is referred to as the "goddess of sustenance" and "honored grandmother." She is the Aztec goddess of the earth and the mother of the corn and flowers. She is usually depicted as a deadly goddess wearing a skirt made of snakes and a necklace of human body parts. According to ancient mythology, this devouring mother was impregnated by a Quetzal feather and so she became the virgin mother of Quetzalcóatl and Xolotl, the god of death. Outraged at their mother's suspicious pregnancy, Coyolxauhqui and her 400 brothers and sisters decided to kill Coatlicue. At that moment she gave birth to Huitzilopochtli, the sun who destroyed his mother's enemies and set them in the sky as the moon and the stars. In some Chicano/a thought, Guadalupe is often referred to as the inculturation or syncretistic manifestation of Tonantzin. The story of Guadalupe never mentions Tonantzin directly even though the Virgin Mary does appear on Tonantzin's holy ground. Guadalupe also does not manifest Tonantzin's deadly side.

—GCG
Lara Medina

References and Further Reading

Anzaldúa, Gloria. *Borderlands La Frontera: The New Mestiza* (San Francisco: Spinsters/Aunt Lute, 1987).

Carrasco, David. "Jaguar Christians in the Contact Zone." *Enigmatic Powers:*

Syncretism with African and Indigenous Peoples' Religions Among Latinos, ed. Anthony M. Stevens-Arroyo and Andres I. Pérez y Mena (New York: Bildner Center for Western Hemisphere Studies, 1995).

De La Torre, Miguel A., and Gastón Espinosa. "Introduction." *Rethinking Latino (a) Religion and Identity*, ed. Miguel A. De La Torre and Gastón Espinosa (Cleveland: Pilgrim Press, 2006).

León, Luis D. *La Llorona's Children: Religion, Life, and Death in the U.S.-Mexicans Borderlands* (Berkeley: University of California, 2004).

León-Portilla, Miguel. *Endangered Cultures* (Dallas: Southern Methodist University Press, 1990).

Medina, Lara. "Nepantla Spirituality: Negotiating Multiple Religious Identities Among U.S. Latinas." *Rethinking Latino (a) Religion and Identity*, ed. Miguel A. De La Torre and Gastón Espinosa (Cleveland: Pilgrim Press, 2006).

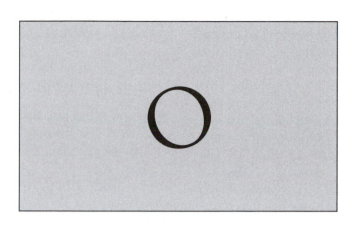

OLAZÁBAL, FRANCISCO
(1886–1937)

Francisco Olazábal pioneered the Latino/a Pentecostal movement in the United States, Mexico, and Puerto Rico from 1916 to 1937. He was raised a pious Catholic until the age of 12, at which time he and his mother (Refugio Velazquez) were converted to Protestantism through the work of itinerant Methodist preachers in Mazatlán, Mexico. They served lay traveling Methodist evangelists in the Sierra Madre Mountains. After visiting family in San Francisco and considering sailing the world as a merchant marine, Olazábal rededicated his life to the Christian ministry through the preaching of George and Carrie Judd Montgomery around 1902–1903. He later attended the Wesleyan School of Theology in San Luís Potosí, Mexico, for three years (1908–1010). He immigrated to the United States in 1911, where he assumed the pastorate of a Spanish-language Methodist Church in El Paso, Texas. Olazábal then traveled to Moody Bible Institute where he studied for one semester before following American evangelist Reuben A. Torrey to Los Angeles, where he was hired to evangelize the Spanish speaking on behalf of the Church of the Open Door. After he left, Olazábal pastored Spanish-speaking Northern Methodist Episcopal churches in Pasadena and later the San Francisco Bay area. In 1916, he was persuaded by the Montgomerys (who had since converted to Pentecostalism after attending the Azusa Street Revival) to convert to Pentecostalism. He was ordained on September 24, 1916, by the General Council of the Assemblies of God and went on to pioneer the work in Los Angeles, El Paso, and throughout Texas. He eventually left the Assemblies of God because (he said) the "gringos have control." As a result, he created the first completely independent and indigenous Latino/a Pentecostal denomination in the United States in 1923 called the Latin American Council of Christian Churches. Olazábal's evangelistic-healing campaigns attracted 250,000 people throughout the United States, Mexico, and Puerto Rico during his 30-year (1907–1937) ministry. He held major evangelistic-healing campaigns in East Los Angeles, San Fernando, Watts, Modesto (California), Nogales (Arizona), Chicago, El Paso, San Antonio, Brownsville, Houston, Laredo, Mexico City, Cleveland, Tennessee, New York City, and San Juan, Puerto Rico. He organized an evangelistic-healing campaign in Spanish Harlem in 1931 that attracted over 100,000 people and another in San Juan, Puerto Rico, in 1934 that attracted thousands of people to the Pentecostal faith. He founded a Bible college in El Paso in 1922, first published the magazine *El Mensajero Cristiano* in 1923, and contributed to the origins of at least 14 denominations. At its height, his council claimed 150 churches and 50,000 followers, with missionaries in Mexico, Puerto Rico, Cuba, Central America, Columbia, Chile, and Spain. After his death in 1937 at the age of 51, due to an auto accident, Olazábal's body was displayed in a gas-vapor-filled casket for viewing by tens of thousands of people in Houston, Spanish Harlem, Chicago, El Paso, and East Los Angeles, where he is buried in Evergreen Cemetery not far from William J. Seymour, the African American founder of the global Pentecostal movement.

Gastón Espinosa

References and Further Reading

Espinosa, Gastón. "El Azteca: Francisco Olazabal and Latino Pentecostal Charisma, Power, and Faith Healing in the Borderlands." *Journal of the American Academy of Religion* 67, no. 3 (Fall 1999): 597–616.

OPERATION PEDRO PAN

Operation Pedro Pan was a joint relief effort from December 1960 to October 1962 on the part of the Catholic Church, the U.S. government, and concerned Cubans that led to the unprecedented exodus of 14,131 children (mostly between the ages of 10 and 16) from Cuba to the United States. In December 1960 the Eisenhower administration noticed that an increasing number of unaccompanied minors were being sent to the United States, typically to Miami, from Cuba by desperate parents in fear of Castro's revolutionary regime and the monopolization of education and businesses by the communist government. This situation was beginning to pose a real humanitarian crisis for the immigrants, especially refugee children who were arriving to the United States alone and in need of basic goods such as food, shelter, and education. As a result, over $1 million was apportioned by the U.S. government in the early 1960s to aid in the relief effort.

The agency chosen to allocate this funding was the Catholic Welfare Bureau of the Archdiocese of Miami. Lead responsibility fell into the hands of its director, Monsignor Bryan O. Walsh. The Reverend Walsh had firsthand experience of this crisis in Miami among the growing number of young Cuban exiles particularly through his encounter with a hungry and homeless 15-year-old named Pedro Menéndez. Working out of the Centro Hispano Católico (Hispanic Catholic Center) housed at a Miami parish school, Walsh enlisted nearly 100 Catholic Charities agencies around

ELIÁN GONZÁLEZ

On Thanksgiving Day, 1999, a five-year-old Cuban boy named Elián González was found off the U.S. coast. Within days, he became internationally known as the child caught in the midst of a custody battle between Cuban Americans and Cubans from the homeland. As the world focused on the political saga, a religious subtext developed. Surrounding Elián's Miami home, Catholics and Protestants gathered to pray. These worshipers claimed to have seen the Virgin Mary hovering over the house and on a bank glass door. Others referred to Elián as the miracle child or Miami's Jesus. The Miami community pointed out that like Jesus, Elián arrived weeks before Christmas, at the end of the millennium. Even the year 2000, the sixth millennium since the supposed creation of the earth, conferred upon Elián, like Jesus, the symbol of hope. For followers of Santería, Elián was a child of Ochún, the quasi-deity of the sea. In spite of Elián's symbolic religious value to Miami Cubans, a predawn raid by U.S. Federal Marshals on his house on April 22, 2000, ended the standoff. Catholic and Protestant ministers denounced the government's sacrilege of violating Holy Week, and called the community to prayer and peaceful demonstration.

—MAD

the United States to meet this humanitarian need. The concerted effort, known as the Cuban Children's Program, served as the domestic counterpart to Operation Pedro Pan.

The goal of the domestic program was to care for the exiled children by finding foster homes for them and providing them with financial assistance. Temporary shelters situated in the Miami-Dade area were established at Florida City, Saint Raphael Hall, Kendall Children's Home, Camp Matecumbe, and Opa-locka. These sites provided immediate housing for the young exiles, along with food, education, and recreation until they were assigned to permanent residences either with family or in foster homes. The relief effort also evolved into an ecumenical and interreligious endeavor that included the Service Bureau for Protestant Children and the Jewish Family and Children Service.

While the Cuban Children's Program addressed the domestic concerns of the exiles, Operation Pedro Pan dealt specifically with the logistical and practical aim of evacuating children from Cuba. The island operation was organized primarily by Monsignor Walsh and James Baker, a U.S. citizen and headmaster of the Ruston Academy in Havana, Cuba. Baker and Walsh shared a mutual concern for the fate of Cuban children under the prospects of communist indoctrination since parochial schools were being closed and parental authority was being threatened under the revolutionary government. They envisioned an evacuation operation whose nomenclature was inspired by J. M. Barrie's *Peter Pan*, a story of children embarking on a flight to a new land of fantastic possibilities unaccompanied by their parents. Baker, along with the assistance of local churches in Cuba, provided a direct line of communication from the United States to an underground network of politically disenchanted Cuban parents on the island, predominantly of middle-class standing. His academy had the responsibility of issuing student visas to children that granted them legal passage to the United States. The collaboration between Walsh and Baker provided the crucial nexus for carrying out Operation Pedro Pan while the financial and political support of the U.S. government and the sponsorship of religious organizations made the dream of this flight possible.

The ideological background of Operation Pedro Pan was shaped by a complex array of religious and political factors, both ancient and modern, revolving around the dramatic narratives of freedom and exile. The political tension underlying the conflicted Cold War period of Pedro Pan was framed by two competing and antagonistic modern social economic orders: the democratic market-driven freedom of the United States and revolutionary Cuba's communist struggle for liberation from class oppression. The alternative visions of history and freedom between these two geographically close countries created a disparate rift issuing in mutual fear that reached its apex during the two-year span of Pedro Pan in such events as the trade embargo, the Bay of Pigs invasion, and the October Missile Crisis. The nuclear threat of the October crisis in 1962, in fact, terminated flights between the United States and Cuba and concluded the evacuation of children under Operation Pedro Pan.

The U.S. government with its strict aversion to communism already had a religious ally in the social teaching of the Catholic Church. In 1937 the papal encyclical *Divino Redemptoris* rebuked communism for stripping humanity of its spiritual dimension and attacking its most original sacred institution, the family. With clergy becoming increasingly marginalized and deported from revolutionary Cuba because of their political opposition, the biblical story of exile became the key religious hermeneutic for understanding the Cuban refugee experience. In December 1961 a replica of the statue of Our Lady of Charity (the Virgin of El Cobre), a prominent religious symbol of Cuban national identity, was transplanted from Havana to Miami. For many, this event marked the origin of the Cuban diaspora. Religious voices addressing the popular piety of Cubans in the United States, such as Bishop Agustín Román of Miami, have referred to the Jewish Babylonian exile (sixth century BCE) as the model for interpreting the Cuban diaspora. The opportunity for catharsis, rejection of idolatry, social justice, hope of return, and restoration have served as guiding principles of self-reflection for the exilic Cuban imagination informed by the Babylonian narrative.

The intent of all parties collaborating in Operation Pedro Pan was to eventually reunite the children with their parents. Although this reality came to pass for many, it did not for every Pedro Pan exile. Yet, on the whole, the children of Pedro Pan have assimilated strikingly well into the professional sector of American society as engineers, business owners, social workers, writers, attorneys, and physicians.

David Manuel Lantigua

References and Further Reading

Conde, Yvonne M. *Operation Pedro Pan: The Untold Exodus of 14,048 Cuban Children* (New York: Routledge, 1999).

CRECED: Final Document (Hato Rey, Puerto Rico: Ramallo Bros. Printing, 1996).

De La Torre, Miguel. *La Lucha for Cuba: Religion and Politics on the Streets of Miami* (Berkeley: University of California Press, 2003).

de los Angeles Torres, María. *The Lost Apple: Operation Pedro Pan on the Streets of Miami* (Boston, MA: Beacon Press, 2003).

Triay, Victor Andres. *Fleeing Castro: Operation Pedro Pan and the Cuban Children's Program* (Gainesville, FL: University Press of Florida, 1998).

ORTEGA, GREGORIA

Gregoria Ortega is co-founder of Las Hermanas, a national organization of Latina Catholics. Raised as a devout Catholic in El Paso, Texas, Gregoria joined religious life at the age of 18 as a member of the Victory Missionary Sisters, commonly known as Victoryknoll. At the age of 39, Ortega accepted a teaching assignment among Chicano youth in Abilene, West Texas. Sister Ortega understood the legacy of racial discrimination toward Mexican Americans in Texas where lynching remained a method of social control into the early twentieth century.

In the early 1970s, when Ortega arrived in Abilene, segregation was commonly practiced in barber shops, beauty salons, cemeteries, bowling alleys, and swimming pools. Even the battle over segregation in public schools continued into the 1970s as some administrators refused to integrate according to federal law. Ortega found herself in the middle of a battle for civil rights as she ministered in the diocese of San Angelo, an area ranking fifth in the nation in terms of where Chicanos were most rigidly segregated. Teaching religious education to high school Chicano youth, Ortega discussed Martin Luther King Jr. and César Chávez with an emphasis on their commitment to nonviolence. When the students could no longer tolerate overt discrimination in their school, they organized a walkout lasting nine days.

Ortega supported them wholeheartedly as long as they remained nonviolent. Her support lasted through the legal case filed by the students and their parents against the Abilene School Board. Sister Ortega's public presence as a religious activist provoked the anger of school board officials and her religious superiors. A newly appointed bishop and local priests decided she should be expelled from the diocese without even having a conversation with her.

Ortega's dedication to the Chicano people and the Church did not stop with her expulsion. After a few months of rest, she returned to San Antonio, Texas, where she received support from a close friend, Father Edmundo Rodríguez, to start an organization of Mexican American religious sisters concerned about the plight of their people. Through Rodríguez, Ortega met Sister Gloria Gallardo of the Holy Ghost Sisters and together they sent out a national invitation to as many Chicana sisters as they could identify. With Gallardo sharing her salary from her work as a community organizer in the Galveston-Houston diocese, the two women struggled to create their vision of a church in support of Chicanos.

Finally in April 1971, 50 primarily Mexican American sisters met in Houston to discuss and pray about the implications of the Chicano movement for the

Catholic Church. After three days of meetings, those present voted to start a national organization under the name of Las Hermanas with the motto "United in Action and Prayer." Within six months, membership grew to 900 and over the next few years Las Hermanas directly challenged the Church to support the efforts of the Chicano movement for civil rights and to improve its own treatment of Spanish-speaking Catholics. Over the following decade, Las Hermanas members involved themselves in the United Farm Worker Movement, helped to establish the first Mexican American Cultural Center in San Antonio, and collaborated with PADRES, an organization of Chicano priests, to push for the appointment of Chicano bishops. Las Hermanas uncovered the exploitation of immigrant Mexican sisters by the Catholic Church, conducted a national survey with findings that exposed the absence of ministry programs for Latinos, and collaborated on the First and Second National Encuentros in 1972 and 1977 organized by Latino/a laity and clergy. Although Gregoria Ortega is no longer a member, Las Hermanas continues to exist with a primarily lay membership focusing on the empowerment of grassroots Latina Catholics.

Lara Medina

References and Further Reading

Martinez, Richard. *PADRES: The National Chicano Priest Movement* (Austin: University of Texas Press, 2005).

Medina, Lara. *Las Hermanas: Chicana/Latina Religious-Political Activism in the U.S. Catholic Church* (Philadelphia: Temple University Press, 2004).

ORTHOPATHOS

Etymologically suggesting "right affections" or "right emotions," the term *orthopathos* (or "orthopathy") is usually considered alongside "orthodoxy" (right beliefs/praise/glory) and "orthopraxy"/"orthopraxis" (right practice) as elements constituting a model for Christian discipleship and spirituality. Deriving their roots largely from Pietistic and Wesleyan paradigms, these three "orthos" are considered to be a holistic approach to Christian discipleship, suggesting the integration of "head," "heart," and "hand" or "knowing," "being," and "doing." This schema attempts to overcome the way that Christianity is often depicted as a disengaged and disembodied faith by placing right belief (which often maintains a place of privilege) on par with elements of an affective and active nature. Such a strategy creates a burden for proponents of this model to give a robust account of the latter two "orthos," as these are more challenging to substantiate than the more familiar and historically prominent notion of orthodoxy.

Whereas liberationist theologians have contributed within the past few decades to the development of orthopraxis, perhaps the most difficult of the three to clarify is *orthopathos*. Several factors contribute to this challenge. Undoubtedly, a rampant suspicion regarding affectional language exists among those cultures indebted to the Hellenistic mind-set so that words such as "emotions," "passions," and "affections" tend to suggest elements that are of a fleeting, irrational, and unmanageable/involuntary nature. Studying beliefs or practices appears to be a much more objectively based endeavor as opposed to the deeply subjective and psychologically complex process of analyzing the affective life. Finally, particularly within the realm of Christian studies, affectional language is usually associated with revivalist settings, those that tend to be avoided or relegated to the periphery by those espousing a more formal and "respectable" understanding of Christianity. When one thinks about the affections and the Christian life, revivalists such as John Wesley (who advocated both a "heart religion" and the pursuit of "perfect love") and Jonathan Edwards (who wrote a famous work entitled *A Treatise Concerning Religious Affections*) come to mind, and yet for many years, such figures were considered first and foremost revivalist preachers and only secondarily theologians.

Several developments within Christianity and Western culture at large have made a term such as *orthopathos* more viable within the academy. The theological disciplines have become more accommodating to a "practical divinity" so that practical theology has come into its own as a specialized field. Also, the heirs of the Wesleyan and Holiness revivals, namely the Pentecostal and charismatic movements, have emerged as viable theological subtraditions within Christianity, especially because of their vast and growing numbers in the Two-Thirds World. Gradually, theologians and others have begun to investigate these global movements with a level of theological sophistication and seriousness that has merited significant attention. Such trends and a general interest within the *Zeitgeist* (spirit of the age) of all things spiritual have helped make spirituality an area of scholarly pursuit, a development leading to new conceptual paradigms that take into account the embodied piety of everyday Christians.

Within this context the Latino voice of Samuel Solivan has emerged. A Pentecostal "New Yorican," Solivan speaks from and to the North American context when he suggests that orthodoxy and orthopraxis are no longer useful in their current usage within the theological guild. For Solivan, orthodoxy has become little more than reified theological statements that help promote the status quo rather than contribute to the humanization of the dehumanized "others" on the margins of society. Additionally, according to Solivan's narration, orthopraxis or praxis more generally has evolved as another intellectual language within academe so that those who talk about liberation and praxis-oriented themes rarely are those who actually engage in the concrete, hands-on work of promoting greater justice and peace in the world. Within this frame of reference, Solivan suggests that *orthopathos* can invigorate the other two "orthos" so that they are not excessively disengaged from the reality of the suffering poor.

What distinguishes Solivan's use of the term *orthopathos* from others is that he is advocating pathos, or suffering/pain, as a key epistemological entryway for theological discourse, especially the kind that attempts to take seriously marginalization, oppression, and injustice. He roots such a notion in God's own pathos (here drawing from the work of the Jewish theologian Abraham Heschel) and the *via dolorosa* (sorrowful way) of the incarnate Son in order to show that God's work makes it possible for the poor and dehumanized to lead lives of fullness and liberation. Solivan believes that the pathos of the suffering poor can become *orthopathos* when the transformative work of the Holy Spirit is active among those who identify and locate themselves in solidarity with the pathos-ridden condition of the marginalized. Such endeavors mirror God's own active and ever-present work among the poor and disenfranchised.

Several reservations could be made regarding Solivan's account. The way he narrates orthodoxy and orthopraxis appears to be excessively sweeping, especially given the complex range of meanings and uses for such broad terms. Solivan also fails to offer a robust historical account for his program, one that could have served in nuancing and substantiating his claims about divine impassibility and the very nature of orthopathic speech. Finally, despite his best intentions, Solivan leaves much to be desired in the way he narrates theologically the logic of moving from pathos to *orthopathos*.

Nevertheless, despite these shortcomings, Solivan's argument still stands. He points to the perpetual difficulty that those who would espouse an account of discipleship based on the three orthos face, namely the challenge of rendering a viable notion of *orthopathos*/orthopathy. From Solivan's vantage point, any account of this oft-neglected element ought to include mechanisms for bringing to consciousness the pain and suffering of those who are on the margins. A theological claim of this kind is rightfully made by a Latino who has been engaged in ministry within such contexts and a Pentecostal who recognizes the work of the Spirit today as transforming the suffering of the poor and oppressed so that they can be freed to lead dignified and hopeful lives.

Daniel Castelo

References and Further Reading

Land, Steven J. *Pentecostal Spirituality* (Sheffield, U.K.: Sheffield Academic Press, 1994).

Solivan, Samuel. *The Spirit, Pathos and Liberation* (Sheffield, U.K.: Sheffield Academic Press, 1998).

Steele, Richard B., ed. *"Heart Religion" in the Methodist Tradition and Related Movements* (Lanham, MD: Scarecrow Press, 2001).

P

PALO

Reglas de Congo (Rule of the Congo), *Regla Conga*, *Regla de Palo*, or *Palo Monte*, *Mayombe* are all variations of the spiritual faith developed mostly in the Congo culture of central Africa of Bantu origin. *Palo* was brought to Cuba, the Americas, and *Hispañola* Island (present day Haiti and Dominican Republic) by African Blacks who were forced into the slave trade. From the 1530s until the abolition of the slave trade in the 1880s, at least 10 million Africans were transported to the Americas of which 4.7 million Africans were transported to the Caribbean (Klein 1986). Between 1810 and 1870, the Spanish colony of Cuba acquired about 600,000 slaves; however, in 1880 Cuba had 200,000 slaves and an entire Afro-Cuban population of 450,000 (Klein 1986). Slaves were ripped from their culture and religious traditions and forced to de-emphasize their faith in Bantu and Yoruban roots. As a result, the process of syncretism occurred (all religions transform and assimilate elements from different cultures); specifically, slaves were forced to emphasize Catholicism. Slaves disguised African gods or spiritual entities in the clothes of Catholic saints and transferred all the power, characteristics, fetishes, and due devotion that belonged to a specific god or spiritual entity. Racism has also influenced the process of syncretism through religious persecution of various religions in Cuba.

Slaves were encouraged to form *cabildos* (social clubs) created along ethnic and linguistic lines by the Whites based on the divide-and-rule strategy to avoid a rebellion. The cabildo served as a religious function and house temples for the emerging Lucumi religion. From the end of the nineteenth century, the houses of Lucumi and Palo Monte priests (*los negros brujos*) were special targets of police raids intended to do away with *brujeria* (witchcraft). In 1884, the Good Government Law was passed, forbidding all cabildos from meeting or organizing festivals. *Negros brujos* and ordinary

Afro-Cubans became "icons of fear" between the emancipation of slaves in 1886 and the first years of the new Republic. At that time, brujeria was considered as the cause of social delinquency and the ritual murder of White children for their blood.

By 1910, all Black organizations were outlawed for fear of a race war. However, intensive reinvestigation of the states' witch-hunt cases against brujos found that hysteria, masquerading as evidence, and racism contributed to brutal executions of innocent elderly African men by *garrote*. Therefore, all variations of Palo keep secret societies that do not seek to convert new members or interact religiously with other groups. The secrecy is rooted in the oppression endured previously, which continues to exist in Cuba. Palo lacks a highly decentralized governing religious body without a formal central instructional structure. Practitioners and believers of Palo residing in Cuba, Dominican Republic, and Afro-Latin communities in the United States, Venezuela, Colombia, and Puerto Rico are unknown. It is unknown how many followers practice Catholicism or another religion in addition to Palo.

Palo's central belief system is human association with certain spirits of the dead. In Palo, Nsambi is the Supreme Creator and Regla de Palo is initiated by worship of the spirits of ancestors—the dead, and the nature spirits or supernatural beings, *mpungus*, that dwell in natural forces, such as trees, rivers, and the sea. The word "Palo" refers to "stick" in Spanish and the sticks or branches from the forest are used by *paleros* (practitioners) as a magical element in spells. Some scholars consider Palo as the "dark side of *Santeria*." Palo has been associated with brujeria or *bilongo*, the Spanish

words for witchcraft, and its practitioners insist that Palo can be used for both good and evil. Alcohol, tobacco, and gunpowder are used in divination rituals, which are supremely important elements of Palo. Specifically, to divine, to see the future, to organize life in a rapid and effective manner, is a priority in the cults of Bantu origin. Quick and reliable divination and the palero's efficacy in this profession guarantee his prestige in the Congo religion.

The Congo liturgy's core is in the *nganga* in which all animistic powers are concentrated and have various levels of energy depending on the amount of time that it has resided in it as part of its message. Anthropologist Lydia Cabrera explains that nganga is a spirit, a supernatural force as well as a receptacle itself (a three-legged iron cauldron) that contains various objects placed in the now distant past (i.e., earth from the cemetery and crossroads, sticks, insects, animal bones), which provide the material foundation for the Father or Mother (palero) of the nganga to carry out his/her orders. All of the *mpungus*, saints or supernatural beings, are condensed within the nganga like a microcosm. *Prendas* are forces secondary to the nganga and may be talismans or amulets, which can be found in any object or thing (i.e., trees, stones, shells, gourds, horns). The ngangas contain good and bad spirits similar to the sacred stones of the Lucumi.

Palo Mayombe or Palo Monte are the most widely known and popular rites, and some consider these to be used for evil or are referred to as "Jewish" (*nganga judía*) rather than "Christian" (*nganga christiana*) witchcraft. The nganga judía is primarily about power and uses a symbol of a railroad spike. The attempt is to work with spirits of criminals and the insane and attempt to extract vengeance, humble, or domesticate one's enemies. Such practices can cause illness, break up marriages, create financial difficulties, or even death to one's enemy. The nganga christiana operates with spirits of good people and uses the symbol of a crucifix to cure the sick, bring peace and harmony, and help those who are distressed.

Sarah J. Rangel-Sanchez

References and Further Reading

Barnet, Miguel. *Afro-Cuban Religions* (Princeton, NJ: Markus Wiener Publishers, 2001).

Brown, David H. *Santeria Enthroned: Art, Ritual, and Innovation in an Afro-Cuban Religion* (Chicago: The University of Chicago Press, 2003).

Cabrera, Lydia. *Reglas del Congo, Palo Monte, Mayombe* (Miami: Peninsular Printing, 1979).

De La Torre, Miguel A. *Santeria: The Beliefs and Rituals of a Growing Religion in America* (Grand Rapids, MI: Wm. B. Eerdmans Publishing Co., 2004).

Klein, Herbert S. *African Slavery in Latin America and the Caribbean* (New York: Oxford University Press, 1986).

LA PASTORELA

The Catholic Church has historically introduced medieval cyclical dramas known as mystery, miracle, and morality plays into its seasonal liturgies. Mystery plays deal with the life of Jesus, miracle plays recount the lives of the saints, and morality plays depict the ongoing battle between good and evil. Las Pastorelas fall into all three of these categories.

Across the centuries, Las Pastorelas provided the faithful of the Catholic Church with visual imagery of the articles of the faith in a jargon that they could understand. It was not until the cyclical church dramas began to be presented that ordinary lay people slowly began to recognize holy writ. By carefully listening to the dialogues of the characters of these folk dramas, they slowly began to understand how their faith was manifested in their daily lives. As the faithful began to experience "the Word made flesh," they began to take on a more active role in the presentation of Las Pastorelas. The actors in these folk plays were not seasoned performers. They were ordinary day laborers who would memorize volumes of dialogue and concoct their own costumes from readily available materials.

Just before Midnight Mass on Christmas Eve the village would gather quietly as they listened to voices singing from outside the church door. The door would be flung open and in would come the figure of Saint Michael the Archangel leading the shepherds. All would process in double file, with the most important shepherds walking closest to Saint Michael. The first following Saint Michael would be the chief shepherds Bato and Tubal; Gil and Lipio were next, followed by Bacirio and Cojo. All bore shepherds' crooks decorated with flowers, ribbons, and tinfoil. Next to process would be the figure of Gila. She was the shepherdess who, in the spirit of purity, would be clad all in white. The last two figures, farthest from Saint Michael, were Hermitaño and Bartolo. Hermitaño represents the universal man who seeks sanctity but who is led astray by the riches that the world offers. Bartolo represents all lazy men who do not want to make a solitary effort at work, but who expect payment, albeit undeserved.

At the start of the folk play, all the shepherds enter singing and thus reveal their identities in poetic verse. They gather to sup and sleep. They sing about the cold weather while Gila prepares the evening meal. Thus, it seems that all is well and they lie down for the night. Only Lipio and Tubal keep watch over the flocks by night. Suddenly, the Evil One, Luzbel, appears among them. In an eloquent speech he states that he is going to try to confound them so that they will not know of the birth of the Baby Jesus. Luzbel tries to trick both the shepherds and the audience throughout the play. Luzbel has incredibly long lines. His words are laced with mythological and biblical allusions as well as poetic lines lifted straight from the work of poet Luis de Góngora.

Luzbel is the Gongoresque Devil that must be subdued and vanquished by his opponent Michael the Archangel. Both spirits must do battle throughout the drama for the souls of the shepherds. They must also contend with the corruption or redemption of the shepherdess Gila and the holy man Hermitaño. Luzbel tempts Hermitaño, seducing him with his smooth logic so that he will steal away Gila: "What need have you of that cross and that rosary . . . ?" he asks. The obvious question that springs forth is this: How can the hermit have a cross since Jesus has not even been born, let alone died on it? Saint Dominic has yet to be born and so the rosary has not been invented yet. Neither has become a salvific symbol yet. The answer to these paradoxes is that both of these objects are anachronistic, existing out of ordinary time. Since the play is a metaphorical one based on the struggle between Good and Evil, it makes perfect sense to the Christians watching it.

Hermitaño, trying to atone for his shortcomings, keeps watch by night. Suddenly, he hears an exquisite song of joy. He believes that brother Tubal is singing in the fields. Just then Lipio and Tubal rush in, proclaiming the good tidings told to them by the angels. Alas, Luzbel too has heard the glad tidings. Finally, after a brief struggle, Saint Michael vanquishes Luzbel and binds him for a thousand years. He comforts the shepherds with smooth words, and they begin to prepare rustic gifts to take to the Infant God. They are all eager to go to Bethlehem save for Bartolo, who prefers to stay in bed. By use of hilarious parody, they finally convince him to go worship the Infant God. Saint Michael ties up Luzbel and all ends well.

There are many manuscripts of the Las Pastorelas in various collections in the American Southwest. If we compare these manuscripts with the peninsular manuscripts from Spain, we will note some prominent differences. Luzbel, for example, has Satan as his helper as well as a whole host of devils. He declares war on the Virgin Mary. This is a scene transferred to another New Mexico folk play called *El Coloquio de San José*. The cry of "Alarm!" pronounced by Luzbel finds its echo in another drama here titled *Los Moros y los Cristianos*. The role of Bartolo is relegated in the peninsular script to Borrego and that of Gila, to Eliseta. The role of Hermitaño is relegated to a character named Laureano. Only the character of Bato remains constant in both the peninsular and New Mexico manuscripts.

Larry Torres

References and Further Reading

Cole, M. R., ed. *Los Pastores: A Mexican Play of the Nativity*. Memoirs of the American Folklore Society, Vol. IX. (New York: Houghton, Mifflin and Company/ American Folklore Society, 1907).

Ravicz, Marilyn Ekdahl. *Early Colonial Religious Drama in Mexico: From Tzompantli to Golgotha* (Washington, DC: The Catholic University of America Press, Inc., 1970).

Torres, Larry. *Six New Mexico Folkplays for the Advent Season* (Albuquerque: University of New Mexico Press, 1999).

PENITENTES, LOS HERMANOS

La Fraternidad Piadosa de Nuestro Padre Jesús Nazareno (pious fraternity of our father Jesus the Nazarene), more commonly known as the *Penitentes* (penitent ones), *Los Hermanos* (brothers), or *Los Hermanos Penitentes* (penitent brothers), is an organization of Roman Catholic laity that emerged in northern New Mexico and southern Colorado. Members of the *La Hermandad* (brotherhood) commit themselves to performing acts of corporal and spiritual penance and to providing aid to members and others. In some villages, the Penitentes built the churches and provided religious education. Although the organization has been predominantly composed of men, a few women have become members. La Hermandad established a number of *Moradas* (chapters). Each Morada elects its own *Hermano Mayor* (head penitent), who presides over the chapter. Since 1947, the administrative center of La Hermandad has been *La Mesa Directiva*

(governing board), which is presided over by the Archbishop of Santa Fe. Nineteenth-century reports estimated that 85 to 95 percent of the Roman Catholic male population of this area belonged to the Brotherhood (Weigle 1976, 98)

Scholars have sought to establish the origins of the Penitente Brotherhood, only to admit that they do not know—and are not likely to ever know—the precise origins of the Hermandad. Historical records, however, indicate that European settlers accompanying Spanish explorer Don Juan de Oñate were performing acts of self-flagellation in northern New Mexico in 1598. In 1826, *Padre* (Father) Antonio José Martínez became the pastor of the Taos area, which actually included much of northern New Mexico from Ranchos de Taos into present-day southern Colorado. In 1833, Martínez suspended their public activity and wrote to Bishop Zubiría of the Archdiocese of Durango about the presence of *La Hermandad de la Sangre de Cristo* (brotherhood of the blood of Christ)

who make exercises of penance during the Lenten seasons principally on Fridays, all of Holy Week, Fridays from this time until Pentecost, and other days of such significance in the year. These exercises consist of dragging wooden crosses, whipping themselves with scourges that they have for the purpose, piercing their backs with sharp stones or flints until the blood flows; and other rigorous means. . . . (T)hey do this everywhere by day, but in the processions of Holy Week, they have the custom of marching in front of the images in the manner described, so that they cause a great spectacle to the bystanders. They say that thus it has been granted to them from time immemorial. (Wroth 1991, 172–173)

Zubiría responded quickly in support of Martinez's position, stating that although performing private acts of penance in moderation could be spiritually beneficial, he prohibited all organized, public, and penitential activities of the Brotherhood. The *Hermanos* were instructed to do all of their acts of penance in the *privacy* of the church or their homes. Despite Zubiría's directive, the Hermandad did not disband. Archival evidence suggests that Jean Baptiste Lamy, who eventually became the first Bishop of Santa Fe, visited Pope Pius IX in Rome in 1854, and received a directive to disband the Hermandad. The papal directive, however, did not suppress the actions of the Penitentes. Consequently, Lamy expanded the rules governing the Penitentes, demanding that the Hermanos subject themselves to the authority of the bishop and that all of the proceedings, meetings, and acts of penance be done in *secrecy*.

In 1885, Archbishop Jean Baptiste Salpointe, successor of Lamy, attempted to revive the Third Order of Saint Francis, originally called the Order of Penance, and declared that the practices of the Hermandad had their origins in the Third Order. He demanded that the Hermanos return to their Franciscan roots. Alberto López Pulido argues that Salpointe constructed this link as a way to gain control over the Brotherhood. According to Pulido, pastors were told to refrain from celebrating Mass in the Morada and to withhold the sacraments from Penitentes if they refused to submit to the rules.

The Brothers resisted Salpointe's attempt to subsume the Hermandad into the Third Order. Salpointe's successors in the last part of the nineteenth century and early years of the twentieth century continued to denounce public acts of penance and to threaten offenders with denial of the sacraments and the impossibility of becoming God-parents. These same years were also characterized by an increase in attention from Presbyterian, Methodist, Congregationalist, and Baptist ministers and their communities who were moving into the territory. Perhaps the most well known among them was Rev. Alex M. Darley, who titled himself the "apostle of the Colorado Mexicans."

Thanks to the ongoing pressure by the archbishops of Santa Fe to keep Penitente activities private or secret and to the increased negative publicity of Protestant commentators such as Darley, the Penitentes increased the level of secrecy surrounding their membership and their activities. In 1946, Don Miguel Archibeque organized the Moradas into one association and effected a "reconciliation" with the Roman Catholic Church. Archbishop Edwin Vincent Byrne approved a new set of rules for the Hermandad. Although Archibeque was not able to obtain unanimous approval, Byrne announced the creation of the Archbishop's *Mesa Directiva* in 1947.

Byrne declared that the Brotherhood was not a "fanatical sect apart from the church." He also affirmed the Brothers' practice of "corporal and spiritual penance," maintaining that it was mandated by Jesus himself as a "necessity" for salvation. . . ." Nonetheless, the archbishop reaffirmed the position of previous archbishops that their penitential practices must be done in moderation and in private, so as to avoid scandal and pride.

David M. Mellott

References and Further Reading

Darley, Alex M. *The Passionists of the Southwest or the Holy Brotherhood: A Revelation of the "Penitentes"* (Glorieta, NM: Rio Grande Press, 1893, 1968).

López Pulido, Alberto. *The Sacred World of the Penitentes* (Washington, DC: Smithsonian Institution Press, 2000).

Steele, Thomas J., ed. and trans. *Archbishop Lamy: In His Own Words* (Albuquerque: LPD Press, 2000).

Weigle, Marta. *Brothers of Light, Brothers of Blood: The Penitentes of the Southwest* (Santa Fe, NM: Ancient City Press, 1976).

Wroth, William. *Images of Penance, Images of Mercy: Southwestern Santos in the Late Nineteenth Century* (Norman: University of Oklahoma Press, 1991).

PENTECOSTALISM

Pentecostalism, now a worldwide movement numbering over 600 million people on six continents, began in the United States in the early twentieth century. It was founded by Charles F. Parham (1873–1929) and the Black Holiness minister William J. Seymour (1870–1922) in the early twentieth century. The first Latino/as converted to the movement were at the Azusa Street Revival in 1906.

Pentecostalism represents the coming together of four major theological streams in late nineteenth-century U.S. Christianity: (1) the Holiness and Wesleyan idea of entire sanctification, (2) the Reformed idea of power for Christian service, (3) dispensational premillennialism, and (4) a robust belief in faith healing. Pentecostals emphasize the spiritual gifts (*charismata*) listed in 1 Corinthians 12 and 14: wisdom, knowledge, faith, healing, miraculous powers, discernment of spirits, tongues, interpretation of tongues, and prophecy. The belief in tongues as the physical evidence of Holy Spirit baptism is the teaching that separates Pentecostalism from other branches of Christianity.

The largest Pentecostal denominations in the United States include the General Council of the Assemblies of God (AG—1914), the United Pentecostal Church (UPC—1917), the Pentecostal Assemblies of the World, the International Church of the Foursquare Gospel (4-Square—1927), the African American Church of God in Christ (COGIC—1897, 1907), the Church of God, Cleveland, TN (1886, 1907), and the Church of God of Prophecy (1923). The largest Latino-serving Pentecostal bodies in the United States are the Hispanic Districts of the Assemblies of God, the Pentecostal Church of God, the Assembly of Christian Churches, the Apostolic Assembly of the Faith in Christ Jesus, the Church of God, Cleveland, TN, the Church of God of Prophecy, the Foursquare Church, the Latin American Council of Christian Churches, the Damascus Christian Church, Victory Outreach, and Calvary Chapel.

Growth of the Latino Protestant Pentecostal Movement

The Hispanic Pentecostal/Charismatic movement has grown from a handful of Mexicans at the Azusa Street Revival in Los Angeles (1906–1909) to more than 164 million men, women, and children throughout Latin America and the United States in 2007. About 27 percent (151 million) of all Latin Americans and 28 percent (9.2 million in 2004;

AZUSA STREET REVIVAL

Located at 312 Azusa Street in Los Angeles at a leased African Methodist Episcopal building, the Azusa Street Revival (1906–1909) marks the iconic event that helped make the Pentecostal-charismatic movement a global phenomenon. Led by the African American pastor William J. Seymour, the revival proved to be a racially and ethnically diverse worship setting as well as a center for missional activity. Whereas usually the events at the Apostolic Faith Mission are thought of in terms of Black and White attendees, other groups were present, including Hispanics. Prominent examples include Susie Valdez (mother of the evangelist A. C. Valdez), who after testifying of her healing in the revival went on to lead her family in evangelistic and social outreach efforts, and Abundio and Rosa de López, who became important figures both within the life of the mission (Abundio was ordained by Seymour) and through open-air, evangelistic services in the Mexican Plaza District of Los Angeles. Apparently, a falling out occurred between the leadership and the Mexican constituency of the mission so that the latter left around 1909. Nevertheless, the Pentecostal message was preached by and among Latino/as throughout the borderlands and beyond by many who were linked in one way or another with Azusa.

—DC

12.88 million in 2008) of all U.S. Hispanics are either Protestant Pentecostal or Catholic Charismatic (Espinosa 2004, 266).

Despite varying levels of apostasy, fragmentation, and competition, the Latina/o Protestant Pentecostal/Charismatic movement is still growing rapidly in a number of countries. There are 72 million Protestant Pentecostal/Charismatic Christians in Latin America, which make up the majority of Latin America's 100 million Protestants. Nearly 35 percent of all Pentecostals around the world live in Latin America. Today, 17 percent of all Latin Americans are Protestant, largely Pentecostal. The Catholic Church estimates that 8,000–10,000 Catholics convert to Protestantism every day throughout Latin America. On any given Sunday in Latin America, scholars now report that there may be more Protestants than Catholics attending church (Espinosa 2004, 267). Furthermore, scholars predict that as early as 2010 one in three Latin Americans may be Protestant or non-Catholic, largely Pentecostal or Evangelical.

Pentecostal growth in Latin America has been uneven. Mexico, for example, has one of the lowest percentages of Pentecostal Protestantism per national population in all of Latin America. Despite this fact, there are 7 million Protestants (out of a national population of 99 million) in Mexico, the second largest number in Latin America after Brazil. The 1990 Mexican Census found that 76 percent of all non-Catholics were Evangelical (largely Pentecostal) and that they have experienced the largest growth in regions like Tabasco and Chiapas, where they make up 17 and 15 percent of the population, respectively. Mexican Pentecostals are served by more than 166 Pentecostal denominations of which approximately 159 are completely independent and indigenous (Espinosa 2004, 267).

Mexican Pentecostals and Protestants are contributing to the growth of Latino/a Protestantism in the United States. Scholars found that 15 percent of all Mexican immigrants arriving in the United States are Protestant or other Christian. They are contributing to the growth of the more than 9.2 million Latina/o Protestants in the United States in 2008. The Hispanic Churches in American Public Life (HCAPL) survey also found that although nearly 800,000 U.S. Hispanics indicated they "recently converted" or returned back to Catholicism from another non-Catholic denomination or no religious tradition, it also found that over 3.9 million Latino/as recently converted from Catholicism. Thus, for every one Hispanic that has returned to Catholic Church, four have left it. Furthermore, a clear majority of Latino/as (57 percent) that "recently converted" from Catholicism to Protestantism were second- or third-generation U.S. citizens (Espinosa 2004, 266–268).

Not all countries in Latin America have experienced Mexico's low Protestant growth rate. Drawing on figures from the year 2000, Protestants make up 29 percent (50 million) of all Brazilians, 27 percent (4 million) of all Chileans, 25 percent (2.8 million) of all Guatemalans, 22 percent (1.4 million) of all El Salvadorians, 22 percent of all Puerto Ricans (867,000), 20 percent (7 million) of all U.S. Latinos, 19 percent (950,000) of all Nicaraguans, and 18 percent of all Hondurans (1.1 million) and all Panamanians (520,000). Brazil has witnessed the most dramatic numerical growth, going from 12.8 percent (12.3 million) of the national population in 1970 to 50 million

in 2000. The largest Protestant denomination in Brazil (and Latin America) is the Assemblies of God, which reportedly has over 20 million affiliates. Scholars in Brazil now claim that there are twice as many Assemblies of God congregations (85,000) as Catholic congregations (35,598) (Espinosa 2004, 268–269). The numerically largest Latino/a Protestant denomination in the United States, Brazil, Argentina, Chile, Colombia, Guatemala, El Salvador, Nicaragua, Costa Rica, Panama, and the Dominican Republic is Pentecostal, often the Assemblies of God or an independent indigenous Pentecostal tradition.

Pentecostalization of U.S. Latino and Latin American Catholicism

By 2007 there were 78 million Catholic Charismatics in Latin America and 6.8 million Latina/o Catholic Charismatics in the United States. In fact, the vast majority of the world's 119 million Catholic Charismatics are located in Latin America south of the U.S. border, where they participate in an estimated 102,873 weekly prayer groups and are supported (although not necessarily directed) by more than 2,000 priests, 100 bishops, and tens of thousands of lay leaders. The movement has witnessed uneven growth throughout Latin America and the United States over the past four decades. It has experienced the largest numerical growth in Brazil (35 million), Colombia (11 million), Mexico (9 million), the United States (6.8 million), Argentina (5 million), Venezuela (3 million), Chile (1.6 million), and Ecuador (1.2 million) (Espinosa 2004, 271–275).

The Latin American Catholic Charismatic movement traces its roots back to

NICKY CRUZ (1938–)

Ex-gang leader turned evangelist, Nicky Cruz (b. December 6, 1938, in San Juan, Puerto Rico) has spent nearly 50 years ministering to troubled teens engaged in gang life, drugs, and alcohol. An ordained Assembly of God minister and much sought-after speaker, Nicky Cruz is founder of "Nicky Cruz Outreach" (www.nickycruz.org), a ministry that targets at-risk urban youth with a message of hope found in Jesus Christ. The author of more than a dozen books, Nicky Cruz is best known for his autobiography, *Run Baby Run* (originally published in 1968), which has sold over 14 million copies worldwide and chronicles Cruz's troubled life from Puerto Rico, where he was raised by abusive parents, to the gang-ridden streets of New York City. In the mid-1950s Cruz became leader of a notorious inner-city gang. Then at the age of 19 his life was transformed through the ministry of evangelist David Wilkerson, founder of "Teen Challenge." Wilkerson's account of the conversion of Nicky Cruz is the subject of the best-selling book, *The Cross and the Switchblade* (1963), which was later adapted into a movie by the same title in 1970.

—*DAR*

the United States and to Bogotá, Colombia. The movement's four primary origins are the following: (1) the U.S.-based Catholic Charismatic Renewal (CCR) in 1967, (2) a Bogotá, Colombia, based Catholic Charismatic prayer group in 1967, (3) the U.S.-based Charisma in Missions Catholic Evangelization and Renewal Society in 1972, and (4) Latin American Catholics who defected to Pentecostalism and then later returned to Catholicism over the past century.

The Catholic Charismatic Renewal began at Duquesne University, United States, in 1967 after two lay instructors in the department of theology named Ralph Keifer and Patrick Bourgeois became interested in the Pentecostal movement after reading John Sherrill's *They Speak with Other Tongues* (1964) and Assemblies of God evangelist David Wilkerson's *The Cross and the Switchblade* (1963), which presciently depicted the conversion of an im-poverished Latino named Nicky Cruz to Pentecostalism. Keifer became so curious about the Pentecostal movement that he began attending a Charismatic prayer group held in the home of a Presbyterian laywoman. He soon received the baptism with the Holy Spirit. Shortly thereafter, Keifer, Bourgeois, and their students organized the first Catholic Charismatic prayer group at Duquesne University. This series of events helped birth the Catholic Charismatic renewal movement in the United States. The renewal spread to other Catholic universities such as the University of Notre Dame in South Bend, Indiana, where Ralph Martin and Stephen Cook, two recent graduates of Notre Dame, quickly became leaders of the fledgling movement. The first nationwide Catholic Charismatic convention took place at the University of Notre Dame on April 7–9, 1967. By the early 1970s, the Catholic Charismatic movement attracted the support of national and international Catholic leaders like

Father Kilian McDonnell and Belgian Cardinal Leon Joseph Suenens.

Little is known about the Catholic Charismatic prayer group that began in Colombia. However, we do know that the Charisma in Missions renewal and evangelization society was organized by two former Assemblies of God missionaries to Colombia named Glenn and Marilynn Kramar in the Los Angeles area in 1972. They first began evangelizing and spreading the Pentecostal message in Colombia in 1967 before they returned to the United States. After receiving a pastoral blessing from Cardinal Timothy Manning in 1982, they opened the Charisma in Missions headquarters in the Los Angeles area. They brought some of the evangelistic strategies and spirituality they practiced in the Assemblies of God into the Catholic Charismatic movement. They also spread their version of the Catholic Charismatic movement throughout the United States, Mexico, Colombia, and Central and South America by organizing prayer groups, conferences, and selling workbooks and an estimated 2 million cassette tapes in Spanish.

From these two origins and others, the Catholic Charismatic movement quickly spread to Puerto Rico (1969), Venezuela (1969), Mexico (1971), Brazil (1971), Argentina (1972), Chile (1972), Guatemala (1972), El Salvador (1977), and throughout the rest of Spanish-speaking Latin America by 1977. Vatican II, the *Cursillo* movement, and the theology of liberation movements all helped pave the way for the Catholic Charismatic movement because of their emphases on spiritual renewal, lay leadership, and faith-based empowerment.

Many scholars are surprised to hear that there are more Catholic Charismatics than Protestant Pentecostals in Mexico. In fact, 9.2 million of Mexico's 13.5 million Pentecostal/Charismatic Christians are Roman Catholic. The movement has grown very rapidly since it began in Mexico City in June 1971. Although, as Chesnut points out, some clerics are critical or ambivalent about the movement, it has garnered strong support from more than 700 priests and 53 bishops. It is largely the small but growing institutional support that has enabled it to hold national services like the one conducted at the Azteca Stadium in Mexico City that attracted 71,000 participants.

The movement has also witnessed notable growth on the island of Puerto Rico, where it has also grown from a handful of people in 1969 to over 215,000 people (one-third of which were under the age of 25) attending 850 weekly prayer meetings by 1997. There is little reason to doubt that the immigration of Catholic Charismatics from Mexico and Puerto Rico has not contributed to the growth of the movement among U.S. Latina/os. By 2008, there were 6.8 million U.S. Latino/a Catholic Charismatics, making it one of the largest overlooked popular grassroots religious movements in the United States (Espinosa 2004, 274).

In South America, Brazil, Colombia, and Argentina have witnessed significant Catholic Charismatic growth over the past four decades. The country that has witnessed the most notable numerical growth is Brazil. The movement has grown from a small prayer group in 1971 to more than 35 million affiliates in 2000. Together with Pentecostal and Charismatic Protestants, there are 76 million Pentecostal/Charismatic Christians in Brazil. In fact, 15 percent of all

Pentecostal/Charismatic Christians in the world today are located in Brazil. The Brazilian Catholic Charismatic movement sponsors 60,000 weekly prayer groups and is supported by over 500 priests, five bishops, and thousands of lay leaders. In São Paulo, annual renewal events have attracted 120,000 participants (Espinosa 2004, 279–280).

Regardless of its staying power, it would be inaccurate to conclude that the Catholic Charismatic Movement has simply brought Protestant Pentecostalism wholesale into Latin American Catholicism. They have reinvented and rearticulated their Charismatic beliefs in light of traditional Catholic teachings and encyclicals on spiritual renewal. Precisely because they have been accused of being too lay driven and of serving as a Trojan horse for Protestantism, Catholic Charismatics have been very careful to emphasize that they are faithful Catholics who wholly support the doctrines, discipline, and hierarchy of the Roman Catholic Church. In fact, many see themselves as the new vanguard for Catholic evangelization and renewal. Despite this fact, the hierarchy has stressed that the Charismatic renewal (which is often led by women) must remain under clerical control and should avoid interacting with Pentecostal and Charismatic Protestants.

Indigenization of U.S. Latino/a and Latin American Pentecostalism

The growth of the largely overlooked independent and indigenous Hispanic Pentecostal movement helps explain the rapid growth of Pentecostalism throughout Latin America and the United States. There are three major reasons why this process took place so early in Latin American Pentecostalism. First, many early Pentecostal missionaries like Henry C. Ball (1896–1989), who was the Superintendent of the Assemblies of God work in Latin America in the 1940s, pushed for self-supporting, self-propagating, and self-governing indigenous churches. Second, indigenous "independent" U.S. Latino/a Pentecostal preachers from the Azusa Street Revival like Abundio L. López, A. C. Valdez, Susie Villa Valdez, Brígido Pérez, Luís López, and Juan Martínez Navarro, along with other later evangelists like Juan Lugo, Francisco Llorente, Antonio Castañeda Nava, Francisco Olazábal, Carlos Sepúlveda, Matilde Vargas, and Leoncia Rosado Rosseau began conducting evangelistic work in the United States, Puerto Rico, and Latin America in the early twentieth century. Third, Pentecostal churches and districts went through a number of schisms and fragmented or developed into new independent and indigenous denominations (or *concilios*—councils), which in turn did the same. It is precisely the indigenization, fragmentation, and localized rearticulation of Pentecostalism in the regional vernacular language, culture, and customs of the people that help explain its phenomenal growth.

The chronic fragmentation and indigenization of the Pentecostal movement in Latin America is one of the primary reasons why the movement has been able to adapt and spread throughout Latin America over the past 100 years. In fact, the majority of Latin American Pentecostals are now part of independent (38 million) rather than classical (34 million) Pentecostal denominations. Most scholars have overlooked the rapid growth of independent Pentecostalism. The vast majority of Latin America's

---

FRANCISCO LLORENTE (1890–1928)

Francisco Llorente founded the Oneness Pentecostal movement among Latina/os in the United States and began the Asamblea Apostólica de la Fe en Cristo Jesús, Inc. (Apostolic Assembly of the Faith in Christ Jesus, Inc.). Born in Acapulco, Mexico, he traveled to San Diego, California, in 1912, where he was converted to Pentecostalism through the preaching of Azusa Street Revival evangelist Juan Navarro Martínez. Shortly thereafter he was ordained an evangelist and began preaching in migrant farm labor camps throughout southern California. He and other converts like Marcial de la Cruz and Antonio Castañeda Nava converted many Mexicans to the Pentecostal movement and set up congregations and missions in Colton, San Bernardino, Riverside, Los Angeles, and Watts. Although most African American and Anglo-American Oneness bodies ordain women, the Apostolic Assembly prohibits the ordination of women, requires women to wear a head covering when in prayer, and requests that they not wear pants, cosmetics, or cut their hair short. In 1925, Llorente was named the first president of the Apostolic Assembly. He served in this capacity until 1928, by which time the Assembly counted 15 congregations.

—GE

1,991 Pentecostal denominations and councils are independent (1,767) rather than tied to classical (224) Pentecostal bodies with historic ties to the United States. This fragmentation thesis hypothesizes that Pentecostal leaders invoke direct unmediated experiences with God as a pretext and basis for splitting off from an existing denomination to form another in an effort to restore Christianity back to its Apostolic roots described in the book of Acts (Espinosa 2004, 266, 276).

Contrary to popular perception, one of the first Latin American countries to indigenize the Pentecostal message was Mexico. Although the Pentecostal movement in Mexico was shaped by Anglo-American and Swedish Pentecostal missionaries like Clarissa Nuzum, George and Carrie Judd Montgomery, H. C. and Sunshine Ball, Alice E. Luce, and Axel and Ester Andersson, as eluded earlier, the first Pentecostal evangelists to spread the movement to Mexico and organize a church were independent Latino/a Pentecostals from the United States. After attending the Azusa Street Revival in Los Angeles in 1906, Mexicans like Abundio L. and Rosa López, A. C. Valdez, Brígido Pérez, Luís López, and Juan Martínez Navarro spread Pentecostalism to Mexicans living along the U.S.-Mexico border between 1906 and 1909, some of which no doubt returned to Mexico with their newfound faith. Furthermore, Romanita Carbajal de Valenzuela left the Spanish Apostolic Faith Mission in 1914 (and possibly earlier) in Los Angeles to spread the Pentecostal message in her hometown of Villa Aldama, Chihuahua, Mexico, where she converted a Methodist pastor named Ruben Ortéga to Pentecostalism and helped plant the first permanent Pentecostal church in Mexico. The independent and indigenous Mexican work received a shot in the arm when

JUAN LEÓN LUGO (1890–1984)

Juan León Lugo pioneered the Pentecostal movement in Puerto Rico and New York City. He converted to Pentecostalism through the work of his mother, Juana, and by Rev. Frank Ortiz on Oahu, Hawaii, in 1913. Ortiz was converted through the preaching of Azusa Street Revival missionaries en route to China and Japan around 1912. Lugo spread the Pentecostal message to immigrants in the San Francisco Bay area and Los Angeles from 1913 to 1916. He was ordained on January 16, 1916, by the Assemblies of God in San Jose, California. He was commissioned by Bethel Temple in Los Angeles to serve as a missionary to Puerto Rico. He arrived on the island on August 30, 1916 and began evangelistic work in Santurce and Ponce. Frank Ortiz Jr., Solomon and Dionisia Feliciano, Frank and Aura Finkenbinder, and Isabel, his future wife, soon joined his evangelistic work. He planted a number of churches on the island before pioneering the work in New York City in 1931. He founded Mizpa Bible Institute on the island in 1937. In 1940, he left the Assemblies of God to work with the Assemblies of Christian Churches and thereafter other Pentecostal bodies.

—GE

Francisco Olazábal returned to his homeland in the 1920s and 1930s to hold large evangelistic campaigns in Mexico City, Ciudad Juárez, Nogales, Mazatlán, and other parts of Mexico. Not long after the Mexican Revolution simmered down, after 1930 the Mexican government required that all foreign denominations hand over the leadership of their movements to Mexican nationals. This led to the nationalization and indigenization of almost all Anglo-American and Swedish-controlled Pentecostal and Protestant denominations in Mexico. Subsequently, it led to a number of internal struggles for control of the new denominations and to denominational fragmentation that birthed a number of new independent and indigenous denominations.

Today there are more than 159 independent and completely indigenous Pentecostal denominations in Mexico that have no administrative, financial, or emotional ties to the United States. They serve more than 4.3 million Protestant Pentecostals in Mexico (Espinosa 2004, 274, 278, 281). However, a growing number of indigenous Mexican denominations like the Apostolic Church of the Faith in Jesus Christ have set up churches and missions among the Mexican diaspora living in the United States.

A similar indigenization process took place in Puerto Rico. Although an Anglo-American woman was probably the first person to preach the Pentecostal message in Puerto Rico in 1909, the first person to plant lasting Pentecostal work on the island was Juan León Lugo (1890–1984). After being converted to the Pentecostal movement by some Puerto Ricans, who were themselves converted by Azusa Street Revival (1906–1909) participants who stopped off in the Hawaiian Islands, he took the Pentecostal message to California (1913) and New York City (1916) before taking it to his native Puerto Rico in August 1916. He spread the Pentecostal message throughout the island and

MAMA LEO (1912–2006)

Born as Leoncia Rosado Rousseau in Puerto Rico on April 11, 1912, Mama Leo received the "baptism of the Holy Spirit" during the revival of the 1930s among the Christian Church (Disciples of Christ) in her homeland. On September 22, 1935, she moved to New York with her husband, Rev. Francisco Rosado. After serving as Evangelists, the couple started the Iglesia Cristiana Damascus (Damascus Christian Church) in the Bronx. During these years, they were in contact and associated with Latino Pentecostal key figure Francisco Olazábal. When her husband was drafted by the military, Mama Leo became the pastor of the church and probably was the first Latina Pentecostal pastor in New York. Working among gang members and drug addicts, especially within the Puerto Rican neighborhoods, became the core of her ministry, not only through preaching in the street but with the establishment of rehabilitation programs. Out of this concern, Mama Leo, with her husband, founded the "Damascus Youth Crusade" in 1975. This drug and outreach program benefited many in the inner city who were considered outcast and marginalized, and it proved to be a model for other Christian drug programs across the Americas. Mama Leo passed away on October 5, 2006.

—*HMV*

incorporated his work in 1922 as the Pentecostal Church of God in cooperation with the Assemblies of God. In 1931, he helped pioneer the Pentecostal work among the Puerto Rican diaspora living in New York City.

That same year Francisco Olazábal arrived in Spanish Harlem. At the invitation of some of his converts in New York City, in 1934 and in 1936 he conducted two large-scale evangelistic healing campaigns in Puerto Rico. Thousands were converted. His campaign broke the monopoly that Juan Lugo and the Assemblies of God enjoyed over the Pentecostal work on the island. His campaign also led to the creation of a number of indigenous Pentecostal bodies.

Twenty years later in 1957, the Pentecostal Church of God based in Puerto Rico split off from the Assemblies of God in the United States because their leaders believed they were being discriminated against. The Pentecostal Church of God is now the largest Protestant denomination on the island, followed by the Seventh-day Adventists, the Assemblies of God, and the Jehovah's Witnesses. Today there are 63 Pentecostal denominations in Puerto Rico, 57 of which are independent bodies. In 2000, more than 1.1 million Puerto Ricans (28 percent of the population) on the island were part of the Protestant and Catholic Pentecostal/Charismatic movement, 867,000 of which were Protestant (Espinosa 2004, 275–279).

Despite the growth of independent Pentecostal denominations in Mexico and Puerto Rico, the country that has experienced the most rapid independent Pentecostal growth is Brazil. Today there are 50 million Protestants in Brazil, the vast majority (41 million) of which are Pentecostal or Charismatic. They make up almost one-third (29 percent) of all Brazilians today. Although the Assemblies of God is the largest Protestant body with approximately 20 million affiliates, the next five largest Protestant denominations (with 1.8 million adherents or more) in Brazil are independent and indigenous Pentecostal denominations like the Universal Church of the Kingdom of God, the God Is Love Pentecostal Church, the Cornerstone Gospel Church, Brazil for Christ, and the Christian Congregation of Brazil (Espinosa 2004, 277–280). Furthermore, there are another 400 independent and indigenous Pentecostal denominations operating in Brazil. The HCAPL national survey found that the top three largest Latino/a Protestant traditions in the United States are all Pentecostal and two of these are independent.

Latin American Evangelization of U.S. Latina/os

One of the most important results of the rapid growth of the Pentecostal movement in Latin America is the decision of a growing number of independent and indigenous Pentecostal bodies to send missionaries to evangelize Hispanic citizens and immigrants in the United States. Although there is no official count of how many independent and indigenous denominations in Latin America have sent missionaries to the U.S. mainland, I would estimate this number to be well over 150. Among independent Latin American Pentecostals, it is a status symbol to say that you have missionaries and churches in the largest and most powerful country on earth.

Perhaps the best example of the "back to the future" phenomena of Latin American Pentecostals returning to the United States to spread Pentecostalism is the Universal Church of the Kingdom of God. The second largest Protestant

body in Brazil after the Assemblies of God, the Universal Church has grown from the preaching of Edir Macedo (1944–) in a largely empty funeral parlor in 1977 to more than 4 million people in 2000. He came to the United States in 1986 to personally initiate the work. Since then, the Church has planted at least 25 mother churches and a number of preaching points in most of the major Spanish-speaking barrios in the United States. Most of these churches serve as the basis for planting new churches throughout a given metropolitan area. There are at least two Universal Church bishops residing in the United States that oversee the work. The Universal Church is also targeting English-speaking Anglo-Americans and African Americans. In addition, they publish *¡PARE de Sufrir!* (Stop Suffering!), which has a U.S. circulation of 50,000. The Universal Church is exporting its "high octane" version of Pentecostalism to the United States, with evangelistic crusades, divine healing services, and public exorcisms. They also use the latest technology, radio, and television to spread their message (Espinosa 2004, 280–281).

Not nearly as media driven, yet no less determined, are the hundreds of missionaries from Mexico's Apostolic Church of the Faith in Jesus Christ, the Light of the World Church, Puerto Rico's Pentecostal Church of God, MI (Movimiento Internacional), Guatemala's Church of Christ, Final Call, and other Latin American Pentecostal denominations that are setting up missions and churches among the Latin American diaspora in the United States. They and other independent Pentecostal denominations are aggressively competing for the heart and soul of the Latino/a community along with Anglo-American and native U.S.

Hispanic Pentecostal denominations like the Hispanic Districts of the Assemblies of God, the Assembly of Christian Churches, the Apostolic Assembly of the Faith in Christ Jesus, Victory Outreach International, and other Pentecostal/Charismatic traditions.

These new Latin American imports are theologically and socially diverse. For although the Light of the World Church requires men and women to sit on different sides of the aisles and requires women to wear a veil, refrain from cutting their hair, and avoid wearing cosmetics, jewelry, or pants, the Universal Church of the Kingdom of God uses drama, skits, Christian pop music, radio, and television to reach young and old alike. Comportment does not seem to be a major issue for them. Furthermore, although some foreign imports like Apostolic Church of the Faith in Jesus Christ are non-Trinitarian and Oneness in theology, others like the Universal Church of the Kingdom of God are Trinitarian.

Another important development is the influence that Latin American Pentecostalism is having on Anglo-American Pentecostalism. Perhaps the best example of this is the fact that the founders of the Toronto Blessing Revival in Canada trace their spiritual genealogy back to the Pentecostal revival in Argentina. The Toronto Blessing, the longest such revival in North American history, has in turn helped inspire and influence the Brownsville Revival in Florida. This revival had a direct impact on American and Canadian Pentecostal subcultures. In many respects, we are witnessing a back-to-the-future phenomenon with Latin American Pentecostal evangelists taking their Azusa Street–like message of salvation and divine healing on speaking tours in Anglo-American Pentecostal churches across the United States and Canada.

The four most famous Argentine evangelists that minister in the United States are Carlos Annacondia, Claudio Friedzon, Alberto Mottessi, and Omar Cabrera. Their enormous churches and revival services, which have drawn up to 60,000 people in Argentina, have been closely followed in American Pentecostal circles and have received major multipage coverage in the most important interdenominational Pentecostal magazine in the United States, *Charisma*. The attention that Annacondia, Friedzon, Mottessi, and Cabrera have received through their speaking tours, books, videos, and revivals in Latin America and in the United States has prompted a growing number of American Pentecostal leaders to adopt their strategies and even to travel to Latin America to visit their churches in order to bring back to the United States new methods and strategies for their own ministries. American and Canadian Pentecostal leaders are also following similar revival movements in Brazil and Guatemala. Finally, although we lack time to fully explore here, there is anecdotal evidence to suggest that Latin American Catholic Charismatics are contributing to the spread of the Catholic Charismatic movement among U.S. Latinos (Espinosa 2004, 282).

The result of Latin American Pentecostal missionary work in the United States, along with high levels of immigration from countries with large Pentecostal/Charismatic populations, is that a very high percentage of U.S. Latina/os are Pentecostal/Charismatic. The HCAPL national survey found that Latino/as of Mexican, El Salvadorian,

Guatemalan, Colombian, and Cuban descent are Pentecostal/Charismatic at a higher rate than found in their country of origin. This may be due to Protestant Pentecostals and Catholic Charismatics immigrating to the United States at a higher rate than non-Pentecostal/Charismatics. Although evidence is lacking for all of Latin America, scholars have recently found that Mexican Protestants immigrate to the United States at more than twice (15 percent) the percentage of the national Mexican population (7.2 percent). This may also be true for Latin Americans that come from countries with large Protestant populations (e.g., Guatemala, El Salvador) and/or from countries where there is acute discrimination, persecution, and other forms of historic social disenfranchisement (e.g., Cuba, Mexico, Colombia). In total, there are 20 million Pentecostal/Charismatic Protestants and Catholics in the six largest Latin American countries sending Latin Americans to the United States (Espinosa 2004, 283–284).

Catholic-Pentecostal Cooperation

The growth of Protestant Pentecostalism has prompted some Catholic leaders to seek out creative ways to work together on common causes. This is an incredibly difficult task because of the deep animosity that exists between Pentecostal Protestants and Catholics in Latin America. This animosity is hard to overcome when, as religion scholar Brian H. Smith notes, Pentecostals accuse the pope of being the "Antichrist" and Catholics of practicing "idolatry" because they "worship" the Virgin Mary and the saints. Still others insult Catholic leaders

by claiming that the devil runs "rampant" in Catholic convents and monasteries, where "nuns have abortions" and "priests spread homosexuality." In similarly sharp rhetoric, in 1992 at the Latin American Conference of Catholic Bishops, Pope John Paul II accused Pentecostals and other "sects" of being "rapacious wolves" and "pseudospiritual movements" that were devouring Latin American Catholics and causing "division and discord in our communities" (1998, 4, 60–64, 92–95).

Despite the real hostility that exists between Hispanic Protestants and Catholics in the Americas, there is a small but growing trend toward ecumenical/interdenominational cooperation. Smith notes that Pentecostals and Catholics have joined forces on moral issues in a number of Latin American countries to promote family values, oppose any measures to legalize abortion or homosexual marriage, fight corruption and military dictatorships, and champion human rights and social justice. In Costa Rica, for example, a number of Catholic and Pentecostal ministers joined forces in 1993 to oppose a legislative proposal that would instruct high school students on how to have safe sex outside of marriage. Similarly in Chile in 1995, some Catholics and Pentecostals worked together to oppose a new law that would grant equal rights to gays and lesbians. In Central America, some Pentecostals collaborated with Catholic Christian Base communities to aid those attacked by Right Wing militias. In Brazil, Bishop Manoel de Mello of the Brazil for Christ denomination praised Catholic bishops for speaking out against human rights violations and sharply criticized Evangelicals for remaining silent. There are also other examples of Catholic and Protestant scholars working together in seminary education and in writing church histories (Smith 1998, 95–97).

Smith argues that there are three possible future scenarios for Catholic-Pentecostal interaction: (1) mutually reinforcing flight from the world whereby they focus on inward spirituality and neglect social responsibilities; (2) conflicting religiopolitical agendas whereby Catholics would support existing government structures while Pentecostals would defend free-market capitalism and political democracy; and (3) prophetic social catalyst moving in tandem for moral reform and social and political change. The transdenominational and transnational Pentecostal/Charismatic movement may be one of the most important ecumenical bridges available today. However, anti-Catholic bigotry and mandates from the Catholic hierarchy that Catholic Charismatics should not invite Protestant Pentecostals to speak at Catholic Charismatic Church–sponsored events undermine this potentially important ecumenical/interdenominational bridge in Catholic-Pentecostal relations (Smith 1998, 15–19, 85–99).

This movement toward ecumenical/interdenominational cooperation between Latino/a Pentecostals and Catholics is moving ahead at a much faster pace in the United States. A number of seminary programs, institutes, and conferences like the former Hispanic branch of the Fund for Theological Education (FTE), Hispanic Summer Program, AETH, the Hispanic Theological Initiative (HTI), and the HCAPL study have brought Latina/o Catholics, Mainline Protestants, Evangelicals, and Pentecostals students and/or faculty together for funding, seminary training, ministry workshops and seminars, and networking opportunities (Espinosa 2004, 285–286).

Gastón Espinosa

References and Further Reading

Camp, Roderic Ai. *Crossing Swords: Politics and Religion in Mexico* (New York: Oxford University Press, 1997).

Chesnut, R. Andrew. *Born Again in Brazil: The Pentecostal Boom and the Pathogens of Poverty* (Piscataway, NJ: Rutgers University Press, 1997).

De Leon, Victor. *The Silent Pentecostals: A Biographical History of the Pentecostal Movement among Hispanics in the Twentieth-Century* (Taylors, SC: Faith Printing Company, 1979).

Espinosa, Gastón. "El Azteca: Francisco Olazabal and Latino Pentecostal Charisma, Power, and Faith Healing in the Borderlands." *Journal of the American Academy of Religion* 67, no. 3 (Fall 1999): 597–616.

Espinosa, Gastón. "'Your Daughters Shall Prophesy': A History of Women in Ministry in the Latino Pentecostal Movement in the United States." *Women and Twentieth-Century Protestantism*, ed. Margaret Lamberts Bendroth and Virginia Lieson Brereton (Champaign, IL: University of Illinois Press, 2002).

Espinosa, Gastón. "The Pentecostalization of Latin American and U.S. Latino Christianity." *Pneuma: The Journal of the Society for Pentecostal Studies* 26, no. 2 (2004): 262–292.

Espinosa, Gastón. "Ordinary Prophet: William J. Seymour and the Azusa Street Revival." *The Azusa Street Revival and Its Legacy*, ed. Harold D. Hunter and Cecil M. Robeck Jr. (Cleveland, TN: Pathway Press, 2006), 29–60.

Sánchez-Walsh, Arlene. *Latino Pentecostal Identity: Evangelical Faith, Self, and*

Society (New York: Columbia University Press, 2003).

Smith, Brian H. *Religious Politics in Latin America: Pentecostal vs. Catholic* (Notre Dame, IN: University of Notre Dame Press, 1998).

Villafane, Eldin. *The Liberating Spirit: Toward an Hispanic American Pentecostal Social Ethic* (Washington, DC: University Press of America, 1992).

PILGRIMAGE

"Pilgrimage," or in Spanish "peregrinación," comes from the Latin words "per" and "ager" (to wander about). The religious concept of pilgrimage, however, is not to wander about aimlessly, but to go a great distance for the purpose of worshipping in a specific place, usually a shrine or tomb where some type of theophany (divine revelation or manifestation) has occurred. Pilgrimage seems to be a part of every major religion and is an important tradition in the three religions that come from Abraham: Judaism, Christianity, and Islam.

Pilgrimage in Judeo-Christian Tradition

From ancient times, pilgrimage has been tied to cultic centers or shrines and to offering or sacrifice. Pilgrims would travel to a shrine to celebrate a specific holiday (holy day) in honor of a certain god or sacred being. While there, the pilgrim would offer part of her/his produce (fruit, vegetable, or animal) in supplication or thanksgiving. In the Hebrew Scriptures, we find the Israelites being called to come before God in three pilgrim festivals (solemn and joyful occasions). These are Passover, Pentecost, and the Feast of Booths.

The Jewish practice of going on pilgrimage to these holy places was so strong that even during the exile, pilgrimage to Jerusalem continued. Despite the fact that the Ark of the Covenant had been lost, faithful Jews continued to "go up to" Jerusalem to offer prayers of supplication and thanksgiving to the God of Abraham, Isaac, and Israel. In the Christian Scriptures, Jesus and the Holy Family, being faithful Jews, also went up to Jerusalem in pilgrimage to offer sacrifice (Luke 2:22, 41). As an adult, Jesus continued the practice of going on pilgrimage to Jerusalem with his disciples (John 2:13). His triumphal entry into Jerusalem on Palm Sunday can be seen as part of the pilgrim ritual of his disciples.

As Jews, early Christians seem to continue the practice of going on pilgrimage to Jewish Shrines in Palestine; however, with the destruction of the Temple in Jerusalem (70 CE) Christian pilgrimages to the Holy Land took on less of a religious tone in favor of a more historical interest in the places where Jesus had lived. Christian pilgrimages to the Holy Land also seem to have been occasions to visit and aid the impoverished Christian communities still living in Palestine. The conversion of the Emperor Constantine in the fourth century gave freedom of worship to all Christians. With the end of persecution, the places of Christian martyrdom as well as the tombs of famous Christian martyrs became places of pilgrimage for those who could not travel to the Holy Land. The places of Christian pilgrimage slowly became organized around types of locations: shrines to Jesus' life, Christian martyrdom, and radical monastic life. As time

CHIMAYÓ

A town and valley 28 miles northeast of Santa Fe, New Mexico, Chimayó and its famous chapel, the *Santuario*, are destination sites for yearly pilgrimages, especially during Holy Week. Steeped in folklore, Chimayó has been associated with several major legends relating to the supernatural and miraculous. One such legend involves a pit in the ground of which the dirt (called *tierra bendita*, "blessed earth") is said to have healing power. The tradition stems back to precolonial days when the Pueblo Indians found the fertile land to be sacred, and later this myth came to be fused with a legend of Guatemalan descent surrounding a crucifix known as the *Señor de Esquípulas*. Both the pit, *El Posito*, and the crucifix were centralized when Bernardo Abeyta, a member of the *Penitentes* brotherhood, received permission to build a private chapel in 1814; the present structure was built by 1816. Over 300,000 people visit Chimayó each year to partake of its chiles and fruits, support its famous weaving industry, and visit the Santuario, as well as the *Capilla del Santo Niño de Atocha*, to search for a miracle and to draw closer to God. Because of its folkloric heritage, the Chimayó valley is one of the most important religious sites in the American Southwest.

—DC

passed, a fourth type of pilgrimage site became important: shrines to apparitions of Jesus, Mary, or a Saint. Most of today's Christian shrines belong to this fourth category.

Shrines and Other Holy Places

Shrines are places tied to the holy or the sacred. According to Crumrine and Morinis, they are "revered *places* which cultures have often erected in the most awe-inspiring locations, honored with the highest manifestations of their arts and crafts, revered as the earthly seat of God, and given much blood, sweat, tears, and money to visit" (1991, 2). Above all, they are sites that have witnessed the action of God in a particularly powerful way through either miracles or martyrdom. Besides the places of Jesus' life, the Christian community in the fourth century began to distinguish certain catacombs around the Roman Empire as

shrines because of the martyrs buried there. As knowledge of them grew, these shrines became important centers of international travel.

As the centuries passed, every important region of Christendom desired to have its place of pilgrimage. Legend, miracles, and ancient documentation led to the discovery of various martyrs in Europe and the Middle East. The most famous of these was the discovery of the body of the Apostle James, the son of Zebedee and "brother" (cousin) of Jesus. His tomb was discovered in the year 830 in Galicia (Spain) at Campus Stellae. The Shrine came to be called Santiago (Saint James) de Campostela, and it the most famous of Spain's 1,014 shrines. According to Christian legend, the body of Santiago was buried because, in his efforts to preach the Gospel to the ends of the earth, he had journeyed to Hispaniola. When he had founded the Church in Spain, the Virgin Mary appeared to him on a Pillar in Zaragosa. She told him Jesus wanted him to return to Jerusalem to be martyred in witness to the faith. Before leaving for Jerusalem, he established a Shrine to Santa María del Pilar as a place of pilgrimage for Spanish Christians.

He left for Jerusalem, and after his martyrdom in 44 CE his body was taken back to Spain and buried. Eventually the location of his tomb was forgotten until the hermit Pelagio discovered it in a miraculous manner. Almost immediately it became a place of pilgrimage. Since then, Christians have been making their way to Santiago de Compostela in the far northwestern corner of Spain in an area that used to be known as *finis mundi* (the ends of the earth). Before the so-called "discovery" of the Western Hemisphere, it was thought that this was the place Jesus referred to in Acts 1:8 when he sent his disciples to preach the Gospel to the "ends of the earth."

Another famous pilgrimage location in Spain is that of Santa María de Guadalupe in Extremadura. In the mid-thirteenth century, the shepherd Gil Cordero miraculously discovered a Lucan statue of Mary hidden during the Moorish invasion of Spain. A shrine was built for it and pilgrims soon began to come to venerate the holy image. It was from this location that the Christian concept of shrines and pilgrimage moved to America.

Probably the most famous Christian American shrine is that of Our Lady of Guadalupe at Tepeyac (Mexico City). This shrine dates back to 1531 and is erroneously named after the shrine to Guadalupe in Spain. Still, this happy

Large crowd outside the Old Basilica of Guadaloupe during the annual pilgrimage to the shrine of Mexico's patron saint, the Virgin of Guadalupe. (Danny Lehman/Corbis)

accident demonstrates how in America the European, African, and Indigenous ideas of pilgrimage and shrines would come to influence how Americans, especially Latino/as, understand these two concepts.

Pilgrimage in Europe was a penitential act. In Latin America it is often with a vow (promesa/manda) in mind. Pilgrimage in the Latina/o mind-set is a mixture of devotion, belief, bartering, gratitude, ritual, and travel. Iconography and myth are essential to pilgrimage. Normally, Hispanic pilgrims will travel short or great distances to see for themselves the location of a mythic event like the apparition of María to Juan Diego at Tepeyac or the survival of the image of Christ (Señor de los Milagros) on the only wall of a chapel that remained standing after a great earthquake in Lima, Peru.

According to Crumrine and Morinis, Mayan and other Indigenous religious and cultural pilgrimages in Latin America "take on cosmological significance, as journeys to shrines are identified with macrocosmic cycles of movement among astral bodies." The Christian influence on pilgrimage is one of conversion. The visit to a shrine moves one from the familiar world of home to the unfamiliar world of the holy place and back again, hopefully as a new person. Pilgrimage is meant to be done with an open heart and "is an exercise in humble supplication, surrender, and prayer in which the qualities of the Christian heart are cultivated" (1991, 5, 14).

Besides connection to the mythic and cosmological, pilgrimage brings the pilgrim into contact with a spiritual and often cultural icon. The pilgrimage shrine and its image of Christ, Mary, or one of the Saints often belongs to a particular culture and needs to be familiar to that culture. But, because it is transcendental in nature, it needs to differentiate itself enough from the cultural norm that it becomes special, awe-inspiring, and transforming. Anthropological and social studies have shown that "pilgrimage can work to reinforce the social image and identity of a group within a diversified ethnic population" (Crumrine and Morinis 1991, 7). When Latina/os are unable to go back to their homeland, the venerated image of the shrine becomes a pilgrim and travels to a local parish in the United States, where the Hispanics of the area can come and visit. At times these pilgrimage images stay in a local area and become miraculous in and of themselves, thus beginning a new Latin American shrine in the United States. For example, the shrine of the Virgin de San Juan de Los Lagos in Mexico became La Virgen de San Juan de los lagos del Valle de Texas and the shrine to the Virgen de la Caridad del Cobre in Cuba became the Ermita de la Caridad in Miami, Florida.

Conclusion

The three Abrahamic religions, Judaism, Islam, and Christianity, hold pilgrimage as an important and hopefully life-changing event. It should not be undertaken as a tourist or as simple travel, rather a pilgrim needs to undertake his/her pilgrimage as an act of faith and a connection to the mythic events and peoples of faith. Christian Latino/as seeking pilgrimage do not have to travel to the Holy Land or Europe as shrines and places of pilgrimage abound in the Americas. There are between 57 and 111 shrines in the United States; Mexico has 223 shrines; Brazil has 121; Peru has

106; Argentina has 93; Ecuador has 91; Chile has 74; Colombia has 68; Canada has 52 shrines, including 1 to Our Lady of Guadalupe; Bolivia and Venezuela have 41 holy places each; Uruguay has 16; El Salvador has 14; Guatemala has 12; Honduras has 9; Puerto Rico has 7; the Dominican Republic, Nicaragua, and Panama have 5 shrines each; and finally, Cuba has 3, Paraguay has 2, and Costa Rica has 1 place of pilgrimage (Crumrine and Morinis 1991, 22).

Gilberto Cavazos-González

References and Further Reading

Crumrine, N. Ross, and E. Alan Morinis, eds. *Pilgrimage in Latin America: Contributions to the Study of Anthropology* (Westport, CT: Greenwood Press, 1991).

LaBande, Edmund René. "Pilgrimages: Medieval and Modern." *New Catholic Encyclopedia*, 2nd ed. (Washington, DC: Gale Cengage, 2003).

McCarthy, Maria Caritas. "Pilgrimage: Early Christian." *New Catholic Encyclopedia*, 2nd ed. (Washington, DC: Gale Cengage, 2003).

Polan, Stanley Morris. "Pilgrimage." *New Catholic Encyclopedia*, 2nd ed. (Washington, DC: Gale Cengage, 2003).

POLITICAL INVOLVEMENT

Political participation on behalf of groups and individuals is an integral function of democratic societies, both sustaining and challenging the decisions and powers of governmental bodies. Historically, scholars have differentiated between conventional means of political engagement such as voting, lobbying, campaigning, or running for office, or more direct means via protests, demonstrations, and forms of civil disobedience as methods to ensure an equitable and efficient distribution of scarce resources.

From a Latino/a perspective, a lack of scholarly focus has led to erroneous assumptions about the nonexistent influence of religion on civic participation amongst the community. This stands in stark contrast to the gamut of existing information on the role of the churches and religious organizations on African American political involvement during slavery, Jim Crow, and the post–civil rights era. Gaps in scholarly literature (as well as depictions and reports by mainstream media sources), have aided long-held perceptions that Latina/os are politically passive, with most historically affiliated to a Catholic church that perpetuated the status quo and refrained from assisting the community amidst structures of oppression (Espinosa, Elizondo, and Miranda 2005, 4).

However, while recent scholarly observations acknowledge the truths to past accounts, they also reveal untold stories of religious organizations and spiritual leaders actively engaging in social and economic justice issues, likewise using faith as vehicles for political activism. At the same time, the "modes" of political participation in which Hispanics engage, from less controversial methods like voting and discussion forums to more direct action initiatives like rallies, protests, and walkouts, often vary by religious affiliation. Overall, studies show most Latino/as wish their churches were more politically active from the local to state and national levels. In addition, Hispanics express interest in seeing their religious leaders talk more about politics, especially Evangelicals in comparison to Catholics and other religious affiliations.

COMMUNITIES ORGANIZED FOR PUBLIC SERVICE

Founded in 1974 by Ernesto Cortéz Jr. and other San Antonio, Texas, activists, Communities Organized for Public Service (COPS), as its name indicates, is concerned with the everyday issues facing the Latino/a community. COPS was organized as an association of 26 Catholic parishes located in the predominantly Hispanic neighborhoods of San Antonio. Each parish became an important building block whose leaders also became the leaders of COPS. Avoiding divisive social issues, COPS concentrated on the basic needs of the community, i.e., proper drainage, traffic problems, good relationships with the police, or clearing dumping grounds within Hispanic neighborhoods. Their efforts also helped block the construction of a Bandera freeway that would have negatively affected the Latina/o community. While remaining nonpartisan, COPS participated in voter registration drives of Latina/os that eventually translated into electing Hispanics to public office. Through their efforts, they were able to participate in the election of San Antonio's first Latino mayor, Henry Cisneros, who was also the first Latino mayor of a major U.S. city.

—*MAD*

However, the extent and mode of political participation largely depends on the policy issues that most impact the community, with immigration largely at the center of past and contemporary debate.

Brief Historical Development

The historical intersection between Latino/a religion and political involvement can be traced back to the initial U.S. invasion of Mexican territory (1846–1848). The Treaty of Guadalupe Hidalgo (1848), which ended a bloody war and drew borders between the two nations, set the legal framework for the United States to occupy over 50 percent of Mexican land. Followed by the Treaty of Mesilla (1854), which settled disputes over remaining sections of the Southwest, areas representing present-day states such as Arizona, California, Colorado, Nevada, New Mexico, Texas, Utah, and Wyoming were all brought under the auspices of the U.S. government.

Initially, the 1848 treaty was supposed to guarantee citizenship and property rights to Mexicans who chose to stay in occupied Mexico, but racially motivated violence spread against them and attempts of integration into U.S. institutions was met with resistance. Outright exclusion of property ownership and political disenfranchisement created the foundations for what Juan Gonzalez (2001) likened to a system of apartheid in his book *Harvest of Empire*, given that Mexicans and other minority groups outnumbered the colonizing Euro-Americans but had little or no access to resources and power structures.

During the initial era of Southwest colonization, historical accounts show that the Catholic Church at times remained silent, concentrating more on spreading Christianity than challenging the oppressive social conditions their predominantly Mexican congregants faced. Meanwhile, Protestants were likewise disinterested, focusing instead on converting Euro-Americans who followed the country's path of westward expansionism. However, there is evidence that some Hispanic clergy resisted the discriminatory attitudes and actions of occupying European religious officials, subsequently inspiring congregants to do the same. Public ethnoreligious celebrations were also products of this resistance, proudly organized to honor the Catholic traditions of their ancestors prior to colonization. In addition, by the late nineteenth century, Latino clergy experienced displacement by European clergy purposely recruited to meet the spiritual needs of growing Euro-American populations in the Southwest. This diluted any progress by church leaders in organizing against worsening economic conditions for Latina/o populations.

During the 1900s, Latino/a workers' rights campaigns, with well-known leaders like Dolores Huerta and César Chávez, are thought to have been largely "secular" movements. However, while most scholars have compared Chávez to Dr. Martin Luther King Jr. for their shared belief in advocating nonviolent action, they largely ignore that the Catholic Church and faith were instrumental in Chávez's struggle for social justice. Likewise, during the latter part of the Bracero Program, a government-sponsored guest worker program that recruited nearly 5 million Mexicans from 1942 to 1964, a broad coalition of unions, churches, and research centers put pressure on the U.S. government to improve the housing and labor conditions workers faced.

In the 1960s and early 1970s, Chicanos, Puerto Ricans, and other Hispanics formed advocacy groups utilizing the concept of identity politics, a powerful organizing tool to build group solidarity in order to address historical and present-day experiences of racism, prejudice, and discrimination. In some localities, churches opened their doors as safe houses for Latino/a students and community groups, while others turned their backs to them. Recently depicted in the film *Walkout* and based on actual accounts, thousands of East Los Angeles High School students organized and mobilized in the spring of 1968 to protest unequal treatment, with local churches often serving as meeting grounds for organizers. As a result, the walkout movement spread across the country, influencing the need for educational reform. Nevertheless, as in the case of the Puerto Rican youth movement and organization the Young Lords, a local East Harlem church (the First Spanish Methodist Church) was seized by the group because it was empty six days a week, turning it into La Iglesia de la Gente. For 11 days the church became a makeshift community center, where primarily local people of color came to engage in testimonials, poetry, music, song, and other activities in protest of economic conditions and institutionalized oppression.

After a surge in undocumented immigration due to political unrest in Latin America during the 1980s, the Sanctuary Movement emerged across the United States. Over 500 congregations, including those of both the Catholic and Protestant denominations, joined forces to aid and shelter Central American immigrants from the Immigration and Naturalization Service authorities. The Reverends John Fife and Jim Corbett, aware of the devastating effects of civil unrest in Guatemala and El Salvador, began opening up churches in South Texas under the

CATÓLICOS POR LA RAZA

Started in 1969 by a Loyola Marymount University law student, Ricardo Cruz, Católicos por la Raza (CPLR) was a political organization that protested how the Catholic dioceses, specifically the Los Angeles diocese, spent church funds in wealthier and whiter neighborhoods while ignoring poorer Hispanic neighborhoods. CPLR was also concerned that the Catholic Church was neither appointing Hispanic clergy in leadership positions nor paying attention to other concerns raised within Latina/o parishes. Although originally established as a response to the closing of a predominant Mexican girl's school, Our Lady Queen of Girl's High School, its first public protest occurred during the 1969 Christmas Eve Mass at Saint Basil located in Wilshire. Then Cardinal James McIntyre spent close to $4 million for the event. Hundreds protested by leading a march to the Mass—picketing outside while service continued inside. Eventually, several entered the church, leading to 21 of the protestors being arrested, including Ricardo Cruz. Citing "moral corruption" for his activities in leading the march, Cruz's admission to the California State Bar was postponed. Although the Catholic Church criticized the Christmas Eve actions of CPLR, they did respond by appointing several Latinos as cardinals throughout the southwestern United States. Additionally, the use of Spanish and Hispanic culture (specifically Mexican) was incorporated into the church, along with official support to organizations like the United Farm Workers.

—MAD

medieval law of "right to sanctuary." During the fourth to seventeenth century, law officials did not have the legal right to arrest criminals in a place of religious worship. Church leaders used this argument to help protect those who needed asylum from bloodshed in their native countries. The Sanctuary Movement soon gained momentum and became popular in Arizona, Illinois, Texas, Pennsylvania, and California. In protest against mid-1980s American interventionist policies in Latin America and other Third World regions, many university campuses also adapted the manifesto of "right to sanctuary." By 1987, 440 locations across the United States were declared as refuges for Central American immigrants.

At the end of the millennium, religion and politics also played an integral role during the Elián González custody battle,

one that reached worldwide media attention. As Miguel De La Torre (2003) pointed out, not only had the Cuban exilic community used religion to justify their overall political and economic power over time, but religious symbols and biblical comparisons of the coming of a Christ child, as well as support from influential local Catholic clergy, were largely instrumental in prolonging the international custody battle.

More recently, a resurgence of nativism and xenophobia has largely been fueled over the growing presence of undocumented immigrants from Latin America. As Congress debated immigration reform in May 2006 and 2007, immigrant rights marches involving thousands from Los Angeles to New York were largely organized or sponsored by local and national faith-based groups and advocacy organizations. A

Hundreds of protesters wave flags at the "Americans for Elian's Freedom" rally at the Miami courthouse on May 11, 2000. The demonstrators demanded that Elian Gonzalez be allowed to stay in the United States. (Getty Images)

similar organization inspired by faith-based initiatives in the 1980s named "The New Sanctuary Movement" was created to offer support to undocumented immigrants. However, their aims have shifted from offering asylum to undocumented immigrants to providing low cost and free legal aid.

The Impact of Religion on Latina/o Political Participation —Results from Studies

Over the past decade political scientists have begun to pay more attention to the growing Latino/a community's role and impact on the U.S. political process. Studies that examine group political participation largely rely on testing the theoretical premises of "social capital," loosely known as the organizational networks in which groups engage in order to sustain the structures of modern pluralistic democracies.

According to a 2008 study by the Pew Forum on Religion and Public Life, most Latino/as see religion as a moral compass to guide their own political thinking, expressing their concern about the need for political participation both inside the confines of the church and in everyday life. Additionally, a vast majority of those surveyed saw the pulpit as an appropriate place for the expression of political views. Not only did an overwhelming two-thirds of Hispanics of differing nationalities and denominations opine that religious beliefs should be raised in church, they also commented that political leaders, both at the local and national levels, do not express their own religious views frequently enough. This backed an earlier 2002 survey of 260 church leaders and members in six major cities in the United States and Puerto Rico (Marquez and Wainer 2002). The study found that church members do not necessarily participate in politics other than voting and that church leaders largely condemn direct action such as rallies, protests, and demonstration, instead encouraging nonpolitical social and community involvement. The authors suggested their findings are largely explained by their churches' avoidance of partisan politics. However, Hispanic churches' commitment to community and social engagement increases different forms of political activism on behalf of their members, thus creating the foundations for future political participation at state, national, and international levels.

When assessing political participation by religious affiliation, studies reveal divergent results. Evangelicals were most likely to apply personal religious beliefs to their political thinking. According to the Pew study, 66 percent of evangelicals reported religion as the most important factor in political decisions as compared to 44 percent of Catholics. Whereas only 10 percent of evangelicals reported that religion and politics should remain disparate, over 30 percent of Catholics reported that religion had no influence in their political lives. A possible reason for this difference is that Evangelicals tend to place higher value on spirituality in all aspects of life. As historian David Bebbington posits, one hallmark of evangelicalism includes conversionism, or the belief that lives need to be changed. Through the mouthpiece of evangelicalism, believers may use politics as a

means to better their own personal situations, whether locally or globally (Espinosa et al. 2005, 15).

In their article, "Religion and Latino Partisanship in the United States," Nathan J. Kelly and Jana Morgan Kelly discovered that the number of hours spent in church had a direct influence on the religious influence upon politics. They suggest a reason for this is that churches provide an important social context in which political information is exchanged. Therefore, Latina/os affiliated with a specific congregation within their religious community are likely to adopt partisan attachments that are consistent with the messages received (88). The Pew study backs this finding. Over 40 percent of Evangelicals attend church services at least three times a week and over 60 percent frequent services at least one time per week. Fifty-one percent of Catholics reported that they attend church on a sporadic basis, and 30 percent reported that participation was limited to a particular religious event, such as a baptism or a wedding. Because frequent, even daily, church attendance (as in the case of Evangelicals like Pentecostals) is encouraged, religion and politics seem to remain inseparable in the Evangelical church as compared to their Catholic counterparts. Religion may continue to have a substantial effect upon political thinking due to a sharp decline in Catholicism and exponential increase in Evangelicalism and Protestant affiliation since the 1980s. The authors postulated that many Christians were finding Protestantism more attractive due to a closer-knit church community, more egalitarian gender roles in the church, social gatherings outside the church, and a more relaxed church atmosphere. If this

LATINO PASTORAL ACTION CENTER

Founded in 1992 by the Reverend Dr. Raymond Rivera, the New York City–based Latino Pastoral Action Center (LPAC) is a national Christ-centered faith-based organization that aims to educate, equip, and empower Latino and other urban churches to develop holistic ministries. The vision of LPAC is to energize civil society and rebuild social capital. They seek to strengthen the Four Pillars of Community Life™: Families, Schools, Community-based Organizations (CBOs), and Churches, which they insist collectively make up the foundation of a healthy community. In addition, they apply a model developed by Rev. Dr. Rivera called the Four Principles of Holistic Ministry™: Liberation, Healing, Community, and Transformation to develop cadres of strong, independent, articulate leaders who legitimately represent and are accountable to their communities. These individuals gain a greater sense of self, and serve as resources to their peers and communities. In turn, they work with others to strengthen the Four Pillars of Community Life. To rebuild social capital, LPAC operates community-based, citywide, national, and international ministries, while serving as a model of holistic ministry for urban leaders in the United States and around the world. Through these ministries, LPAC aims to revitalize the community by guiding children, youth, and adults to a lifelong calling of personal and community growth.

—EDR

trend continues, one may predict a trend toward the coalescence of politics and religion.

The breadth and extent of political topics discussed in church settings has also received examination. According to the Hispanic Churches in American Public Life Survey (2008), 54 percent of Latino/as believed that they have a say in government decisions. So strong is the connection between religion and politics in the Hispanic community that when compared to Euro-American (White) Christians, Latino/as who consider themselves as "spiritual but not religious," still perceive a stronger connection between these two factors. According to the Pew study, over 50 percent of secular Hispanic Catholics felt that American politics were lacking spirituality, whereas only 30 percent of White Catholics reported the same.

When asked specifically what issues were most personally relevant, 80 percent reported concerns with U.S. immigration policy. Immigration is a particularly fervid political topic among Latino/as in America who have not yet attained legal status. According to the Hispanic Churches in American Public Life Survey, 74 percent of Latina/os want their churches to support undocumented immigrants, even at the risk of breaking the law. Subsequently, 80 percent of undocumented Hispanics reported that their churches should become more involved with immigration law, at both the grassroots and the national levels.

Issues such as gender equality, taxation, and government aid are more readily discussed in the Protestant denomination. As Larry Hunt states, "Protestantism may offer more opportunity for access to leadership roles and stimulate more religious and social participation among Hispanics by offering a smaller and more intimate sense of community'' (2001, 142). Protestant churches tend to be smaller, more participation-oriented, and congregational (as opposed to the noncommunity-based organization, i.e., Episcopalian). Thus, under the protection of the close-knit church communities, spiritual leaders and churchgoers feel more open to probity, especially regarding political issues. In the Catholic Church, only 20 percent reported that women's rights were discussed, and in the Protestant church that number was nearly tripled. Although topics such as abortion and homosexuality remain controversial among Latino/as, 58 percent of Protestants, including Evangelicals, reported they were discussed openly in church, whereas 45 percent of Catholics reported that both were discussed in a more evasive manner.

Alan Aja and Anne Hoffman

References and Further Reading

De La Torre, Miguel. *La Lucha for Cuba: Religion and Politics on the Streets of Miami* (Berkeley: University of California Press, 2003).

Espinosa, Gaston, Virgilio Elizondo, and Jesse Miranda. "Hispanic Churches in American Public Life: Summary of Findings." Center for the Study of Latino Religion, *Interim Reports*, Vol. 2003, no. 2 (March 2003): 1–29.

Espinosa, Gaston, Virgilio Elizondo, and Jesse Miranda. *Latino Religions and Civic Activism in the United States* (New York: Oxford University Press, 2005).

Fraga, Luis R., John A. Garcia, Rodney E. Hero, Michael Jones-Correa, Valerie Martinez-Ebers, and Gary M. Segura. "Su Casa Es Nuestra Casa: Latino Politics Research and the Development of American Political Science." *American Political Science Review* 100, no. 4 (November 2006): 515–522.

Hunt, Larry R. "Religion, Gender, and the Hispanic Experience in the United States: Catholic/Protestant Differences in Religious Involvement, Social Status, and Gender-Role Attitudes." *Review of Religious Research* 43, no. 2 (December 2001): 139–160.

Jones-Correa, Michael, and David Leal. "Political Participation: Does Religion Matter?" *Political Research Quarterly* 54 (December 2001): 751–770.

Kelly, Nathan J., and Jana Morgan Kelly. "Religion and Latino Partisanship in the United States." *Political Research Quarterly* 58, no. 1 (March 2005): 87–95.

Marquez, Frances, and Andrew Wainer. "Latino Religion and Civic Engagement: How and Where do Congregations Encourage Participation." Paper presented at the annual meeting of the American Political Science Association, Boston, August 28, 2002.

Pew Hispanic Center. *Changing Faiths: Latinos and the Transformation of American Religion* (Washington DC: Pew Forum on Religion and Public Life, 2007).

POSTCOLONIALISM

Even though the definition of the term "postcolonialism" is debatable, we can at least say that postcolonialism, as a tool of critical analysis, seriously considers the historical implications of centuries of imperialism and colonialism. Postcolonialism recognizes that liberation did not come with the end of the wars of independence fought throughout the Two-Thirds World, which fell victim to the colonial process. Rather, imperial structures of oppression continue to this day manifested as militarism, economic globalization (neoliberalism), and the normalization and legitimization of the cultural Eurocentric norms. The social, economic, political, and religious narratives produced at the center of Eurocentric thought maintain oppressive global structures that define a reality that continues to benefit the former colonizers. Part of this constructed reality defines the identities of the colonized in relation to the colonizer. By defining and classifying the existence of the colonized, it makes their subordination to the self-defined "superiority" of White Christian European existence and thought possible. Therefore, part of the liberationist project is to define one's group identity, as a people, apart from the definitions created by the colonizers of yesteryear and of today. Postcolonialism becomes a methodology by which the colonized speaks back to Eurocentric colonizers about how they have defined the identities, cultures, and customs of the colonized.

Although a multitude of systems and structures exists to colonize the minds of the oppressed, for purposes of this entry, the cultural text that concerns us revolves around the religious narrative, specifically a Christianity practiced by Latina/os that can subconsciously reinforce their own subjugation. Inhabitants of the Western Hemisphere who first experienced the Spanish conquest, then the colonization by various European powers, and the hegemony of the United States must ask how theological thought and the biblical text were used and misused to produce a religious ideology that not only justified but encouraged the subjugation of one people by another, usually along race and ethnic lines. Likewise, postcolonialism examines the types of theological and biblical interpretations

that can foster anti-imperialist resistance to the colonial narrative.

It would seem that Latino/a theologies of liberation would be open to postcolonial critical analysis. After all, the term "liberation" as used within religious circles came into vogue during the late 1960s when many colonized groups throughout the world begin to construct a theological response to the exploitation of Two-Thirds World people (including those within the United States), an oppression manifested as racism, classism, sexism, and heterosexism. As such, postcolonial theories arose from anticolonial struggles for liberation from injustices and the suffering caused by empires. Nevertheless, many of the early Hispanic religious scholars were suspicious of postcolonial theories, disregarding them as another Eurocentric intellectual venture. This perception may be because many, who were among the first generation of Latino/a scholars, focused almost exclusively on Catholic thought and, to a lesser extent, on Protestantism. This was expected, for after all, the vast majority (over 90 percent) of the Hispanic community identified with Christianity. Many of these early Latina/o scholars were trained at Christian seminaries and/or divinity schools and served or continue to serve in ministry. The worldview they developed was formed by both modernity and church teachings. Hence, hesitancy exists in addressing the connection between the colonialization project, along with its religious dimension, and their Christian faith and field of study.

By contrast, the more recent Latina/o religious scholars entering the academic guild come from a very different social location. Since the 1990s, these scholars began to recognize the complexities that any discourse on differences concerning sexual identity, ethnic and racial groups, and cultural and national origins have upon any conversation concerning Liberationist thought. Recognizing that Hispanics were not a monolithic group was not enough. The ambiguities of differences complicated oppression as overlapping levels of subjugation began to be considered. Most of these newer Latina/o scholars, who were university trained, who probably never served as a minister or a priest, and who may have claimed no faith allegiance, began to explore these differences in earnest. In exploring these differences, they were more receptive to employing critical theories like postmodernity and postcolonialism.

Hispanics who use a postcolonial methodology are keenly aware that the relationship between the colonizer and the colonized is not a simple dichotomy. No neat division exists between the boundary that separates the colonizer from the colonized. What exists is a space of exchange producing multiple conflicting identities, histories, and cultures. The postcolonialist looks toward what is hidden between these binary poles. Hence, much attention is given to the concept of hybridity. We are not simply Hispanic or Anglo, White or Black, male or female; rather we exist where these binary poles connect, merge, conflict, and create. This space becomes the product of rape, violation, massacres, invasion, and conquest, in short, a colonized space. Postcolonialism attempts to move beyond that space, hence the "post" in postcolonialism. Hybridity forces the Latino/a religious scholar to be conscious of how her/his own construction of liberative discourses might at times participate in its own oppressive ideologies. Through such self-critique of complicity with oppressive structures, postcolonial thoughts achieve its most critical contribution to the liberative discourse. The use of postcolonial critical theory by Latina/os also forces the Eurocentric academy to seriously consider their own complicity with theological presuppositions informed by subjective colonized assumptions that are accepted as objective.

Those Hispanic scholars who employ postcolonial analysis in their work do so with an understanding that it provides a way of understanding why and how oppressive global structures operate. This knowledge is helpful in the very struggle for justice. Thus, Latino/a based liberation theologies and postcolonial theories are not at odds with each other. Instead, the latter can help bring in the implementation of the former.

Miguel A. De La Torre

References and Further Reading

Dube, Musa W. "Postcolonialism & Liberation," *Handbook of U.S. Theologies of Liberation*, ed. Miguel A. De La Torre (St. Louis: Chalice Press, 2004).

Keller, Catherine, Michael Nausner, and Mayra Rivera, eds. *Postcolonial Theories: Divinity and Empire* (St. Louis: Chalice Press, 2004).

Segovia, Fernando F. *Decolonizing Biblical Studies: A View from the Margins* (Maryknoll, NY: Orbis Books, 2000).

POSTMODERNISM

Postmodernism is notoriously difficult to define. It is sometimes used to describe the period since the late 1960s, an epoch that—allegedly—follows and is distinct from modernism. The term entered the lexicon with Jean-François Lyotard's publication of *The Postmodern Condition* (1979). Theoretical discourses of modernism, from René Descartes through the Enlightenment to the social theories of Karl Marx and Max Weber, championed reason as an adequate source for discovering and systematizing all knowledge and for building a progressive, free, and egalitarian society. Yet for all its "accomplishments," modernism also produced immense suffering for its victims, ranging from colonial genocide to oppression of the workers by capitalist industrialization, exploitation of women, and marginalization and exclusion of entire peoples, including U.S. Latino/as. Modernism produced disciplines, institutions, and modes of discourse, which legitimate various forms of domination and control. Postmodern thinkers such as Lyotard and Jean Baudrillard claim that the historically unprecedented social developments in technology, media, and socioeconomic configurations require new theories and concepts.

Postmodernism refers not only to a historical period but to a diffuse set of discursive challenges, critical approaches, and rhetorical practices that aggressively attack traditional society, theory, and culture. Not social theory per se, it combines fragmentary insights and methodologies from literary studies, historical theory, and philosophy in its attempts to challenge established paradigms. While postmodern discourses address a diverse and baffling array of topics, they share a critique of modernism. Modernism is criticized for making totalizing and universalizing claims, assuming the existence of a foundation for all knowledge, and presenting its findings as absolute truth. More specifically, postmodern theory challenges the modern notion that

theory reflects reality, emphasizing the perspectival, contingent, and relative nature of knowledge. Moreover, it examines the interplay of knowledge and power and the role of power in the production and authorization of knowledge.

U.S. Latino/a Critiques of Postmodernism

U.S. Latino/a religious scholars mostly reject the postmodern project and have been hesitant to seriously engage the movement. This rejection stems from a suspicion that postmodernism, as the outworking of modernism, serves the same agenda of modernism—to justify the systematic exclusion and exploitation of U.S. Latino/a people. More particularly, these scholars critique postmodernism's radical relativism, internal inconsistency, and parochial character. First, they commonly claim that postmodernism's relativism leaves no foundation from which to critique power structures. If every perspective constitutes a viable truth claim, then no means exist for criticizing any one perspective, even if one position directly leads to oppression. Thus, the postmodern position eliminates any basis for challenging the oppressive status quo, trivializing the suffering of U.S. Latino/as and other marginalized people. Second, though postmodern theory challenges universalizing and totalizing claims, ideologies, and unchanging truths, and denies the veracity of any grand explanatory narrative, it dogmatically holds relativism as universally valid. For postmodernism, the only universal truth is that there is no truth. Finally, postmodernism is found primarily in metropolitan centers of the modern world, former seats of colonial power. Though postmodernism recognizes the parochial character of all knowledge and human enterprise and challenges modern myths used to justify the oppression of others, it ironically remains narrowly concerned with European interests.

U.S. Latino/as scholars' rejection of postmodern theory should not be interpreted as romantic nostalgia for modernism. Like others who suffered under the aegis of modernism, they have much to celebrate in its demise. They have little reason to hope that postmodernism will turn out differently. Yet, they also recognize the ambiguity of modernism: though it provided ideologies of oppression, it also contained the impulse toward emancipation from oppression. Many "discoveries" of postmodern theory, such as the uncovering of epistemological limits of modernism, have long been visible to those on the underside of modernism. U.S. Latino/a religious scholars have anticipated many of the elements that form part of current postmodern theory.

U.S. Latino/a use of Postmodern Theory

Although many U.S. Latino/a religious scholars dismiss postmodernism on the whole, some recognize the need to engage in these currents, given the pervasiveness of postmodernism in the theoretical currents of the North American Academy. They read postmodern texts carefully, wrestle with the postmodern turn in critical theory, and face the challenges to totalizing gestures of theological texts and religious systems. They combine and connect the Iberian, indigenous, and African thought forms of their U.S. Latino/a heritage to the traits of postmodernism. They link the symbolic-cultural concept of *mestizaje* to hybridity,

the diasporic, alien, and exile categories of identity to alterity, and the interpretation of meaning through communal praxis to intersubjectivity. They take seriously, for example, the postmodern theorists' insight into the reduction of spatial distances through advances in travel and communication and perceive its effects in the transnational, fluid movements of religious practices, rituals, and icons on the borderlands. However, they do not indiscriminately adopt the entirety of postmodernism; rather they cautiously and critically appropriate elements of postmodernism's critique of modernism that resonates with their work. The significance of postmodernism rests on its deployment and reformulation with the concrete postcolonial contexts of U.S. Latino/a faith communities. Against those who argue that postmodernism truncates the possibility of liberation, Manuel Mejido Costoya counters that unless U.S. Latino/a religious thought critically engages postmodern conceptions, the liberationist impulse to transform society will be reduced to the level of hermeneutics, merely conversation about liberation (2006, 277).

Concluding Assessment

Even as U.S. Latino/a religious thought has anticipated many of postmodernism's critiques of modernity, many of its assumptions and themes remain in need of postmodern scrutiny. For example, the concept of liberation, as a central aspect of Hispanic religious thought, to the extent that it envisions a wide-scale social emancipation, rests on modernist progressivism and hermeneutic reduction. Despite all vociferous attacks against postmodernism's radical relativism, internal inconsistency, and parochial elements, U.S. Latino/a religions bear a surprising affinity with postmodernism. For example, postmodernism's eschewing of essentialism and the reification of an unequivocal self in favor of the experience of hybridity, fluidity, and intersubjectivity of identities deeply resonates with the forefront of contemporary U.S. Latino/a religious projects. Increasingly they are acknowledging these connections and reformulating religious thought to contend with postmodern challenges.

Rodolfo J. Hernández-Díaz

References and Further Reading

Best, Steven, and Douglas Kellner. *Postmodern Theory: Critical Interrogations* (New York: Guilford Press, 1991).

Goizueta, Roberto S. "Rationality or Irrationality? Modernity, Postmodernity, and the U.S. Hispanic Theologian." *Caminemos con Jesús: Toward a Hispanic/Latino Theology of Accompaniment* (Maryknoll, NY: Orbis Books, 1995).

González, Justo L. "Metamodern Aliens in Postmodern Jerusalem." *Hispanic/Latino Theology: Challenge and Promise*, ed. A. M. Isasi-Díaz and F. F. Segovia (Minneapolis: Fortress Press, 1996).

Mejido Costoya, Manuel J. "The Postmodern: Liberation or Language?" *Handbook of Latina/o Theologies*, ed. E. D. Aponte and M. A. De La Torre (St. Louis: Chalice Press, 2006).

Rivera, Mayra. *The Touch of Transcendence: A Postcolonial Theology of God* (Louisville, KY: Westminster John Knox Press, 2007).

PREFERENTIAL OPTIONS

In 1979, at the Third General Conference of the Latin American Episcopate (CELAM) meeting at Puebla de Los Angeles, Mexico, the expressions "preferential option for the poor" and "preferential option for the young" entered the ecclesial vocabulary of the Roman Catholic Church. The option for the poor becomes a staple of Catholic Social Teaching and a defining principle for Latin American and U.S. Hispanic theologies. The option for the young receives significantly less attention.

The preferential option for the poor is born out of the experience of the Latin American church. The concept is reflected in the final documents of the CELAM meeting at Medellín, Colombia, in 1968. There the bishops affirm that they have heard the cries arising from the suffering poor and commit to a solidarity that "ought to bring us to a distribution of resources and apostolic personnel that effectively gives preference to the poorest and most needy sectors" (1970, no. 9). This commitment to being a "Church of the poor" is articulated explicitly at Puebla and, as Roberto Goizueta observes, marks a "transposition of social justice from the realm of ethics to the realm of epistemology and theological method."

To make a preference for the poor is to respond to the multiple oppressions inflicted on people because of material poverty. It is not an optional commitment but finds grounding in biblical imperatives to align with those who are marginalized. The option for the poor calls for evaluation of economic, social, and political systems, structures, policies, and life-styles from the perspective of those most devastatingly impacted by their outcomes. This preference does not imply the exclusivity of divine love or attention. Yet it situates the church with the poor, who are agents of their own history as well as evangelization, challenging the church to conversion, action, and solidarity.

The phrase entered the papal lexicon in 1980 in John Paul II's address to the Brazilian bishops. From this point forward it began to appear with increasing frequency in papal, regional, and national episcopal articulations of social teaching across the globe. In Latin American liberation theologies the option for the poor is central to the thought of Gustavo Gutiérrez and others such as Elsa Támez and Jon Sobrino who influenced Oscar Romero, the martyred archbishop from El Salvador.

In the United States, the option for the poor is among the hermeneutic stances employed by Catholic and some Protestant Latino/a theologians. In some of these theologies, the option expands beyond socioeconomic factors to include the oppression experienced by Hispanics because of the denigration of Latino/a cultures and popular religious expressions within the U.S. context.

The final document from Puebla explicitly discusses a preferential option for young people in the section that follows an explication of the option for the poor. As with the poor, the young emerge as those who are both evangelized and evangelizers. The absence of the option for the young in theological reflections after Puebla draws the attention of the Congregation for the Doctrine of the Faith, which notes the significance of the silence. The option for the young finds limited expression in U.S. documents related to the third Encuentro and in the 1988 *National Plan for Hispanic Ministry*. This commitment for Hispanic youth in particular is fueled by a concern for experiences of marginalization that are intensified by poverty and issues of cultural identity. Like those of the bishops at Puebla, these references regard youth as treasure and prophetic voice.

Carmen M. Nanko-Fernández

References and Further Reading

Congregation for the Doctrine of the Faith. "Instruction on Certain Aspects of the Theology of Liberation." August 6, 1984. http://www.vatican.va/roman_curia/congregations/cfaith/documents/rc_con_cfaith_doc_19840806_theology-liberation_en.html.

Goizueta, Roberto S. "The Preferential Option for the Poor: The CELAM Documents and the NCCB Pastoral Letter on U.S. Hispanics as Sources for U.S. Hispanic Theology." *Journal of Hispanic/Latino Theology* 3, no. 2 (1995): 65–77.

Nanko, Carmen Marie. "Justice Crosses the Border: The Preferential Option for the Poor in the United States." *A Reader in Latina Feminist Theology: Religion and Justice*, ed. María Pilar Aquino, Daisy L. Machado, and Jeanette Rodríguez (Austin: University of Texas Press, 2002).

Second General Conference of Latin American Bishops (CELAM). *The Church in the Present Day Transformation of Latin America in Light of the Council: II Conclusions*, ed. Louis Michael Colonnese (Bogotá, D.E.-Colombia: General Secretariat of CELAM, 1970).

Third General Conference of Latin American Bishops (CELAM). "Evangelization in Latin America's Present and Future: Final Document." *Puebla and Beyond: Documentation and Commentary*, ed. John Eagleson and Philip Scharper; trans. John Drury (Maryknoll, NY: Orbis Books, 1979).

PRIVATE RELIGIOUS SCHOOLS

According to the 2000 Census, Hispanics are the largest minority group under the age of 18, representing 16 percent of U.S. school-age children or one-third of the Hispanic population. This school-age population is growing faster than any other racial or ethnic group, probably due to two factors. First, the median age of Latina/os is 26.6 years younger than any other U.S. group. And second, 20 percent of all newborn Americans are Hispanic. It is not surprising that the public education system has become an important concern to the Latino/a population. Unfortunately, the public schools where Latina/os are usually enrolled continue to be mostly segregated, overcrowded, understaffed, and underfunded. Private religious schools can serve as an alternative to public education. These private religious schools provide students with religious instruction throughout the curricula. Many faith traditions (i.e., Protestants, Jewish, Muslim, Evangelicals, Catholics, etc.) provide elementary and middle-school education to children whose parents are looking for an alternative to the public school system and can afford it. In addition, some private schools offer a high school education. The reasons for placing a child in a private religious school vary.

For some, these private schools ensure that more financial resources will be used in the classroom, thus supporting the claim that private schools provide a superior education. Attending private school is seen by some as an advantage when competing for acceptance into prestigious colleges. Others choose religious schools as an alternative to what is perceived to be the threat of teaching secular humanism in the public school system. Parents who believe that public schools are tolerant, if not advocates, of homosexuality and/or abortion, while being hostile to religious instruction (i.e., banning prayer in school in 1963), may wish to shield their children from such influences. Private religious schools that reflect their own personal beliefs become in their minds the means of transmitting their values to their children. Yet for others, due to the cost of a private education, they believe that private schools are a safeguard to racial exclusivity. Many Christian schools established during the Civil Rights era were founded for the sole purpose of providing a loophole to the Supreme Court's mandate of desegregation. And finally, some parents are attracted to the discipline provided in private religious schools. In areas with high rates of crime and drug use, where public schools might be plagued with violence, the discipline of religious schools can provide a sense of security and safety for parents worried about the safety of their children. This is not to say that all private religious schools agree that their existence is based on such reasons; nevertheless, among the many reasons why parents choose a private religious education over a public school, these are among the prominent motivations.

One of the consequences of the expense to attend private schools is that mainly parents with economic privileges are able to send their children to these institutions. Because Latina/os are predominantly located at the lower economic stratums, few have the financial means to afford private education for their children. Relegating poor Hispanics in economically deprived neighborhoods to public schools may prove disadvantageous to Latina/o youth. For those attending the public school system, the prospects of graduating high school remain dismal. In 2003, Euro-American high school completion rate stood at 84 percent. Compare this with Mexican Americans at 48.7 percent, Dominican Americans at 51.7 percent, Puerto Ricans at 63.3 percent, or Cuban Americans at 68.7 percent. Of those who do graduate from high school, only 36.5 percent pursue a college education.

Hispanics attending public education face a history where the educational system was designed to "Americanize" Latina/os by attempting to erase the Hispanic cultural heritage, along with the Spanish language. Additionally, these schools (specifically in the Southwestern United States) mainly offered agricultural classes, industrial training, and home economics. In other words, they were designed to train Latina/o children to be farmhands and domestic help. For most Latino/as who attended public schools prior to the 1980s, memories of corporal punishment for speaking Spanish or of being counseled to attend vocational schools to learn how to perform menial jobs remain vivid. Furthermore, there is a lack of proper role models among public school teachers where only 4 percent of them are Hispanic. For these reasons, private religious school seems to provide an alternative for those who can afford it.

Among private religious schools, the faith tradition with the most numerous institutions is the parochial schools attached to Roman Catholic parishes. Parochial schools have existed within the Americas since the Spanish conquest in the sixteenth century. They were originally established with the goal of converting the indigenous people to Christianity. With time, because of the lack of education for the children of the early settlers, religious orders started to provide educational instruction to non-Indians. The Catholic exclusive hold on education in the Americas began to loosen during the early nineteenth century with the rise of secularization movements. Nevertheless, the importance of parochial schools was reaffirmed by Vatican I (1869–1870), which viewed public education under state supervision with suspicion.

Meanwhile in the United States, Euro-American parochial schools flourished during the 19th century, mainly as a response to the dominance of Protestantism within the public school system. These schools basically provided a twelfth grade education to Catholics that was divided into two parts: kindergarten through eighth grade, followed by a ninth through twelfth grade secondary education. Classes were usually taught by nuns, students wore uniforms, and Mass attendance was mandatory. With the ecumenicalism brought about by Vatican II (1962–1965), parochial schools ceased being exclusively for Catholic students. In addition, responding to concerns over academic rigor, lay teachers began to be hired to teach major portions of the curriculum.

Even though the vast majority of Hispanics are Roman Catholics (70 percent according to the Hispanic Churches in American Public Life), only 20 percent attend Catholic schools. Still, for the few who do attend, their schooling can provide opportunities that are more difficult to attain by those receiving a public education. Private religious schools in Hispanic enclaves seem to thrive in nurturing and sustaining the Latino/a culture and training the next generation of leaders. For example, with the expulsion from Communist Cuba of the Jesuit priests who ran Havana's top private schools during the 1960s, many reestablished those same schools in Miami, Florida. The renowned Havana school Belén Jesuit, which was founded in 1854 (the school from which Fidel Castro graduated), was reestablished in Miami in 1961. With a strong emphasis on bilingual education, private schools like Belén Jesuit, LaSalle, and Loyola have helped form the next generation of Latino/a religious and community leaders. One of the critiques leveled against these types of schools is they reinforce elitism because they cater mainly to boys from families with economic means.

Miguel A. De La Torre

References and Further Reading

Milián, Alberto. "Parochial Schools." *Encyclopedia Latina: History, Culture, and Society in the United States*, ed. Ilan Stavans (Danbury, CT: Scholastic Library Publishing, 2005).

Vélez, William. "The Educational Experiences of Latinos in the United States." *Latinas/os in the United States: Changing the Face of América*, ed. Rodríguez, Havidán, Rogelio Sáenz, and Cecilia Menjívar (New York: Springer, 2008).

PROCESSIONS

"Processions," the English word for "procesiones," are religious displays of veneration and adoration that have traditionally been done by Catholics for centuries. In the Great American Southwest these processions tend to follow the liturgical calendar year. Beginning with the time of Advent, procesiones in honor of Nuestra Señora de Guadalupe are wont to take place amid bonfires called luminarias in Spanish and Native villages. Her feast day always falls on December 12. This procesión recalls and honors the apparitions of Our Lady of Guadalupe to the Indian Juan Diego on Tepeyac hill near Mexico City in 1531. The procession is unique in that amid the pageantry and choral singing of village voices, rifles are fired off to mark each of Guadalupe's four apparitions. In recent years, gunshots have been replaced by firework displays.

The start of Lent varies from year to year, depending on lunar cycles. What never changes, though, is the fact that it is the time of year held to be most sacred

At sunrise on Good Friday, members of Tucson's Los Dorados organization raise a white cross on a mountain peak near the city. (Stephanie Maze/Corbis)

POSADAS

La Posadas is one of the best known Latino/a Advent celebrations. "Posada," which means "resting place," is the name for "inn." In the Advent celebration it is meant to recall the inns that rejected José and María as they traveled to Bethlehem to be counted in the census declared by the Roman Emperor Caesar Augustus (cf. Luke 2:12–5). Las Posadas originated in Mexico during the second half of the eighteenth century. At that time the Church hierarchy decided to do away with the boisterous masses called Misas de Aguinaldo (Masses of the Gift). These masses were held during the nine days of the Magnificat's "O antiphons" and acted out the nativity story recalling God's gift in Jesus. The bishops, however, became concerned that the festive flair of these masses had gotten out of hand. The laity then took the reenactments they had seen in church to their houses. Approximately 200 years later las Posadas are still being celebrated. Traditionally pilgrims carrying images of Joseph, Mary, the angel, and the donkey go to three or four different homes asking for room in the inn (Posada). Only the last house gives it to them, and a celebration of food and song ensues.

—GCG

---

by Catholics in villages of the Southwest. The first day of Holy Week is called Palm Sunday. Procesiones del Domingo de Ramos held on this day commemorate Jesus' triumphant entrance into Jerusalem on the back of a donkey while people waved palm branches and yelled "hosanna in the highest." These types of procesiones are usually led by a holy confraternity of men collectively known as "Los Hermanos Penitentes de Nuestro Padre Jesús Nazareno." They gather to explain Lenten ritual symbolism to the faithful and to unravel the upcoming mysteries of Holy Week.

Toward the end of Holy Week, on Holy Thursday, the village priest leads a church procesión for the Reposition of the Blessed Sacrament immediately following Mass and in preparation for services to be held on Good Friday. El Viernes Santo, as Good Friday is known, is marked by ritual procesiones to sacred sites. Such sites often include a devotional visit to the Santuario de Chimayó, which is held to be the most sacred spot in the American Southwest. It houses the miraculous image of the healing Lord of Esquipulas. Processions to Chimayó on this day focus on the miraculous dirt on the chapel, which is believed to contain healing powers.

The beginning of May marks procesiones led by children who are going to receive their First Holy Communion. They strew flower petals along the processional way around the church, singing songs of the season. They are sometimes helped along by older confirmandi, that is, children who will be confirmed later that season. Procesiones in May are always held in honor of the Blessed Virgin Mary. The procesiones culminate with the coronation of the Virgin Mary as Queen of May. The children who participate in them are called Niños de María. May is also the time of year during which the Feast of San Isidro falls. Saint Isidore or Saint Cedric, as he is also recognized in English, is the patron saint of agriculture. Procesiones held in honor of San Isidro will often carry small statues of the saint praying while angels plow his fields for him with a pair of oxen. Sometimes another statuette is also carried next to San Isidro. It is the image of Santa Inés del Campo or Saint Agnes of the Fields. In certain villages she is honored as mistress of growing plants. In Spain, an even more interesting object is carried in such processions. It is the disembodied head of María Toribia or Santa María de la Cabeza, as she is known. Pious legend holds that she was the wife of San Isidro himself. Procesiones of this type tend to meld Catholic tradition with ancient fertility rites.

Las procesiones de Corpus Christi take place in late May or in early June. They honor the humanity of Jesus with processions that visit several outdoor pavilions or folk altars set up by various leagues and confraternities in the village. They are held with much pomp and they are always visited by the priest carrying the Blessed Sacrament in a monstrance underneath a canopy. May processions used to include la Fiesta de la Santa Cruz. The Feast celebrating the Triumph of the Holy Cross has been transferred to September now in the liturgical calendar of events.

Mid-June is the time traditionally dedicated to Saint Anthony of Padua. San Antonio is almost universally recognized as the saint who is invoked whenever something is lost and must be found. In certain places he is also invoked by girls who hope to find suitable husbands. His feast day on June 16 is marked with choral processions that laud his miracles and wonders. According to the Catholic Encyclopedia entry titled "St. Anthony of Padua," when these procesiones come to a shady spot, all listen as his story is told:

> Saint Anthony of Padua, in Padua you were born [Anthony was actually born in Lisbon, Portugal]. You donned the habit, girded loin and studied night and morn. When first you gave a sermon, revealed was this to you: Your father would be hanged that day, by witnesses untrue. As you went to defend him your prayer book lost became. The Most High found and wrote within a promise in your name. "I speak to you, dear Anthony," a voice three times exclaimed. "Within your book a promise penned for all who call your name: Whatever's lost; soon found shall be, forgotten; recalled verily, and what is far, brought close to thee if in thy name, be made the plea."

Larry Torres

References and Further Reading

Dal-Gal, N. "St. Anthony of Padua." *The Catholic Encyclopedia* (New York: Robert Appleton Company, 1907).

Montaño, Mary. *Tradiciones Nuevo Mexicanas* (Albuquerque: University of New Mexico Press, 2001).

Weigle, Marta, and Peter White. *The Lore of New Mexico* (Albuquerque: University of New Mexico Press, 2003).

PROTESTANTISM

The religious landscape of the Hispanic population in the United States has become as complex and diverse as it is among the general population. The denominational and religious expansion among the broader population is also reflected within the Latino/a population.

No longer simply Catholic or Protestant, Hispanic religious identities and traditions reflect a strong presence of "evangelical," Pentecostal, and other historic religious groups, such as Jehovah's Witnesses and Mormons, as well as religious identities beyond Christian denominations, such as Jewish, Muslims, and Buddhists. Thus, to understand Latina/o Protestantism it is important to recognize the religious environment in which it lives and the historical context from which it has emerged.

Historical Context and Origins

Hispanic Protestants are among the oldest religious groups beyond the Catholic within the Latino/a population. Although there were Spanish Jews among the settling Spanish population in the Southwest, their presence tended to be more secretive and even underground. It is common knowledge that the early settling Spanish population was Catholic, migrating from their native Spain at the time when the Spanish Inquisition was at its peak. At the core of the Spanish inquisition was a Catholicism that did not tolerate religious differences among the population. Loyalty and faithfulness to the Catholic Church had to be publicly proclaimed and practiced. Any religious belief or practices other than Catholicism were not tolerated and subject to persecution. Thus, to be Spanish was to be Catholic. Such an environment of religious intolerance shaped the early beginnings and much of the experience and formation of Latina/o Protestantism in the United States.

Spanish Catholicism during the settlement of the Americas shaped the religious and social environment of the Spanish settlers and communities. The assumption was that all Spanish settlers and their descendants were Catholic. The colonial Catholic Church was physically at the center of Spanish settlement. It was also at the center of social and cultural life, including the economic and political dynamics of the Spanish communities. It shaped personal and community identities. The Church shaped community life and dictated its communal and ritual life. Spanish communities took on Catholic religious symbols, names, and festivals. In the Mexican territories that are now part of the United States, Catholicism was the official religion. To believe and practice any other type of religious life was prohibited and extremely difficult. Jews had to go underground in order to practice their religious traditions while publicly practicing Catholicism. In that religious climate, Protestantism was not allowed, as well. It was in such a religious climate that Hispanic Protestantism was born and it was such a climate that shaped how Latino/a Protestantism was to be perceived and lived.

Connection to Spain

A direct historical connection of Hispanic Protestantism to Spain or the Spanish Reformation has not been documented. While Latino/a Catholicism's connection to Spanish Catholicism is clear and well documented in history, as well as the presence of Spanish Jews who brought their religious faith and practices to the new world, no direct connection has been documented for Hispanic Protestantism to Spanish sources or roots. No documented case has been discovered that suggests some form of Spanish Protestantism being brought to the Spanish territories from Spain. At this point, there is no institutional or continuation of any Spanish Protestant religious activity connecting the Americas and Spain.

The one connection to religious events in Spain was the Spanish Bible. The work of Juan de Valdez and Casiodoro de Reina led to the Spanish translation of the Bible, and this was a crucial contribution to Protestant missionary work in the Americas. The distribution of the Bible in Spanish was a key factor in the conversion of many Hispanics to Protestantism. However, neither Spanish translator is known to have migrated in exile to the Americas. Instead, they exiled to Portugal and Italy. Nor do we have historical evidence of any person or group coming to the Americas engaged in missionary or religious work based on the work of the Spanish translators. However, without the Spanish Bible, Latino/a Protestantism would have had to wait.

Anglo Protestant Missionary Work

This suggests that Hispanic Protestantism is a product of the sociohistorical realities of the new world. The historical scene was the western expansion of the American population who brought their Protestantism with them. Protestantism was introduced to the Spanish and Latino/a mestizo population by Anglo Protestants moving westward in the middle to late nineteenth century. As this population pushed the western frontier, it did so under the influence of Manifest Destiny, the notion that the Anglo Protestant peoples, cultures, and their Protestant religious faith were superior to the Native American peoples, but also to the early Spanish settlers and their culture and religious Catholic faith tradition.

From the very beginning, American Protestantism held a sense of superiority over Spanish Catholicism and later, Hispanic Catholicism. Catholicism was viewed as an inferior and defective religious system.

Although the expanding Anglo population did not initially intend to minister unto the Spanish population, social contact was almost unavoidable and exposure to the Protestant faith occurred. In addition, isolated cases of religious outreach did occur, especially in Texas, New Mexico, Colorado, and California. Anglo Protestant missionaries became active with major support from national Protestant denominations such as the Baptists, Presbyterians, and Methodists. Among these missionaries were Sumner Bacon, Melinda Rankin, Alexander Sutherland, Frank Onderdonk, Thomas Harwood, and E. F. G. Nicholson. It is interesting to note that the American missionary zeal had two core motivations. One was religious conversion grounded in the belief that the Protestant faith was clearly superior to Catholicism and was more enlightened. Catholicism was defined as deficient and responsible for the poor spiritual and social condition of Latina/os. The preaching of the gospel was intended to free these people from the "yoke" and tyranny of Catholicism. The Anglo believed that the Protestant faith was the one true gospel.

The second motivation was the acculturation and Americanization of the Mexican population. There was a strong interest in making Hispanics not only good Christians but also good Americans. A close connection was made between Catholicism and inferior life conditions and unacceptable behavior among the Hispanic population. Protestantism was viewed as a means of

ESCUELA DOMINICAL

While the modern Sunday School had its beginnings in 1781 in England, its incorporation into Hispanic Protestantism would not follow for well over a century. Prior to the 1880s, most Anglo Protestants considered Hispanics to be effectively "Christianized" due to Roman Catholic ecclesiological hegemony over Mexico and Central and South America. It was not until the 1860s and afterward that Bible societies and Colporteur agencies made serious efforts to introduce Hispanics to Protestantism. With the beginning of the first Hispanic Protestant churches on U.S. soil in the 1880s, Sunday Schools soon followed. From their beginning Escuela Dominical, or Sunday Schools, have been indispensible to Latino/a Protestant congregations. Perhaps as an alternative to the Roman Catholic Catechism system, they have been used to inculcate Christian doctrine to children and adults alike, to train and equip future lay leaders, and to fulfill their sense of the Great Commission by evangelizing newcomers into the faith. It is estimated that 75 percent of Hispanics who join the Protestant church do so because of the influence of the Escuela Dominical. While some churches have abandoned the traditional Sunday School, most mainline Hispanic churches in the United States continue to see it as upholding the Judeo-Christian tradition of family instruction.

—RDG

improving life conditions and leading to better behavior and acceptable citizenship. Hispanics needed social uplifting through education and acculturation, in addition to religious conversion. Thus, American Protestant denominations invested in the conversion, education, and socialization of the Latina/o population. In addition to churches, Protestant missionaries established schools, educational institutions, and settlement houses throughout the Southwest to serve the Hispanic population. Some of these educational institutions include Lydia Patterson Institute in El Paso, Texas; Holding Institute in Laredo, Texas; McCurdy School in Espanola, New Mexico; Presbyterian Pan American School in south Texas; and Harwood School in Albuquerque, New Mexico. Settlement houses include the Wesley community centers throughout the Southwest. The primary mission of Protestant settlement houses and later community centers was the social betterment of the Latino/a community through social work and social activities that led to a responsible and acceptable social behavior. In other words, missionary work included the acculturation of the Hispanic population.

The most effective missionary strategy in reaching the Hispanic population was the introduction and exposure to the Bible in Spanish and Spanish religious tracts. Apparently, Spanish Catholics had no personal or direct knowledge of the Bible. Catholic priests were the only persons in the settlements who owned and had access to the Bible. The distribution of Spanish Bibles became a major Protestant activity. When the Protestant Bible became available to the Latina/o community, religious conversion soon followed. The Bible became a highly prized possession, the center of family life, and discussion focus of small circles of interested persons. In many cases, the Protestant Bible had to be hidden so as

---

BAPTIST SPANISH PUBLISHING HOUSE

Since its founding by missionary J. E. Davis, in Toluca, Mexico, in 1905, the Baptist Spanish Publishing House (aka Casa Bautista de Publicaciones, Editorial Mundo Hispano, Hispanic World Publishers) has been making its contributions to both reflect and produce cultural changes. Moved to the border city of El Paso, Texas, in late 1916 because of unsettled times in Revolutionary Mexico, it has become an international institution, governed by an International Board of Trustees and led by an international staff of editors and administrators. Its offices and plant have been located at 7000 Alabama Street (in El Paso) since 1938. From its inception, materials for Bible study in Hispanic evangelical churches (in México, the United States, and as many as 40 other countries) have occupied a major place in its publication program. But it also offers a wide range of books—both originals in Spanish and translations from English and other languages.

—JTP

---

not to cause problems with the local priests. The Spanish Bible became the major tool of introducing religious intrigue and initiating a search for more religious and biblical knowledge. Bible study was central in the birth of Hispanic Protestantism and became an important part of its heritage and culture. The Bible was central to the life of the Protestants and became the symbol of early Latino/a Protestantism.

The first missionaries among the Hispanic population were Anglos. However, the most effective missionaries were newly converted Latina/os. These newly converted Hispanics knew the people, the territory, the culture, and had a personal history with the Catholic experience. Protestant denominations were quick to provide education and support for these new indigenous religious leaders. Many young Hispanic ministers were mentored by Anglo missionaries. Latino/a converts became Hispanic missionaries. They became missionaries to their own communities. Although they used terms like evangelists and ministers, they were known as "hermanos" within

the Hispanic Protestant communities and were successful in establishing many Protestant congregations both in urban areas and in villages across the Southwest and West Coast. Some of these hermanos were pioneers such as Alejo Hernández and José Policarpo Rodríguez in Texas, as well as Gabino Rendon and Benigno Cardenas in New Mexico.

The response of the Catholic Church to the conversion of Latina/os was not well received. The Catholic Spanish population was living at the northern edges of the Spanish and Mexican territories and was underserved by the Catholic Church due to the scarcity of priests. The lack of priests suggests that the population was not adequately trained in their religious faith nor properly ministered to in their religious tradition. In many cases, lay Catholics would serve congregations, and isolated priests acted with little or no supervision from Catholic authorities. When religious conversions began to occur, the Catholic Church reacted in protest and an equally negative promotion of Protestantism. Catholic priests prohibited laity from reading the Bible or attending Protestant Church worship or activities. Catholics were not allowed to enroll in Protestant schools. This was a particular issue in northern New Mexico where Presbyterian schools attracted many local Latina/os and became a means for religious conversation. In many cases, Catholics were excommunicated for sending their children to Protestant schools.

As a result of the mutually negative propaganda, a strong anti-Catholic and anti-Protestant climate quickly emerged not only between the religious bodies but also within the Hispanic population. Latino/a Catholics and Hispanic Protestants took on the attitudes taught by their respective religious traditions. Latina/o Protestants viewed Hispanic Catholics with the same negative attitudes as the Anglo Protestants held. Latino/a Catholics viewed Hispanic Protestants through the same lenses as the Catholic Church taught. Latina/o families were divided and friendships broken because of the Catholic-Protestant rift. Mutual distrust and mutual demonization was commonplace. Religious intolerance was a powerful reality at the birth of Hispanic Protestantism.

Yet, Protestantism took root within the Latina/o population. Early missionary efforts resulted in conversions and eventually in the establishment of Latino/a Protestant congregations among Presbyterian, Baptist, and Methodist Churches, especially in New Mexico and Texas. Similar efforts developed in Puerto Rico and Cuba, which produced a significant Latino/a Protestant population that became part of this country through immigration and influenced the North, East, and Florida regions. Today, Hispanic Protestants are found in every Protestant denomination and Protestant religious movement in the United States. These include Baptist denominations, Methodists, Presbyterians, United Church of Christ, Lutherans, Reformed, and others. Likewise, Mormons and Jehovah's Witnesses have been quite successful with Latina/os.

Protestant Significance

For generations, the common term for all non-Catholic Hispanics was "protestantes." This was especially true among Catholics, who also referred to Protestantes as "sectas." Within the Latino/a Protestant communities the more common term for self-definition is "evangelicos." The historic use of the term "evangelicos" has a different meaning from today's usage of "evangelical" in English. Today, "Evangelical" in English refers to a particular theological and ecclesiastical tradition more associated with Pentecostal, charismatic, and "nondenominational" traditions. Non-Catholic Hispanic religious traditions have diversified into three major clusters: Evangelical/Pentecostals, Mainline Protestants, and others, especially Mormons. The Jehovah's Witness movement has also attracted a number of Latino/as. Mainline Protestant traditions include the more historic Protestant denominations such as the United Methodist Church, Presbyterians, Lutherans, Baptists, Reformed, and United Church of Christ. With regard to presence in the Hispanic population, 15 percent identify as Evangelical and approximately 10 percent as mainline Protestant.

The significance of the presence of Latino/as within mainline Protestant denominations is historical, sociological, and even theological. The brief historical summary in the previous section points

First Hispanic Baptist church in Santa Barbara, California. (Cynthia Odell)

to the significant contributions that mainline churches have made through their early efforts in reaching out to Hispanics and to the establishment of Latina/o congregations. The establishment of Hispanic congregations is highly significant. Latino/a Protestant congregations had their own Hispanic clergy and lay leadership. Congregational structures and their administration resulted in the emergence of Latino/a leadership. The demand for Hispanic clergy led to the education of scores of Hispanic persons with liberal arts education and theological training. Many of the first Hispanics to attend colleges and universities were preparing for ministry in Protestant denominations. Lay leaders also developed with organizational skills. They learned how to run

meetings and make reports. Laity became Sunday school teachers and local church officials. All of this led to leadership development, as well as a strong dosage of self-respect and dignity.

In addition to the establishment of local Latino/a congregations, denominational judicatories were developed to coordinate Hispanic ministries and congregations. These are geographic structures established for the purpose of supervising and coordinating the religious work of the denomination, and they required top-level administrators and supervisors, most of whom were Hispanic. For example, the Methodist Church created annual conferences and one, the Rio Grande Annual Conference, still exists, covering Texas and New

MARCHA

Metodistas Asociados Representando la Causa de los Hispano Americanos (MARCHA) is Spanish for the organization Methodists Associated to Represent the Cause of Hispanic Americans. Established in the early 1970s, MARCHA serves as the officially recognized caucus of Latino/as within the United Methodist Church (USA) and the Methodist Church of Puerto Rico. It also maintains relations with Methodist churches in Latin America. The primary purpose of MARCHA is to address and advocate for issues and programs of importance to Latino/as within the denomination, as well as beyond. Its membership is composed of Hispanic individual laypersons and clergy of the United Methodist Church and the Methodist Church of Puerto Rico, as well as representatives of various church bodies and regional caucuses. MARCHA holds annual national meetings to conduct its business, provide training and continuing education, and facilitate networking and action related to denominational and social issues of significance to Latinas/os. In partnership with other ethnic caucuses, MARCHA plays a major role in the life of the denomination advocating for church legislation and addressing issues of discrimination, injustice, and ministry within the church and society.

—DMJ

Mexico. In Texas, Baptists created the Mexican Baptist Conventions of Texas, and the Presbyterians had the Texas-Mexican Presbytery for administering the Hispanic work; these existed until recent times.

The creation of Latino/a congregations and judicatories is also significant in that it generated Hispanic organizational leadership and facilitated structures of self-determination. After the Anglo-American conquest, it was the Protestant denominations that facilitated and supported the creations of Latina/o structures that were owned and operated by Hispanics. Protestant churches were some of the few community structures and organizations that were thoroughly Latino/a owned and operated. Hispanics owned and managed their church buildings and facilities. These were early models of self-help community organizations.

Mainline Protestantism also brought a new religious reality and new religious options for Latina/os. The establishment of Protestant congregations meant that Hispanics had a religious choice. The Latino/a population was no longer a homogeneous religious community. In addition, there was not just one Protestant denomination. Hispanics could choose from several Protestant churches. Protestantism brought religious diversity to the Latino/a population. In fact, many Latina/o Protestants took on strong denominational identity, pride, and loyalty.

Religious diversity and choice brought religious and theological themes into family and community conversations and debate. Religious diversity suggested that there was more than one way to understand God, the church, and religious life. Religious understanding was no longer a monopoly taught by one church and one set of clergy. The Christian faith was now open for discussion and was even open to differences of opinion. The Protestant-Catholic divide and

BISHOP MINERVA G. CARCAÑO (1954–)

Minerva G. Carcaño, a native of Edinburg, Texas, is the first Latina to be elected to the episcopacy of the United Methodist Church, serving as Bishop of the Phoenix Episcopal Area, Desert Southwest Annual Conference. Additionally she is the official spokesperson for the Council of Bishops on immigration. Bishop Carcaño is a 1975 graduate of the University of Texas Pan American with a BA in Social Work. She received a Master of Theology degree from Perkins School of Theology of Southern Methodist University in 1979. Carcaño had several pastoral appointments in Texas and California. In 1986 she became the first Hispanic woman to be appointed a district superintendent in the United Methodist Church, serving the Western District of the Rio Grande Conference in west Texas and New Mexico. Carcaño spent four years (1992–1996) as the organizing pastor of the South Albuquerque Cooperative Ministry. She then served as director of both the Mexican American Program and the Hispanic Ministries Program at Perkins School of Theology. Subsequently, Carcaño became superintendent of the Metropolitan District of the Oregon-Idaho Annual Conference of the UMC. Carcaño also was the chair of worship resources on the committee that prepared *Mil Voces*, the United Methodist Spanish-language hymnal.

—EDA

the new multiplicity of Protestant denominations generated much religious debate and conversation.

Issues and Challenges

Although mainline Protestant denominations initiated religious work among the Hispanic population and had early successes, many challenges remain or have emerged for the mainline Protestant denominations, as well as for the Latino/a mainline Protestant congregations. History has not resolved all of the issues, and the current social/religious realities present new challenges for Hispanic Protestantism.

Stagnant Membership. As with the general churches from mainline Protestant traditions, the Latino/a mainline churches have experienced recent stagnant membership. In many cases, especially in small towns and rural areas,

Latina/o Protestant churches have been closed. For decades small membership congregations were supported by the denominations as mission churches. However, as the denominations also faced stagnant or dropping memberships, financial strains have led to the reduction of mission support for Hispanic congregations. Given the historic small membership of many Latino/a congregations, a drop in mission support made it difficult for many Latina/o churches to financially support themselves. As a result, the most current strategy has been to focus on major cities or metropolitan areas for religious work. Among some major mainline Protestant denominations, support for Hispanic ministries has become a difficult debate.

Cultural Realities. An important characteristic of many mainline Latino/a congregations is the level of acculturation among its membership, especially among the younger generations. Many second- and third-generation mainline Protestant Latino/as do not speak Spanish or have difficulty with it. As a result many of these congregations have bilingual worship services or programs that are totally in English. It is not uncommon for acculturated mainline Hispanic Protestants to join Anglo congregations. This results in a membership, leadership, and financial drain for Latina/o Protestant congregations. It also presents stressful issues of language and culture that affect older generations. Many Hispanic Protestant congregations struggle with the issue of cultural identity and cultural competence. Initially established to serve the Spanish-speaking population, they now serve English-speaking Latino/as and struggle with the issue of mission and purpose. To what extent is Spanish central to being a Hispanic congregation?

Immigrant Outreach. A current challenge facing many Latino/a mainline Protestant churches is reaching out to the Latina/o immigrant population. It has been extremely difficult for established Hispanic Protestant congregations to successfully attract immigrants. The acculturation of mainline Latino/a congregations and the extensive use of English may explain part of the challenge for attracting immigrants who need a Spanish language program. Cultural and identity issues may also go beyond language. It is a common perception that many mainline Protestant Latina/o congregations have developed a middle-class mentality and culture. Such a congregational cultural climate may present a challenge to immigrants who may be poor.

Racial-Ethnic Realities. In spite of acculturation, Hispanic Protestants still retain their ethnic identity. Latino/a Protestant congregations are essentially ethnic congregations. Even when the congregation has become essentially English speaking, the membership will be Hispanic. Within the denominational structures, networks, and membership, Latina/o Protestants are still defined as an ethnic minority population and thus are different from the dominant Anglo Protestant membership. Racial and ethnic attitudes and relations in the broader social environment tend to be reflected within the denominational life. Some mainline denominations have special structures and offices to deal with ethnic ministries and issues. For example, the United Methodist Church has the Commission on Religion and Race with one of its tasks being to monitor racism within the denomination. Many mainline denominations will have ethnic caucuses, including Latino/a caucuses.

Socioeconomic Realities and Hispanic Clergy. Although many Latina/o mainline congregations may have a middle-class mentality and culture, economically the membership comes from a history of poverty and financial marginalization. Financial pockets are not deep and many are first-generation middle-class and high school or college graduates. With such poverty background and small memberships, Latino/a congregations struggle to meet denominational expectations and become self-supporting. Limited funds are left for meaningful ministry beyond paying utilities and paying the pastor's salary. Pastors of Latino/a congregations receive among the lowest salaries in the denomination. Many congregations cannot support a full-time pastor. Many seminary-trained Hispanic clergy seek higher-paying congregations; some serve

Anglo congregations. As a result, mainline Protestant Latino/a congregations struggle to fill their pulpits with seminary-trained Hispanic pastors. As a result, many churches will employ pastors from non-mainline traditions and struggle with theological fit. Thus, Latina/o Protestant congregations struggle with issues that are essentially financial and struggle to keep their educated clergy. Not surprisingly, Hispanic congregations and ministries tend to play marginal roles in mainline Protestant denominational life.

Theological Orientation and Attitudes. Hispanic mainline Protestant theological perspectives tend to be shaped by the blending of the denominational theology and doctrines, sociopolitical ethnic realities, and the broader Latino/a religious culture. As part of broader mainline denominations, Latina/o Protestants tend to reflect some of the liberal and ecumenical orientation of Protestant denominations, especially seminary-trained Hispanic clergy. However, most Latino/a Protestant laity would probably reflect a leaning toward the more moderate to conservative end of the theological continuum. With regard to social attitudes, Latina/o Protestants would also tend toward the moderate, with the exception of issues related to civil rights and racism. In such areas, they would be liberal and supportive of social justice.

Although many of the larger and historic Hispanic congregations tend to reflect the historic traditions of their mainline denominations especially with regard to worship and music, which tend to be grounded in their European roots, Latino/a congregations nonetheless are part of the larger Hispanic religious reality. Latina/o Protestants have maintained their Hispanic ethnic identity. Latino/a Protestant congregations are increasingly influenced by the more culturally grounded Latino/a music and worship. "Coritos" and more informal worship have become more common. This is especially true among smaller congregations and those served by immigrant clergy or clergy not trained in a denominational seminary in the United States.

Pentecostal Success. The growth of Latino/a Pentecostal and nondenominational Evangelical congregations has impacted Hispanic mainline Protestantism. They are no longer the only option to Catholicism. Latina/os can choose from a wide variety of theologies, worship, music, and congregational cultures. Pentecostal and Evangelical churches offer enthusiastic worship and attractive theologies that address the daily lives of Hispanics. Such churches are finding success in reaching out to Latino/as, while mainline Protestant churches struggle to do so. The Pentecostal influence upon Mainline Protestants is real. The growth of Pentecostalism within the Latino/a population has gotten the attention of mainline Latina/o Protestants. However, the Hispanic Protestant response has been diverse. Although Protestant clergy leadership and laity are forced to ask the question of why Pentecostalism is apparently attracting so many Latino/as while they struggle to stay open, not all agree on what the lessons are. Protestants have significant theological, liturgical, and structural issues with Pentecostalism and do not seek to duplicate them. Protestant liturgical traditions and theological roots are strong. Yet, Protestant worship has incorporated some of the enthusiastic nature of Pentecostal worship, but usually within a traditional Protestant worship service.

As this entry suggests, Hispanic mainline Protestantism has an important history of contributions to Latino/a religious life. Latina/o mainline Protestants were the first converts to Protestantism within the United States, and they paid a painful price within their families and communities. Hispanic Protestants established congregations and produced generations of Latino/a religious and lay leadership. These leaders led their congregations in self-determination and paved the way in defining what Latina/o Protestantism was to become. Today, it faces many new challenges. The challenges have to do with cultural and linguistic identity, mission, and purpose, as well as congregational culture and worship. However, the hope for Latino/a Protestantism is that its future is in the hands of Hispanic leadership.

David Maldonado Jr.

References and Further Reading

Banker, Mark T. *Presbyterian Missions and Cultural Interaction in the Far Southwest 1850–1950* (Urbana: University of Illinois, 1993).

Barton, Paul. *Hispanic Methodists, Presbyterians, and Baptists in Texas* (Austin: University of Texas Press, 2006).

Barton, Paul, and David Maldonado Jr. *Hispanic Christianity within Mainline Protestant Traditions: A Bibliography* (Decatur, GA: Asociacion para la Educacion Teologica Hispana, 1998).

Brackenridge, R. Douglas, and Francisco O. Treto-Garcia. *Iglesia Presbiteriana: A History of Presbyterians and Mexican Americans in the Southwest* (San Antonio: Trinity University Press, 1974).

Hernandez, Alberto. "Historic Mainline Protestants." *Handbook of Latina/o Theologies*, ed. Edwin David Aponte and Miguel A. De La Torre (St. Louis, Missouri: Chalice Press, 2006).

Maldonado, David, Jr. *Protestantes/Protestants: Hispanic Christianity within Mainline Traditions* (Nashville: Abingdon Press, 1999).

Maldonado, David, Jr. *Crossing Guadalupe Street: Growing Up Hispanic and Protestant* (Albuquerque: University of New Mexico Press, 2001).

Maldonado, David, Jr. "The Changing Religious Practice of Hispanics." *Hispanics in the United States*, ed. Pastora San Juan Cafferty and David W. Engstrom (New Brunswick, NJ: Transaction Publishers, 2000).

Maldonado, David, Jr. "Hispanic Protestantism: Historical Reflections." *Apuntes* 11, no. 1 (Spring 1991): 3–16.

Martinez, Juan Francisco. *Sea La Luz: The Making of Mexican Protestantism in the American Southwest, 1829–1900*. Denton: University of North Texas Press, 2006.

Sylvest, Edwin, Jr. "Hispanic American Protestantism in the United States." *Frontera: A History of the Latin American Church in the USA Since 1513*, ed. Moises Sandoval (San Antonio: The Mexican American Cultural Center, 1983).

Walker, Randi Jones. *Protestantism in the Sangre de Cristos 1850–1920* (Albuquerque: University of New Mexico Press, 1991).

PUERTO RICANS

According to Eileen Findlay, "The mottled past still haunts Puerto Rico" (1999, 1). Though a small island, Puerto Rico has been the center of historical and cultural struggles far exceeding its geographically narrow shores. Spanning just 100 miles by 35 miles in the Caribbean Sea, the island's landscape is as diverse as its people. Under the shadow of Spanish and then American political

VIEQUES

Vieques is a small island municipality of the Commonwealth of Puerto Rico, an unincorporated and nonsovereign territory of the United States in the Caribbean. During World War II, the U.S. government expropriated most of the Vieques territory for military purposes. Vieques became an important sight for naval exercises and military operations of the U.S. Navy Atlantic Fleet, NATO, and South American and Caribbean allied forces. U.S. military interventions were rehearsed in Vieques: Dominican Republic, Panama, Granada, Haiti, Balkans, Iraq, and Somalia. Vieques is a 51 square mile island where the navy was in control of two-thirds of its land and civilian residents used to live squeezed between an ammunition depot and a maneuver area. In April 1999 a navy jet mistakenly dropped bombs on the wrong target, killing one guard and a civilian employee of the base. This accident generated a massive protest that developed during the next years into a broad-base nonviolent civil disobedience movement with local, continental, and international support. Many Latino/a religious leaders helped organize and participated in these protests. On May 1, 2003, President George W. Bush ordered the navy to cease operations in Vieques. The people of Vieques are still struggling with the challenges of land sovereignty, economic development, health issues, and a major environmental cleanup.

—*LRR*

control, Puerto Ricans have long struggled to craft a sense of national, cultural, and religious identity in the wake of Spanish colonialism and American neocolonialism. Heirs of the often violent encounters of indigenous, African, and Spanish cultural forces, Puerto Ricans are colonial subjects in a postcolonial world, citizens in a foreign nation, a nation within a nation.

Historical Background

Long before Columbus's consequential "discovery" of the island he christened "San Juan Batista," Puerto Rico's native inhabitants crafted societies of great cultural depth. Unfortunately, the island's first inhabitants, the Taínos, are now lost to us except for a few archeological remnants and national monuments erected in their memory. Though their naming of the island as Borinquen remains as Puerto Ricans regularly call one another "boricuas," cultural influence between Taínos and modern Puerto Ricans is indirect at best. Disease, conquest, and enslavement ensured that links between Taínos and Puerto Ricans were severed early. The historical reconstruction of these peoples is difficult and tinged by ideological aims. In other words, the influence of Taíno culture upon Puerto Ricans emerged much later in the island's history as these Puerto Rican ancestors were rediscovered in the island's cultural narrative.

Columbus's arrival on November 19, 1493, marked the eventual end of the Taíno, as well as the advent of long-standing Spanish rule. The first governor of the island, Juan Ponce de León, arrived in 1508 and soon the island's shores were fortified, providing safe harbors and trading hubs in the "rich ports" of Puerto Rico. Spanish domination remained unabated throughout the nineteenth century but lifted slightly just a year before the critical political shifts of 1898 as partial autonomy was granted to the island and its inhabitants.

Autonomy, limited as it was, proved fleeting. Puerto Rico's colonial masters changed as a result of the U.S.'s victory in the Spanish-American War. In 1898, political ownership of Puerto Rico shifted as the looming hegemony of the U.S. grew in the Western Hemisphere. The political situation of Puerto Rico changed radically. The integration of this Caribbean island within the fabric of American power was tenuous, consistently prioritizing American sensibilities. For example, the 1901 Supreme Court assessment of Puerto Rico's place within the American nation proved paradoxical and U.S.-centered, describing the island as "foreign to the United States in a domestic sense."

The shape of politics in Puerto Rico shifted radically in 1917 when the U.S. government extended citizenship to Puerto Ricans, a move precipitated at least partly by World War I and the country's need for soldiers. In the coming decades, the privileges of American citizenship would inaugurate a significant migration. Reaching a peak in 1953, many Puerto Ricans left the island for the promises of life in the United States, especially in New York City. The 2003 census found more Puerto Ricans living on the U.S. mainland than in Puerto Rico.

The question of the island's political status in relation to the United States remains the primary barometer of Puerto Rican politics. The *Partido Nuevo Progresista* (PNP) advocates statehood, while the *Partido Popular Democrático* (PPD) rallies behind the continuation of the political status quo. In addition, the *Partido Independentista Puertorriqueño* (PIP) represents an important minority voice in public discourse, calling for Puerto Rico's complete independence. In 1998, a nonbinding plebiscite revealed a highly divided populace, nearly evenly split between statehood and the continuation of the status quo. The recent debate over the presence of the U.S. Navy on the island of Vieques has only exacerbated these political divisions.

Ambivalence over the island's political status also defines the life of Puerto Ricans living in the United States today. Statistically among the poorest and least-educated ethnic groups, many Puerto Ricans have found it difficult to tap into the American Dream that has drawn so many to "jump the puddle" (*brincar el charco*). Though able to evade to a large degree the contentious issue of immigration, Puerto Ricans living in the U.S. find themselves on the margins of American culture.

Puerto Rico's Mottled Past, Present, and Future

Perhaps no other factor is as complex, yet definitive, in the analysis of Puerto Rican culture than the elusive notions of race and ethnicity. The negotiations of race and ethnicity were a critical component in the encounter of Europeans, indigenous populations, and Africans in Latin America. Puerto Rico has acquired a paradoxical reputation as a racial paradise. Along with Brazil, Puerto Rico has long been lauded as a jewel of ethnic integration, a paradise in which racial dissension is absent. In the past, the myth of "racial democracy" was the natural

---

OUR LADY OF PROVIDENCE

"Our Lady of Providence" is a title for the Virgin Mary that originated in Italy during the thirteenth century. In Roman Catholicism, Mary is the helper and protector of Jesus and of all creatures in need. The word "providence" represents divine care and guidance. The term also conveys God's sovereignty, agency, and superintendence over human life. The Regular Clerks of the Congregation of Saint Paul, Barnabites, were founded in Italy, in 1530, by Saint Anthony Mary Zaccaria, and adopted the devotion of the Virgin of Providence. Soon this cult disseminated throughout Italy, France, and Spain, where devotees built a shrine in Tarragona, Catalonia. Popes, Gregory XVI in particular, made frequent visits. An Italian depiction of Mary leaning over the Child, who peacefully sleeps on her lap while she holds his left hand between her own hands folded in prayer, is now the classic image of this Virgin. In 1854, the Bishop Gill Esteve y Tomás introduced the devotion to the Providence in the Cathedral of San Juan, Puerto Rico. In 1969, Paul VI declared her the Patroness of Puerto Rico and by papal decree unified the celebration of the arrival of the image, on November 2, with the "discovery" of Puerto Rico, which occurred on November 19, 1493.

—*VLC*

---

explanation for Puerto Rico's seeming racial harmony. Instead of rigid boundaries, racial divisions have appeared to both outsiders and internal ideologies as porous, permitting the so-called "mulatto escape hatch"; "whitening" thus became a mode of social ascendancy. That is, an improvement in social class via marriage, higher education, and/or social advancement had a "lightening" effect upon the individual's perceived race. Thus, for some cultural critics, Puerto Rico has come to represent an ethnic utopia worthy of emulation. While such an assignment seems to celebrate the island's cultural diversity, it disguises the racial strife that defines the frequently bitter negotiations of Puerto Rican identity. More than providing an insight into Puerto Rico, such assessments often emerge from the inability to think beyond the racial dyad of Black and White so prevalent in the United States.

The reclamation of indigenous identity also provides a fascinating insight into Puerto Rico's cultural negotiations. In particular, Puerto Rico's construction of national identity reveals the central function of race and ethnicity in the definition of its cultures. Though Puerto Rico's native population was eradicated by war and disease, the reclamation of Taínos as the pre-Colombian ancestors of modern Puerto Ricans occurred in the twentieth century at the intersection of ideology and archeology. Evidence of their history, culture, and rituals being sparse, archaeological reconstruction of Taínos is largely an ideological project hoping to define the Puerto Rican people. Ultimately, the Taíno is not a physical presence on the island today, but an ideological notion constructed at the end of an archaeologist's spade.

As critical as race and ethnicity are to the construction of Puerto Rican identity, one ought to remember that they are not

---

NUYORICAN

The approximately 500,000 Puerto Ricans or people of Puerto Rican descent who live in the New York metropolitan area are referred to as Nuyoricans. The word "Nuyorican" demonstrates this hybrid identity, combining the English word "New" from New York with "Rican" from Puerto Rican. Their various religious practices (Catholic, Pentecostal, Seventh-day Adventist, Jehovah's Witness, often combined with aspects of Santería) are a product of the island's history. In 1899 after Puerto Rico became a U.S. territory, missionaries from U.S. Protestant churches divided the island into nine fields. Today less than 50 percent of Puerto Ricans on the island and in U.S. urban centers is Catholic and the majority of Protestants is Pentecostal. In 1951, a report to New York's Cardinal Francis Spellman stated that while 800 Puerto Rican Protestant ministers served in New York, there were no Puerto Rican Catholic priests. Puerto Ricans, who did not feel welcomed in the English-speaking Catholic Masses, turned to smaller Spanish-speaking Protestant churches. Prominent Nuyorican Piri Thomas's family included a Pentecostal mother, *espiritista* stepmother, and "deathbed" Catholic father. Nuyorican also refers to the "Spanglish" spoken by Puerto Ricans in New York and to the intellectual movement of poets, musicians, and artists such as Tito Puente, Jesús Colón, and Esmeralda Santiago, whose work deals with their dual culture often including a hybrid religious culture.

—AA

---

isolated phenomena. It is quite difficult, if not impossible, to analyze these critical categories without also recalling how gender, social status, religion, and class are inextricably tied together. The power of the confluence of sexuality and race are most potent in that they together shaped everyday power relations and became explicitly politicized in the construction of Puerto Rican identity. Ultimately, one cannot comprehend the cultures of Puerto Rico without grappling with these difficult yet essential cultural facets. The very definition of "Puerto Ricanness" is inseparable from the complex ethnic negotiations that have punctuated the island's history.

Important Moments in Puerto Rican Religion

Until 1898, the dominance of the Roman Catholic Church in Puerto Rico was virtually unchallenged. Within a decade of Columbus's arrival, the first ecclesiastical province in these newly "discovered" lands was established in the neighboring island of Hispaniola. By 1511, San Juan hosted one of the first three dioceses in the "New World" and was the first with a local prelate. The following year Puerto Rico became host to the earliest and one of the most substantial library collections of Western learning. Ultimately, the colonizing of Puerto Rico was not only a political activity spearheaded by the Spanish crown but also a religious mission sponsored by the Roman Catholic Church. Fortified by political support, the church and the Spanish state were inseparable foundations of the Puerto Rican colony. Among the many ecclesial leaders who helped shape Puerto Rico in the years of Spanish rule, the ascension of Juan Alejo de Arizmendi as the first Puerto Rican born

---

MADRE MARÍA DOMINGA (1897–1991)

María Dominga was born in Puerto Rico. In 1913, she entered the congregation of the Dominican Sisters of the Holy Cross, in Brooklyn, New York. She performed her ministry first as a parish school teacher and later as a foundress and first Mother General of Las Hermanas Dominicas de Nuestra Señora del Rosario de Fatima on November 3, 1949, the second native congregation of religious women to be founded on the island of Puerto Rico. From the beginning Madre Dominga insisted that in order to serve the poor, one must give concrete witness to a life of poverty and a deep spiritual life. The sisters opened and maintained missionary houses throughout the Caribbean, Central America and the United States. They opted to work in the community to strengthen the values of the Puerto Rican family, and thus, their motto: *Llevar a Cristo a la familia y la familia a Cristo* (To bring Christ to the family and bring the family to Christ). Madre María Dominga died at the age of 96 in 1991. Soon after her death, her case for canonization was formally introduced and is being studied by church officials.

—ADS

---

bishop in 1804 was a particularly historical and symbolic moment for the development of Puerto Rican national identity.

The massive political shifts that followed upon the U.S.'s possession of Puerto Rico were accompanied by concomitant changes in the geography of Christianity on the island. Just two years after the 1898 Treaty of Paris ended the Spanish-American War and granted the United States possession of Puerto Rico and Cuba, the Foraker Act became law and established a civilian government. Simultaneously, President William McKinley enacted a legal proposition already augured by the arrival of American troops on Puerto Rican soil. McKinley expressly ordered the separation of church and state, effectively breaking the unequivocal legal buttresses of the Roman Catholic Church on the island. No longer a *de facto* partner in the political machinery of Puerto Rico, the Catholic Church could not receive financial and juridical support from the new civilian government.

At the turn of the century, American influence was growing around the world, perhaps best exemplified by the possession of islands around the world, which projected this burgeoning power. To familiarize Americans with these various possessions, a pictorial description of *Our Islands and Their People* was published in 1899. Puerto Rico, as one of the featured islands, and its economic struggles entered the American psyche thanks to the recent refinements of photography. Other media reports reinforced these characterizations and helped shape American perceptions of Puerto Rico, its people, and its history.

From the perspective of American missionaries and politicians, Roman Catholicism and Spanish monarchical rule functioned in a fateful symbiosis, an arrangement now deemed catastrophic for the Puerto Rican people and arcane thanks to the advent of American democracy. Protestant denominations from the United States were primed to introduce "pure" religion in Puerto Rico

CARLOS MANUEL RODRÍQUEZ (1918–1963)

Carlos Manuel Rodríquez, or Charlie, as he was best known to his friends and colleagues, was born in Caguas, Puerto Rico, on November 22, 1918. He was badly wounded when he tried to rescue his one-year-old cousin from the attack of a rabid dog. The severe bites led to serious intestinal problems during his entire life and most likely his untimely death of intestinal cancer on July 13, 1963. Charlie attempted a baccalaureate degree, which he was forced to abandon because of bad health. He ultimately dedicated all of his time to the Catholic University Center, becoming a Catholic lay minister. He organized the *Círculo de Cultura Cristiana* and published *Christian Life Days* as a tool for university students to enjoy the liturgical seasons. He belonged to the Holy Name Society and the Knights of Columbus, and as a member of the Brotherhood of Christian Doctrine, he taught catechism to high school students. Anticipating the liturgical changes brought about by Vatican II, Charlie encouraged liturgical renewal among the clergy and the laity, working for active participation of the laity and the use of the vernacular language. On April 29, 2001, he was beatified by Pope John Paul II.

—*ASD*

in a new, implicit symbiosis between Protestantism and American democracy. Nevertheless, these same denominations were uninterested in a competitive struggle for the souls of Puerto Ricans. After all, the wider aim of bringing "true" Christianity to the island's people abated grand denominational designs. In addition, American Protestants hoped to engender the ecumenical spirit of the time upon the people of Puerto Rico.

These various trajectories prompted a pivotal "comity" agreement. While the large cities of San Juan and Ponce were denominational neutral grounds, the rest of the island was cleaved into four exclusive sections for the missionary activities of Presbyterians, American Baptists, Congregationalists, and Methodist Episcopalians. Eventually, the Christian Church (Disciples), the Christian and Missionary Alliance, the United Brethren in Christ, and the Evangelical Lutheran Church also gained a part in the comity compact. Many of these denominations partnered to found the Seminario Evangélico de Puerto Rico (Evangelical Seminary of Puerto Rico) in 1919.

Despite these denominational machinations, Roman Catholicism remained a crucial religious touchstone in Puerto Rico. Magnificent Catholic churches still dominate the town centers of Puerto Rico. In addition, Pentecostal Christian faiths have thrived, adding yet another dimension to the history of Puerto Rican religion. In recent years, the dual dominance of mainline Protestant churches and Catholicism has given way to a far more fractured situation in which independent churches and faiths have complicated an already tangled web of religious belief. In a certain sense, however, this diverse religious landscape is not new. Popular Puerto Rican religion has often combined elements of ecclesiastically approved Christian dogma with elements of Taíno and African religions. This syncretistic blend of traditional dogma and elements of the occult is known as espiritismo (spiritism). Although not recognized by official church institutions, spiritists beliefs such as Santería influence the daily religious practices of Puerto Ricans.

Recent years have seen the burgeoning of Puerto Rican scholarship on religion and theology. In a recent essay, Luis Rivera-Pagán outlines some of the most important contributions to and studies of Puerto Rican theology. Rivera-Pagán provides "four hermeneutical paths" that succinctly summarize and assess the various trajectories of Puerto Rican theology. First, reflecting the diversity of Puerto Ricans themselves, a single, monolithic Puerto Rican theology proves elusive; in fact, one of the defining marks of Puerto Rican theology is its diversity. Second, he affirms Luis Rivera Rodríguez's distinction between *teología puertorriqueña* and *teología puertorriqueñista*. The former is a primarily historical effort that considers how Puerto Ricans have experienced God and self within their historical particularity. The latter "is that reflection from Christian faith and praxis about God and the human condition and destiny in the Puerto Rican experience and context made . . . with an option for *puertorriqueñidad*." The first is more of a descriptive effort while the second is more prescriptive, asking how the Puerto Rican experience can reassess theology. Third, we must recognize that male theologians have dominated the enterprise of Puerto Rican theology and that its continued vitality requires the cultivation of feminist interpretations of puertorriqueñidad. Finally, Puerto Rican theology reflects the continuing influence of liberation theology as well as the shifting definitions and criteria of a liberationist perspective. Though many have too quickly pointed to the demise of liberation theology, Puerto Rican theology suggests that liberation theology is instead experiencing a great deal of transformation and diversification (2006, 144–151). Despite these four defining points, Puerto Rican theology remains difficult to pinpoint, especially because Puerto Ricans living on the island and those living in the mainland of the United States bring differing, though often complementary, perspectives.

In conclusion, Puerto Rican religious cultures are shaped at the critical intersection of history, ethnic identity, and religion proper. As a profound expression of a people's hopes and fears, religion reaches to the very core of cultural identity in a cultural discourse inextricable from a people's sense of history and self. This is particularly true in Puerto Rico where politics, culture, identity, and the nation are tenuous and disputed notions.

Eric Daniel Barreto

References and Further Reading

Duany, Jorge. *The Puerto Rican Nation on the Move: Identities on the Island and in the United States* (Chapel Hill: University of North Carolina Press, 2002).

Findlay, Eileen. *Imposing Decency: The Politics of Sexuality and Race in Puerto Rico* (Durham, NC: Duke University Press, 1999).

Gotay, Samuel Silva. *Protestantismo y política en Puerto Rico, 1898–1930: Hacia una historia del protestantismo evangélico en Puerto Rico* (San Juan, PR: Editorial de la Universidad de Puerto Rico, 1997).

Haslip-Viera, Gabriel, ed. *Taíno Revival: Critical Perspectives on Puerto Rican Identity and Cultural Politics* (Princeton, NJ: Markus Wiener Publishers, 2001).

Picó, Fernando. *History of Puerto Rico: A Panorama of Its People* (Princeton, NJ: Markus Wiener Publishers, 2006).

Rivera-Pagán, Luis N. "Puertorriqueños/as." *Handbook of Latina/o Theologies*, ed. Edwin David Aponte and Miguel A. De La Torre (St. Louis: Chalice Press, 2006).

Rodríguez León, Mario A. *El Obispo Juan Alejo de Arizmendi: Ante el proceso revolucionario y el inicio de la emancipación de América Latina y el Caribe* (Bayamón, PR: Centro de Estudios de los Dominicos del Caribe, 2003).

Stevens-Arroyo, Antonio M. *Cave of the Jagua: The Mythological World of the Taínos* (Albuquerque: University of New Mexico Press, 1988).

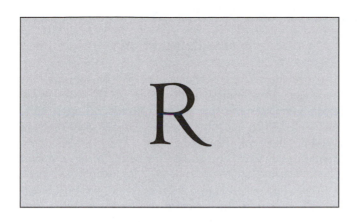

RAZA CÓSMICA

The phrase *raza cósmica* first entered the public consciousness of Mexicans and Chicano/as as an expression of cultural and religious identity deriving from the 1925 publication of *The Cosmic Race: The Mission of the Ibero-American Race* by Mexican politician and Minister of Education José Vasconcelos Calderón (1882–1959). Although criticized for its connections with the racial ideologies of the late 1800s and early 1900s, Vasconcelos's racial project in *La Raza Cósmica* affirmed the cultural uniqueness and humanitarian potential of the racial mixing (*mestizaje*) that occurred, following the Spanish and Portuguese conquests, between European colonists and the indigenous peoples of the Western Hemisphere. While the literal English meaning of the Spanish term *raza* is "race," in the Mexican sociopolitical context of the 1920s the term signified more precisely the idea of a "people" or a "civilization" whose *mestizo* origins were not to be interpreted as a mark of racial

impurity or postcolonial shame, as stereotyped by all Euro-Western racial ideologies. Instead their racial features and Latino identity were to be interpreted, and celebrated, as a sign of the growing Ibero-American mestizo and Hispanic peoples' important roles in the future of the human race.

Vasconcelos's conceptualization of the Cosmic Race was influenced by many of the major intellectual currents of the times, and by lesser ones, like Theosophy, which today is associated with the New Age Movement. When he was appointed Rector of the Universidad Nacional Autonoma de Mexico (UNAM) in 1920, Vasconcelos petitioned the governing board and received permission for a new university motto: *Por mi Raza hablará el Espiritú*, which translates as "The Spirit shall speak through my People." Given his strong Roman Catholic background, Vasconcelos most likely was alluding to the Holy Spirit's empowering role in the history of Salvation. However, his universalism was influenced also by nineteenth-century

---

BLANQUEAMIENTO

The concept of blanqueamiento, "whitening" or "becoming white," was a Spanish colonial administration policy from the 1500s to the 1800s. Given its historic conflict with dark-complexioned North African Berbers, Moroccans, and Arabs during the *Reconquista* (ca. 711–1492), Spain developed racialized class structures and social prejudices whereby "whiteness" signified a person's Spanish or Christian "purity of blood" (*pureza de sangre*), while "blackness" signified a person's Moorish "impurity" or Muslim heritage. The lack of Caucasian women throughout the colonies motivated many Spanish soldiers and settlers to take wives or concubines from among the indigenous population. Offspring from these unions encountered upper-class prejudices favoring lighter complexions against the diverse shades of skin color resulting from racial mixing. African slaves were at the bottom of this matrix. Concerned about racial imbalances and class struggles, Spain offered land grants to poor White settlers and their families whose presence then ensured more "whitening" opportunities among the colonial population. Dark-complexioned colonial subjects motivated by internalized oppression often sought lighter-skinned marriage partners for "whitening" the family's racial and social status (*mejorar la raza*). Local manifestations of this colonial legacy linger across contemporary Central and South America, which immigrants from Latin America often bring with them to the United States.

—AH

German Idealism, particularly Georg W. F. Hegel's philosophy of history and Johann G. Fichte's notions of self-consciousness. He was quite fond of reading Friedrich Nietzsche and Arthur Schopenhauer. In addition, he was familiar with Oswald Spengler's two-volume history of modern Europe, *The Decline of the West* (1917), which used biological categories to ponder the rise, growth, and decay of Western civilization. Vasconcelos believed the application of Charles Darwin's doctrine of natural selection to the social and political arenas was highly problematic because these zoological-racial ideologies, first developed in England by Herbert Spencer and later expanded by German scientists and nationalists, despised the interracial sexual unions that had populated and enriched vast regions of the world where ancient civilizations once flourished outside the immediate reach of Caucasian Europe—areas like Latin America, Asia, and Africa. Vasconcelos, and other Latin American intellectuals and religious leaders, critiqued these racialized worldviews as divisive and dehumanizing theories, which culminated in the myth of Aryan supremacy and the threat of Nazi expansionism.

In contrast, Vasconcelos believed, with deep conviction, that he had detected a divinely ordained trajectory in the history of the past five centuries whereby the various races of the human family were intermixing at a gradually increasing pace that would result in the appearance of a "new human type," which he called "the Cosmic Race." He believed the "melting-pot" phenomenon in the United States, and similar trends in Argentina, were evidence of humanity's emerging multiracial future. His evolutionary views of human history were also influenced by his understanding of Darwinism and by his personal interest in the esoteric ideas of the Russian Theosophist Helena Petrovna Blavatsky. Vasconcelos borrowed Madame Blavatsky's notions about a great migration of people all over the earth after the fall of Atlantis from which sprang the great civilizations of the ancient world like Egypt and Greece, as well as the indigenous civilizations of the Americas like the Mayas, Incas, and Aztecs. Against the prevailing four major racial categories of his day based on skin color —White, Black, Red, and Yellow—he posited the emergence of a fifth race, "the Cosmic Race," from the interracial mixing common in Mexico and Latin America as *mestizaje*. Vasconcelos's predictions, while uplifting Hispanics, Spaniards, and Latin Americans of mixed racial ancestry, also pitted this "Ibero-American race" against Anglo-Saxon and Germanic Caucasians, and his attitude toward the role of "Blacks" in this scheme was ambivalent and outdated.

All contemporary criticisms of Vasconcelos's racial project aside, it is extremely important to note that at a time when not only Germany and Japan but much of the world seemed intoxicated by ideologies of race and nationalistic exclusivity, he criticized the myth of racial purity by emphatically maintaining that racial mixing and the development of syncretistic cultures had been part of human history since the very beginnings of civilization during the latter stages of the Neolithic Era. During the first half of the twentieth century, his theory of *La Raza Cósmica* inspired intellectuals and activists from a wide spectrum of cultures yearning for social justice and liberation from Eurocentric racism: first in Mexico, then throughout Latin America, and eventually across the Hispanic communities of the southwestern United States. Despite his tendency to romanticize the Spanish and Roman Catholic heritage, Vasconcelos was acutely aware of the lingering negative effects of the Iberian colonial legacy among the peoples and nations of the Americas. His use of the term "raza" and affirmation of mestizaje influenced social justice efforts in Mexico and among Chicano/as in the United States. Finally, just as Karl Marx's emphasis in the mid-1800s on the growing role of economic relations and financial institutions in world history is today seen as a prophetic understanding of future trends, Vasconcelos's vision in the 1920s of an increasingly multicultural and interdependent planet was prophetic of contemporary trends in Latin America and the global community.

Albert Hernández

References and Further Reading

Graham, Richard, ed. *The Idea of Race in Latin America: 1870–1940* (Austin: University of Texas Press, 1990).

Miller, Marilyn Grace. *Rise and Fall of the Cosmic Race: The Cult of Mestizaje in Latin America* (Austin: University of Texas Press, 2004).

Vasconcelos, José. *La Raza Cósmica: Misión de la Raza Iberoamericana* (Barcelona, Spain: Agencia Mundial de Librería, 1926).

Vasconcelos, José. *The Cosmic Race/La Raza Cósmica*, bilingual ed., trans. Didier T. Jaen (Baltimore: Johns Hopkins University Press Paperbacks, 1997).

RECONQUISTA

Reconquista is the Spanish term for the epic struggle fought on the Iberian Peninsula by Spain and Portugal from the Moorish invasion of Gibraltar on July 19, 711, to the fall of the Nasrid Caliphate of Granada on January 2, 1492. Although modern Spanish nationalism often misrepresented the conflict as a continuous religious war against a unified foreign conqueror, the Spanish Reconquest was actually a series of intermittent military campaigns against widely divergent Arab, Berber, and Muslim factions from North Africa spanning nearly eight centuries. Although numbering very few actual Arabs or Muslims among their ranks, the indigenous North African, dark-skinned Berber warriors who accompanied General Tariq ibn-Ziyad's invasion forces in 711 would forever be known in Spanish history as *los Moros* (the Moors). Their arrival was immortalized in the master narrative of Spanish history as "The Moorish Conquest," hence, the mythic counterattack known as the *Spanish Reconquest,* and the term for the romantic heroism of medieval Spanish knights and mercenaries known as *Conquistadores.*

Since the Spanish Reconquest began nearly four centuries before the more familiar Crusades to the Holy Land (1095–1291), some historians interpret these Iberian wars as an earlier phase of the medieval Western European phenomenon of Christian "crusading" against Islam, while others have interpreted the Reconquista as a series of conflicts unique to Spanish feudalism and the multicultural situation in medieval Iberia. Whatever interpretive framework we apply to understanding this struggle, its effect on the formation of medieval and early modern Spanish national consciousness, and its subsequent impact on Spain's imperial objectives and colonization of the indigenous peoples of the Americas after 1492, had a lasting influence in Spain, as well as in Latin America and the Hispanic American religious cultures of what was once known as Spanish North America, and these trajectories still influence a number of contemporary cultural and political issues around the world.

Historical Development

The Romans called the Iberian Peninsula *Hispania* and in early medieval times its inhabitants were still called *Hispani*, hence the term "Hispanic," from which the English term "Spaniard" is also derived. After the fall of the Roman Empire in 476 CE, the Visigoths controlled most of the Iberian Peninsula until an Arab-Berber alliance with military and political ties reaching all the way back to Damascus's Umayyad Caliph, Abu al-Walid I (ca. 668–715), crossed over from North Africa. Commanding an army of 7,000 Berber and Arab soldiers from Morocco, the young Berber general Tariq ibn-Ziyad burned all of his ships so that the troops would accept nothing short of total victory in the conquest of Hispania, a dramatic historical act repeated in 1519 by Hernán Cortés (1485–1547) as he landed in Mexico and burned his ships before conquering the Aztec Empire. The famous geographic feature on the tip of the Iberian Peninsula facing the North African coast of Morocco, the Rock of Gibraltar (*Jebel al-Tariq*), which in Arabic means "Tariq's Rock," was named after this cunning young general. Superbly organized with light cavalry and strong infantry, the invaders overthrew the Visigoths throughout most of present-day southern Spain and Portugal. The final blow for the Visigoths came in July 711 when Tariq's forces defeated the army of Spain's last Visigothic ruler, King Rodrigo, at the Battle of the Guadalete River. A few months later Toledo, the Visigoth capital, fell and almost the entire peninsula soon came under Moorish rule. As the Moors consolidated their victories, the southern and western portions of Iberia were divided into a series of small kingdoms governed by various Berber or Arab emirs. The newcomers renamed the area "al-Andalus," meaning the "land of the Vandals," after another Germanic tribe they confused with the Visigoths. Later known to Spaniards as "Andalucía," the region's romantic charm and rich cultural legacies have endured into the present.

The surviving Spanish-Visigoth feudal nobility, along with their subjects, retreated to Iberia's northwestern regions in Asturias and Galicia, while others sought safety from the advancing Moorish forces in towns and villages located high in the Pyrenees Mountains. Spain's patriotic counterattack was first launched from the Kingdom of Asturias when the region's founder and hero, Don Pelayo, defeated the Moors at the Battles of Alcama and Covadonga sometime between 718 and 725. While much of Pelayo's story seems legendary, his kingship and military victories mark the traditional and historic starting point of the Spanish Reconquest. These legends seem largely a creation of later Spanish generations whose nationalistic concerns regarded King Pelayo as the royal patriarch of Leon and Castile, powerful medieval kingdoms that developed later

from the Kingdom of Asturias. The stark political reality for both Spanish and Moorish leadership is that neither side fared very well in Iberia from 718 until about 756. The Umayyad Caliphs of Damascus (modern Syria) showed little interest in Andalucía after 720, and the Abbasid rulers of Baghdad (modern Iraq) were even more distant from Iberia than their Umayyad predecessors. Factional rivalries, civil war, and territorial disputes produced a highly unstable political situation across Andalucía and North Africa for 40 years following Tariq's victories.

The decisive turning point in the history of Hispano-Arabic Andalucía, however, occurred on Friday, May 14, 756, when a surviving Arab prince from Damascus's recently massacred Umayyad Dynasty, Abd al-Rahman I, declared himself leader of the people and heir to his family's dynastic claims by establishing the Umayyad Caliphate of Cordoba. His support grew when local leaders realized his mother was also a North African Berber princess. Regarded as the "Golden Age" of Islamic civilization on European soil, economic prosperity, scientific knowledge, and education thrived in Cordoba for the next two centuries. Under the successful and creative leadership of Abd al-Rahman and his strong successors, the Cordovan State flourished until about 1031 when internal corruption, factional dissent, and the growing power of several independent warring states, known as the Taifa Kingdoms, destabilized political and economic conditions across Andalucía. By 1083 Seville had replaced Cordoba as Iberia's major city and center of Islamic culture.

The demise of Cordoba's Umayyad Caliphs presented a unique military and territorial opportunity for the Christian kingdoms situated across the northern half of the Iberian Peninsula. Leading the Spanish forces under the banner of a united Leon and Castile, King Alfonso VI (1079–1109) conquered Toledo in 1085, a military victory that alarmed Islamic rulers across the Mediterranean region. While dealing a serious setback to Hispano-Arabic political and military objectives, this event's cultural impact on Western European civilization helped spark the so-called "Renaissance of the Twelfth Century" as many ancient Greek and Roman classics and scientific works believed lost after the fall of the Roman Empire were translated from Arabic into Latin during the 1100s and brought to the attention of scholars in Europe's rapidly growing cathedral schools and universities. King Alfonso VI also employed Spain's most famous warrior of the Reconquest, Rodrigo Díaz de Vivar (ca. 1044–1099), whose legendary military skills earned him the honorary title, "El Cid the Champion" among Muslim and Christian knights. According to several accounts, El Cid and King Alfonso both admired the Greek and Roman classics and recognized the contributions of Arab scholars to the preservation of knowledge.

In 1086, however, a rival faction of Islamic fundamentalists crossed over from North Africa conquering Seville and Cordoba, and most of Andalusia. They called themselves the Almoravids, from the Arabic phrase *al-Murabitum*, literally meaning "people of the *ribat*," Arabic for a religious community analogous to a "monastery." Believing the Cordovan Empire's collapse was the result of excessive worldliness and lack of piety, the Almoravids refused lofty titles like "caliph" or "emir" and followed an austere way of life. The Spanish kingdoms retained control of Toledo while continuing the Reconquest against this latest North African opponent whose primary weaknesses stemmed from their poorly organized central government back in Seville. Besieged from the outside by the growing power and military successes of the Spanish Reconquest and from the inside by factionalism and dissent, the Almoravids were overthrown in 1148 at Seville by local Hispano-Arabic leaders who appealed for assistance to the rising Almohad faction from North Africa. By 1155 the Almohads ousted the Almoravids from both Cordoba and Granada and became the dominant Islamic power in Iberia for a century.

Meanwhile, Christian Spain and Portugal had been gradually consolidating their power base among their own factions and feudal kingdoms. In 1147 King Alfonso Enriquez of Portugal, known as *El Conquistador*, captured Lisbon from the Moors with the help of crusader knights from Leon and Castile, Cologne, Flanders, and England. By 1149 Catalonia's last Muslim outposts fell to Spanish forces led by the Counts of Barcelona. The most decisive victory of the Reconquest was fought on July 16, 1212, at the Battle of Las Navas de Tolosa as King Alfonso VIII of Castile united the kingdoms of Leon, Aragon, Navarre, and Portugal against the Almohad Empire. Alfonso's successor, King Fernando III of Castile, led a series of campaigns against the major urban centers of Almohad power in Iberia. He succeeded by first taking Cordoba (1236) and Valencia (1238), and then paving the way for the siege of the Almohad capital at Seville, which surrendered on November 23, 1248. A key Spanish-

Christian strategy in this phase of the Reconquest was their use of "divide-and-conquer" tactics, which pitted rival Arab and Muslim factions against each other and further weakened the overall political and military effectiveness of the Almohads. On December 22, 1248, King Fernando III and his allies entered Seville as conquerors of the most religiously and culturally diverse kingdom on European soil. The Reconquista had achieved most of its goals in a little over 500 years and was regarded by many of the figures of that era as a mission accomplished and closed.

However, during the decisive Mediterranean conflicts of the thirteenth century, the Christian kingdoms and feudal factions of the Iberian Peninsula witnessed the rise of the violently expansionist and highly skilled seafaring House of Aragon, which began its own program of conquest first by attacking the Balearic Islands in 1229 and then seeking control of Corsica, Sardinia, and Sicily with the broader aim of eventually taking Naples and Rome. In the 1300s the Aragonese forged an alliance with Castile and Portugal aimed at controlling the Iberian Peninsula once and for all by conquering Granada and toppling the Nasrids. The project had two major objectives: the final expulsion of Muslim rule from Christian Europe, and the emergence of the royal House of Aragon as a major power among the Christian nations of Europe. These actions on the part of Aragon revived the Spanish Reconquest and culminated in the surrender of the Caliphate of Granada to Spain as Europe's first, modern nation-state under the unified rule of King Ferdinand II of Aragon and Queen Isabel I of Castile on January 2, 1492.

Major Doctrinal Points

Although the Spanish Reconquest was a military and political process spanning centuries, its cultural and religious effects took on the nature and fervor of nationalistic doctrine as its objectives became inextricably tied to the formation of Spanish national identity and Spanish Catholicism. Under King Ferdinand and Queen Isabel's powerful joint rulership the Reconquest took on the nationalistic symbolism and intolerant proportions for which it became infamous in the colonization of the Americas and in the varied histories of Hispanic American religious cultures.

For example, Spain's famous patron saint, Santiago de Compostela (St. James), whose traditional pilgrimage route was one of the most famous practices in medieval Christendom, was also known throughout the Reconquest as *St. Santiago Mata Moros*, literally "St. James, the Killer of Moors." The epithet made this beloved, pious saint a favorite figure among the Conquistadors who came to the Americas searching for gold and enslaved the indigenous peoples of the Western Hemisphere. Furthermore, by defeating the Muslims in 1492 after so many centuries of war in what appeared to most other European nations and the papacy as an apocalyptic struggle, and which coincided with news of Christopher Columbus's epic discoveries in an unknown land, Spain developed a distinct sense of "National Messianism," which propelled it to the pinnacle of European political and colonial power over the next two centuries. Indeed, whenever and wherever Spanish colonial power was threatened, the image and memory of the Reconquest was called upon to inspire the troops and rally the people into defeating the opposition, such as in Santa Fe, New Mexico, when a statue of the Virgin Mary rescued from a burning church during the 1680 Pueblo Indian Revolt returned in 1692 as *La Conquistadora* (Our Lady of Conquering Love) at the head of an army led by Don Diego de Vargas who resettled the region for the Spanish Crown.

Racialization is another legacy of the Spanish Reconquest that had a lasting impact on the modern world. Spain's racialized prejudices about the superiority of white skin tones versus dark skin tones developed from the fear and violence spawned by its early encounters between North Africans and Europeans, and eventually included taboos against interracial marriages, which were signified first by the religious identities of light-skinned Christians versus dark-complexioned Moors, Muslims, or Arabs. Later in the 1300s and 1400s, these prejudices were signified by more intentionally racialized and legal categories for Spanish national identity. Race and religion became objectified categories of exclusion and oppression that were used with legal force to keep Christian Spaniards from intermingling with Jews and Muslims, categories later deployed with lethal force in all Spanish colonies that contributed much to the racism and classism that permeated Latin America and Hispanic American culture.

Not all aspects of the Spanish Reconquest produced negative results or dealt with warfare. Arab and Moroccan influences filtered in from North Africa and from as far away as Damascus and Baghdad. A rich blending of Islamic, Christian, and Jewish cultural influences known as *convivencia* (living together) occurred in the art and architecture, poetry and literature, and music of Medieval Spain, which can still be seen and heard everywhere in the country today. The long struggle against the North African factions caused the premature end of feudalism in Iberia and led Spain to become Western Europe's first modern nation-state. Finally despite the Spanish Empire's social taboos and legal sanctions against interracial mixing, the Latin American and Hispanic American racial mixing known as *mestizaje,* has much older, deeper historical roots during the Golden Age of Hispano-Arabic Andalusian civilization and the Spanish Reconquest than its alleged first appearance in sixteenth-century colonial Mexico and Peru has led the general public to believe.

Albert Hernández

References and Further Reading

Fletcher, Richard. *Moorish Spain*, 2nd ed. (Berkeley: University of California Press, 2006).

Glick, Thomas F. *Islamic and Christian Spain in the Early Middle Ages*, 2nd rev. ed. (Boston: Brill, 2005).

Lowney, Chris. *A Vanished World* (Oxford: Oxford University Press, 2006).

Mann, Vivian B., Thomas F. Glick, and Jerrilynn D. Dodds. *Convivencia: Jews, Muslims, and Christians in Medieval Spain* (New York: George Braziller, Reissue Edition 2007).

Menocal, María Rosa. *The Ornament of the World: How Muslims, Jews, and Christians Created a Culture of Tolerance in Medieval Spain* (Boston: Little, Brown & Company, 2002).

O'Callaghan, Joseph F. *Reconquest and Crusade in Medieval Spain* (Philadelphia: University of Pennsylvania Press, 2003).

RELIGIOUS AFFILIATION

The Hispanic population represents a major component of the American life and culture. The U.S. Census Report of 2000 stated a total population of 281.4 million residents (excluding Puerto Rico and the U.S. islands). Hispanics comprised 35.3 million (12.5 percent); 27.1 million (76.8 percent) of Hispanics live in seven states (California, Texas, New York, Florida, Illinois, Arizona, and New Jersey), with California (11 million) and Texas (6.7 million) being the states with the strongest Hispanic presence. This growth and rapid expansion of the Hispanic population is shaping the religious panorama of the United States.

Although the U.S. Census Bureau remains the main source of information and statistics regarding the American population, the Census Bureau fails to provide data about the religious affiliation of the people living in the United States. The Census is prohibited by Public Law 94-521 to ask questions on religious preferences. Consequently, although religion plays a vital role in the American life, especially among Latino/as, it is impossible to determine the religious affiliation of people in the United Sates in general and of Hispanics in particular. Nevertheless, research studies conducted by the Pew Research Center and the Barna Group, along with the ongoing work of the Hartford Institute and the Church Council of Churches, provide a general description of Latina/os and their religious inclinations.

The Pew Research Center published one of the most comprehensive studies about Hispanic religion in the United States in 2007. The report *Changing Faiths: Latinos and the Transformation of American Religion* was produced with the collaboration of the Pew Hispanic Center and the Pew Forum on Religion and Public Life. This report states that Latino/as are transforming the nation's religious landscape because of their growing numbers and strong religious practices, which differ from non-Hispanics who are more widely distributed among various religions and Christian denominations.

The Pew report describes six major religious traditions among Hispanics: Roman Catholics, Evangelical Protestants, Mainline Protestants, other Christians (Jehovah's Witnesses, Mormons, or Orthodox), other Faiths (Muslims and other non-Christian faiths), and Seculars. Approximately one in ten Hispanics do not claim any religion affiliation (8 percent). Therefore, it can be argued that a religious inclination represents an important ethos for Hispanics. More than two-thirds (68 percent) of Hispanics identify themselves as Roman Catholics. The next largest category is made up of evangelical Protestants with 15 percent. No one denomination comprises more than 7 percent of the total. The denominational distribution of Latino/a Protestants is as follows: Pentecostal (6.9 percent), Baptist (3.1 percent), Independent or nondenominational (3.1 percent), Congregational or Church of Christ (0.7 percent), Presbyterian (0.3 percent), Methodist (0.3 percent), Lutheran (0.2 percent), Episcopalian (0.2 percent), Denomination not specified (3.8 percent).

According to the Pew report, Jehovah's Witnesses are the largest religious group related to Christianity with 1.9 percent of the Hispanic population in the United States. Hispanic Mormons represent 0.7 percent, and only 0.1 percent claims a religious affiliation with the Orthodox Church. Less than 1 percent (0.9) of Hispanics identify themselves as members of Jewish, Muslim, or other non-Christian religions, while 1.1 percent of Hispanics refused to disclose their religious affiliation to the Pew Research Center.

Catholicism in the United States is stronger among Hispanics than among other racial groups (either Whites or Blacks). First-generation Hispanics tend to be affiliated with Roman Catholicism more than with other religions or Christian denominations. Among foreign-born Hispanics, 74 percent of adults are Roman Catholics compared with 58 percent of native-born Hispanics. Since immigration has increased significantly in the past few years, the Pew Report projects that Hispanics will become an ever-increasing segment of the Catholic Church in the United States.

In 2001, the Barna Research Group conducted a study about Hispanic religious affiliation. They published the report "The Faith of Hispanics Is Shifting" based on surveys among more than 4,000 adults in the United States. Of those adults, 468 identified themselves as Latina/os. This study argues that the religious affiliation of Hispanics is gradually shifting from its traditionally Roman Catholic affiliation to a more diverse "spiritual hybrid." Although Roman Catholicism continues to be the major religion preference among Latino/as, other Christian groups are attracting large numbers of Hispanics. According to this research, Hispanics have a higher tendency than non-Hispanics to attend Charismatic and Pentecostal churches.

In order to completely comprehend the Hispanic religious affiliation in the United States, it becomes imperative to comprehend the religious dynamics of Latin America. According to the U.S. Census in its publication "The Foreign-born Population in the United States," in 2002, 35.2 million foreign-born people reside in the United States (11.5 percent of the total American population). Of the American foreign-born population, 52.2 percent comes from Latin America, with 36.4 percent from Central America (including Mexico), 6.2 percent from South America, and 9.6 percent from the Caribbean (Puerto Ricans are considered American by birth).

Samuel Escobar, a well-known Peruvian theologian, discusses key characteristics of Christians in Latin America. The term "evangelical" describes the majority of Protestants such as those who belong to what is considered "historical" churches that came from Europe and North America, independent churches established from independent missionaries, and classic Pentecostal churches.

The Roman Catholic Church continues to be the dominant religious organization in Latin America, although it has been declining both numerically and influentially in society. Meanwhile, Evangelical numbers are growing. For example, in 1968 only 85,000 Evangelicals lived in Colombia (0.43 percent of the population), but in 2000 this number grew to 2 million (5 percent of the population). According to a study from the Catholic University in Chile, 13.9 percent of the population in that country identify themselves with evangelicals. Escobar argues that since the America's Synod that met in Rome in 1997 with the presence of 300 Catholic Cardinals and Bishops from Latin America, the United States, and Canada, the Roman Catholic Church has emphasized the "new evangelization." The Catholic Church is now emphasizing conversation and more collaboration between North and South America.

A religious movement that Escobar calls "almost-evangelical" (para-evangélico) is becoming a preponderant religious force in Latin America. This movement comes from charismatic Roman Catholics, charismatic mega-churches in the United States, and groups from traditional Protestant churches. According to Escobar, these groups are becoming a religious force different from Catholics and Evangelicals.

Conclusion

Religion is a central element in the Latina/o culture. The main religious affiliation for Hispanics is the Roman Catholic Church. In 2002, the Official Catholic Directory states that there are 65,270,444 Catholics in the United States, to which 72.6 percent (almost 26 million) of Hispanics belong. Yet, only 64 percent of Hispanic Catholics attend services regularly. Even though the majority of Latino/as identify themselves with Christianity, Hispanics are not well represented among Christian denominations in the United States. The Presbyterian Church (U.S.) has 330 Hispanic congregations with a total membership of over 40,000 people. Hispanics represent a small number compared with the 2.3 million members and more than 10,000 congregations. In 2002, the United Methodist Church had 600 communities of faith in 52 conferences and started 75 new Hispanic congregations in 35 conferences. The total Latino/a membership in the United Methodist Church in 2002 was 45,417, a small number compared with a total

membership of almost 8 million. The Southern Baptist Convention in 2005 had 48,884 churches and church-type missions and a total membership of 15,065,076, of which 2,827 churches are Hispanic with a membership of 175,752 people.

Octavio Javier Esqueda

References and Further Reading

Barna, George. "The Faith of Hispanics is Shifting." *The Barna Update* (January 3, 2001). Available at www.barna.org.

Escobar, Samuel. "Los Evangélicos en América Latina Hoy." *Apuntes Pastorales* XXII-1 (October–December 2004): 10–14.

Pew Hispanic Center. *Changing Faiths: Latinos and the Transformation of American Religion* (Washington, DC: Pew Research Center, 2007).

Sánchez, Daniel. *Hispanic Realities Impacting America* (Fort Worth: Church Starting Network, 2006).

U.S. Census. "The Hispanic Population 2000." Available at www.census.gov.

RENEWALIST MOVEMENT

Renewalist Christianity is one of the largest and fastest growing movements within Christianity worldwide. In general, renewalist Christianity emphasizes the intervention of the Holy Spirit in the daily lives of Christian believers. "Renewalist" becomes a term that encompasses Pentecostals and charismatic Protestants and Catholics. These groups believe that the movement of God's Spirit becomes manifested through metaphysical phenomena that includes, but is not limited to the following: (1) *glossolalia* the act of speaking in tongues, specifically a human language the speaker does not know or a heavenly language that is only understood by God and God's angels; (2) the performance of miracles, specifically the healing of the sick and, in some cases, the raising of the dead; (3) the act of prophesying, specifically the utterance of a word from God that may or may not contain an element of foretelling; and (4) the participation of exuberant worship services, complete with spontaneous displays of emotional enthusiasm, such as shouting, dancing, clamping of hands, raising of hands, jumping, uncontrollable laughter, uncontrollable shaking, and speaking in tongues. Central to the renewalist movement is the concept of "baptism of the Holy Spirit," also known as the "second baptism" or the "second blessing." This event signals the first moment that the Spirit indwells a believer. It is usually accompanied with some supernatural manifestation of the Spirit, as in the case of glossolalia.

Within the United States, Latino/as identify with renewalism at higher rates than non-Hispanics. Those Hispanics who prescribe to renewalist thought are more likely than their non-Hispanic counterparts to: (1) regularly read the Bible; (2) take a literal view of the biblical text; (3) share their faith for the purpose of evangelizing; (4) adhere to the teachings of the "prosperity gospel," specifically that God blesses believers with financial success and good health; and (5) believe that Jesus' second coming will occur within their lifetime. Hispanics with lower levels of education are more likely to be renewalists, as are those who are foreign born.

Among Hispanic Catholics, a majority (54 percent) describe themselves as being either charismatic or Pentecostal,

compared to the rest of the non-Hispanic Catholic population where only about one in ten uses these labels for self-identification. These Hispanic Catholics are more likely than non-Hispanic Catholics to: (1) speak in tongues or prophesy, and (2) to witness or participate in an exorcism, that is, the casting out of demons from those possessed. Even Latina/o Catholics who do not self-identify as charismatic or Pentecostal still report experiencing or participating in Spirit-led metaphysical experiences. It appears that this renewalist movement has not displaced Catholic identity, but rather, has been incorporated by Hispanic Catholicism. Not surprisingly, Latino/a Catholics practice a different type of Catholicism than non-Hispanics, a Catholicism that incorporates many charismatic or Pentecostal behaviors.

An example of the incorporation of charismatic elements within Catholicism while maintaining a Catholic identity can be found in the influential movements among Hispanics known as *Cursillos de Cristiandad*. Originating in Franco's Spain in 1944, cursillos began as a conservative and hierarchical movement that focused on the sacraments. By the mid-1960s, the movement spread to every part of the United States where Hispanic Catholics resided. Cursillos are retreat-type events where participants renew their commitment to the faith through an "encounter" with the mysteries of the *kerygma* (core of the Gospel). Participants are encouraged to emotionally experience the mystery of the Divine through an experience akin to being "born-again" for Catholics.

A majority of Latina/o Protestants (57 percent) can be classified as belonging to this movement, compared to the non-Hispanic Protestant population where one in five uses the labels "charismatic" or "Pentecostal." Among non-Catholic Latino/a faith traditions, the three traditions with the highest concentration of Latino/as are Pentecostals. They are the Assembly of Christian Churches, the Pentecostal Church of God, and the Apostolic Assembly of Faith in Christ Jesus, which, respectively, ranked third, fourth, and tenth.

Ethicist Eldin Villafañe attempted to explain how Latina/os within the renewalist movement understand the working of the Spirit. The charismatic and Pentecostal revival experience among Latina/os can be seen as a liberative theological response to the social and economic repression they suffer. By interpreting Galatians 5:25, Villafañe believes that to live in the Spirit (a theological self-understanding) is to also walk in the Spirit (an ethical self-understanding). Through the power and manifestation of the Spirit, the Latino/a disenfranchised can challenge the structures of sin and evil as the whole congregation receives charismatic empowerment and the spiritual resources to encounter the social and discriminative struggles they face daily. For after all, this is the historical project in which the Spirit is engaged, to facilitate believers' participation in the reign of God—a reign that is concerned with establishing justice, restraining evil, and fostering conditions for an ethical moral order.

Miguel A. De La Torre

References and Further Reading

De La Torre, Miguel A. *Religion and Religiosity*, ed. Havidán Rodríguez, Rogelio Sáenz, and Cecilia Menjívar, eds. *Latinas/os in the United States: Changing the Face of América* (New York: Springer, 2008).

Espinosa, Gastón. "Methodological Reflections on Latino Social Science Research." *Rethinking Latino(a) Religion and Identity*, ed. Miguel A. De La Torre and Gastón Espinosa (Cleveland, OH: Pilgrim Press, 2006).

Pew Hispanic Center. *Changing Faiths: Latinos and the Transformation of American Religion* (Washington, DC: Pew Forum on Religion and Public Life, 2007).

Villafañe, Eldin. *The Liberating Spirit: Toward an Hispanic American Pentecostal Social Ethic* (Grand Rapids, MI: William B. Eerdmans Publishing Company, 1993).

SALSA WORSHIP

The origins of the term "salsa" as an umbrella concept to refer to distinctive or combined musical expressions, styles, and sounds—primarily but not exclusively from Cuba—are debatable. Arguably the contemporary popular use, inclusive nature, and homogeneity of the term and its various musical forms in significant sectors of the Hispanic world can be traced back to the richly diverse Latin music scene in New York City during the late 1960s and the 1970s. Besides its contribution to the marketing of salsa as a genre and its internationalization, the creation of the *Fania All Stars* in 1968 became especially influential in the formation of a popular salsa consciousness primarily grounded in the urban experience of the *barrio*. Johnny Pacheco, a Dominican and a founding member of the Fania All Stars, once defined salsa as Cuban music with a New York influence. This meant, in part, there were "more aggressive arrangements" than the traditional Cuban *guaguancó*, *guaracha*, or *son montuno*, but also the rich influence of musicians of "different nationalities" upon the emergent sounds. Given the strong presence of artists of Puerto Rican origin in New York and among the ranks of the Fania All Stars, salsa as a classic genre also became inclusive of traditional *bomba* and *plena* forms from the island. The influence of various jazz forms in arrangements and improvisations can add yet another layer of complexity to salsa.

As a means of popular religious expression, salsa music explores a variety of experiences and themes. Cuban and Nuyorican singers Celia Cruz and La India—known, respectively, as the queen and princess of salsa—delve into Yoruba-based African-Caribbean religious roots. In Celia's *Canto a Yemaya* (*Afro-Cubana*, 1998), the singer presents a syncretism of African and Roman Catholic themes by addressing Yemaya as the spiritual guide and Virgin to whom the poor pray for peace. Inspired in the religion of *Santería*, La India pays homage to the sister spirits *Yemaya y Ochun*

Ruben Blades in concert. (Neal Preston/ Corbis)

(*Llegó La India via Eddie Palmieri*, 1992), referring to them as mother and saint. In *Para Ochun* (*El Sabio*, 1980), Puerto Rican salsa star Héctor Lavoe, whose drug addiction and depression once led him to seek the aid of a *santero*, sings of bringing flowers to the Queen's altar to seek her protection. Nuyorican trombonist and bandleader Willie Colón's *Aguanile* (*El Juicio*, 1972, sung by Héctor Lavoe) and his *Un bembe pa' Yemayá* (*The Winners*, 1987 sung by Celia Cruz) are Santería-influenced chants. *Aguanile* in particular mixes Santería chanting with the Christian Greek liturgical rubric "Lord, have mercy . . . Christ, have mercy" (*Kyrie eleison . . . Christe eleison*), prayers to the Holy and Immortal God, and references to Christ's crucifixion. In collaboration with Colón, Panamanian singer Rubén Blades's

Maria Lionza (*Siembra*, 1978) offers a tribute to the people of Venezuela through a description of the myth and popular cult of the goddess from Sorte Mountain in Yaracuy.

The subversive political use of religious themes is commonplace in salsa. Rubén Blades's composition about an outspoken pacifist priest, *El Padre Antonio y el monaguillo Andrés* (*Buscando América*, 1984)—a classic tribute to El Salvador's assassinated Archbishop Óscar Arnulfo Romero—stood as a defiant affirmation of the church's solidarity with the oppressed at a time in history when dictatorial and totalitarian regimes ruled in many Latin American countries. His musical adaptation of a partly Christianized *Chilam Balam* Mayan prophetic text (*La Rosa de los Vientos*, 1996) speaks of the final judgment but also points to the utopian hope for a new *América*—like the one Simón Bolivar dreamed of as Blades points out in other songs (e.g., *Plástico*, in the album *Siembra*, 1978). Drawing on another apocalyptic theme, Blades's *La canción del final del mundo* (*Escenas*, 1985) is a deceptively joyous criticism of nuclear proliferation with an accompanying urgent call to save the earth from destruction. Blades's *Maria Lionza* is hailed as a Queen—a Virgin Mary–like figure—who watches over the destiny of all Latina/os and looks after their unity and liberty.

Salsa serves as a powerful vehicle for expressing more traditional Christian themes, for example, conversion, in the context of popular religiosity or through adaptations of biblical stories. In the account of her musical career *La dicha mía*, a Johnny Pacheco composition (*Celia Cruz & Friends: A Night of Salsa*, 1999), Cruz thanks blessed Santa Bárbara and prays to all the saints for her good fortune as a singer. Cruz's improvisations are interspersed with a recurrent chorus of thanksgiving to the Lord: *Esa dicha me la dio el Señor*. In *El Nazareno* (*Traigo de todo*, 1974), the *sonero mayor* (premiere improviser) of Puerto Rico, Ismael Rivera, affectionately Maelo, offers a tribute to the Black Christ of Portobelo, Panamá, who gives good advice and protection and to whom he attributes a conversion experience that turned him from a life of drugs, partying, and hypocrisy to a life of happiness, good fortune, and service to the downtrodden and enemies. Héctor Lavoe's classic *El Todopoderoso* (*La voz*, 1975) uses the Lenten motif of Christ's passion (used previously in the song *Aguanile*) as a call for solidarity in a selfish world. Rubén Blades's *Noé* (*Mucho mejor*, 1984) tells the story of Noah and God's judgment through the flood to an unbelieving people with a humorous comment here and there about urban life, e.g., after the flood, the ark ends up in New York's 110th Street!

Of central significance in the conception and popularity of "Christian salsa," not only for Christians but also for the general Latino/a public, is the long-term collaboration of Nuyorican pianist Ricardo "Richie" Ray and vocalist Bobby Cruz. Already popular musicians in the New York music scene of the 1960s, Ray's announcement of his becoming a born-again evangelical Christian in the mid-1970s, with his friend Cruz's conversion following soon afterwards, led to the creation of many salsa hits. *Juan en la Ciudad* (*Reconstrucción*, 1976) tells the biblical story of the prodigal son who squanders his inheritance on worldly pleasures but is accepted into the loving arms of a forgiving father. *Timoteo* (*El bestial sonido*, 1999) is a call to people who are self-secure in their works to seek the Lord's forgiveness before it is too late. Although the chorus, *Faltas tú, faltas tú, Timoteo faltas tú*, reminds the irreligious man that he is the only one left in the family without the Lord, the song does not end with a happy conversion but with the sad and sudden death of Timoteo without the benefit of salvation. *Los Fariseos* (*El bestial sonido*, 1999) gives an account of Christ's last moments before his death with a dramatic chorus of the Pharisees asking for the release of Barabbas. Some mainstream salsa artists such as Fania star Ismael Miranda (*Buscando el camino*, 2008), Toni Vega (*Cuestión de fe*, 2004), and Dominican Juan Luis Guerra (*Para Ti*, 2004)—a *merengue* singer who occasionally sings salsa—have released songs related more closely to faith in Christ. There are now artists who focus exclusively on Christian salsa such as José "Papo" Rivera (*Salsa cristiana*, in the album *Unplugged—Evento histórico*, 2005) and Puchi Colón (*Salsa Praise*, 2002; *Lo mejor de mi para Él*, 2004; *Salsa Praise 2*, 2008). Others such as Roman Catholic singer and composer Cuco Chávez (*La nueva misa caribeña*, in his album *Caribe*, 1993) or the Lutheran group *Classic Son* (*Misa cubana 2*, 2002) from Cuba have set traditional liturgical orders of worship to a variety of Caribbean rhythms.

Leopoldo A. Sánchez M.

References and Further Reading

Orovio, Helio. *Cuban Music from A to Z* (Durham, NC: Duke University Press, 2004).

SALVADORANS

El Salvador, the smallest of the five Central American nations, is one of the most densely populated countries with more than 5 million people in an area of roughly 8,000 square miles. Democracy has been absent for most of the country's history, and this has led to civil unrest and extensive periods of political and social violence. In 1992, the country reached a period of political peace and stability through a United Nations Peace Accord between leftist guerillas and the Salvadoran army. The country continues, however, to struggle with high levels of postwar violence. Salvadorans in the United States reflect the country's sociopolitical instability as well as the connection between U.S. policies in the region.

Political Connections

Salvadoran immigration to the United States is a fairly recent phenomenon. In contrast with other immigrant groups that have a long history of immigration to the United States, the first wave of Salvadoran immigration began in the 1980s propelled by the civil war, which devastated the country for 12 years. Since 1980, thousands of Salvadorans have immigrated, escaping political persecution, massacres, death squads, human rights violations, poverty, and postwar violence. In many ways, their immigration reflects the intertwined sociopolitical connection between the two countries.

During the 1980s, the United States financed the Salvadoran government and trained military personnel to defeat the perceived threat from communism. At its peak, U.S. support included a military package of more than $1 million per day in counterinsurgency aid. U.S. military aid proved ineffective and spawned tragic consequences. Many ex-graduates of American military schools perpetrated gross violations of human rights, including the assassination of the Archbishop of San Salvador, Óscar Arnulfo Romero in 1980; the massacre of more than 500 civilians in El Mozote in 1981; and the execution of six Jesuits, including the president of the Catholic University and two workers in 1989. These violations perpetrated by American-trained personnel ultimately contributed to the immigration of thousands of civilians to the United States.

Religious Connections

The influx of Salvadoran immigrants has transformed the religious landscape of U.S. Latino/a communities in two ways. First, the repression that forced refugees to flee and the federal immigration policy that would have denied them political asylum ignited the Sanctuary movement in the 1980s. Many congregations across the United States responded to immigrants' pleas for humane assistance by offering social and political support in the form of social services, advocacy support and legal challenges to federal immigration policies. By sheltering or hiding families inside congregations, offering food services to those in need, and providing legal counsel to families, these congregations resisted U.S. policies.

The Sanctuary Movement of the 1980s has inspired many groups working with immigrants in the United States today. Groups such as the New Sanctuary Movement continue working with immigrants by accompanying and protecting them from violations of their human

---

EL SALVADOR DEL MUNDO

Salvadorans take part in a nationwide week-long celebration to honor their patron, El Salvador del Mundo, Jesus Christ the "Divine Savior of the World," after whom they named their country. This celebration was instituted in the official Catholic calendar in 1457, and celebrates Jesus' transfiguration at Mount Tabor, as described in the Christian gospels. In the colonial times, the newly funded city of San Salvador adopted this celebration as its own. According to the chronicler Fray Francisco Vásquez, San Salvador honored its patron with great solemnity and arcs made of flowers, altars, sermons, street parades, and other cultural expressions. The main festivities to honor El Divino Salvador del Mundo take place on August 5 and 6 every year. For a week, Salvadoran Catholics celebrate their patron with parades, dances, cultural events, and religious ceremonies both inside and outside the country. During the main religious celebration on August 6, thousands in San Salvador, Los Angeles, Washington, San Francisco, and other cities with significant Salvadoran presence, celebrate their religious and cultural heritage. This patron saint reflects the changing reality of border and cultural crossing among Salvadorans in the twenty-first century.

—*SLA*

---

rights such as hatred, workplace discrimination, and unjust deportation. Borrowing from the tradition of the Sanctuary Movement of the 1980s, these movements attempt to respond to the new realities of immigration.

Second, Salvadoran immigration to the United States transformed the religious landscape of the Latino/a community by providing new elements of popular religiosity. Every year on March 24, millions of Americans, Salvadorans and non-Salvadorans, commemorate the life and martyrdom of Archbishop Óscar Romero of El Salvador. On this day, congregations, students, unions, and other nonreligious groups honor Romero's commitment to peace and justice through marches, service learning projects, vigils, prayers for peace, and protests. In the second week of November, religious communities across the nation meet at Fort Benning, Georgia, to perform acts of civil disobedience and peaceful demonstrations at the School of the Americas, now Western Hemisphere Institute for Security Cooperation, in commemoration of the killing of six Salvadoran Jesuits and two workers by U.S. trained military personnel. In August, many Catholic denominations in the United States celebrate El Divino Salvador del Mundo, patron of San Salvador and one of the main religious figures for Salvadorans. In all, these celebrations reveal the connection between religion and sociocultural realities in the United States and in El Salvador.

Cultural Connections

Culturally, Salvadoran immigration underlines the connection between cultural transmigration through the phenomenon of youth gangs. Youth gangs initiated in the United States by Latino/a youth such as Mara Salvatrucha and

Sur 13 have crossed the border again, but this time in reverse, from the United States to El Salvador. Many Salvadoran youths who found refuge in the United States during the 1980s were later deported back to their country of origin under the Immigrant Responsibility Act of 1996, which allowed for the deportation of any legal resident convicted of a felony that carried a punishment of at least one year in jail. Salvatrucha and Sur 13 traveled with many of the deported youth, giving them a sense of identity and belonging through violent initiation rites, symbolic representation outside of society, a spoken dress code, and their own unique language, in many cases a mix of Spanish with English words. In addition, they organized the youth in clicas, or cells, with clear roles and responsibilities for each member.

In a country with a long history of war and postwar violence and low investments in its youth, these underground groups spread rapidly throughout El Salvador, and they now control entire communities through the exercise of vigilante justice, taxation, drug trafficking, and other illegal activities. With more than 20,000 members, these gangs are the de facto power in many communities and cities across the country as they provide security, organize revenge killings for victims of crime, and empower their members through violence and a sense of belonging.

In many ways, gangs are the other face of the intercultural and political relations between the United States and El Salvador. Many of these youths grew up in poor communities within the United States and are now living in poor communities in El Salvador. They had escaped cycles of violence from their countries, and are now back into a new cycle of postwar violence. They use globalization to spread their message, but maintain a local presence across El Salvador and the United States.

Salvador Leavitt-Alcántara

References and Further Reading

Alvarenga Venutolo, Patricia. *Cultura Y Ética De La Violencia: El Salvador 1880–1932* (San José: Editorial Universitaria Centroamericana- EDUCA, 1996).

Anderson, Thomas R. *Matanza: The 1932 "Slaughter" That Traumatized a Nation, Shaping U.S.-Salvadoran Policy to This Day*, 2nd ed. (Willimantic, CT: Burbstone Press, 1992).

Gill, Lesley. *The School of the Americas: Military Training and Political Violence in the Americas* (Durham, NC: Duke University Press, 2004).

SANCTUARY MOVEMENT

During the 1980s, U.S. policies in Central America created military conflicts in places like El Salvador and Guatemala. For some, staying in their native land meant death, usually at the hands of the government. Many sought a safe haven in the United States as refugees. Refugees, by legal definition, are those who fear persecution due to their race, religion, nationality, political views, and/or their association with political or social organizations. By 1980, the Salvadoran military killed over 10,000 people, including Archbishop Óscar Romero and four churchwomen from the United States. Church leaders and workers were usually targeted for arrest, rape, torture, and disappearance (a euphemism for killing). Guatemala, on the other hand,

---

NEW SANCTUARY MOVEMENT

In September 2006, Elvira Arellano, a 32-year-old undocumented cleaning woman, walked into Adalberto United Methodist Church in Chicago and requested the right of sanctuary, an ancient practice of seeking refuge in a sacred place. Her actions were a desperate attempt to avoid separation from her seven-year-old son, Saul, who is a U.S. citizen. She was eventually deported on August 19, 2007. Her act of disobedience sparked the New Sanctuary Movement, a coalition of congregations responding to the perceived injustices faced by the undocumented. The movement is reminiscent of the Sanctuary Movement of the 1980s, which occurred during the height of Central American Civil Wars. The New Sanctuary Movement consists of interfaith religious leaders and participating congregations who open their church doors to undocumented immigrants residing in the United States. Those associated with the movement attest that all people share basic common rights to a livelihood, to maintaining family unity, and to physical and emotional safety. Yet they believe that the immigration policy of the United States violates these rights through its policy of separating children from their parents demonstrated in unjust deportations and in the exploitation of immigrant workers.

—*MAD*

---

witnessed over 50,000 deaths, over 100,000 disappeared, and 626 village massacres.

Nevertheless, the Reagan administration refused to grant refugee status to those attempting to escape persecution, taking the stance that these migrants were simply coming to the United States seeking economic opportunities. For the Reagan administration, refugee status was determined by whether the government from where the asylum seekers originated was on good or bad terms with the U.S. administration. Because Cuba and Sandinista-led Nicaragua had hostile relationships with the U.S. government, those leaving these communist/socialist nations were routinely granted refugee status. But because El Salvador and Guatemala were receiving military aid from the Reagan administration, and saw these armed conflicts as the front of the Cold War, applicants for political asylum from those nations were routinely denied refugee status. Less than 4 percent of all

applicants would be approved. Unable to meet U.S. legal requirements for migration as refugees, these applicants, who were usually poor peasants, were denied legal entry, leaving them with the alternative of facing persecution or death.

In response, Jim Corbett (a Quaker) and John Fife (a Presbyterian) cofounded the Sanctuary Movement. The Sanctuary Movement lacked a central command or hierarchical structure. It consisted of loose connections among faith-based communities, human rights groups, and secular organizations. Shortly, the movement was represented by various denominations and traditions, including Baptists, Jews, Mennonites, Methodists, Presbyterians, Quakers, Roman Catholics, and Unitarian Universalists. On March 24, 1982, Reverend Fife, pastor of Southside Presbyterian Church in Tucson, Arizona, along with five churches in San Francisco, declared their worship space a sanctuary for those

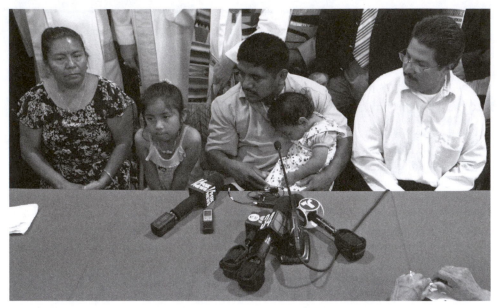

A family of undocumented immigrants from Guatemala facing deportation answer questions from the media after the public launch of the New Sanctuary Movement in Los Angeles. Calling for a moratorium on immigration raids and deportations that have separated hundreds of illegal immigrants from their U.S.-born children, the New Sanctuary Movement is opening churches and places of worship to harbor families who risk being torn apart. (Danny Moloshok/Reuters/Corbis)

fleeing the violence in El Salvador and Guatemala. It was no coincidence that they chose the second anniversary of the assassination of Archbishop Romero to mark the start of the Sanctuary Movement. Soon afterward, Corbett asked the Chicago Religious Task Force on Central America to set up an "underground railroad" that moved refugees seeking sanctuary away from the heavily patrolled border area of the southwestern United States to the less patrolled North.

The practice of setting aside a space of refuge has it roots in the biblical text. When the Jews entered the Promised Land, six levitical cities were designated as cities of refuge, places that provided absolute security to fugitives (Joshua 20:7-9). In the event of accidental homicide, the person charged could seek asylum from avengers. This tradition of setting aside a site of refuge became part of American tradition during slavery. An underground railroad was established composed of safe houses, which served as havens for runaway slaves journeying north toward freedom.

Eventually, some 400 religious congregations and 12 universities joined the Sanctuary Movement, establishing safe havens where over 70,000 refugees could find refuge. Local municipalities were encouraged to adopt ordinances that expressed solidarities with those refugees seeking asylum, even if it meant a refusal to cooperate with the federal government's efforts to enforce immigration laws. Twenty-two cities and one state (New Mexico) joined the movement's call to set up sanctuary spaces. Church leaders and laity faced arrest (up to five years in prison) and fines ($2,000 for each refugee harbored) for declaring their worship space a true sanctuary. In 1985, 11 sanctuary movement activists were indicted on alien-smuggling charges. After a six-month trial in Tucson where they were not permitted to reference El Salvador or Guatemala, eight were convicted of various felonies and three were acquitted. All eight convicted received probation. Their "crime" was providing refugees with emergency housing, legal and social services, job training, and English classes. The Sanctuary Movement insisted that they were not engaged in "civil disobedience," but rather "civil initiative," that they were upholding the laws on how to treat war refugees—laws that the U.S. government was refusing to uphold. Their "civil initiative" raised consciousness concerning the plight of these migrants and how the United States contributed to their conditions, inspiring similar actions to be taken in other countries.

Miguel A. De La Torre

References and Further Reading

Bau, Ignatius. *This Ground is Holy: Church Sanctuary and Central American Refugees* (Mahwah, NJ: Paulist Press, 1985).

De La Torre, Miguel. "For Immigrants." *To Do Justice: A Guide for Progressive Christians* (Louisville, KY: Westminster John Knox Press, 2008).

De La Torre, Miguel. *Trails of Hope and Terror: Testimonies on Immigration* (Maryknoll, NY: Orbis Books, 2009).

Golden, Renny, and Michael J. McConnell. *Sanctuary: The New Underground Railroad* (Maryknoll, NY: Orbis Books, 1986).

SANTERÍA

The religion known as Santería has its origins in the West African religious traditions that were introduced to the New World through the Atlantic slave trade. Large concentrations of ethnic Yoruba peoples largely from the geographic area that today incorporates the Federal Republic of Nigeria and the Republic of Benin arrived in Cuba between 1830 and 1886. The last official documented accounts of slavery date to 1886. Yoruba populations were also exported to Virginia, United States. Between 1517 and 1880 Cuba had imported more than 1 million slaves from 80 different African cultures. The Spanish colonial island economy relied on the cultivation of coffee, tobacco, and labor-intensive sugar plantations. Most of the slave populations were located in rural plantations, while others supplied growing demands for domestic labor. Yoruba peoples were preferred for domestic labor. Slaves, considered a human commodity, were imported upon approval of the Roman Catholic Church of Spain, hereinafter referred to as the Church, and processed by the government. Roman Catholic baptism of all slaves constituted legal entry into the island colony.

A shortage of Roman Catholic clergy and churches disadvantaged broad efforts to evangelize slaves throughout the country, particularly in rural areas. White plantation owners and populations living in rural areas were mostly located in significantly remote places away from nearby urban parishes. Studies of geography and commodity trade routes strongly suggest that most rural slaves were never exposed to churches or clergy. The domestic slave and free labor force living

IFÁ

Ifá is the oracle religion of the Yoruba people. It originated from Orunmila in Ile-Ife, the second of the three Yoruba Supreme Beings. It is a system of divination based on the 16 basic and 256 derivative figures obtained either by the manipulation of 16 palm nuts or by the toss of a chain of eight half seed shells. Origins of *Ifá* come from West African regions, but can be seen practiced in Latin America. In Cuba, it is seen through the practice of Santería, while it is seen through Candomblé in Brazil and Voudoun in Haiti. The divination act is performed by a Babalawo, and the purpose of it is to obtain divination through the spirits. The Yoruba believe that through the teachings of Ifá, fate can also be controlled to a large extent. It is through the performance of certain propitiatory sacrifices and magic prescribed by the Babalawo that this can be achieved by grouping palm nuts in one hand and shifting them to the other. As this goes on, the Babalawo makes single or double marks in wood powder (saw dust) of seeds that fall out during hand transfers and spreads powder on the divination tray until one of the 256 *odus* is created to explain the future.

—SJR & RHR

in, or near, developing townships like the port of Regla, Cuba, were influenced and monitored for evangelization purposes. African indigenous religions were outlawed, though strategic toleration was practiced. Clergy had the state-sponsored authority and mission to evangelize, teach the Spanish language, reeducate, indoctrinate all people of color, investigate, and ensure that slave protection laws were observed. The long-term paternalistic power of the Church gained an unknown number of converts mainly in urban centers.

The colonial system provided weekend leisure time on the plantations. Slave privileges served as a mechanism for evangelization, at times permitting limited African religious expressions. Periodic leisure time was afforded and justified under a psychological scapegoat criterion. To avoid communication between slaves in neighboring plantations during religious leisure time, they used an alternating system between the plantations. An important advantage was that slaves could purchase their freedom; however, it depended on clergy approval. In some cases a conditional prefreedom credit system took place. The slave owner at times provided a conditional freedom that allowed the slave to seek employment and pay for his/her freedom by committing to an installment plan. The free slaves also had the right to purchase slaves. Many free slaves in rural areas relocated to urban centers seeking port, manufacturing, and domestic jobs. The urban population came closest to Roman Catholic acculturation.

The Church's records strongly suggest that the sponsoring of religious syncretism by the Cuban church would be a viable means to advance religious conversion over time. Cultural and religious syncretic expressions contributed to the legal establishment of urban Afro-Cuban social organizations called *Cabildos*. This was a colonial strategic policy suitable for containment of free slave

ASHÉ

"Ashé" is a Yoruba word introduced to the Americas via African slavery in the Caribbean. It can best be understood as a sacred energy that becomes the power, grace, blood, and life force of all reality, embracing mystery, secret power, and divinity. As a transcendent world force, it is absolute, illimitable, pure power, nondefinite, and nondefinable. This energy current is amoral, neither good nor bad. It is unable to be seen or personified, a neutral cosmic energy undergirding every aspect of existence. All that has life or exhibits power has ashé. The movement of the wind, the elements of plants, fire, and moving water expends ashé. When a candle is lit to an orisha, a quasi-deity within Santería, the act releases power—the power of fire, smoke, and burning wax. This ashé is able to feed and empowers the orisha. The most potent ashé can be found in the spilling of sacrificial blood. Within some Hispanic communities, the term "ashé" has become a form of greeting or a term equivalent to "amen."

—*MAD*

populations that were permitted to operate under a secure affiliation and monitoring system by urban parishes. Members of these organizations frequently participated in Church events, religious services, and sacraments and maintained an interfaith relationship with their local Catholic priest.

The relationship was reciprocal. It was customary for Cabildos to support Catholic feast days and religious events. They also encouraged participation in Catholic sacraments, holy masses, and the superficial association of saints with Yoruba deities. Catholic priests were known to participate in Cabildo-sponsored socioreligious events and preserved a trusting relationship. The Catholic attempt to stamp out African retentions through religious assimilation and conversion over time failed. Moreover, many overlapping ethical and moral code values and religious similarities were identified and preserved. Other features that were radically dissimilar to core African beliefs were dismissed. The integration of Whites

into African religions by way of popular piety made a considerable contribution to the survival of Yoruba indigenous religion. The academic operational term Afro-Cuban Santería, known variously as Saint Worship, Regla de Ocha-Ifá, and/or Lukumí, referred to the popular expressions accommodated by early Yoruba people and first-generation descendants.

During the Spanish Inquisition the word "Santería" was used to denote a deviated Catholic worshipper, which excluded African traditions by definition. Any person worshipping a Catholic saint outside the narrow institutional orthodoxy of the times was labeled a *santero*, therefore, addressing the rising concerns about Spanish Santería or Folk Catholicism. If expressions of popular piety incorporated beliefs and practices beyond institutional acceptance, the characterization of *brujo* (witch) or *brujería* (witchcraft) was used to denote a person practicing witchcraft. In Cuba, the words Santería or Santero/a became a popular New World operational label

BABALAWO

Babalawos are the *Ifá* (system of divination) priests that are seen more commonly in the Yoruba cultures that are native to the West African countries (such as Nigeria, Togo, Benin—formally known as Dahomey, and Cote d'Ivoire). Babalawos refer to Ifá for purposes of divination by use of palm nuts. The Babalawos are seen as the embodiment and soul of the Yoruba Nation. They serve as a link from past generations to present ones. Often, Babalawos are held in high esteem, especially in king and tribal councils. Babalawos usually have the last words in decisions that will affect the tribe as a whole. Ifá is consulted at almost every juncture and important occasion. Although Babalawos originate from West Africa, they are also found in countries such as Cuba, Brazil, and Panama, as a result of the slave trade. In Cuba these Babalawos are apparent through the practices of Santería, while in Brazil they are seen through the practices of Candomblé. Although traditions vary from country to country, they all share the same origins and fundamentals that relate them to one another. The basic use of pine nuts, divination chains, and trays remains vital to the practice of Babalawos.

—SJR & RHR

extending the definition to any person who fused Catholicism with African religions and various forms of European Spiritism. Over time, fostering a whitening process of an undetermined number of Afro-Cubans, primarily in urban settings, into the new social order, customs, education, and language somewhat succeeded in social terms. However, a religious juxtaposition diagramming operational Catholic equivalences with cultural fusion began to form. Reciprocity in gender relations, biracial marriages, common-law unions, adultery, prostitution, domestic labor influences, and White immigration were some of the many undercurrents that account for cultural fusion in Cuban colonial and republican lower-income groups.

The Republican Period from 1902 to 1959 accounts for important social and religious changes. National labor movements founded in 1925, and legalized in 1938, recruited many Afro-Cuban members who held leadership positions.

Central to their platforms was a schism between Blacks as nationals challenging the traditional racial minority classification. The new constitution of 1940 included clauses prohibiting racial discrimination. Economic and social upward mobility among Afro-Cubans permeates a religious revitalization and preservation consciousness movement. Popular piety among the marginalized Whites becomes a joining empowerment force where reverse religious conversion of Whites takes root. As the marginalized population moves up the social strata, it begins to gain and expand White sympathy, adherents, and converts reaching all levels of society. Therefore, the *africanization* of marginalized Whites proliferated. The evolving trend led to an internal religious process of converting Yoruba oral traditions into a unifying Spanish language production of monographs, books, and academic discourse. By the late 1940s and early 1950s, the first two Spanish language versions

ORISHAS

Followers of the Afro-Cuban religion known as Santería believe that the supreme God Olodumare created quasi-deities called orishas to serve as protectors and guides for every human being. Their roots can be traced to Africa, brought to the Caribbean by those destined to be slaves. In order to continue worshiping their African gods under the constraints of slavery, slaves hid their deities behind the masks of Catholic saints, identifying specific orishas as specific saints. These orishas provide guidance and security to humans, whom they adopt as their children. Today, each santero/a is consecrated to a specific orisha. Because Santería is shaped and formed by earth-centered forces of nature, these forces are personified as orishas. Besides being understood as quasi-deities and forces of nature, these orishas also represent archetypes, personalities, energies, and elements. Since physical elements of existence reflect spiritual principles, the believer is assured that they do not exist in a universe that lacks reason or direction. All that is, whether seen or unseen, exists in totality where orishas protect all of creation. They provide structure to reality, and without them, human existence cannot develop. Orishas were the first to walk the earth, and from them all humans are descended.

—MAD

of Ifá Odu (Lukumí-Yoruba canon/scripture) by Ogún priest Pedro Arango were internally circulated in Havana. Other books that focused on philosophy, Yoruba-Spanish vocabulary, and divination systems became readily available in the marketplace.

Santería in America

Fidel Castro's revolutionary triumph in 1959 initiated economic tension between Cuba and the United States. By 1961 the United States imposed an economic trade embargo and the revolution was declared socialist. Castro's declaration caused an abrupt exodus of Cubans to the United States. Most exiles were of the White middle and upper social class. They settled in large numbers in New Jersey, New York, and Miami, with an overflow settling in Puerto Rico.

Priesthood ordinations in New York and Puerto Rico began in 1961–1963 followed by Miami in the late 1960s. With the growing influx of exiles during this period came an increasing number of priests and priestesses who began reconnecting through small groups at each location. Home worship was transformed into centers that operated as an extended family. The constant stream of new arrivals, displaced from their homeland, generally did not know the language, laws, and the American way of life. Their private dwellings and rental apartments called *ile* soon developed into an exile community network system. The networks as support centers ministered on religious matters, maintained contact with Cuba, facilitated links and strengthened relations with groups in other cities, and provided a significant social services role.

Economic development took shape from the onset of *ile* networks. The rapid necessity to meet expanding ritual and ceremonial demands amalgamated a complex industry of readily available market products and the manufacturing

A Santería altar and religious objects belonging to Santería priest Jose Merced in Euless, Texas. (AP Photo/Matt Slocum)

of religious items that depended on priestly craft. Localized products and natural resources had varied limitations based on geographical location. Travel between cities and postal services facilitated the acquisition of raw materials. The free-market principle of supply and demand created new specialized jobs, increased consumption of a wide range of products in local markets, and increased imports and exports.

By the end of the 1960s and early 1970s, the informal economic subsystem developed into a structured American business phenomenon known as the *Botánica* that did not exist in Cuba. These are specialized retail religious supply stores. The stores' client base was connected to local religious leaders. A rapid commodity consolidation process began to unfold in the various communities. The exile Lukumí religion and

marginalized Latino/a community started to merge. As the merging of communities took place, the Botánicas absorbed the product needs of popular piety found in predominantly Catholic Spanish-speaking communities. The Botánica product line surpassed Lukumí and embraced the needs of popular Catholic and *Espiritismo* traditions. Out of the expansive nature of the business grew the practicality of the wholesalers that consolidate manufactured goods throughout the diaspora and supply Botánica's nationally. Stores are generally located in moderate to high concentrations of Latino-Hispanic communities.

The infusion of Cuban Santería into the overwhelmingly Christian American culture transgresses Cuba's paradigm. The religion has become multicultural, multiethnic, and globalized. Most members are self-denominated White representing all socioeconomic levels. Superficial ties are maintained with Cuba, but the religion as professed in the United States is self-dependent. There is a generational gap where many reject the colonial classification of the term "Santería" and its association with Roman Catholicism; thus, "Lukumí" is the preferred name for the religion.

Doctrinal Points

Lukumí-Yoruba is a pre-Christian faith that does not rely on Christianity or the Bible. It believes in one almighty creator known as "Olodumare" and a hereditary core of deified emissaries named orishas that have delegated or borrowed power. The orishas are worshiped as sacred dimensions each with a representing archetype and group types containing anthropomorphic characteristics that govern a complex structure of natural life

---

BEMBÉ

"Bembé" is a loosely used term that means live musical fiesta, or drum dancing. "Bembé" signifies "to be" or "to live." In the context of Lukumí religious events bembé can be any festive drums that have not been consecrated, therefore, drums used for informal socioreligious musical events associated with thanksgiving celebration. The festive events include drum percussion called Lúlu and Yonkóri, which are rhythmic songs honoring Lukumí-Yoruba deities called orisha. The Akpón is a soloist singer that initiates sets of songs and stimulates audience participation. A chorus known as Ankorí is randomly formed and leads dances among congregants. Bembé in the form of celebration are generally one day events lasting less than seven hours. Altars consisting of food offerings to the deities and ancestors are constructed. Minor rituals are done to spiritually purify sacred spaces. Bembé celebrations in excess of one day are called batamún, lasting several days, and batá drums are employed. The batá are three sand-clock shaped log drums of different sizes. Each wood log is perforated, cut to specific external and internal measurements. Each drum contains two open mouths covered by leather. Other instruments like the maraca, called Acheré, are generally used by the Akpón.

—EP

---

domains. There are deified culture heroes and martyrs. Ancestor worship is recognized and practiced.

The religious canon or sacred text is called "Ifá" consisting of odu, which are 16 primal chapters and 240 subchapters. It is an extensive corpus of history, myths, legends, folktales, verses, and proverbs. Ifá is used as a complex divination system for individual, community, and religious guidance. Ifá-odu governs the ethics, morals, and theological principles by which priests and adherents live and worship.

Core beliefs include a concept of reincarnation and the fulfillment of destiny assigned by Olodumare. Human reason and purpose is conceptualized within a framework connected to nature worship, sacredness of Olodumare's planetary creation, free will and fate, universal laws, and the recognition of binary principles of constructive and destructive forces that may be natural and supernatural. The beliefs include the sacredness of a small group of sacrificial farm animals that form an integral part of Olodumare's mandates.

The religion has no concept of the Christian Satan or Devil power authority, or concept of hell. The philosophy centers on the here and now—balance and resolution of life trials and tribulations. It is not based on the idea of miracle or life after death paradise. Central to the core beliefs is that Olodumare distributed knowledge; therefore, all religions have truth but none hold a monopoly on truth. The distribution of knowledge includes human science and technology. A concept of religious diplomatic relations is believed and practiced. Superficial contact with the religion does not require a person to assimilate and internalize Lukumí or instantaneously dismiss themselves from their ongoing religious tradition in order to benefit or receive guidance. In this regard, the lack of a rigid evangelization model has been perceived as syncretism. However, if the

CHURCH OF THE LUKUMÍ BABALÚ AYÉ

Church of the Lukumí Babalú Ayé was incorporated in the state of Florida in 1974. It is the first known Lukumí-Yoruba church within the United States. The founders were Carmen Plá Rodriguez and Ernesto Pichardo. Both were born in Cuba and migrated to the United States in 1961, shortly after Castro's revolution. They settled in Miami, Florida. During the first decade of the church's incorporation, its founders formed a small ad hoc group for the primary purpose of research and structural studies. An official membership drive began in 1984. The first organizational group was established in 1986, charged with the goal of opening its first house of worship in the City of Hialeah, Florida. The church leased a commercial property with the option to buy in mid-1987. Upon public announcement of intent to establish the nation's first Lukumí-Yoruba church, it encountered intense political and religious opposition. The initial obstacle was the acquisition of a certificate of occupancy from the city. Additionally, elected officials passed resolutions and three ordinances prohibiting religious animal sacrifice. On June 11, 1993, the U.S. Supreme Court overturned lower court decisions in favor of the church. This landmark decision is considered an important religious freedom case of American history.

—*EP*

person is destined by Olodumare to become an adherent or priest/ess, he/she is expected over time to acculturate, assimilate, and internalize the Lukumí way of life by adhering to the spiritual principles and mandates of Olodumare.

Ritual Structures

Priests and priestesses are called olorisha or olosha as subsequent ordained extensions of their individual tutelary orisha. The general olorisha priesthood hierarchy is based on ordination seniority and specialization through long-term traditional oral apprenticeship and experience. There is one separate henotheistic priesthood order, known variously as babalawo, oluwó, omó-odu, Ifa priest, or priest of the deity Orunmila, that claims hierarchal religious seniority and canon authority. Ordination into the priesthood is a complex process that requires preordination rituals, ordination ceremonies, and postordination completion rituals over a period of one year.

The religion has its holy and celebrative days associated with each African orisha archetype. Priests and priestesses also celebrate their respective ordination day annually. These are elaborate socioreligious events that generally take place in homes. Altars are constructed corresponding to the priest's tutelary orisha, food offerings are placed at altars, food is consumed by the congregants, and at times live religious musical presentations are included honoring the orishas.

Major community events are called "drumming" and are officiated by specialized religious musicians. Orisha possession is frequently experienced by ordained members, whereby the orishas randomly advise congregants. Natural communication and guidance relies on two complex divination systems known as dilogún, in which 16 cowry shells are employed and, the ikín 16 kola nuts or opele divining chain. Both systems are used to interpret canons for individuals and community. Herbal medicine, prayer, invocation, protective charms, hymns, praise songs, baptism, marriage, birth and death rites, as well as food and selective sacred animal offerings are all part of this religion. Religious canon regulates all rituals and ceremonies, dietary laws, and taboos. There is an elaborate construct of rituals and ceremonies utilized for faith healing, and as means of alternative therapy or crisis intervention, the exorcism of spiritual malady, thanksgiving, petitioning, and for general health, safety, and prosperity of all humankind.

Key Figures

There are many notable Cuban Lukumí priests that made instrumental contributions during the 1960s. In 1961, New York records the first olorisha priesthood ordination in America by Mercedes Noble. The officiating priest of the deity Obatalá was Obá Oriaté Victor Manuel Gomez. He also became Miami's first officiating Obá Oriaté in the late 1960s. Arriving in New York from Cuba in 1962, Obatalá priest Benigno Dominguez De La Torre ordained four people by 1964. He moved to Puerto Rico and became Puerto Rico's top olorisha progenitor between 1965 and 1970. In the month of November 1963, Shango priest Juvenal Ortega ordained the first olorisha in Puerto Rico.

The progenitor in the United States of the first two babalawo ordinations was Carlos Ojeda. Bobby Bolufer was one of the first two ordained in 1969 and became Puerto Rico's first officiating babalawo. The organization of babalawos led by Carlos Ojeda and Diego Fontela became official in 1974. In January 1974, olorisha Carmen Plá Rodriguez and Obá Oriaté Ernesto Pichardo founded the Church of the Lukumí Babalú Ayé in Hialeah, Florida. The church won a landmark U.S. Supreme Court First Amendment case in 1993, recognizing constitutional protection for religious animal sacrifice.

Dieties

Babalú-Ayé

Babalú-Ayé, Cuba's version of the African Ewe-Fon-Dahomey deity, is Nigeria's Obaluaye (king of the earth), Omolu (the Lord's son), and Chankpana, god of contagious disease who punishes or afflicts with severity. Since he descended to earth from the supreme Olofi, he requires submission to his authority. Babalú-Ayé's devotee dresses in jute and sackcloth in replication of an ancient symbol of distress and sickness. He has a bag strung across his chest in which he carries his favorite foods and is accompanied by a dog that licks the wounds of the sick. This unkempt-looking creature is dreaded for his association with a variety of sicknesses and their agents, but he is also respected for what he can do to anyone who antagonizes his devotees. Myth has it that Babalú-Ayé works miracles and is strict and unforgiving to devotees who break their pledges. He symbolizes Saint Lazarus or Saint Baba, and his cult followers in Cuba perform his flagellation sacrifice with frequency. On the 17th of each month, his devotees dress in sackcloth and fulfill a pledge in his honor (on December 17 his feast day) that is now traditional in Havana.

—NSM

Changó

Changó is one of the main *orishas*, or quasi-deities, of the *Yoruba* pantheon (Africa) and the religion Santería. This orisha is very popular among Cubans and Cuban Americans. He is the god that rules over thunder and lightning, fire, electricity, and semen. Being one of the patrons of warriors, he simultaneously represents many human virtues and vices. Changó is known for being in constant battle with his nemesis and brother Oggún, the god of war. Although he is admired by friends for being virile, brave, loyal, hardworking, as well as a skilled dancer, he is also known for having a terrible temper and is prone to womanizing, bragging, gambling, and lying. He is credited with having 44 wives: his main wife being Obba and his main mistresses being Ochún, the love goddess, and Oyá, the ruler of the cemetery. Oyá, previously Oggún's wife, is his favorite lover. In present-day Nigeria, the former Yoruba territory, it is believed that the king of Oyó committed suicide and now rules as Changó. According to many ancient legends, he is the son of Aggayú, ruler of volcanoes and their rivers of molten lava. Within Santería, Changó has several manifestations, the most common being Santa Bárbara, a martyred teenage girl of the third century.

—VLC

Eleggua

Eleggua (Elegbara/Eshu) is the trickster orisha who victorious Cuban revolutionaries celebrated in 1959 as they marched from Oriente into Havana, wearing his necklaces and waving his red and black flags. This triumphant mythological warrior orisha holds a prominent place in Santería culture. As the most influential santo in Cuba, the fearless deity ruler of roads opens and closes paths. He is present at the opening of all ceremonies and is given incantations at the end, in request for permission to perform initiations. Santero/as seek his blessings before executing magic spells and give him first place in ritual sacrifices. Eleggua represents Saint Martin and Saint Anthony and is naturally fond of children. Not surprisingly, a headpiece carved of cowrie shells with boyish bulging eyes and ears is his lead representation. In Cuba, Eleggua is a magician whose spells are not easily broken, and he can divine the future even without sacred tools. He personifies destiny, good luck, human desire, as well as tragedy. His medium tells jokes, often curt ones, engages in mischievous activities, smokes a large cigar, loves alcohol, and eats his gourmet foods (which includes smoked fish, roasted possum, and male chickens).

—NSM

Obatalá

Called Oddua and Orisha-nla, Obatalá is the chief of the orishas and one who shares the character of the supreme deity, Olodumare. Obatalá walks many paths: the creator of humankind and the world, source of all beginnings, supreme judge, principal messenger, husband, and wife. As creator, he is responsible for all human deformation and peculiarities. The West African deity is androgynous, he is Olofi's son and Olodumare's wife, and thus has multiple personalities; he appears in as many as 16 female and male characters. In spite of Obatalá's varied names and shifting gender personae, her feminine personality called Oddua is dominant. In Santería she is associated with the Our Holy Lady of Mercy and regarded as the goddess of purity, truth, justice, mercy, wisdom, and peace; she is represented by a white dove. Obatalá's special feast day is September 24, the birthday of Our Lady of Mercy. Her devotees carry her lucky number, 8, and dress in her color, white. The hills and mountains of Cuba are hers because they produce her special herbs. In Santería worship, the masculine Obatalá is number one. He is the ritual head, and the color white symbolizes his majesty and purity; his *iyawo*, or initiate, must spend an entire year wearing white as a sign of his rebirth within the Santeria faith.

—*NSM*

Oggún

Oggún is the python deity representing earth-based technologies (blacksmith, steel, mining, smelting, and minerals) and war in West Africa, and is one of the oldest spirits in the orisha pantheon. The mythological power originated in Ogun-Oyo, Nigeria, and adapted to New World slave religion. This shrewd but mischievous deity is the brother of Eleggua, Ochosi, and Changó—orishas with whom he competes for the goddess Ochun. In Santería and Vodou religions, Oggún represents Saint John the Baptist and Saint Peter who holds the symbolic keys to the kingdom of heaven. Oggún's avatars wear sacred beads with his favorite colors; they have an appetite for his gourmet dishes, smoke big cigars, showcase his cultural symbols of automobiles, tanks, railways, and metal tools; and they wield a machete for clearing underbrush and symbolically engaging battle. He has many sacred herbs and is the first orisha to dine at the Bembé feast when there is an animal sacrifice. Oggún carries an air in Afro-Hispanic culture because he is loved by farmers, taxi drivers, police officers, and other professionals. He became an interracial cultural icon and a system of spirituality with a strong cultic following throughout the Americas.

—*NSM*

Olodumare

As the Great One and God of the Yoruba people of Nigeria, Olodumare is known by many other names throughout Africa. He is the supreme deity and mighty creator of the world. Also, he is the source and originator of all things, sovereign ruler, and repository of the destinies of all creatures, divine and natural. Olodumare made a pantheon of intermediate beings (named *vodu* and orisa) to work on his behalf in the natural and spiritual worlds. He gave the divinities specific tasks for governing the world and holds them responsible for its order and chaos. Issuing from Olodumare through the divinities and ancestors is a cosmic energy of *ashe* that links and animates everything with the spiritual force. Although God is the central character in myths recalling the creation of the world, he is a hidden or distant controller of the universe. In Afro-Caribbean religions, Olodumare is honored as God mainly during initiation rites or other special occasions. Cuban and Puerto Rican devotees do not make him the center of their worship. Their objects of ritual actions are orishas who, in return for devotion, mediate powerful *ashe* to their human devotees. Practitioners believe Olodumare gives everyone a destiny or road map in life.

—*NSM*

Orúnla

A creole version of the African divinity Orunmila of Ife, Orúnla is regarded as the master of all secrets, knowledge, and concentrated magical science. This mythological ruler of divine realms is the ancestral father of all spiritual mysteries and patron of babalawo priests endowed with his gift of knowledge of the cowry shells. Orúnla, the only orisha to witness the creation of the universe and the setting of human destinies, is the source of *ifa* divination, entrusted to him by the creator Olodumare. As custodian of human knowledge, he owns the table of Ifá, the chief instrument used in divining the future. Followers of Santería religion revere Orúnla for his spiritual powers; though he resides in heaven as each initiate chooses his or her destiny, he comes to earth and incarnates in his human mediums. Orúnla is also the double of Saint Francis of Assisi, whose special day is October 4 and who is known for his piety. Sometimes this wise and intuitive deity gets cantankerous and, with an iron will, makes rash decisions. However, he is a greatly loved orisha whose avatars wear his number 16 on yellow and green, eat his special food, and use his many sacred herbs to communicate with other orishas.

—NSM

Oyá

Oyá is one of the quasi-deities of the Yoruba pantheon (Africa) and the religion *Santería*. She is patroness of the cemetery, queen of the realm of death, and mistress of the flame. As guardian of the underworld, she is one of the most fearsome orishas. Originally her domain was the sea, but she was tricked by Yemayá into making a trade. In Africa, Oyá is the goddess of the Niger River, but her power over natural phenomena, such as tornadoes, is what provokes fear all over the Yoruba territory. In Cuba, Oyá is known as the goddess of the winds of change and storms. According to the ancient legends, Oyá was married to Oggún, god of war, brother and also rival of Changó, god of thunder. One day, while riding a magnificent horse near Oggún's house, Changó seduced and abducted Oyá. She became his lover, who as a female warrior often goes into battle as his companion. Together with Changó, they make fierce love and war. Beautiful and prone to violence, she is represented as a warrior-goddess, carrying a "machete" or sword. She is best known as the manifestation of Santa Teresa de Jesús and Our Lady of Candlemas.

—VLC

Yemayá

Called mother of all that exists, Yemayá is a sister of the deity Ochun and a favorite orisha in Afro-Caribbean religions. The model mother and giver of life, protector of maternity, goddess of oceans, and patron of mariners, she is symbolized by the Atlantic ocean. As if to debunk American stereotypes of Black inferiority, ignorance, and low IQ, Cubans see the Black Yemayá as the goddess of rational thinking, good judgment, and intellect. Her temperament is as complex as her wisdom: She wears seven alternate blue and red beads; she dances as vigorously as angry waves and is like a wild tempest, but can be calm and peaceful. She is majestic, haughty, and salacious but protects her children with motherly grace. Since her face is always masked, Yemayá is only revealed in dreams; the anchor, half moon, and silver sun announce her presence. Like Ochun, Yemayá is one of Changó's wives and is associated with Christian saint Our Lady of Regla. Devotees wear her blue and white colors and are fond of her special foods (fruits, bananas, male goats, poultry, and fish). Her statue is a beautiful matron with a prominent voluptuous breast that bespeaks a dream of fertility for Cuba's land of want and hardship.

—*NSM*
Ernesto Pichardo

References and Further Reading

Ayorinde, Christine. *Afro-Cuban Religiosity, Revolution, and National Identity* (Gainsville: University Press of Florida, 2004).

Brown, David H. *Santería Enthroned Art, Ritual, and Innovation in an Afro-Cuban Religion* (Chicago: The University of Chicago Press, 2003).

De La Torre, Miguel A. *Santería the Beliefs and Rituals of a Growing Religion in America* (Grand Rapids, MI: Wm. B. Eerdmans Publishing Co., 2004).

Mason, Michael Atwood. *Living Santería Rituals and Experiences in an Afro-Cuban Religion* (Washington, DC: Smithsonian Institution Press, 2002).

Murphy, Joseph. *Working the Spirit: Ceremonies of the African Diaspora* (Boston: Boston Beacon Press, 1994).

SECULARISM

Hispanics who trace their roots to Spain or Latin America are influenced by a history that has normatively blurred the lines between political and religious institutions. Catholicism's dominance within society created a union of church and state. As early as 1474, Isabella, queen of Castile, secured the right to fill high ecclesiastical posts within her domain from the papacy, a right her husband, Ferdinand, would eventually use during the conquest of the Americas. By 1494, a mere two years after the "discovery" of the so-called New World, Pope Alexander VI (of Spanish origin) negotiated the Treaty of Tordesillas, dividing the lands to be conquered in the Western Hemisphere between Spain and Portugal. All ecclesiastic powers operating in what was called New Spain became subservient to the crown. For example, through *patronato real*, the king was given the right to appoint the high ecclesiastical offices (including bishops) of the churches in the Americas. Also, the king took the responsibility of administering the *diezmo* (tithes) and church expenses. In effect, the king of Spain became a vice-pope. This created difficulties in Latin America during the independent movements of the nineteenth century when the struggle against the state also meant a struggle against the church. Although some of the independent movements adopted anticlerical dimensions, most revolutions displayed indigenized Eurocentric icons (i.e., la Virgen de Guadalupe in Mexico or la Virgen del Cobre in Cuba) to rally the masses.

The secularization process did not begin with the U.S. conquest of lands held by Spanish-speaking people. Catholic missions throughout what would become the southwestern United States were initially secularized by the Mexican Congress in 1833 to meet the economic demands of Mexican citizens living close to the mission. The purpose of secularizing these missions was to break the Church's economic prominence in what was then the frontier. These missions quickly fell into neglect and disrepair. A century would pass before restoration projects would be undertaken, mainly by Euro-Americans, for the sake of tourism.

As the United States conquered lands held by Spanish speakers (i.e., Florida and Puerto Rico from Spain and the southwest from Mexico), the new rulers imposed the U.S. concept of "separation of church and state." Although religious biases toward the predominantly Catholic inhabitants of the land were manifested in a multiple of cultural, political, and social ways, the ideology created a new way of being, or not being, religious within a Eurocentric political system. While Hispanics have a historical tradition that merges politics and religion, these traditions are manifested and dealt with differently within the United States from the Euro-Americans.

For some, political structures become a way to bring relief and liberation to Hispanics who live in poverty and oppression. It was common for political movements, like the United Farm Workers Union, to use banners adorned with Hispanic religious symbols. Not surprisingly, a 2007 poll conducted by the Pew Hispanic Center found that most Latino/as (66 percent) see religion as a moral compass that guides their political thinking. Similarly, most Hispanics (65 percent) believe it is appropriate to address political and social issues from the pulpit.

Those who refer to themselves as secular say that they have no specific religious affiliation or consider themselves as agnostic or atheist. While a large number of Latino/as who call themselves secular (44 percent) and say that religious beliefs are not important in influencing their political thinking, a substantial minority (37 percent) say that religious beliefs play an important or somewhat important role in influencing their political thinking. Similarly, half (50 percent) of those who call themselves secular say that churches should stay out of political matters, while 43 percent believe that political views should be expressed from the pulpit.

The same poll found that 7.8 percent of those questioned about their faith labeled themselves as secular—a figure that is less than non-Hispanic Whites (11.4 percent) and slightly higher than non-Hispanic Blacks (7.7 percent). Of the Latina/os who convert to a new faith, 28 percent reported moving away from all forms of religious expression. Almost two-thirds (65 percent) of those who identify as Latino/a secular claimed to have practiced a religious faith at some earlier point in their lives, with 39 percent saying that the faith tradition they practiced was Catholicism. Latina/os who call themselves secular are predominantly male (66 percent) and younger than those who identify with a faith tradition. These converts to secularism are relatively wealthy, with about a third of them earning over $50,000 a year (compared to just 17 percent of all Latina/os). More than half (54 percent) were born in the United States; a majority (68 percent) speaks English or are bilingual; and 20 percent have a college diploma (compared to 10 percent of all Hispanics). Those claiming to be secular are disproportionately Cuban (8 percent claim to be secular but Cubans represent 4 percent of Hispanics) and Central American (14 percent claim to be secular but Central Americans represent 9 percent of Latina/os).

These Latina/o seculars are evenly split among political ideologies with

28 percent identifying themselves as conservatives (compare to 9 percent of non-Hispanics), 29 percent self-identifying as moderates (compared to 43 percent of non-Hispanics), and 33 percent calling themselves liberals (compare to 42 percent of non-Hispanics). It is interesting to note that 29 percent of those who claim to be secular say that religion is still very important to them, with 8 percent of them attending weekly church services. Nevertheless, those who specifically claim to be atheists are viewed more negatively by Hispanics than the general public. Only 19 percent of Latino/as view atheists favorably compared to 35 percent of the favorable view of atheists by the general public.

Miguel A. De La Torre

References and Further Reading

Rodríguez, Havidán, Rogelio Sáenz, and Cecilia Menjívar, eds. *Latinas/os in the United States: Changing the Face of América* (New York: Springer, 2008).

Pew Hispanic Center. *Changing Faiths: Latinos and the Transformation of American Religion* (Washington, DC: Pew Forum on Religion and Public Life, 2007).

SEXUALITY

One of the stereotypes by which Latina/os are described concerns their so-called sexual fecundity. Although it is true that Hispanics have larger families than Euro-Americans (3.59 average household size compared to 2.59), how that data have historically been interpreted has contributed to oppressive structures. To represent Hispanics as having high fertility rates is to depict them as overly sexually active. Images of hot-blooded Latin lovers and hip-swinging spicy señoritas have dominated popular imagination, a possible attempt to project Euro-American self-denying fantasies upon a Hispanic other.

These stereotypes are not limited to popular culture. For example, the eminent Harvard professor Samuel P. Huntington, in his book, *Who Are We? The Challenges to America's National Identity* (2004), claims that Latino/as pose a threat to the United States on many fronts, including being overly fertile (224), in other words, oversexed. When this image exists in a Euro-American culture that has historically maintained a philosophical dualism between the purity of the mind that must transcend the carnal pleasures of the body, then Hispanics, by definition, are seen by the dominant culture as being more physical and less intellectual. Add to this the sexual dualism developed early within Christianity between spirit and flesh, where the spirit is incorruptible and the flesh is associated with sin. After all, lust does become one of the seven deadly sins. The result is a Latina/o body that is relegated to being instinctively "passionate," if not sinful. Hispanic bodies can therefore be offered up as pleasurable objects or, worse, as deserving the imposition of strong techniques in sexual seduction (if not abuse).

Ironically, rather than fitting the licentious stereotypes imposed upon Hispanics by the dominant Euro-American culture when it comes to issues related to sexuality, Latina/os appear to be more conservative than their Euro-American counterparts. Ignored are the roles that honor/shame play within the Hispanic culture and their impact on suppressing sexual desire. The same philosophical and religious influences that have shaped the Euro-American construction of

OCHÚN

Ochún is the African patron goddess of love and sexual pleasure, luxury, and beauty. Also, she is ruler of oceans and fresh waters. As one of the most popular and venerated deities, she is called the giver of life, mother of the orishas, and possessor of feminine virtues that guard women's pregnancy. The accomplished dancer Ochún typifies the "sensuous saint" and controls the knowledge and art of lovemaking. She loves everything yellow and her ornaments and necklaces reveal an expensive taste for fine clothes, jewelry, and an assortment of exotic foods. Legend has it that Ochún seduces other male orisha lovers, although her main consort is Changó. She is known widely as Cuba's patron saint and mother, la Virgin (Our Lady of Regla) de la Caridad del Cobre, whose feast day the church celebrates on September 7. The public statue of this goddess of the erogenous and wealth symbolizes the graces of Cuban women and, as Kole Kole, represents children and the poor and needy and shows great patience and kindness. Ochún has become a national identity symbol of hope in a distressed Cuba and, since 1960, a metaphor for peace and reconciliation among ethnic Cubans in the American diaspora.

—NSM

sexuality have been dominant within the Hispanic community and their nations of origin. The dominant Catholic and evangelical influences upon the Latino/a community have also associated any form of sex outside of heterosexual marriages as sinful and depicted sexual excess as contrary to Christian teachings.

For example, according to a 2007 poll conducted by the Pew Hispanic Center, more Latino/as oppose gay marriage (56 percent) than non-Hispanics (42 percent). The vast majority of Latina/o evangelicals oppose gay marriage (86 percent), while Hispanic Catholics are more divided with 52 percent opposing gay marriage and a significant minority (32 percent) in favor of it. On another issue related to sexuality, abortion, 57 percent of all Latino/as state that it should be illegal to have an abortion, significantly higher than non-Hispanics at 40 percent. Again, Latino/a evangelicals appear to be more conservative with 77 percent opposing abortion compared to 54 percent of Hispanic Catholics. Of

course, understanding these attitudes about homosexuality and abortion cannot be limited to membership in a religious faith tradition. Studies have shown that recently arrived immigrants and those for whom Spanish is the dominant language tend to be more conservative on social issues. It appears that as English proficiency is acquired, a more liberal shift occurs.

A self-imposed stereotype that has also negatively impacted Latino/a understanding of sexuality is the Virgin-Whore dichotomy that has been imposed upon Latina bodies. Influenced by dualistic thinking, Latinas are provided with two models. The first is the Virgin Mary, or La Virgen de Guadalupe. The Virgin functions as the ideal model of Latina femininity that emphasizes the so-called female virtues of motherhood, nurturer, and caregiver. Because this model is a Virgin, purity and a lack of sexuality is added to the qualities of the ideal Latina. The other choice offered is the Whore, usually in the symbol of la Malinche,

TLAZOLTEOTL

Tlazolteotl is the deity of sexuality in the sense of both procreation and eroticism. Originally a Mayan Huastec deity from people along the Gulf of Mexico, who came under Aztec rule about 1450, Tlazolteotl is the patroness associated with both fertility and sexual pleasure. She is most often depicted giving birth and protecting both pregnant women and midwives, as well as the herbs they need, including those herbs used for abortion. Together with Xochiquetzal, "beautiful like a flower," who was the patroness of ritual and illicit sexual relations, Tlazolteotl, "eater of dirt," was one of the deities who cleansed the people of the sins they confessed through ritual, including auto-blood sacrifice. Feminine deities who protected abortion and sex for purposes other than procreation, as well as to whom the people confessed, presented a challenge to Christian sensibilities at the time of European contact. Like many male Aztec deities, Tlazolteotl can take the form necessary for her cosmological task: Coatlicue, the Serpent who gives birth to the deities and welcomes the dead into her jaws so they become one with the cosmos, or Tonantzin, the Mother Earth who gives life, or Cihuacoatl, the patroness of women who die in childbirth.

—*MVS*

the indigenous woman who has played the role in Latino/a imagination of being Hernán Cortés (the conquistador) lover, translator, and betrayer of her own people. La Malinche functions as a warning against the dangers of unchecked femininity, specifically a sensual, subversive, and treacherous femininity. A dichotomy developed within Latino/a culture between the "good" girl and the "bad" girl, between the sacred and the sensual, between la Virgen and la Malinche, between the Virgin and the Whore.

A larger Hispanic family is not the consequence of hypersexuality. Views on abortion, along with Catholic teachings on contraception, may partially explain the higher fidelity rates among Hispanics. Additionally, the emphasis and importance that *familia* (family) plays within the Hispanic culture can account for larger families. This concept of *familia* has led to customs among Hispanics, which has contributed to the Euro-American stereotypes concerning the Latina/o sensuality. For example, it is customary for Hispanics to hug and kiss (on the cheek) when greeting each other—even men embrace each other as a common form of salutation. Such *abrazos* (hugs) among Latino men, while disconcerting to Euro-American men's homophobia, do not cast any doubt upon the Latino man's machismo.

Sex among Hispanics is no more excessive than the sexual habits of Euro-Americans—or any other group for that matter—yet stereotypes of overactive libidos, within popular culture and the academy, have contributed to biases that have proven detrimental to Latino/as.

Miguel A. De La Torre

References and Further Reading

De La Torre, Miguel A. *A Lily Among the Thorns: Imagining a New Christian Sexuality* (San Francisco: Jossey-Bass, 2007).

De La Torre, Miguel A. "Beyond Machismo: A Cuban Case Study." *The Annual of the Society of Christian Ethics* 19 (1999): 213–233.

De La Torre, Miguel A. *Out of the Shadows into the Light: Christianity and Homosexuality* (St. Louis: Chalice Press, 2009).

López, Robert Oscar. "Sexuality." *Encyclopedia Latina*, ed. Ilan Stavans (Danbury, CT: Scholastic Library Publishing, 2005).

Pew Hispanic Center. *Changing Faiths: Latinos and the Transformation of American Religion* (Washington, DC: Pew Forum on Religion and Public Life, 2007).

SOUTH AMERICANS

South Americans, along with Central Americans, have historically been labeled as the "Other Hispanics" by the U.S. Census Bureau. Unfortunately, because they have been treated as a monolithic group, they represent the least documented U.S. Hispanic group. Even though South Americans have been migrating to the United States since the late 1700s, it is difficult to find statistical information about them. Throughout the 1800s, many came to the United States fleeing the violence of South America's wars for independence (1810–1824). Others, specifically Chileans and Peruvians, came in search of riches during the 1849 California gold rush.

According to the 2000 Census, South Americans as a group representing nine Latin American countries, comprise 4 percent of the U.S. Hispanic population and 0.5 percent of the overall U.S. population. They are mostly immigrants, with 76.58 percent being foreign born, of which 28.13 percent are U.S. naturalized citizens. The majority of South Americans from predominant Spanish-speaking nations come from Argentina, Bolivia, Chile, Columbia, Ecuador, Paraguay, Peru, Uruguay, and Venezuela. These nine countries can be grouped geographically. Argentina, Chile, Paraguay, and Uruguay comprise the Southern Cone; Bolivia, Ecuador, and Peru represent the central mountain region; and Columbia and Venezuela are located on the Caribbean Sea.

Brazil is not included among South Americans because of the difficulty of labeling them as Hispanics, even though many Euro-Americans do. Brazilians are ambivalent about self-identifying as Hispanic or Latino/as. They were colonized by the Portuguese rather than the Spaniards and, as such, do not share the language or the colonial history of the rest of South America. And while Brazil is one of the major South American countries that influences the continent's politics and economy, and it is recognized that Brazilian culture has also had an impact upon the United States, we do the Brazilians a disservice if we simply lump them together with all South Americans.

South Americans living in the United States have a median age of 33, older than the Hispanic overall median age of 26 but still younger than the overall U.S. median of 35.4. Compared to the rest of the Latino/a population (with the exception of Spaniards), South Americans have attained higher levels of education with 76.11 percent graduating from high school (compared to 52.42 percent of all Hispanics), and 25.18 percent graduating from college (compared to 10.44 percent). South Americans are also economically more stable than Hispanics. The median household income of South Americans is $41,132 per year, significantly higher than the overall Latino/a median income of $33,676, but still

---

AEMINPU

The *Asociación Evangélica de Misión Israelita del Nuevo Pacto Universal* (AEMINPU; Evangelical Association of the Israelite Mission of the New Universal Covenant) is led by Ezequiel Ataucusi Gamonal, who is considered to be the incarnation of the Holy Ghost, the New Christ, the Son of Man, Father Israel, and even a New Inca. AEMINPU is based on an Andean Messianism. This Peru-based church wishes to return to the roots of Christianity, a time before the Romanization of Christianity by Emperor Constantine. Members call themselves Israelite because they identify with God's chosen people and with the "authentic" ritual practices prior to Constantine's reforms. A mixture of Andean Messianism and biblical reinterpretation, the movement is based on what members consider to have been the organization of the Inca Empire. In this way, the movement matches the "old messianic return to the time of the Incas," motivated by the myth of the Inkarri (Atahualpa, the Inca king's promise of returning and reestablishing the Inca Empire just before he was beheaded by the Spaniards). The Israelite Mission has grown to become the largest creed in Peru, second only to Catholicism. Outside of Peru it has spread to Bolivia, Ecuador, Colombia, and among Latinas/os in the United States.

—NM

---

slightly lower than the overall U.S. median household income of $41,994. Yet surprisingly, the percentage of South Americans living in poverty, 15.05 percent, while lower than the overall Hispanic population at 22.63 percent is still disproportionately higher than the total U.S. rate of 12.38 percent.

The largest concentrations of South Americans live in New Jersey (2.18 percent), Florida (1.98 percent), and New York (1.75 percent) with Miami-Dade, FL (7.2 percent), Queens County, NY (7.20 percent), and Hudson County, NJ (7.19 percent) topping the list. Because of the lack of documentation concerning South Americans, it is easy to stereotype them as being mainly White, Roman Catholic, and Spanish speaking. In reality, South Americans represent a very diverse group of people. It is not uncommon to find U.S. Hispanics with South American roots whose primary language is indigenous. Rather than Spanish, they speak Quichua or Aymara. Besides these indigenous roots, there is a strong African presence due to the slavery that was once practiced, especially in northern Columbia and Venezuela. Many South Americans have an Asian background; for example, the former president of Peru, Alberto Fujimori (1990–2000), is from Japanese descent. South America is as diverse as the United States, and as such, there is no typical South American.

South American Migration

Many who migrated to the United States during the 1970s and early 1980s included political refugees fleeing U.S.-backed (and at times installed) right-wing military regimes. Fearing "another Cuba" in the hemisphere, in the early 1960s the United States launched the Alliance for Progress, hoping it would create a middle class. Unfortunately, the emerging middle class that benefited from these earlier attempts of the Alliance for Progress in social and economic

Peruvian Catholics march in a procession honoring Saint Martin de Porres in the East Village, New York City, on May 6, 2007. Saint Martin de Porres, the first black saint of the Americas, was born in sixteenth-century Peru to a Spanish nobleman and a young freed black slave and was canonized May 6, 1962. (Getty Images)

development found themselves in countries unable to absorb their new skills and talents. Frustrated by the inability to advance economically, many migrated to the United States. This exodus of trained professionals caused a brain drain in the countries they left.

The Alliance for Progress was originally designed to modernize and enhance social services (i.e., literacy programs, hospitals, and road construction) but soon morphed into a National Security doctrine. As the Cold War battles moved to the South American continent, preventing "another Cuba" was achieved not through economic development but by supporting dictatorial regimes. A poignant example of this can be found in President Salvador Allende's government in Chile. Elected to one of the oldest democracies in the hemisphere, Allende began to construct a socialist alternative to the Alliance for Progress. With the open support of the United States, specifically the CIA, his government was overthrown and replaced with the brutal dictatorship of General Augusto Pinochet.

The cry to "fight communists" provided political and economic support from the United States throughout Latin America in spite of the atrocities being experienced by the general public. In South America, the life-threatening state terror in Argentina (1976–1983), Chile (1973–1990), Paraguay (1954–1989), and Uruguay (1973–1984) [as well as Brazil (1964–19850)] caused many citizens to find refuge in Europe. Because of the U.S. government's support of these

MARTIN DE PORRES (1579–1639)

Martin de Porres was the illegitimate son of a Spaniard and an Afro-Latina, who was born at Lima, Peru, in 1579. His father eventually recognized him as his son, but when returning to Spain left him in his mother's care. De Porres was baptized by the future saint Toribio de Mogrovejo. At age 12, he became a barber and a medic. At 15 he joined the Order of Preachers (Dominicans) as a "donato." Being illegitimate and mulato hindered him from full incorporation into the Dominicans. He turned the friary into a hospital by taking in the sick off the streets. When the brothers complained that he was breaking cloister, de Porres responded, "It is better to break cloister than to break charity." His reputation as a doctor grew, and he treated rich and poor, people and animals alike. He would say, "I cure you but it is God that heals you." He desired to be a missionary but was not allowed to do so. Missionaries in China and Japan declared that he would appear and encourage them when they felt like giving up. He died in 1639 and was canonized in 1962. He is often depicted with a broom and small animals.

—GCG

military juntas, the United States was not able to publicly recognize the migrants of these South American nations as refugees fleeing persecution. Nevertheless, a few did find a safe haven in New York, Washington, D.C., Chicago, and the San Francisco Bay area.

During the mid to late 1980s, the cause for immigration shifted as South Americans migrated to the United States due to economic reasons. As many of these regimes transition to democracies, economic crises developed due mainly to the neoliberal policies imposed by the International Monetary Fund (IMF). Spiraling inflation, widespread unemployment, and the dismantling of the welfare state led many from the urban middle class to either drop below the poverty line or leave for the United States. This migration, specifically from Columbia, Ecuador, and Peru, consisted of many urban professionals. In addition to the challenges of settling in a new land, they live as neighbors who at times find themselves engaged in the

political quarrels rooted in their nations of origins. For example, continued tensions exist among Columbians, Ecuadorians, and Venezuelans over border disputes or between Chileans and Argentineans over long-standing political conflicts between their home nations.

While many came to make a new life in the United States, others came with the full expectation of eventually returning to their homeland. For example, Columbians escaping the violence of their civil war created an ethnic enclave in Jackson Heights, New York. Disinterested in U.S. social issues, they recreated their homelands on a new land, complete with restaurants and shops. They were more concerned with their children remaining Columbians than with their assimilation to U.S. culture. Aliens by choice, they remained active in the life of their homelands, even voting in their nation's elections, always waiting for the day they could return. For many, that day never came.

VIRGEN DE CHIQUINQUIRÁ

Alonso de Narvaez, the Spanish painter, is credited with painting the sixteenth-century portrait of the Virgin of the Rosary. The portrait was placed in a Columbian chapel where it was exposed to a leaky roof. By 1577 the damaged painting with obscured images was moved to Chiquinquirá, Columbia. According to the story, a pious woman from Seville, Maria Ramos, hung the faded painting in the chapel in 1586 and prayed. On December 26, 1586, the damaged painting completely restored itself. By 1829, Pope Pius VII declared Our Lady of the Rosary of Chiquinquirá patroness of Columbia. The Virgin is also venerated in Venezuela and among Venezuelans in the United States. According to the story, a washwoman during her chores noticed a small slab of wood floating on Lake Maracaibo in the early eighteenth century. Retrieving the wood, she discerned an undistinguishable image. She took the wood home. While working around the house, she heard knocks coming from the slab. Upon investigating she discovered a glowing light that produced the image of Columbia's Virgin de Chiquinquirá. The wood with image is at the Basilica at Maracaibo. Among Venezuelans, la Virgin de Chiquinquirá is affectionately called *La Chinita*.

—MAD

Religious Contributions

The political conditions of South America gave rise to a religious movement that has greatly influenced U.S. Latino/a theologies, along with other non-Hispanic theologies. Known as Liberation Theology, this movement became a religious response to the political and economic sufferings of South Americans. The roots of this South American religious movement can be found during the Spanish colonialization of the continent. Early in the conquest of the hemisphere, the Spanish Pope Alexander VI (1492–1503) granted the king of Spain the right to administer all of the ecclesiastical duties of the Church located in what was then called New Spain. *Patronato real* (the king's patronage) gave the king the right to administer the tithes and appoint high ecclesiastical offices, making Spain's king a vice-pope. Early on, two church structures developed in

South America. One was complicit with the colonial political structures and another was composed of individual priests of various religious orders who chose to be in solidarity with the victims of colonialism—the dispossessed Indians. Thus a two-tiered, informal ecclesiastical structure evolved. Many liberation theologians view these early protestors of colonialism as forerunners for what would develop into the South American liberation theology movement.

The emerging nations that arose as a result of the wars for independence throughout South America during the early 1800s attempted to maintain the same control over the church that Spain previously enjoyed. As a result, Christendom carved out a space for itself from which to operate—a space it could maintain by providing religious legitimacy to the existing political structures. For the most part, the Church found an ally in the right-wing military dictators of the

---

ROSA DE LIMA (1586–1617)

Isabel Flores de Oliva was canonized by Clement X in 1671 as the first saint from the Americas. She is commonly called Santa Rosa de Lima because as an infant her nanny dreamt that her face had become a rose. When she was confirmed at age 11 in 1597, Bishop Toribio de Mogrovejo called her Rosa without any knowledge of the nanny's dream. He would eventually be canonized after her. As a teenager, she disliked being called Rosa and only accepted the name when at 25 she was consecrated as a Dominican. She lived in Lima most of her life, except for a brief period when as a child her parents moved to Quives. It was in Quives that she began her battle with rheumathroid arthritis. Upon her return to Lima, her parents encouraged her to marry, but she refused. She cut her hair and disfigured her face and eventually became a recluse in her own home like Catherine of Siena. She would leave her hermitage only in service of the poor and to go to Mass. At the age of 20 she began her formation as a Dominican sister. She died in 1617 at the age of 31.

—GCG

1970s in their fight against Godless communism. The Castro revolution in Cuba, followed by the expulsion of most of the Catholic clergy from the island, left many within the Church concerned that another Cuba might occur in their homeland. But while much of Christendom found the military juntas as allies, from the underside of Christendom was the church of those being tortured and disappeared, composed mainly of the poor, the peasants, and the marginalized.

The religious response to the suffering of South Americans evolved into a theology. Crucial to the development of this theology was Pope John XXIII's (1958–1963) call for a Second Vatican Council (1962–1965). One of the reasons why the Pope called for this Council was so the Church could come to terms with modernity. To that end it produced a pastoral encyclical called *Gaudium et spes* (1965). The encyclical emphasized the church's responsibility for "those who are poor or afflicted in any way." When the South Americans attending the

Council returned to their homelands, they had difficulty applying the teachings that came from the Council to the South American experience. How does one do Christianity within the context of U.S.-backed brutal dictatorships? How does the Church respond to the suffering of the people? What does it mean to take responsibility for "those who are poor or afflicted" within South America.

In 1968 a conference was held in Medellín, Columbia, to discuss how to implement Vatican II within the South American context. The document that arose from this conference became a blueprint for Liberation Theology. Shortly afterwards, Gustavo Gutiérrez, a Peruvian priest, published *Teología de la liberación* (1971), a reflection on how theology can be formed by learning from the daily struggle of the poor. The book was translated into English in 1973 under the title *A Theology of Liberation*. One of the developments in the implementation of Liberation Theology was the creation of Christian Base Communities (CBCs).

SEÑOR DE LOS MILAGROS

El Señor de los Milagros, the Lord of the Miracles, is a religious mural from Lima, Peru, housed in the Shrine of the Nazarenas. Believed to be painted by a seventeenth-century African slave, the mural portrays Jesus Christ as *Christ Moreno*—a Peruvian of African descent. Rather than a White Jesus who shares the race of the colonizers, the Jesus in the mural finds solidarity with Peru's disenfranchised. When the 1665 earthquake struck Lima, it destroyed all of the walls in the church where the icon was located, except the wall containing the mural. Images of the icon have become a unifying symbol among Peruvians living outside their homeland. During the early 1970s, Peruvians in the northeastern United States started religious brotherhoods to honor el Señor de los Milagros. An image of the icon was housed in the Sacred Heart Church in Manhattan. As the U.S. Peruvian population grew, so did the number of brotherhoods. By 1977, the Organization of Peruvian Catholic Brotherhoods in the USA was established to coordinate the activities of the different brotherhoods throughout the United States, specifically the October 18 annual procession.

—MAD

These base communities were composed mainly of poor people. They were provided with opportunities to appropriate and practice their Christian faith in a new way. These base communities directly reflected on the social, ecclesiastical, and economic marginalization they were facing.

The theology that developed in South America was tied to the social and political needs of the people. For this reason, among the salient goals of Liberation Theology were the following: (1) the goal of achieving liberation from all forms of social, political, economic, and institutional exploitation; (2) the goal of creating a more dignified life by providing human control over determining each person's own destiny; (3) the goal of creating a new person in Christ that is delivered from the consequences of the sin of oppression; (4) the goal of establishing justice; and (5) the goal of forming a new social order based on sociopolitical freedom and redistribution of economic resources.

With the replacement of military dictatorships by civilian governments during the 1980s, with the collapse of the Berlin Wall and its hope in leftist utopias, and with the election of leftist, some of whom were persecuted during the 1970s by the military juntas, questions have begun to arise about the relevance of Liberation Theology in South America. This led Gustavo Gutiérrez to comment during the 1996 conference of the American Academy of Religion that he does not believe in Liberation Theology, rather, he believes in Jesus Christ. Because all theologies are contextual to a certain place and time, they must be abandoned when the theology can no longer address the needs of the people. But because the poor and oppressed will continue to exist, whatever theology arises that addresses their needs and introduces the divine into their struggle, that theological perspective will be liberative.

Although it can be argued that this liberationist perspective already existed within the United States, specifically during the Civil Rights Movement and the contributions made by Martin Luther King Jr. and Malcolm X, the South American version of Liberation Theology impacted and influenced many different U.S. religious movements, including those of Latina/os. What today are known as Hispanic theologies find that many of their tenets are either a result of or have been highly influenced by the many theological perspectives that arose from South America's religious response to political oppression.

Miguel A. De La Torre

References and Further Reading

Berryman, Phillip. *Liberation Theology: Essential Facts About the Revolutionary Religious Movement in Latin America and Beyond* (Philadelphia: Temple University Press, 1987).

Berryman, Phillip. *Religion in the Megacity: Catholic and Protestant Portraits from Latin America* (Maryknoll, NY: Orbis Books, 1996).

Ellacuría, Ignacio, and Jon Sobrino. *Mysterium Liberationis: Fundamental Concepts of Liberation Theology* (Maryknoll, NY: Orbis Books, 1993).

Gutiérrez, Gustavo. *A Theology of Liberation: History, Politics, and Salvation*, rev. ed., trans. Sister Caridad Inda and John Eagleson (Maryknoll, NY: Orbis Books, 1993).

The Hispanic Databook (Millerton, NY: Grey House Publishing, 2004).

Peterson, Anna, Manuel A. Vásquez, and Philip Williams, eds. *Christianity, Social Change, and Globalization in the Americas* (New Brunswick, NJ: Rutgers University Press, 2001).

Richard, Pablo. *Death of Christendoms, Birth of the Church*, trans. Phillip Berryman (Maryknoll, NY: Orbis Books, 1987).

Vasquez, Manuel A. "Central and South Americans, and 'Other Latinos/as.' " *Handbook of Latina/o Theologies*, ed. Edwin David Aponte and Miguel A. De La Torre (St. Louis: Chalice Press, 2006).

SPANIARDS

Spaniards have had a formative influence on the religious culture of Hispanic Americans. Spain has left a rich legacy that is clouded, too, with moral ambiguity and controversy. An examination of the Spanish influences on the formation of Hispanic American religious cultures shows that it is an influence mediated through Latin America, a region, people, and culture formed by the encounter between Spain, the indigenous civilizations of the Americas, and African slaves brought over by the Spanish and the Portuguese. This encounter was marked by conquest, enslavement, and degradation, as well as a powerful encounter among developed and accomplished cultures. Consequently, to assess the Spanish contribution to Hispanic American religious cultures requires an assessment of the many negative legacies of the Conquest, while at the same time acknowledging and celebrating the rich Spanish dimension that remains integral to Hispanic American identity.

Prelude to Conquest

A handful of factors that helped make the Spanish Conquest possible have left lasting consequences. First, the fall of the Kingdom of Granada to Castile and Aragon and the success of Christopher Columbus's first voyage to the Americas both occurred in 1492. Columbus's discoveries could not have been timelier for Spain. The completion of the Spanish reconquest (*Reconquista*) of the Iberian Peninsula from the Moors left Spain possessing a large group of fighting men seeking the next adventure, men who for various reasons lacked any hope for social advancement in the new kingdom, and a zealous Catholic faith borne out of centuries of driving the Muslim out of what was viewed as Christian territory. America would provide a new frontier whereby this pent-up energy could find a new outlet. The crusading spirit of the reconquest was transformed into a new crusading spirit of conquest. Instead of recapturing a known country for glory, honor, and Christianity, the new cause was the exploration and conquest of an unknown land, securing any wealth found there as a reward for daring the unknown, ensuring social advancement denied at home, and converting the indigenous peoples of America to Christianity.

Second, the Spanish brought with them an ambiguous view of race that theologian Luis Pedraja describes as a curious mixture of tolerance and condescending racism. An understanding of the contradictory views the Spanish held of the people they encountered in the Americas can be seen through the lens of their own history. Spaniards share a quality with the Latin and Hispanic American people and cultures they helped give birth to; they too are a mix of the people and cultures that migrated, conquered, and settled in Spain. Besides the first-known residents of the Iberian Peninsula, the Celts, Iberians, Basques, and later arrivals, namely the Phoenicians, Carthaginians, Berbers, Greeks, Romans, Vandals, Visigoths, Moors, and Jews, all contributed to Spanish identity and culture. Many of these later arrivals had evolved from a plurality of backgrounds. For example, Carthage began as a Phoenician outpost, and the Phoenicians, in turn, evolved from the Canaanite civilization in Palestine. Hispania, as Spain was known under Roman rule, was opened to nearly every civilization Rome conquered and incorporated into its Empire. Jorge Gracia adds that the Moors brought to Spain their Arab, Syrian, Egyptian, Nubian, and Berber roots, all united under Islam. Unfortunately, this history did not open the Spanish to consistently seek constructive relationships to the indigenous peoples of America.

Sangre azul, literally "blue-blood," was a racial (and racist) category coined by the Spanish during the reconquest (*Reconquista*) of the Iberian Peninsula from the Moors, employed for political ends to distinguish "real" Spaniards from persons with family bloodlines "contaminated" with Moorish or Jewish elements. According to Gracia, the Christian kingdoms of reconquest-era Spain, countries in a continual state of war against the Moors, had to remain on guard against treason and betrayal. The best security against that were family bloodlines, which served as the basis for every loyalty and political alliance forged during that epoch. Ironically, *sangre azul* developed precisely because everyone knew that Spanish bloodlines inextricably were a mixture of all the peoples who made Spain, including the Moors and the Jews. Tragically, this legal fiction led to the expulsion of the Jews and all remaining Moors for the sake of building up political stability and the religious orthodoxy of a newly united, officially Catholic kingdom. In the Americas, despite the intermarriage of the first waves of Spanish arrivals (overwhelmingly male) with Indian women, and despite the plural roots of Spanish identity, neither could stop the racism that grew out of the fiction of the "pure-blooded" Spaniard. Racism, an abiding concern of Latin and Hispanic Americans, finds its ultimate origin here.

The question of race relations among the Spanish, Africans, and Indians during the Conquest is a history of a missed opportunity to create a truly mixed society and the tragedy of the racism that eventually triumphed. It reveals, too, an important issue that both Latin and Hispanic Americans need to grapple with: the term "Spanish Conquest" is not entirely accurate because the Conquistadors were never exclusively Spanish.

The Conquest

It is commonplace to describe the Spanish Conquest as a catastrophe executed by all-powerful Spanish Conquistadors inexorably overrunning indigenous civilizations, and then introducing African slaves who replaced the decimated Indian populations in the work force. There is much truth to this statement; one dare not underplay nor dismiss the destruction of the Indians, but it glosses over a far more complicated history. That Francisco Pizarro could capture Peru with an army of 200 Spaniards, and Hernán Cortéz could capture the Aztec Empire with fewer than 600 men, points to a historical fact beyond Spanish courage in the face of the unknown and skill in battle. Scholars of the Spanish Empire have recovered an almost-forgotten legacy of the Conquest, where its success depended on *extensive, active aid and military alliances between the Spanish Conquistadors and local Indian tribes.* And, these collaborators sometimes included freed Africans. In other words,

Engraving from about 1600 depicts Spanish invaders battling the Incas in Peru. Francisco Pizarro conquered the empire of the Incas in 1533, claiming their lands for the king of Spain. (Library of Congress)

to argue that the Conquest was a cataclysm that destroyed the existing order, turned the world of the Indian upside down, and precipitated their systematic impoverishment and oppression is a problematic generalization because it would not have been universally held by the Indians themselves.

For example, Pizarro's conquest of Perú is *the* example of Indian collaboration *par excellence*. When Pizarro's expeditionary force landed in Perú, they and the Inca factions who fought with them both took advantage of the fact that the Inca Empire had just come out of a period of civil war. Far from the Conquest being a cataclysm, for many Inca factions the arrival of the Spanish was an opportunity for political and military *gain*. The great irony here was how many

SPANISH-AMERICAN WAR

The Spanish-American War was fought between Spain and the United States from April to August 1898. American politicians, mindful of the Monroe Doctrine yet inspired by notions of Manifest Destiny, had been watching Spain's Caribbean military activities since Cuba's Ten Years' War (1868–1878). When a new phase of the Cuban Revolution broke out in 1895, American politicians declared support for the Cuban patriots amidst a rising tide of anti-Spanish propaganda in U.S. newspapers. Spain's alleged intentional sinking of battleship USS *Maine* in Havana harbor on February 15, 1898, triggered the outbreak of war. Most of the fighting occurred on the islands of Cuba and the Philippines, while President William McKinley asked for and received Congressional approval for annexing Hawaii. Although in decline for over a century, the war marked the end of the Spanish Empire in the Americas and the end of Spain's naval presence in the Pacific. By gaining Cuba, Puerto Rico, Guam, and the Philippines from its victory over Spain, the United States emerged as an international power. During the U.S. occupation, Roman Catholic Hispanics in these islands were introduced to Protestantism by American missionaries, marking an important moment in the religious history of these islands and their people.

—AH

of the Inca allied themselves with Spanish in the conquest of their own empire. Pizarro's conquest was an opportunity for Perú's tribes to overthrow the hegemonic rule of the Inca and replace it with a complicated and uneasy relationship with the newly arrived Spanish power. Indian-Spanish relationships took a variety of forms ranging from military alliances to a mutual understanding where the territory conquered by the Spanish was viewed by neighboring tribes as legitimate conquests by a powerful new arrival. The first Indian revolts that happened in the decades immediately following the Spanish Conquest were not revolts against an oppressor, but wars amongst tribes and the Spanish against each other's territorial incursions. With the loss of the Inca hegemony, the Conquest evolved into a situation resembling a civil war, with tribes warring with each other and with or against the Spaniards, under an emerging but incomplete Spanish hegemony.

Indigenous collaboration with the Spanish was the norm throughout the Conquest. In Mexico, many Indian chiefs took for themselves the title of "conquistador" and individual cities would write memorials to Philip II on how they assisted the Spanish in the Conquest. Cortez's conquest of Mexico resembled Pizarro's in that his Indian allies consistently tipped the balance of power in his favor. In the Yucatan, Mayan clans took pride in their alliance with the Spanish against rival Mayan clans and their role in creating the new Spanish Empire in America. Henry Kamen argues that the Conquest did not *initially* bring about Indian desolation, but something more complicated. The indigenous response to the Spanish invasion was based on political calculus of self-interest similar to Spanish decisions, and their responses varied between collaboration and resistance. Indigenous cultures showed great resilience and adaptation, treating the Conquest as an opportunity to create a new world.

The catastrophic destruction and dispossession of the Indians by the Conquest developed in the two centuries following the arrival of the Spanish. What began as a mutual acceptance and melding of the Spanish and Indian cultures broke down and hardened into a racially stratified society.

The openness the Spanish first displayed to the Indians can be seen in the spectrum of relationships between the new arrivals, who were entirely male, and Indian women. Many historians fall into the trap of caricaturing all relationships between Spanish men and Indian women as exploitative. But Kamen cautions that the status of indigenous women must not be reduced to the generalized status of "kept women" for the conquerors. Upon arrival, the Spanish did not display much prejudice, immediately accepting the need to take indigenous women as companions, and were delighted to meet women, who impressed the Spanish by their ability to defend themselves. J. H. Elliott suggests that consensual unions were as prevalent as forced ones. Intermarriage between Spanish Christian men and Indian women (and later Spanish Christian women to marry Indian men) was officially encouraged by the Spanish crown to facilitate communicating, teaching, and learning between the two peoples, to learn how to work their lands and manage their property, and to convert the Indians to the Catholic faith and Spanish ways of living. Therefore, it can be reasonably concluded that although exploitation certainly was a factor in many Spanish/Indian relationships, sincere and loving marriages must have been just as prevalent for the Spanish conquest to have succeeded. Without the active support and collaboration of the Indian women with their Spanish husbands, life for the invaders would have been impossible.

Unfortunately, this intermarriage of Spanish and Indians, instead of creating a *cultura mezclada*, an authentic melding of Spanish and Indians races and cultures, broke down into a stratified society based on race and class. Intermarriage between the Spanish and Indians gave rise to children of mixed race and, as with the Indian women, Spanish men had a range of responses to their mixed-race children. Elliott points out that Spanish fathers often tended to raise such children as their own, especially if they were sons, to the point that they were culturally absorbed into the new elites of Latin America. However, the fact that many mestizos were born illegitimately, coupled with the inability to classify mestizos in a hierarchical society shot through with the idea of *sangre azul*, contributed to an increasing exclusion of mixed-race people. What developed was a system of social stratification based on ethnicity and class, whereby skin color becomes lighter as one goes up the class ladder. Individual exceptions proved this general rule. This racial and class stratification was solidified further by the Spanish response to indigenous rebellions during the eighteenth century. The catastrophe suffered by the Indian population as a whole did not occur with the Conquest itself, but when the Spanish and mestizo elites stopped the melding of cultures in an effort to consolidate their position of power.

Institutional Contributions

The conquest was sponsored by the united thrones of Castile and Aragon, which formed the nucleus of a united monarchy for a united Spain. However, despite the fact that the expeditionary forces that conquered the Americas carried the legal sanction of the Crown, it was left to the Conquistadors themselves to finance and make provision for their respective enterprises. Much of the origin of another problem faced by Latin and Hispanic Americans, the relationship between the political power at the center and those who live disenfranchised on the periphery of power, can be found here.

Historically, the Spanish political reality is nearly as complex as their ancestry. Gracia points out that the unified Kingdom of Spain is an amalgamation of kingdoms and regions, many of which possessed unique cultures and dialects. Centered on the united thrones of the kingdoms of Castile and Aragon, Spain would eventually incorporate, besides the Moorish Kingdom of Granada, the kingdoms of Majorca, Navarre, and Valencia, the Principality of Barcelona, the Basque Provinces, Galicia, and the Canary Islands. Beginning in the sixteenth century, the Spanish monarchy sought to amass greater power onto itself at the expense of a nascent parliamentary system that had existed since 1188, and the traditional medieval rights held by individual towns and regions (e.g., the *fueros,* or rights held by the Basques). Subsequent history would prove that this effort was never entirely successful. Spanish history would be marked by a constant tension, which often boiled over into conflict and sometimes war, between the Crown at the center and the constituent regions of Spain over how the country ought to be governed, that exists to the present day.

The unresolved issue of the political balance of power between the Spanish Crown and authorities subordinate to that power extended to their American empire. Over the three centuries between Columbus and the Wars of Liberation, the Spanish Crown and its American governors could never adequately control the Creoles (Spanish subjects born in Latin America) who ran colonial economic and political affairs on the ground. Essentially, the cause of the Crown's difficulties with the Creoles lay with the latter's belief that the conquest and settlement of the continent was gained through their own sweat and blood. Kamen argues that the Creole position was entirely correct. Although the Spanish expeditionary forces that conquered the Americas had the legal endorsement of the Crown, the financing, provisioning, and execution of these expeditions was underwritten as a private enterprise. Conquistadors carefully planned their expeditions with detailed strategies and goals, adequately provisioned their army, and manned it with trusted personnel consisting of men who could trust each other, and who often came from the same family, town, or province. In lieu of financial support, the Crown gave these expeditions of conquest legal sanction by granting its leaders military commands and the authority to receive and distribute the majority of the spoils of conquest to defray costs and profit from their efforts. The Creole descendants of these Conquerors saw themselves as heirs to this achievement, and this attitude was reinforced by their development of the political and economic structures on the continent. They thought both of these things won them the right to govern their lands as they saw fit even as they pledged their allegiance to the king. This attitude was one reason why attempts by the Crown to reform and improve the condition of the Indians failed. The other reason was distance between Spain and her American empire made the enforcement of any laws difficult without Creole cooperation. Therefore, in the eighteenth and the early nineteenth centuries, the Crown sought to establish more direct control over the empire, which would serve as a major contributing factor for the Creoles to fight to liberate and rule their respective territories for themselves.

Ironically, Latin American independence did not bring democratic, liberal forms of government to the people. Instead, what developed was a government more centralized and authoritarian than their former Spanish masters. *Caudillismo* is a term coined by Glen Dealy to describe the core idea behind how much of Latin America was governed since independence. The caudillo is "the surrounded man" who rules through interpersonal relationships, specifically by the granting of favors in exchange for continued loyalty. Born out of the Creole's self-proclaimed right to rule, Caudillismo led to the creation of a system where the government and the economy were controlled by a small elite consisting of a large handful of families. This disenfranchised the majority of Latin Americans from the political and economic life of their nation. Oligarchic governments, stunted economic growth, restrictions on economic opportunity, the political upheaval caused by the internecine conflicts among the elites, and attempts to overthrow the oligarchy through revolutionary means, all

contributed to the forced exiling of Latin Americans to the United States to find economic opportunity, justice, and freedom. The Hispanic American tradition of grassroots political organization and activism against social, political, and economic injustice of every stripe finds part of its inspiration in this memory of suffering socioeconomic and political disenfranchisement in the hands of Latin American oligarchies, which held to the habit of maintaining centralized, authoritarian power inherited from Spanish rule.

Besides this memory of marginalization and oppression under the tyranny of oligarchy, Hispanic Americans have received resources to assert their identity as a people from the Spanish. Though introduced into America as part of the Spanish Conquest, these resources possess an integrity of their own, which can transcend that historical baggage.

The Contribution of Language

The Spanish language, which arrived in America as a the language of conquest, has been appropriated by Hispanic Americans as a means to maintain their community identity. Theologian Roberto Goizueta argues that of all the qualities any culture possesses, including the Hispanic American culture, the language symbolizes communal identity. Its power lies in the ability of language to shape culture and one's reality as a member of a community. Moises Sandoval offers an example that confirms Goizueta's argument. One of the earliest campaigns Hispanic Americans fought to gain a place within the Catholic Church in the United States dealt with the issue of allowing the people to worship in Spanish—the Mass, sacraments, and other pastoral ministries to be given by priests in

SAN JUDAS TADEO

The patron saint of hopeless causes, for Latino/as, is San Judas Tadeo, Apóstol. Judas had the bad fortune of sharing his name with Judas Iscariot who betrayed Jesus, and this is why in English he is known as Jude. In the New Testament he is referred to as an Apostle and is called Judas of James. This relationship to James may indicate that he was a member of Jesus' family and has linked him with the letter of Jude. According to Esusebius's History of the Church, Judas Thaddeus is intimately tied to the first icon of Christ, the Edessa Image. The ailing king of Edessa is reported to have sent Jesus an invitation to visit him. He hoped the Lord would heal him of a chronic illness. Instead, Jesus sent a cloth with his face miraculously etched on it. Jude is said to have taken the image to the king and cured him. Because of his namesake Judas Iscariot, Judas Thaddeus soon became the forgotten saint. Veneration of him began in nineteenth-century Spain and Italy and spread to the Americas at a time to help people deal with the turmoil of revolutions and the effects of the great depression.

—GCG

Spanish. Additional evidence for appropriation is found within the language as spoken by Hispanic Americans themselves. Spanish, like any living language, incorporated features of other languages it encountered. (The 700 years of Moorish rule gave Spanish a significant Arabic influence, which contributed approximately one-quarter of the former language's vocabulary.) The Conquest opened Spanish to receive influences from all the indigenous languages it encountered, to the point that Hispanic Americans can trace their Latin American ancestry by means of linguistic archaeology. Differences in vocabulary among the regional varieties of Spanish that grew out of Latin America usually came from the incorporation of indigenous words and phrases, be it the Nahuatl language of the Aztecs or the Guarani of Paraguay. When Hispanic Americans speak Spanish, they both consciously and unconsciously identify with their Spanish and indigenous roots. The free use of Spanish alongside English is a symbol asserting their freedom to be both completely Hispanic and completely American by their command of the two majority languages of both American continents.

The Contribution of Catholicism

Miguel de Unamuno's quip that "Here in Spain, we are all Catholics, even the atheists" is notable for its lack of hyperbole. Beginning in 589, when the Visigoth King Recarred declared Spain to be Catholic instead of Arian, the Catholic faith integrated itself completely into the fabric of Spanish culture. The reconquest sealed Catholic Christianity's status as both an official and popular religion because it consistently served as the primary unifying principle the Spanish rallied around in their campaigns against the Moors. Ironically, the best evidence for the durability of Catholic Christianity in both Spanish and Latin American culture can be found during the periodic episodes of anticlerical

VIRGIN OF MONTSERRAT

Co-patroness of Catalonia, along with Saint George, the Virgin of Montserrat is venerated inside the monastery of Santa María del Montserrat a few miles north of Barcelona, Spain. Montserrat in Catalonian means "tight or closed-in valley." In the painting, this Dark Madonna is shown against a backdrop of sharp, rocky crags being entertained by altar boys. She is one of many dark-skinned Madonnas venerated throughout Europe, and especially throughout Spain, where Moorish history left its indelible mark. In Catalonia she is known as "Moreneta" meaning "she of Moorish color." This Madonna balances the equally dark-skinned Christ Child upon her lap. Some scholars have suggested that this Madonna (as well as scores of others) was not deliberately dark at the beginning. They suggest that perhaps centuries of veneration among the candles of the faithful have rendered this and many other such Madonnas dark from the soot. Legend holds that Saint Ignatius of Loyola himself prayed before this image and laid down his armaments there before he founded the Jesuit Order. The best-known reflection of dark-skinned counterpart Madonnas in the Americas is Our Lady of Guadalupe whose image from 1531 is about 300 years younger that the twelfth-century image in Montserrat.

—LT

activity against the Church. Despite the fact that the clergy and institutions of the Church can be criticized and attacked to the point of destruction, an elemental sense of the sacred, coupled with a continued respect and appreciation for popular Catholic devotional practices, continues to survive and thrive.

Of course, the Catholic faith offered a major motive and served as the primary catalyst for the Spanish efforts to conquer America. The question that must be asked is, how and why did Catholic Christianity become so successfully integrated into Latin America, and among Hispanic Americans, who are heirs to the Conquest? In another irony, the Indians and their *mestizo* descendants appropriated the faith, but on their own terms. Carlos Fuentes identifies the cause behind this appropriation. The introduction of the Christian idea of a God-man who sacrifices himself for his people even to the point of death won over the Indians of America. Unwittingly, Christianity had reached beyond the native religious demands of sacrifice to the gods to recover the memory that, in the beginning, it was the gods themselves who sacrificed for their sake. The Hispanic American practice of Catholic Christianity is a blending of Spanish and indigenous traditions so pervasive that it affects Protestant Hispanics who take cues from Catholic devotional life.

The Contribution of the Virgin Mary

Mary's central role in Hispanic American religious culture finds its origin in the Spanish tradition of venerating her. Marian devotion, like the Catholic faith that promoted it, was integrated into Spanish culture through the reconquest. She was viewed as the devoted and helping mother as well as a powerful intercessor between humanity and a God who, according to theologian Timothy Matovina, Spanish Catholics feared as a stern and distant being. Her intercession was called upon repeatedly in the war against the Moors to the point that Angus MacKay described the frontier between the Spanish Catholic and the Moorish Moslem a Mariological one. Mary became a warrior figure for the Spanish, symbolizing their triumph over the whole of the Iberian Peninsula.

With the Conquest came Mary, whose intercession was called upon by explorer and conquistador alike to ensure a successful expedition and military victory. In the Americas as in Spain, Mary came as a warrior figure symbolizing the conquering power of the Spanish, and with the subsequent colonization she was called upon for everything from the conversion of the Indians to the protection of crop harvests. Ironically, the Indians, as Linda Hall argues, appropriated Mary on their own terms, despite her original status as an instrument of Spanish conquest. Among the Aztecs, Mary could be appropriated beyond her being the Mother of God and intercessor with God because to invoke her help appealed to their worldview shot through with miraculous, even magical, qualities. Aztec religion contained a strongly held and deeply rooted tradition of the sacred feminine. Janus-faced goddesses, both nurturing and dangerous at the same time, populated the Aztec pantheon. Among the Inca, strong traditions of goddess worship, coupled with the existence of "Chosen Women," beautiful virgins selected to serve the Inca king, existed. These features of Aztec and Inca religion made the Catholic idea of a benevolent, powerful female intercessor with the Divine most compatible.

Fuentes argues that the Indians found in Mary a mother figure that transformed them from the despoiled victims of conquest to the pure children of the Blessed Mother. The Indians appropriated the Spanish idea of Mary as a symbol of God allied and fighting with them, endorsing their belief that despite the Conquest, they remained in God's favor. Latin and Hispanic Americans interpret the 1531 apparition of Mary to Juan Diego as a sign that God's favor is not limited to the conquering Spaniards. Rosa María Icaza points out the way Mary treated Juan Diego showed that God would not treat the Indian as an inferior underclass. Mary called Juan Diego by name, a sign of respect and recognition of him as a person, she entrusted him with a mission and showed patience when he encountered difficulties in fulfilling that mission, and she challenged him to grow as a complete human being to live out his divine call. How God treats those who society labels as least demonstrates a rejection of such marginalization and oppression, and the converse assertion that all human beings are God's people. Hispanic Americans look upon the apparition of Our Lady of Guadalupe as a sign that those who boast Spanish, Indian, and African ancestry are God's people too, and that their mestizo identity is a gift from God.

Marian devotions are part of a larger tradition inherited from the Spanish. According to William Christian, the devotion to the saints is another important tradition. Commonplace upon Hispanic Americans is the practice of seeking out the personal patronage of a saint to call upon for protection or help. This patronage extends to everything from commercial enterprises to entire neighborhoods. Of the many features found in the various fiestas, which are a part of Hispanic American religious life, at least part of their origins can be traced to Spain, too.

Conclusion

Hispanic Americans have inherited from the Spanish a tradition of the Church as a political force. For example, while the Conquest was fully progressing, Francisco de Vitoria and Bartolomé de Las Casas developed a body of natural rights theory in defense of the Indians. Arguing how the Indians demonstrated the human qualities of rationality, demonstrated by their ability to create families, build communities, possess property, and have an economic and political structure, these men helped create modern human rights theory. The work of both men, especially Las Casas, is enjoying renewed attention as a philosophical and theological resource against marginalization and oppression. The Church has remained, despite episodes in the nineteenth and twentieth centuries of sustaining anticlericalism and suffering persecution, a political force in Spain. Beginning with the Catholic Action movement in the late 1950s, which contributed to the Liberation Theology movement in the late 1960s, the Church in Latin America moved beyond being a traditional support of the social and political status quo to become a political force advocating for the disenfranchised poor majority. Among Hispanic American Catholics, the Church has assumed a central role in their political activity too. Michael Jones-Correa and David Leal found that active Hispanic and non-Hispanic Catholic churchgoers generally participated more in politics. The reason lies with the simple fact that the Church serves as the primary center from which Catholics become politically mobilized and civically involved.

The Spanish legacy for Hispanic American religious culture is one that contributed beyond a religious heritage, replete with important social, economic, and political influences. This legacy helps vivify and bind together Hispanic Americans as a community, and link them with a powerful Spanish and Latin American lineage marked by equal parts tragedy and triumph.

Ramón Luzárraga

References and Further Reading

Dealy, Glen Caudill. *The Latin Americans: Spirit and Ethos* (Boulder, CO: Westview Press, 1992).

Elizondo, Virgilio, Allan Figueroa Deck, S.J., and Timothy Matovina. *The Treasure of Guadalupe* (Oxford: Rowman and Littlefield Publishers, Inc., 2006).

Elliott, J. H. *Empires of the Atlantic World: Britain and Spain in America, 1492–1830* (New Haven, CT: Yale University Press, 2006).

Fuentes, Carlos. *The Buried Mirror: Reflections on Spain and the New World* (Boston: Houghton Mifflin, 1992).

Goizueta, Roberto S. *Caminemos con Jesús: Toward a Hispanic/Latino Theology of Accompaniment* (Maryknoll, NY: Orbis Books, 2001).

Gracia, Jorge J. E. *Hispanic/Latino Identity: A Philosophical Perspective* (Malden, MA: Blackwell Publishers, 2000).

Hall, Linda B. *Mary, Mother and Warrior: The Virgin in Spain and the Americas* (Austin: University of Texas Press, 2004).

Jones-Correa, Michael A., and David L. Leal. "Political Participation: Does Religion

Matter?" *Political Research Quarterly* 54, no. 4 (December 2001): 751–770.

Kamen, Henry. *Empire: How Spain Became a World Power, 1492–1763* (New York: Harper Collins Publishers, 2003).

SPIRITUAL HYBRIDITY

Spiritual hybridity began in the late fifteenth century as a cultural mixture of spiritual and/or religious belief systems and practices, in Spanish-speaking Latin America and among Latina/os of the United States as a result of the European invasions and colonization of the American continent and the Caribbean. The use of "spiritual hybridity," rather than "religious syncretism," follows the more recent attempts by culturally mixed and queer peoples to discuss the ambiguous, continual, and multidirectional flow of cultural influences across power differentials. For example, Gloria Anzaldúa and Laura E. Pérez write on spiritual hybridity, Lara Medina on "nepantla spirituality," and Randy Conner and David Sparks on "queering creole spiritual traditions."

Other parts of the world, such as the Philippines and some of the Pacific Islands, have also experienced cultural hybridity as a result of Spanish and other European imperialisms that are relevant to a broader understanding of Latina/o spiritual hybridity or religious "syncretism." With respect to the influence of the Spanish on the Chamorro people of Guam, Michael Tuncap, during the Ethnic Studies California Graduate Student Conference held in the Spring of 2007, called for an interrogation of what is meant by the term "Latina/o."

Such hybridizations in spiritual beliefs and practices continued throughout the centuries by means of both the imposition and appropriation of Christianity where native populations are concerned; as a result of mixture with traditions brought to the Americas by enslaved peoples from various parts of Africa; by native peoples transported from one part of the Caribbean and/or the Americas to another as labor; and by subsequent immigrations from Europe and various other parts of the world, including China, India, and the Middle East. In more recent times, as a result of the youth culture of the 1960s and 1970s, Latina/os also began to explore Buddhism, Hinduism, and nonhereditary Native American beliefs and practices like their generational peers. Finally, these past four decades have also witnessed spiritual hybridity as Latina/os pick and choose between various Latina/o traditions, such that we see Central Americans or Chicanas now initiated into *santería*, as it disseminates from Afro-Cuban culture, and Caribbean-origined Latina/os practicing Mexica ("Aztec") sweat lodge or other indigenous ceremonies from the American continent.

Further, the nature of colonial-era Spanish religious beliefs and practices must be understood in some cases as already being potentially culturally hybrid. This is particularly evident with respect to the religious cultures of *conversos*, Jews who converted to Christianity during the Inquisition; of hidden Jewish Spanish colonizers (who account for some of the culturally hybrid practices of populations like those of New Mexican *Hispanos*); and of Muslims of Moorish Spain.

Among Latina/os of the United States, incorporated originally through the imperialist wars of expansion of the United States against Mexico (1846–

BRUJERÍA

Brujería (from *Bruja*, witch) is the belief and practice of witchcraft. In the Latino/a worldview, witches are considered as either malevolent sorcerers or benevolent curers. Some are believed to have the assistance of the devil and spirits and extraordinary evil powers (*maleficia*) to change into animal form, and to inflict enemies with suffering, death, financial failure, and sickness through the evil eye (*mal de ojo*), resulting in bewitched victims (*enbrujada*). Curers (*curanderos*), on the other hand, usually have the power to remove the bewitchment through *limpias* (spiritual cleansing). Curers use natural remedies to remove the malevolent influence of bewitchment. Brujería in Latina/o culture is a blend of Spanish witchcraft and Mesoamerican traditions. Spanish witchcraft was based on four basic beliefs about witches, usually female: their pact with the devil, the *aquelarre,* or their mysterious gathering place, flights, and metamorphosis. Most indigenous groups in the Americas believe in some form of sorcery or witchcraft. The Aztecs believed in the *nagual* or *nahualli*, a male witch with magical powers to change into animal form, and Tezcatlipoca was the god of night and their patron.

—FAO & KGD

1848) and Spain for possession of its former colonies in 1898 (Cuba, Puerto Rico, and the Philippines), complex religious hybridities in belief and practice that arise out of centuries of intense renewed and new cultural contacts are further complicated. Latin American–origin peoples of the United States have been placed in contact with Anglo-Protestant dominant cultures (not the least of which through the public educational system) and with European immigrant Protestants, but also with culturally different forms of Roman Catholic practice than that of dominant culture that have been described as Eurocentric and anti-Hispanic. Thus, we might also speak of new kinds of spiritual hybridities as Roman Catholics convert in record numbers to various forms of Protestantism. The complex historically continuous layering throughout the past 500 years of different religious worldviews among Latina/os, both in Latin America and in the United States, is an area of present active interest in a variety of disciplines that promises to enrich our understanding of the various forms of spiritual hybridity that characterize different Latina/o populations in unique ways.

Laura E. Pérez

References and Further Reading

Arrizón, Alicia. *Queering Mestizaje. Transculturation and Performance* (Ann Arbor, MI: University of Michigan Press, 2006).

Conner, Randy, with David Sparks. *Queering Creole Spiritual Traditions: Lesbian, Gay, Bisexual, and Transgender Participation in African-Inspired Traditions in the Americas* (Binghamton, NY: Haworth Press, 2004).

Medina, Lara. "Nepantla Spirituality: Negotiating Multiple Identities and Faiths Among U.S. Latinas." *Rethinking Latino (a) Religion and Identity,* ed. Miguel De La Torre and Gaston Espinoza (Cleveland: Pilgrim Press, 2007).

Pérez, Laura E. "Spirit Glyphs: Reimagining Art and Artist in the Work of Chicana *Tlamatinime.*" *Modern Fiction Studies* 44, no. I (April 1998).

———. *Chicana Art: The Politics of Spiritual and Aesthetic Altarities* (Durham, NC: Duke University Press, 2007).

STRUCTURAL SIN

It is not surprising that a hyper-individualistic culture would reduce sin and salvation to the personal. For many Euro-American Christians, sin is an action, or omission, committed by an individual who now stands guilty before God. This individual action (or lack thereof) creates alienation between the individual and God. Sin becomes universal with "sin" being defined by those in power. The sin of those privileged by the prevailing social structures becomes normative for all humans, ignoring that power relationships mean different groups are tempted in different ways. For example, what is considered a sin for a White male with economic class (i.e., pride) may be a needed virtue for a poor Black Latina woman who is constantly told to be humble. Salvation is also reduced to an individual act. The act needing remedy is the sin committed by the individual, and the act providing the remedy is Jesus Christ's death on the cross. It is therefore common to hear sermons and religious admonitions within Euro-American churches that focus on and encourage personal piety.

Yet sin always manifests itself socially, through laws and regulations that permit the few to live in privilege and the many to live in want. Laws, customs, traditions, moral regulations, and so-called common sense are constructed by society to normalize and legitimize the prevailing power structures. By making sin a private matter, little is done to challenge or change structural sin. Those benefiting from how society is structured may recognize that sin may have been individually committed, but ignore that because we are communal creatures, it affects other humans. Individual biases against those of a different gender, economic class, or race and ethnicity become the collective biases of the society. These biases are codified, institutionalized, and legitimized by the government, marketplace and church. In this way, the social structures are designed to be oppressive toward marginalized communities, which include Latina/os, so that the dominant culture can exist within its privileged space.

For many within the dominant culture, a failure to recognize their complicity with structural sin exists. Sympathy with the plight of oppressed Hispanics is meaningless if those who society benefits remain ignorant of how structural sin maintains and sustains poverty, violence, and oppression within the nation's *barrios*. Even if individuals repent their biases, society will continue implementing oppression in their stead. Complicity to structural sins, regardless of the beliefs and practices of the individual, makes everyone a sinner who benefits by how society is structured, for all sins have individual and communal dimensions.

Hispanics' understanding of sin and salvation is more communal, recognizing that all sins have a social context. While not minimizing the importance of living a moral life as an individual, Latino/as also recognize that sin is not limited to the personal. Sin also exists within the social structures of society. The consequences of oppression and violence can be caused by the acts of an individual, as well as by the normal and legitimate policies, laws, and moral regulations of the social order. These structural sins exist in the economic policies, the cultural traditions, and the legal codes of the society. To simply concentrate on personal piety ignores how sin, in the form of social structures, is designed to privilege a minority group at the expense of those disenfranchised by the social order. Hence all sins, as relational, not only create alienation between the individual and God, but also between the individual and his/her neighbor, the individual and her/his community, and the individual and God's creation. Recognizing the social dimension of sin leads to an understanding of sin not from the perspective of the sinner, but from the perspective of the one sinned against.

Structural sin cannot be redeemed by individual atonement. Atonement ceases to be limited to Jesus Christ's death on the cross. His life and resurrection are just as salvific. For Christ, salvation from sin is not limited to the individual, but also to the community. Individual repentance of sin may be welcomed, but remains insufficient as long as structural sins remain. Individual repentance is insufficient because it fails to change or challenge the status quo. The society as a whole requires redemption, a moving away from structural sins toward a more just society.

Hispanics are not the only ones negatively affected by structural sins. Those who benefit from the status quo are also negatively impacted, and thus in need of salvation. Members of the dominant culture must live up to a false construction of superiority that justifies why they are privileged by the social structures. This false construction requires a complicity with structural sins which usually results in a loss of one's humanity. Not only are those oppressed by structural sin in need of salvation from oppression, those benefiting from structural sins are also in need of salvation—of regaining their humanity. The danger of reducing sin simply to the personal masks the causes and consequences of structural sin and the need of both the privileged and the disenfranchised for salvation.

Miguel A. De La Torre

References and Further Reading

Cortés-Fuentes, David. "Sin." *Handbook of Latina/o Theologies* (St. Louis: Chalice Press, 2006).

De La Torre, Miguel, and Edwin David Aponte. *Introducing Latino/a Theologies* (Maryknoll, NY: Orbis Books, 2001).

González, Justo. "The Alienation of Alienation." *The Other Side of Sin: Woundedness from the Perspective of the Sinned-against*, ed. Andrew Sung Park and Susan L. Nelson (New York: SUNY Press, 2001).

SYNCRETISM

The earliest use of the term "syncretism" occurred when Plutarch chose it to describe how the Cretans would quarrel among themselves but quickly reconcile with foreign enemies. By the sixteenth century, Erasmus used the term to describe the reconciliation achieved among those who theologically disagreed. The term came to imply the mixture of ideas or concepts—specifically religious ideas and concepts—that were incompatible. Today, the term is mainly used among religious thinkers to describe the mixture or fusion of a "pure" religious faith with a "pagan" religion. Usually when a faith tradition is described as syncretistic, the term connotes a certain derogatory quality. Among Latino/as, the term syncretism is mainly used to describe non-Christian faith traditions that use Christian symbols, concepts, and ideas, specifically Santería, but also other traditions with indigenous roots like curanderismo or espiritualismo.

In reality, all religions are syncretistic. When faith traditions like Christianity, Islam, or Buddhism are introduced to a culture, both the culture and the way that religion is understood and practiced are transformed. For a new faith to exist within a new cultural setting, a certain degree of syncretism occurs to reconcile areas of incongruency between the everyday life as experienced by people rooted in social structures that predates them and the new faith that usually asks to live and think in new ways. Sometimes the changes to both the culture and religion are minor, almost unnoticeable. At other times the changes are profound.

Among religious thinkers, the term "syncretism" has historically been used to describe a religion like Santería, but seldom used to describe a religion like Christianity. Part of the reason is that the major religious tradition that has been legitimized and normalized by the culture is seen as "pure" regardless of how much it has borrowed from the multiple cultures it has passed through. Labeling the faith tradition that is not legitimized or normalized by the culture as syncretistic defines it as an impure mixture and subordinates it to the purity of the dominant faith tradition of the culture. Hence a value system is established where the syncretism of the dominant faith is masked while the exposed syncretism of the marginalized faith is labeled as an abomination of the true faith. Within the Latina/o religious milieu, religions like Santería have historically been seen by Christian churches as the merging of Catholic and African beliefs by the so-called confused, primitive mind of child-like Black slaves.

Today, there are Hispanics who worship at a Christian church, more than likely a Catholic Church, who also participate in more indigenous religious rituals like Santería. For some, it is acceptable to offer a sacrifice to one of the orishas (quasi-deities) of Santería on Saturday night and still attend Sunday morning Mass. The Catholic Church has historically seen its role as correcting the confusion of those engaged in Santería's rituals. Other Christian faiths voice a harsher criticism. For example, many Evangelicals—especially Pentecostals—believe that Santería is a Satanic faith that perverts Christian symbols.

While some degree of syncretism occurs within all faith traditions, it would be naïve to simply describe religious expressions like Santería as syncretistic. In a Caribbean culture that has historically oppressed those from African descent, especially through slavery, Africans were forced to find creative ways of keeping their traditions alive. In a predominantly Christian culture that forced slaves to be baptized to accept the religion of the slave masters and prohibited Africans from participating in the religious expressions of their homeland, Africans were forced to keep their true belief systems masked and secret. So, when a slave bowed her or his knees before the statue of a Catholic saint, the slave knew that she/he was really worshipping the orisha whom that statue represented. This merging was not the product of a confused or primitive mind, but rather a shrewd maneuver on the part of the slaves. All the devotion that was due to a particular orisha was projected upon a Catholic saint who signified a particular orisha. In a way, they dressed their African Gods in the clothes of medieval Catholic saints. The Christian overlords were happy because they saw their slaves outwardly worshipping a Catholic saint, for example Saint Barbara, but in reality, all the worship directed by the slave to Saint Barbara was actually for the orisha Changó. It was the Christian overlords, in the minds of the Africans, who were primitive and confused because they lacked the knowledge about the true power that lay behind the statues of Catholic saints.

This type of masking continues today. When a Christian comes to a santero/a for a consultation, the Christian would seldom be told to offer some sacrifice to the orisha Changó. Because the primary duty of the santera/o is to restore harmony in the life of the seeker, regardless of their faith tradition, the santero/a does not enter into a discussion about Yoruba pantheon. Instead, the santera/o might simply explain that Saint Barbara was originally known in Africa as Changó, and what is required now is to offer a sacrifice to Saint Barbara/Changó. With time, after harmony is restored to the life of the seeker, the santera/o can begin to teach the seeker about the cosmic powers behind symbols of Catholic saints. Saint Barbara recedes as Changó becomes more prominent in the seeker's consciousness. The statue of Saint Barbara, which is unimportant to Santería, still serves an important function for the seeker by providing a familiar religious environment where the seeker can find important points of reference. In this way the seeker is transitioned into a new faith. For some, the transition, which can take years, is complete; while for others, a full transition from Catholicism to Santería may never take place, with the believer participating in the rituals of the two different faith traditions.

The term "syncretism" becomes a poor term by which to describe non-Christian, more indigenous faiths of Hispanics. Such religions, like Santería, can best be understood as a faith reality that is different from Christianity and from its original indigenous religion. Rather than using the derogatory term "syncretism," these newer Latina/o religious faiths should be understood as new cultural realities. These so-called syncretistic religions have matured to the point that syncretistic labels can be discarded. Although originally a syncretistic label might have proven helpful in understanding how the religion developed, it hinders the ability to fully grasp the importance of what can be understood to be a present-day transcultural phenomenon. To continue to insist that religions like Santería are some dialectical product of the Yoruba's belief system and Iberian Roman Catholicism, where a "confused" merging of the saints and orishas took place, fails to properly understand that Hispanics are not confused about their beliefs. Distinctions in faith traditions and practices have always been recognized.

Miguel A. De La Torre

References and Further Reading

De La Torre, Miguel A. *Santería the Beliefs and Rituals of a Growing Religion in America* (Grand Rapids, MI: Wm. B. Eerdmans Publishing Co., 2004).

Schreiter, Robert J. *Constructing Local Theologies* (Maryknoll, NY: Orbis Books, 1996).

TESTIMONIOS

In Latino/a churches the practice of giving *testimonios,* public testimonies of God's work in one's life, is common in many of the evangelical and charismatic Protestant worship services. While difficult to trace the origins, there is ample evidence of similar practices in Spanish and Latino/a Catholic traditions. The *retablas* provide visual evidence in the churches of miracles and answered prayers depicted in colorful plaques on the walls. The practice of providing public expressions of gratitude for answered prayers can also be found in many cultures within the Catholic Church. Another possible origin for these practices comes from the evangelical traditions of revivals and Pentecostal Churches, where participants were often given opportunities to give "witness" or "testimony" of God's miracles or salvation. It is probable that the evangelical practices resonated with the Catholic traditions of public acknowledgments of miracles and eventually evolved into the practice of *testimonios* in Latino/a churches, where the practice is more prevalent than in Anglo counterparts.

Within church services, the practice of giving testimonies can vary in form and content. While testimonies are more common in prayer services and worship gatherings at homes, in many instances, a place is provided within more traditional services. In those instances, either the order of service allows an opening for people who would like to share their testimony or the pastor invites them to do so. At the given moment, those who desire to share the testimonies stand and tell their stories, which can vary in length from a brief praise for an answered prayer to a lengthier account of an event or experience. Some testimonies are recurring accounts shared regularly by individuals in the congregation, while others are new accounts of recent events. In most cases, only a few stories are shared before the service continues after an appropriate response by the congregants.

While the content of the testimonies varies, there are several recurring themes that tend to be overarching. One of the most common themes is an account of the congregant's conversion experience. While this is common within evangelical revivals, and may well find its roots in the revivalist tradition where testimonies were common, accounts of conversion experiences enter other forms of worship. Typically, these accounts provide a contrast between one's life before and after the conversion experience, which typically has transformed the life of the individual. Generally, the purpose of these accounts is to encourage others to convert and to highlight the virtues of the new life experienced in Christ. While in most instances these accounts are first-person narratives, on some occasions members share the stories of a close relative or friend who may not be present or able to share.

A second common theme is answered prayers. These accounts tell the story of a particular need or situation for which the person had been praying and how the prayer was answered. While typically the answered prayer presents itself as a resolution to the problem, it is not always answered as expected. In some instances, people share how a prayer was answered in an unexpected manner, which the congregant nevertheless interprets as God's answer to their request. Within Latino/a congregations, the prayer requests and answers at times are for finding employment, for the immigration status of friends and relatives, or for protection from harmful circumstances. Within this genre, one can also find testimonies of healings, which are significant for a community that often has little access to and resources for health care. Testimonies of healing do not necessarily involve a full and miraculous restoration of health, but can also involve temporary or partial

relief. Even in instances where medical intervention occurs, the actual healing is still attributed to God, who is seen as guiding or providing the medical assistance. These testimonies perceive God's action in and through the events that bring either temporary comfort or healing to the individuals involved.

A third form of testimony involves divine intervention of some form. In these instances, divine intervention might have occurred without a prayer being offered or without the person being aware of the circumstances until after the event. These forms of testimonies may involve deliverance from a tragedy or loss, the intervention of someone that brought a perceived blessing, or a timely word of comfort. These testimonies might range from simple happenstance to dramatic events. Within this genre one might also include direct divine intervention in a person's life, such as visions or special awareness that is often shared with the congregation as a message.

Although testimonies vary in nature and this brief typology simply covers some of the more common themes, the practice of giving testimonies serves several clear functions within Latino/a churches. First, testimonies are a didactic tool that instructs congregants on the nature of the faith and in the manner through which God works. Testimonies assist new converts in understanding how God might be at work in their lives and how to interpret events through the lenses of their faith. For instance, members of the church are instructed on how God might answer prayers in a manner that is different from that which they might expect or how a miraculous event can occur under ordinary circumstances.

Second, testimonies offer empowerment to disenfranchised communities.

The stories attest to God's power and work in their midst. While individuals in these congregations might feel marginalized and powerless within the economic and political structure, the testimonies of God's work in their lives provide them with a sense of value and importance. They might be of little consequence to the power brokers and historical forces of the world, but they matter to God and find a source of greater power that sustains them and helps them to transcend the difficulties and struggles of life. It also empowers them to take part in the church, by allowing them to tell their story and to participate in the teaching and life of the congregation in an active manner.

Finally, one can argue that testimonies are a manifestation of popular religion within the Protestant church, since they allow for unstructured and unsanctioned expressions of faith from the people, which allow them to express their understanding of the faith outside of the organized tradition. At times, the extemporaneous nature of the testimonies can take over a service or alter its course as the message resonates with the congregation, forcing the pastor to focus on the testimony itself. Ultimately, they provide a venue for personal expression of individual understandings of the nature of one's faith and God's ongoing work in the life of the congregation.

Luis G. Pedraja

References and Further Reading

Aponte, Edwin David, and Miguel A. De La Torre. *Handbook of Latina/o Theologies* (St. Louis: Charlice Press, 2006).

De La Torre, Miguel A., and Edwin David Aponte. *Introducing Latino/a Theologies* (Maryknoll, NY: Orbis Books, 2001).

Pedraja, Luis G. *Teología: An Introduction to Hispanic Theology* (Nashville: Abingdon Press, 2003).

THEOLOGICAL AND RELIGIOUS EDUCATION

In 2008, the Association of Theological Schools (ATS), the accrediting agency for theological education in the United States and Canada, distributed the *Fact Book on Theological Education* for the academic year 2006–2007. This fact book is designed to provide a concise overview of the current enterprise of graduate theological education in the United States and Canada, and it states the following:

> As of fall 2006 there are 253 member schools. Of these only forty-two member schools offer a Doctorate of Philosophy and/or Doctorate of Theology. The religious affiliation of these PhD granting institutions consists of: 60% Protestant Denominational Schools, 27% Inter/Nondenominational Schools, 10% Roman Catholic Schools, and 5% Orthodox Schools. Out of the forty-two schools, thirty-nine are in the United States and two are in Canada.

The Hispanic population ATS statistics indicate that Latina/os constitute more than 20 percent of the U.S. population, but only 4 percent of the faculty and students at ATS schools are Hispanic. Additionally, about two-thirds of these member schools do not have any Latina/o faculty members. Furthermore, most are not trained in issues that affect this

HISPANIC THEOLOGICAL INITIATIVE

Hispanic Theological Initiative (HTI) was founded in 1996 under the leadership of Justo González. HTI was sparked by demographic inconsistencies between the shifting ethnic composition of the United States and the unchanging makeup of religion faculties. As the number of Latinas/os grew, corresponding growth in theological education was lacking. Prior to the program's inception, there were a mere "69 Latina/o scholars of religion teaching in theological schools, seminaries, and colleges" according to the Association of Theological Schools. Funded by the Pew Charitable Trusts and the Lilly Endowment, HTI has sought to support Latina/o students in theological education, to shape a vibrant community of Hispanic scholars, and finally to have a significant impact upon Latino/a churches. In other words, the aims of HTI have centered around three foci: graduate students, the academy, and the church. Though the shape of the program has changed over time, HTI has primarily provided financial, mentoring, and networking support to doctoral students in religion. In these specific ways, HTI has worked toward alleviating those pitfalls that most commonly obstructed qualified doctoral candidates from completing their education. After a decade's effort, the number of Latina/o faculty has expanded to over 127, at least 58 of which received an HTI fellowship.

—EDB

ever-growing and acutely religious minority group in the United States.

Of the 3,622 full-time faculty in ATS schools in the 2007–2008 academic year, only 124 or 3 percent are Hispanic. Although the percentage is small, the distribution of Hispanic faculty in teaching fields is relatively good: 22 percent are in Biblical Studies, 24 percent in theological/historical studies/ethics, 24 percent in pastoral/practical theology areas. The others are spread across a variety of teaching fields. The ATS database only keeps track of faculty and students at its 253 schools. However, in the Hispanic Theological Initiative database, a scholarship, mentoring, and networking program with the primary mission to increase the presence of Latino faculty —especially tenured faculty—in seminaries, schools of theology, and universities, 162 Hispanic faculty are recorded in the United States.

For 12 years, HTI has worked collaboratively to help students overcome the many challenges Latina/os encounter while pursuing doctoral studies in religious and theological education. Since its inception in 1996, HTI has, as follows: (1) awarded 105 doctoral fellowships; (2) engaged 38 tenured or tenured-equivalent professors as mentors of HTI fellows; (3) supported 55 HTI fellows to the completion of their doctorates; (4) currently provided support to 39 HTI fellows in the pipeline; and (5) maintained an average time-to-degree for HTI doctoral fellows of 4.85 years.

Additionally, among the students who have received HTI fellowships: (1) 13 denominations are represented; (2) 40 percent are Roman Catholic scholars; (3) 60 percent are Protestant scholars; (4) 33 percent are women; and (5) 67 percent are men.

APUNTES

Apuntes, first published in February 1981, is the oldest journal on Latino/a theology. The journal began as a collaborative venture between the Mexican American Program of Perkins School of Theology and Dr. Justo L. Gonzalez, who served as its editor for 20 years. The publication of *Apuntes* almost coincides with the beginning of Latino/a theology in the early 1980s. Within its pages one finds essays, written by prominent figures in Latino/a theology, exploring some of the early formative concepts in what was then called Hispanic theology. The name, *Apuntes*, intentionally alludes to the double meaning of the word in Spanish. First, it can mean the notes or *apuntes* scribbled on the margins of books and Bibles. Hence, the original subtitle of the journal: *Theological reflections from the Hispanic margin*. It was intended to give voice to those at the margins of theology, particularly Latino/as. Publishing not only academic essays, but also essays from pastors, the journal fosters dialogue between the church and the academy. Second, *apuntes* means "to take aim." Thus, the journal has a double aim: to make the voices of the Latino/a church heard and to critique both the theological and the ecclesiastical establishment.

—*LGP*

Among the 55 HTI fellows who now have doctorates: (1) 53 are working and teaching in the academy; (2) 75 percent are in full-time teaching positions; (3) 25 percent are adjunct faculty members or work in administration, research, and the nonprofit sector including ministry; (4) 27 percent have published books; (5) 22 percent are tenured; (6) 25 percent are in tenure-track teaching positions; and (7) five have been appointed as deans.

These results bear witness to the fact that HTI's synergetic and holistic approach (one that provides funding, mentoring, and networking opportunities) has provided an excellence model for academia that continues to serve the Latina/o student community by helping students achieve both a doctoral degree and continued long-term career success. However, while great strides have been made in the past 12 years, there is still much work to be done. The census demonstrates that Latina/os are the least well represented of all ethnic groups among faculty in the United States, in spite of the fact that they are the largest minority in the country. Hispanics are still the least represented group in the faculty and student bodies of ATS schools, and as the Latino/a population continues to grow, the future of these schools increasingly rests with their ability to effectively educate racial and ethnic religious leaders. Indeed, before mid-century, the Hispanic community will be the largest minority group in the United States. Moreover, the majority of Latina/o faculty falls within the lower levels of academic rank; they are disproportionately represented among the "instructor" and "lecturer" categories. This level of academic rank gives them little voice in university policies and practices, makes it difficult for them to mentor doctoral students (because of tenure pressures and lack of status), and

---

PARAL

The Program for the Analysis of Religion Among Latinas/os (PARAL) was launched in 1988 by various Latina/o scholars within the Society for the Scientific Study of Religion. Countering the absence of Hispanic religion from much of social science study, PARAL developed an agenda for interdisciplinary study of Latina/o religion in the United States, resulting in funding from major foundations beginning in 1989. The systematic exploration of Latino religious experience produced PARAL's first conference in April 1993 at Princeton University. Three themes were explored, resulting in three volumes of the PARAL Series: *An Enduring Flame* (1994) examined popular religiosity; *Old Masks, New Faces* (1995) tackled the linkages between religion and cultural identity; *Enigmatic Powers* (1995) reviewed syncretism with indigenous and African religions. A fourth volume with bibliography of pre-1995 works followed. Over the next decade PARAL sponsored conferences, panels, and sessions at scholarly gatherings. The 1996 meeting at the University of California, Santa Barbara examined the impact of popular religious expression in liturgical music and pastoral practice with oral history from Latino/a leaders, producing the award-winning *Recognizing the Latino Resurgence* (1998). In the new millennium, PARAL began collaborating with a documentary series on Latino/a religion.

—*ASA*

---

places them in a vulnerable status. As only 2 percent of all full professors in the academy, they are a scarce resource for Latina/o graduate students. Thus, the underrepresentation of Latinas/os at ATS schools and in religion departments of universities becomes particularly more worrisome, given the high degree of religious participation in the Hispanic community.

Theological schools have their roots in predominantly White denominations and social structures. As the total racial/ethnic population surpasses the total White population in the United States before mid-century, the future of these schools increasingly rests with their ability to effectively educate racial/ethnic religious leaders, and the future of American Christianity is tied to its capacity to serve racial/ethnic populations.

Similar trends exist for Latina/o administrators. The dearth of Latina/os

in key administrative roles, such as college presidents, provosts, deans, and department chairs, may be considered a ripple effect from the very small number of Latina/o academics, because Latina/o administrators in executive positions are primarily selected from the faculty ranks. University administrators are also key in that they often have more decision-making power than do faculty and greater access to budgets, which enables them to have a direct impact on minority student recruitment, retention, and well-being. Hence, the hiring of Latina/o administrators must be viewed as an important priority in raising the profile of Latina/o issues within academe. The reason most often given by hiring committees for not making offers to highly qualified Latina/o applicants was a difference in "style" that did not "fit" with the expectations of the committee. Among the specific style issues were appearance and access to important networks, two attributes that almost certainly were affected by the candidate's ethnicity, not their ability or qualifications for the job.

The lack of Latina/os in the PhD pipeline is a serious concern for the Latina/o community as academicians play an important role within higher education and the community as mentors, scholars, and leading researchers on issues pertinent to the Hispanic community as well as the society as a whole. Because Latina/os are the nation's largest minority group, unless they are able to achieve at the same levels as other groups, not only they, but the society as a whole, will suffer.

There are some reasons for Hispanic underrepresentation. A smaller percentage of the Hispanic community holds baccalaureate degrees and so a smaller pool is available for postbaccalaureate degree programs. The dominant religious expression in the Hispanic community is Roman Catholic, which has a much larger ratio of church members to seminary students than most Protestants. For example, there is one United Methodist in seminary for every 1,500 UMC members but one Roman Catholic in seminary for every 10,000 Roman Catholics. The other dominant religious expression in the Hispanic community—Pentecostal— does not require theological education for ministers. While these reasons contribute to the underrepresentation, the need for more students and more meaningful theological education for Hispanic students is crucial.

What is going on and why are these numbers so low? The myriad reasons for the early and chronic underachievement of Latina/o students have been well documented in many books and articles.

The most notable characteristic of these data is the relatively flat rate of growth in BA and other degrees over the past two decades for Latina/os. With such a small pool of students eligible for doctoral study, it is not surprising that the pipeline slows to a trickle at the level of the PhD.

The majority of Latina/o college students are enrolled in two-year colleges. And transfer rates, especially for minority students, are notoriously low. Only about 3 percent of students enrolled in community colleges actually transfer to four-year colleges annually, in spite of the fact that approximately one-third report intending to transfer when they enroll.

If a student decides to go to a four-year college, the first barrier is getting accepted; after acceptance, the next barrier is that the higher costs cannot be financially met. This makes these institutions much less accessible, and because there are so few Latina/os enrolled, such students often feel marginalized and alone. Also, an institution with limited representation of Latina/o faculty leaves Latina/o students who aspire to these positions with very few role models within postsecondary institutions. Latina/o faculty members provide mentorship to students.

When a Latina/o college student is at a four-year college, he/she learns that these institutions do not promote a positive cultural climate for Latina/o students. The student is always struggling with issues of social self-confidence and academic self-concept, which hinders and always attacks their cognitive, intellectual, and critical thinking skills. Moreover, institutions who remain static with their teaching methods and composition of faculty will not help the student become more comfortable at the institution so he/she can flourish. Nonetheless, the few Latina/o students who eventually do attend selective colleges tend to have higher graduation rates and continue with their education.

What can be done to increase the pipeline? A study performed by Chang showed students who attended racially diverse institutions feel more self-confident, establish an academic self-concept, persist, and are generally satisfied with college. It is critically important for an institution to will and promote diversity throughout the academic structures of the institution to create a positive cultural climate for Latina/o students, which will then produce better cognitive outcomes for students with respect to academic, intellectual, and critical thinking skills. It is also important for an institution to respond and adapt to the pedagogical needs of its students.

Another important and significant contribution that faculty members may provide Latina/o students is an environment that supports their research efforts. A big hurdle for Latina/o students was not an academic one but, rather, the problem of being taken seriously as a scholar by faculty who had rather narrow views of what a future academic should look like. For this reason institutions need diverse faculty. There is an assertion that faculty of color are more inclined to mentor and support diverse students because their comfort level with issues of diversity and their own value for diversity translate into pedagogical practices that validate the presence of students of color.

Here are more ways that academic institutions can increase the pool of PhD candidates: (1) increase the number of Latina/o faculty; (2) increase the proportion of grant money; (3) find ways to ensure that students can successfully transfer to four-year colleges and universities to earn their degrees; (4) make the campus more diverse by diversifying not only the student body but also the faculty and the curriculum; and (5) hire more administrators of color in the higher ranks. By beginning to implement a plan of action to increase the Latina/o pool of PhD candidates and faculty, institutions will have the ability to create a more seamless continuum for Latina/os as they navigate through postsecondary and postgraduate education, and the continued charge of redefining the academy for future generations of Latina/o students.

Joanne Rodríguez-Olmedo

References and Further Reading

Castellanos, Jeanett, Alberta M. Gloria, and Mark Kamimura, eds. *The Latina/o Pathway to the Ph.D.: Abriendo Caminos* (Sterling, VA: Stylus Publishing, 2006).

Chang, Mitchell J. "The Positive Education Effects of Racial Diversity on Campus." *Diversity Challenged*, ed. G. Orfield (Cambridge, MA: Harvard Education Publishing Group, 2001).

Fact Book on Theological Education 2006–2007 (Pittsburgh: The Association of Theological Schools, 2007).

Hurtado, S. "The Institutional Climate for Talented Latino Students." *Research in Higher Education* 35, no. I (1994): 21–41.

Gandara, P., and L. Chavez. "Putting the Cart before the Horse: Latinos in Higher Education." *Latinos and Public Policy in California: An Agenda for Opportunity*, ed. D. López and A. Jiménez (Berkeley, CA: Institute of Governmental Studies, Regents of the University of California, 2003).

THEOLOGICAL ANTHROPOLOGY

From a Latino/a perspective, theological anthropology will privilege what Orlando Espín identifies as *lo cotidano*: the common experiences and struggles of daily life where God is encountered. These experiences, struggles, and encounters with God all occur within the context of a life lived within a community.

The Hispanic understanding of community is not to be understood as individuals contractually united as a free, voluntary association. Roberto Goizueta argues that one is involuntarily born into the community, which is marked by distinctive qualities (e.g., the Spanish language and cultural traits from Spain and Latin America). Anchored by the dense network of immediate and extended family ties and strengthened by interpersonal relationships that link families to the larger community, the Latina/o community is one where individuals gain identity as a Hispanic and a Christian. Individual identity is not intrinsically in conflict with the community, but can only be had by being an integral part of the community one is born into or, as Goizueta argues, accompanied (*acompañado*) by the community and God. Latino/as are born into a community that is a bridge between the cultures of the United States and Latin America. God is encountered as a powerful incarnate presence among Hispanics by virtue of the community's culture and religious traditions that center on the Church. Consequently, God calls on this community to bridge all forms of division and alienation that divide God's people, especially those who are socially and economically disenfranchised.

Constructing a Latina/o theological anthropology presents great challenges due to the pluralism inherent in Hispanic identity and life experiences. For example, there exists a debate among Latina/os whether the term "Hispanic" best represents the identity of the people or if the term "Latino" is the better alternative. Debates aside, a credible theological anthropology must encompass a plurality of economic, national, religious, political, and social experiences, including those of women and social minorities within the Hispanic population. It must deal with issues that reveal a creative tension between the unity and diversity inherent in Latina/o identity and life, and show how each reinforces the other.

Priest and scholar Virgilio Elizondo correctly identifies all Hispanics as *mestizaje*. The Spanish cultural root all Latino/as share originates from a mix (*mezcla*) of the peoples and their cultures that migrated and settled in Spain. The Spanish conquest of Latin America, and the centuries following that event, incorporated indigenous American civilizations, Africans, and other European migrants into the mix. Consequently, as Miguel Díaz argues, Hispanics, by virtue of their broad ancestral background, can be as White as any European Caucasian and as Black as any West African, and every shade in between. This is theologically significant because God calls Latina/os to combat barriers of human division and alienation, and they can do so because cultures are bridged in their very being as a people. Hispanics are in a unique position to bridge many parent cultures, without denying the contributions of each, and thus herald the advent of a new humanity.

Popular religious practices are decisively important for understanding Latino/a theological anthropology because they serve as perhaps the most obvious and powerful demonstration of identity. Catholic or Protestant, such practices have the common denominator of coming up from the community, centered in the church. Theologian Jeanette Rodríguez argues that the church is central for Hispanics because that institution forms and maintains communal bonds centered on understanding God's saving and integrating presence among the people in daily life. That is manifested through the rich Catholic sacramental and devotional life (especially Marian devotions), and the *coritos* (simple hymns with refrains), praise and worship styles, and testimonials of faith practiced amongst Protestant congregations. Catholic and Hispanic Protestants mutually influence each other's religious practices. Indigenous religious practices, done under the guise of Catholic saints and symbols, often exercise an important role in Latina/o religious practices, too.

Hispanics share the social trait of the struggle (*la lucha*) for liberation, which manifests itself in many forms. Primary is the struggle against marginalization and oppression in both society and the church. This situation was born out of the fact that nearly all Latino/as are exiles or the descendants of exiles to the United States from the chronic political and economic problems of Latin America. For Mexican Americans, the struggle occurs in their ancestral homeland, the Mexican territory annexed by the United States following the Mexican-American War. Hispanics have found their religious traditions frowned upon by the American Christian mainstream, and have also suffered exclusion from participating in the official ministries of the church. Struggle takes on a different form with the commonplace occurrence of Latina/os who have attained full sociopolitical enfranchisement, economic security, and acceptance in the church. There, the question of how to maintain one's identity as a Hispanic while integrating oneself into the church and American society comes to the fore. Latino/a theological anthropology argues that God sides with the marginalized, calls on the people to resist their marginalization and oppression, and calls, too, on Hispanics who have already overcome both to work with those who continue to suffer under marginalization and oppression and remove its causes.

Women are an anchor of Hispanic American identity. *Mujerista* theology, pioneered by Ada María Isasi-Díaz, adds to Hispanic American theological anthropology by calling for a realization of this fact through the inclusion of women who struggle to gain their rightful place as subjects and participate to the full in their families and the community. The objectification of women through overwork, *machismo*, and other abuses that degrade women as persons is resisted.

Theologians Espín and Sixto García both see Hispanic theological anthropology as an imitation of the Triune God. Following how the plurality of the persons of the Trinity sustains the unity of God without becoming a monolith, a Hispanic American theological anthropology can demonstrate how diverse Hispanic identities and experiences become a dynamic unity, without collapsing a people into a monolithic unity. This can serve as a sign of how Latino/as can be true to God when they are true to their identity.

Ramón Luzárraga

References and Further Reading

Aponte, Edwin David, and Miguel A. De La Torre, eds. *Handbook of Latina/o Theologies* (St. Louis: Chalice Press, 2006).

Diaz, Miguel H. *On Being Human: U.S. Hispanic and Rahnerian Perspectives* (Maryknoll, NY: Orbis Books, 2001).

Garcia, Jorge J. E. *Hispanic/Latino Identity: A Philosophical Perspective* (Malden, MA: Blackwell Publishers, 2000).

Goizueta, Roberto S. *Caminemos con Jesús: Toward a Hispanic/Latino Theology of Accompaniment* (Maryknoll, NY: Orbis Books, 2001).

Isasi-Díaz, Ada María. *Mujerista Theology: A Theology for the Twenty-First Century* (Maryknoll, NY: Orbis Books, 1996).

TRANSNATIONALISM

Transnationalism refers to modes of being and belonging—worldviews, practices, social relations, and institutions—which span two or more nation-states, making it possible for individuals to be multiply embedded, often developing alternative and/or hybrid identities. Applied to Latino/as, the term describes the need and ability of immigrants to be integrated into the social and cultural structures of the society of settlement (often the United States), while maintaining close ties with the countries of origin in Latin America.

The concept of transnationalism is not new. Randolph Bourne used it in his 1916 article "Transnational America," which appeared in *Atlantic Monthly*, to describe the changing ethnoracial landscape in the United States as a result of the massive immigrant waves in the late 1800s and early 1900s and to characterize the young nation's place in the emerging architecture of interstate relations in the wake of World War I. Moreover, because the United States and Mexico have been closely intertwined since at least the 1848 Treaty of Guadalupe Hidalgo, which left some 80,000 Mexicans in newly acquired U.S. lands, we can say that both Mexican immigration and, particularly, the Southwest border region have always been strongly transnational, long before the term became popular in academic circles.

Nevertheless, the concept became significantly rearticulated in the 1990s in response to the successive waves of Latin Americans (as well as Africans and Asians) who came to the United States following the Immigration and Reform Act of 1965, which eliminated a quota system favoring immigration from Central and Northern Europe. Dislocated by the sociopolitical turmoil and the rapid and unequal economic development that have dominated the region from the late 1960s forward, many of these immigrants have settled in the United States, not only securing jobs, but eventually forming families, purchasing houses, sending their American-born children to school, and paying taxes, all activities that weave them into the fabric of everyday life in the United States. Simultaneously, these immigrants make use of new advances in the fields of transportation and communications, such as inexpensive air travel, the Internet, discounted phone cards, and an increasingly globalized mass media. These advances allow them not only to send remittances to and travel with relative frequency to Latin America but to keep abreast of daily events in their communities of origin.

To characterize this simultaneous embeddedness, anthropologists Linda Basch, Nina Glick Schiller, and Christina Szanton Blanc offer the now classic definition of transnationalism: "the processes by which immigrants forge and sustain multi-stranded social relations that link together their societies of origin and settlement. We call these processes transnationalism to emphasize that many immigrants today build social fields that cross geographic, cultural, and political borders" (1993, 7). Basch, Glick Schiller, and Szanton Blanc call those immigrants engaged in multiple social relations spanning national borders "transmigrants." They argue that "transmigrants take actions, make decisions, and develop subjectivities and identities embedded in networks of relationships that connect them simultaneously to two or more nation-states" (Basch, Glick Schiller, and Szanton Blanc 1993, 7)

So, a Salvadoran mother who has immigrated to the United States to work as a maid or a nanny in Los Angeles, Houston, or the Washington, DC area, leaving behind her young children under the care of her mother, is engaged in a transnational social field. In addition to sending monthly remittances to ensure her children are well-fed and go to school, she very likely places daily calls to her hometown of Intipucá or Chirilagua in Eastern El Salvador to discipline them and to make sure that they do not become members of transnational gangs (*maras*), which are now present among immigrant and nonimmigrant young people throughout Central and North America (Vásquez and Marquardt 2003, 119-144). If she feels her children are in danger of engaging in destructive behavior, she may work two or three jobs to send them to private school or she might decide to bring them to the United States, although this move might give the children increased freedom and further challenge her authority. In other words, this Salvadoran mother is parenting transnationally, making crucial decisions about the future of her family that have an impact on the societies of both origin and settlement (Hondageneu-Sotelo and Avila 2003).

Another example of transnational livelihoods might be a Brazilian Pentecostal pastor who collects the tithes in his thriving church in Somerville or Framingham, Massachusetts, to support missionary activities in Governador Valadares, his community of origin in the state of Minas Gerais (Levitt 2001). His congregation's missionary work might involve seeding sister churches in Brazil or among Brazilian immigrants in other countries like Spain, Portugal, or the United Kingdom, creating a polycentric transnational religious network through which videotaped sermons, itinerant preachers, self-help books, and gospel music groups circulate. This transnational exchange of ideas, personnel, resources, and material culture, in turn, transforms the religious landscapes in both the United States and Brazil contributing to their vibrancy and pluralism. The same applies for a Mexican town association in Silicon Valley or in New York City, whose members contribute to the annual feast of their village's patron saint in Oaxaca or Puebla, or to the upkeep of the local chapel and cemetery, where they hope they will be buried when they die. In fact, one of the most important functions of these transnational home associations is the repatriation and proper burial of the bodies of their deceased members.

These examples show that transnationalism is about what anthropologist Roger Rouse (1991) calls "bifocality," the ability of Latin American immigrants to zoom in and out of different spaces and times according to the demands of the transnational social field in which they are involved. Bifocality may lead to the juxtaposition of identities and practices or to hybridity, the creation of new cultural and religious expressions blending different aspects across the transnational network. For example, rural Dominican Catholicism in the neighborhood of Jamaica Plain, Boston, may tend toward a Pan-Latinismo, when Nuestra Señora de la Altagracia, the patroness of the Dominican Republic, comes to be venerated alongside other national saints, such as Saint John the Baptist (Puerto Rico), the Lord of the Miracles (Peru), or *el Divino Niño* (Colombia). Simultaneously, Dominican immigrants may take back to their villages of origin a more formalized Catholicism learned from the Irish American or Italian American priests ministering to them in Boston. So, their relatives and friends in the Dominican Republic might now demand that mass be said on time, lasting exactly one hour, and that confession take place at the appointed regular times, as it is done in the United States (Levitt 2001).

These examples of transnationalism also demonstrate that religion is often central in the creation of transnational social fields. This is not surprising given that most religious traditions, by virtue of their goal of bridging personal conversion and renewal with universal salvation, have historically operated at multiple scales from the local to the global. Sociologist Peggy Levitt argues that religious organizations enter transnational processes according to at least three configurations. First, "extended transnational religious organizations" basically "broaden and deepen a global religious system that is already powerful and legitimate" (Levitt 2004, 6). The prime example here is the Catholic Church, with its centralized and hierarchical yet tentacular structure linking the Vatican, global religious orders, regional and national episcopal bodies, and the parish, all buttressed by a universalizing doctrine. The second type is "negotiated transnational religious organizations" that present a more flexible and decentralized form of organization. In these organizations, "relations between sending and receiving country churches evolve without a strong federated institutional structure or rules. Instead, individuals and organizations enter into informal agreements with one another that have weaker connections to political circles but are more flexible constituted" (Levitt 2004, 8). The example here would be many small transnational Pentecostal churches but also African-based religions, such as Santería and Candomblé, which rely on loosely connected houses led by charismatic *padrinos/madrinas* or *pais/mães de santo*. Finally, there are "recreated transnational religious organizations," formed by "groups with guidance from home-country leaders," which seek to replicate local practices, beliefs, and modes of organization abroad. "[T]hese are franchise-like groups [that] are run by migrants who receive periodic resources, financing, and guidance from sending-country leadership while chapters are supported and supervised regularly by those who remain behind" (Levitt 2004, 11–12). Examples of this last category would be the *Igreja*

Universal do Reino de Deus, which emerged in Rio de Janeiro, Brazil, and the *Iglesia La Luz del Mundo*, established in Guadalajara, Mexico, both of which have temples throughout Latin America and in the major cities in the United States.

The various morphologies of transnational religious organizations point to another dimension of transnationalism. Thus far, the literature has tended to emphasize "transnationalism from below" or "grassroots transnationalism," that is, the activities carried out by individuals as they negotiate daily life. Such an emphasis has generated the impression that transnationalism is automatically emancipatory, that it necessarily entails resistance to the normalizing power of the nation-state (Smith and Guarnizo 1998). While the transnationalism has an undeniable transgressive and creative thrust, it is important to keep in mind that institutions, too, can engage in "transnational from above."

In particular, the state, although challenged by globalization, has also benefited from transnationalism. Throughout Latin America, states have, for example, tried to harness the remittances that immigrants send in order to subsidize economic restructuring projects that are often against the interests of the poor and working classes, from which many of the immigrants come. To facilitate this process, the state may recognize dual citizenship or allow immigrants abroad to vote. Haitian or Dominican politicians may be actively campaigning in the United States, leading to what Nina Glick Schiller (2005) calls "long-distance nationalism." In a transnational setting, long-distant nationalism is "a set of ideas about belonging that link together people living in various geographic locations and motivate or justify their taking action in relation to an ancestral territory and its government" (Levitt and Glick Schiller 2004, 1020). Further, and arguably more dramatic, is evidence of the power the state is provided by the current divisive debates over undocumented immigration. Both the United States and Latin American countries have actively tried to regulate transnational immigration as a part of a new regime of closure and mobility connected with neoliberal capitalism.

In that sense, the term "transnationalism," as opposed to "globalization" with which it is often wrongly conflated, does not connote that the nation and the state have disappeared or are irrelevant in the emerging social and geopolitical cartographies. Instead, transnationalism points to the need to go beyond "methodological nationalism," the dominant notion in the social sciences, which posits that the natural unit of analysis is the nation-state, that all the important action takes place within the fixed container of the nation-state (Wimmer and Glick Schiller 2003). What transnationalism does is to historicize and contextualize the nation-state, to show that its borders are porous and contested yet binding. Transnationalism embeds the nation-state in ongoing social, political, economic, cultural, and religious dynamics that crisscross it as well as enable and constrain it.

The enduring power of the state to control the borders of the nation and to manage populations means that, as sociologist Alejandro Portes writes, "not all immigrants are 'transmigrants' and claims to the contrary needlessly weaken the validity of empirical findings on the topic. It is more useful to conceptualize transnationalism as one form of economic, political, and cultural adaptation that co-exists with other, more traditional forms" (2001, 182–183). Instead, in a more likely scenario, immigrants might be able to engage in transnational activities of different intensity, extensity, and durability, depending on the specific needs of the life cycle and the structural constraints they face. Thus, some scholars distinguish among "core transnationalism": those activities that "(a) form an integral part of the individual's habitual life; (b) are undertaken on a regular basis; and (c) are patterned and therefore somewhat predictable [and] 'Expanded' [or 'broad'] transnationalism which, in contrast, includes migrants who engage in occasional transnational practices, such as responses to political crises and natural disasters" (Levitt 2001, 198). According to this classification, transnational motherhood will very likely involve core transnationalism, while voting in a presidential election in the country of origin might be part of an expanded transnationalism.

Overall, transnational frameworks are very valuable in challenging the received idea of American exceptionalism, which views the United States as a radically different society and culture, unaffected by regional and global processes such as colonialism, imperialism, the slave trade, and immigration. The notion of American exceptionalism is built on a denial of coevalness that views Latin American societies as inherently static, corporatist, patriarchal, and authoritarian by virtue of their Catholic background, while the United States is construed as a progressive and democratic society informed by an Anglo-Protestant stress on freedom of conscience and voluntary congregationalism (Vásquez 2005). By highlighting spatiotemporal simultaneity, transnationalism relativizes the hard,

ahistorical dichotomies set up by the thesis of American exceptionalism. In turn, challenging this thesis is crucial to a fuller understanding of the history, religion, and contemporary life of Latino/as in the United States. It allows us to see Latina/os and Latin Americans as existing in a common space and time, as sustaining rich historical and ongoing connections, with powerful transformative effects throughout the hemisphere. Transnationalism makes possible a hemispheric vision that does not gloss over the continued importance and specificity of the nation-state and the creativity and diversity of local life in Hispanic communities throughout the United States.

Manuel A. Vásquez

References and Further Reading

Basch, Linda, Nina Glick Schiller, and Christina Szanton Blanc. *Nations Unbound: Transnational Projects, Postcolonial Predicaments, and Deterritorialized Nation-States* (New York: Gordon and Breach, 1993).

Glick Schiller, Nina. "Long Distance Nationalism." *Encyclopedia of Diasporas: Immigrant and Refugee Cultures Around the World*, ed. Melvin Ember, Carol R. Ember, and Ian Skoggard (New York: Kluwer Academic/Plenum Publishers, 2005).

Hondagneu-Sotelo, Pierrette, and Ernestine Avila. "'I'm Here, But I'm There': The Meaning of Latina Transnational Motherhood." *Gender and U.S. Migration: Contemporary Trends*, ed. Pierrette Hondagneu-Sotelo (Berkeley: University of California Press, 2003).

Levitt, Peggy. *Transnational Villagers* (Berkeley: University of California Press, 2001).

Levitt, Peggy. "Redefining the Boundaries of Belonging: The Institutional Character of Transnational Religious Life." *Sociology of Religion* 65, no. 6 (2004): 174–196.

Portes, Alejandro. "Introduction: The Debates and Significance of Immigrant Transnationalism." *Global Networks* 1, no. 3 (2001): 181–194.

Rouse, Roger. "Mexican Migration and the Social Space of Postmodernism." *Diaspora* 1, no. 1 (1991): 8–23.

Smith, Michael Peter, and Luis Guarnizo, eds. *Transnationalism from Below* (Piscataway, NJ: Transaction Publishers, 1998).

Vásquez, Manuel A. "Historicizing and Materializing the Study of Religion: The Contributions of Migration Studies." *Immigrant Faiths: Transforming Religious Life in America* (Lanham, MD: AltaMira Press, 2005).

Vásquez, Manuel A., and Marie F. Marquardt. *Globalizing the Sacred: Religion across the Americas* (New Brunswick, NJ: Rutgers University Press, 2003).

Wimmer, Andreas, and Nina Glick Schiller. "Methodological Nationalism, the Social Sciences, and the Study of Migration: An Essay in Historical Epistemology." *International Migration Review* 37, no. 3 (2003): 576–610.

TRINITY

Contemporary Latino/as understand and celebrate the Trinity through the experience of community. This Latino/a concept of the Trinity—in development over 500 years—may be at odds with traditional considerations. Traditional Trinitarian notions are rooted in philosophical categories and systems that primarily consider the nature of God within God's self, unrelated to history and human experience. Contemporary Hispanic communities develop some of these classic Trinitarian concepts, such as divine immanence and economic Trinity, as well as introduce new categories that understand the presence of God within history and culture, and the relationship between this presence and the structure of Latina/o communities.

Philosophical conceptions of the Trinity, based on Greco-Roman systems and categories, came into contact with Taíno and Nahua peoples throughout the fifteenth and sixteenth centuries through Spanish explorers and missionaries. Spanish military technology enabled these explorers and missionaries to subjugate the Taíno/Nahua peoples and colonize them, and catechetical techniques used to form the newly conquered peoples had varied results. Nonetheless, creative constructions of God developed, as Taíno/Nahua experiences based on their own religious sensibilities, such as ancestral lineage and cyclic stories of death/rebirth, found their way into trinitarian concepts. These cultural experiences eventually developed into religious formulations on God, incarnation, revelation, salvation, etc.

Contemporary Hispanic communities developed conceptions of God by stressing the communitarian qualities of the divine and the means through which these qualities break through history and make possible liberation. It is through the movement of God in history as love shared and concretized through vital families, communities, and institutions that the Trinity is present in the world, ever enveloping these communities in love, in turn serving as continued witness to God's presence in the world. This character of the Trinity is found in the reality of all people, as well as all human institutions and communities, as they participate in developing structures of life and justice. Latina/o communities consider oppressive societal structures, whether these be families, communities, or institutions, to be dysfunctional Trinitarian systems, as these frustrate or oppress the essential quality of the Trinity, an enveloping experience of love and justice given and received. Examples of dysfunctional Trinitarian systems are communities and institutions that engender any type of discrimination, whether religious, ethnic, cultural, economic, racial, or sexual.

A number of Hispanic theologians have developed the notion of *familia* to understand the Trinity. Based on both Roman and Popular Catholic conceptions, the experience of familia integrates what Zaida Maldonado Pérez refers to as the "sociocentric organic," wherein individuals develop meaning within a network of relationships. In turn, life is encountered via relationships, rendering this life unique and set apart—holy—in the sense of the Hebrew Scriptures. This experience of familia extends not only to those individuals of a particular culture or ethnicity, but to all who have experienced and rejected egocentric contractual societies, systems that promote an individual's development through means of competition and transitory, mutually beneficial liaisons, and endeavor toward strengthening communal bonds and understanding themselves within communal relationships. This concept of familia is comprehensive, not only pertaining to nuclear family systems, but including the mundane, what Pérez refers to as *lo cotidiano, la lucha, el meollo*. These Spanish and Portuguese expressions encapsulate the understanding that purpose and meaning reside within the daily experience of living in

relationship with others, all of whom are committed to the continued development and growth of la familia, particularly those who live in the midst of systemic injustice and marginalization.

In addition to those aspects heretofore mentioned, Luis Pedraja develops the conception of the Trinity from the consideration of the relationship between those with and without power, particularly political and societal power. Drawing upon Cappadocian theological reflection, Pedraja develops the iconoclastic dimension of the Trinity, stressing that the Trinity cannot be conceived of simply as the Father, or the Son, or the Holy Spirit, but instead includes all of these and more, not residing in a model that can be manipulated for the gain of a particular political or societal entity. Throughout Christian history, particular aspects of God have been promulgated and embraced as normative, such as overly spiritualized or rationalized conceptions of God, outside the experience of those without spiritual sensibilities, or the uneducated, to the oppression of particular peoples and the detriment of the entire community of faith. From the perspective of the marginalized, such conceptions of God ought to be rendered as they are—particular and incomplete conceptions that demand interaction and engagement with other conceptions. In addition, a constitutive quality of the Trinity is diversity. Uniform and monolithic structures that compel conformity are radically challenged. Particular mores and values are typically derided and dismissed by dominant cultures, belying the dominant society's predisposition for their own conceptions of God —stolid, stagnate, and uncommunicative. The Trinity communicates that diversity reveals the divine, not chaos or confusion, stressing the necessity for sharing and communication.

Oswald John Nira

References and Further Reading

Diaz, Miguel H. *On Being Human: U.S. Hispanic and Rahnerian Perspectives* (Maryknoll, NY: Orbis Books, 2001).

Espín, Orlando O. *The Faith of the People: Theological Reflections on PopuCatholicism* (Maryknoll, NY: Orbis Books, 1997).

González, Justo L. *Mañana: Christian Theology from a Historical Perspective* (Nashville: Abingdon Press, 1990).

Pedraja, Luis G. "Trinity." *Handbook of U.S. Theologies of Liberation*, ed. Miguel A. De La Torre (St. Louis: Chalice Press, 2004).

Pérez, Zaida Maldonado. "The Trinity." *Handbook of Latino/a Theologies*, ed. Edwin David Aponte and Miguel A. De La Torre (St. Louis: Chalice Press, 2006).

U.S. POLITICAL PARTIES

As the Hispanic population increases, sheer numbers will create political power that can potentially influence both the U.S. political process and the two major political parties—Republican and Democrat. Of particular interest is how the religiosity of Latina/os affects political decisions, which in turn can impact the two major parties. For years, Hispanics have faced xenophobic laws and regulations. Many are discovering that an effective response to structural discrimination is obtaining U.S. citizenship and the right to vote. During the 2006 mass Hispanic demonstrations throughout the country to pass comprehensive immigration reform, many chanted, "Today we march, tomorrow we vote." To make this a reality, many Latina/o leaders have attempted to conduct voter registration drives to place as many Hispanics as possible on the voting rolls. Although Hispanic political participation had historically lagged behind Euro-Americans and African Americans, the 2008 presidential election demonstrated a new Latina/o voting force that impacted results in states like Nevada, Virginia, and Florida.

As more Latina/os enter the political process, they are becoming a crucial swing voting bloc that can affect the final outcome of elections. Politicians are recognizing this potential. Consequently, most presidential contenders are repeatedly making campaign stops in California, Texas, and Florida (states with large Hispanic populations), greeting their audiences in Spanish. This growing political strength helps explain why in 2007, for the first time in U.S. history, both the Democratic and Republican parties held presidential primary debates in Spanish prior to the casting of the first vote in the Iowa Caucus and the New Hampshire Primary.

According to the research conducted by the Pew Hispanic Center, Hispanics, with the notable exception of Cubans (24 percent), tend to prefer the

NATIONAL HISPANIC PRAYER BREAKFAST

In 2002 Nueva Esperanza led by the Reverend Luis Cortés Jr. hosted the first National Hispanic Prayer Breakfast, which has become an annual event in Washington, D.C. The first gathering had been scheduled for the fall of 2001, but was moved in the wake of the terrorist attacks of September 11. Now hosted by Esperanza USA, of which Cortés is president, the National Hispanic Prayer Breakfast brings together Hispanic clergy to pray for the nation and for the Latina/o community. The organization also seeks to gather Latino/a faith leaders and elected officials to discuss and advocate issues that are important to the Hispanic community. The National Hispanic Prayer Breakfast and Conference has expanded from a single event to include three days of activities. Typically, during the breakfast program, Hispanic clergy and community members hear from a variety of national political leaders and international speakers highlighting the Hispanic faith community's presence and contributions to the United States. Speakers over the years have included President George W. Bush, Governor Howard Dean, chairperson of the Democratic National Committee, Senator Hillary Rodham Clinton, and Senator Mel Martinez. Four special awards are given at the breakfast to noted public advocates for the Latino/a community: the Esperanza Leadership Award; the Esperanza Partner; the Esperanza Spirit Award; and the Esperanza Advocate Award.

—EDA

Democratic Party. In 2007, 43 percent of Latino/as considered themselves to be Democrats, 20 percent claimed to be Republican, and 20 percent said they were Independent (7 percent listed some other political affiliation). A gender gap seems to exist where Latinas tend to be more liberal and Democratic than their Latino counterparts. Overall, it appears that the Republican Party is making little inroad into the non-Cuban Hispanic population. Still, it is important to note that while Democrats have maintained a two-to-one advantage since 1996, Republicans have been able to narrow that gap during the 2000 and 2004 presidential races and the 2006 midterm elections when Hispanics voting for Republicans ranged from 30 to 40 percent. Nevertheless, these inroads seem to have been dwarfed during the 2008 presidential election where

CNN exit polls showed 67 percent of Latino/as going for the Democratic candidate.

When party affiliation was examined based on religious affiliation, the 2007 Pew study showed that Hispanic evangelicals are twice as likely to consider themselves Republican as Latina/o Catholics. Yet, when focus solely on the Hispanic Evangelical voter registration, Republicans hold no advantage when compared to non-Hispanic Evangelicals. Among Latina/o Evangelicals, 36 percent are registered with the Republican Party, the same number that is registered with the Democratic Party (19 percent are registered as Independent and 3 percent as other). Compare these figures with non-Hispanic Evangelicals where 50 percent are registered as Republicans as opposed to 25 percent who are registered as Democrats (23 percent are registered as

Independents). Puerto Rican Evangelicals run counter to this trend by favoring Democrats (52 percent) over Republicans (18 percent).

Among Hispanic Catholic eligible voters, those who claim to be Democrats are three times greater than those who claim to be Republicans (48 percent to 17 percent). This holds true when we take into account ideology. While most Euro-American conservatives consider themselves Republican, Latino/a Catholic conservatives still prefer the Democratic Party (40 percent as opposed to 30 percent conservatives who prefer the Republicans). This is significant when we consider that the majority of the Hispanic electorate is Catholic (63 percent). In fact, 70 percent of all Latina/os who claim to be Democrats are Catholics.

When eligible voters were asked during the Pew study as to which party could do a better job on a number of issues, the Democratic Party was overwhelmingly chosen over and against the Republicans with wide margins. These issues included: (1) dealing with the economy (49 percent to 29 percent); (2) improving the educational system (50 percent to 25 percent); (3) dealing with Iraq (48 percent to 26 percent); (4) immigration (49 percent to 22 percent); (5) improving the nation's morality (46 percent to 28 percent); (6) protecting the environment (51 percent to 22 percent); and (7) protecting civil rights (55 percent to 21 percent). It is interesting to note that depending on the issue, 14 to 18 percent thought neither party would do a good job while 3 to 7 percent said either party could do a good job. The only exceptions where the Republican Party was deemed to do a better job than the Democrats by a slight majority was among Evangelical when it came to improving the education system (40 percent to 38 percent), dealing with Iraq (40 percent to 36 percent), and improving the nation's morality (42 percent to 36 percent). On protecting civil rights, the parties were tied with 39 percent each.

One reason why the Democratic Party might have a stronger appeal among Hispanics could be the liberal economic issues with which Latina/os hold strong feelings. Although the religious beliefs of most Hispanics contribute toward a more conservative view on social issues, i.e., abortion (57 percent opposed) and gay marriage (56 percent opposed), they usually take a more liberal stance on economic issues. For example, 69 percent favor government-guaranteed health insurance, while 64 percent believe the poor live difficult lives because of a lack of governmental services. No doubt, the major political parties have taken great strides to reach out to the Latina/o voter. As more of the Latina/o population obtain citizenship, get older, and register to vote, their impact on who gets elected and who does not can become profound.

Miguel A. De La Torre

References and Further Reading

Geron, Kim, and Melissa R. Michelson. "Latino Partisanship, Political Activity and Vote Choice." *Latinas/os in the United States: Changing the Face of América*, ed. Havidán Rodríguez, Rogelio Sáenz, and Cecilia Menjívar (New York: Springer, 2008).

Pew Hispanic Center. *Changing Faiths: Latinos and the Transformation of American Religion* (Washington, DC: Pew Forum on Religion and Public Life, 2007).

UNIVERSAL CHURCH OF THE KINGDOM OF GOD

Originally from Brazil, the University Church of the Kingdom of God (UCKG) is a neo-Pentecostal church emphasizing exorcism and prosperity theology and is the offspring of dissident movements within Pentecostal churches. Modeled on Messianic patterns, it has an entrepreneurial structure with a strong charismatic hero-impresario leader.

A new offshoot of Pentecostalism concerned with divine healing has more recently emerged in the "religious supermarket" as an alternative to Indigenous-Creole Pentecostalism. Exorcism and prosperity are its central elements. Energetic, charismatic leaders exhort huge gatherings and provide continuous worship services in old cinemas and auditoriums, open buildings in which the public meetings are conceived more as public spectacles than as community life and worship. The hymns, sermons, and exhortations are a kind of therapy for the suffering masses. When the leader comes on stage, enough enthusiasm has already been created to generate an almost hysterical explosion of emotion in the congregation. The pastor becomes a moral agent who brings a message of hope and stability. They enjoy messianic authority that extends to areas of life from the economic to the spiritual. Observers have noted that the flexible bond that results from these shared emotions demands little personal commitment and is a welcome alternative to the pain, needs, and conflicts that participants must confront daily. Faced with daily crises, people prefer a moment of ecstasy with this vibrant and untamed Jesus to the silence and existential vacuum of daily life.

From a doctrinal point of view, many prosperity neo-Pentecostals use the Bible as a fetish and a source of magical phrases as they perform exorcisms and divine healings. Rarely is the Bible actually studied, since the central acts of faith are healing and liberation, as well as thematic reflections with moralistic emphasis, more than biblical teaching.

The Universal Church of the Kingdom of God in Brazil is organized as a religious transnational enterprise and is by far the most successful divine healing prosperity movement coming from Latin America. The Universal Church of the Kingdom of God, founded by Bishop Edir Macedo in 1979, developed its model of mission from different ecclesiological presuppositions, assuming some traditional Pentecostal doctrines and adding his own theological and doctrinal tenets, but rooted in divine healing and prosperity theology. Bishop Macedo started this movement with a small group of followers that every Saturday joined him in praising, Bible study, and prayers of intercession, particularly exorcisms to heal people possessed by evil spirits and negative forces.

Soon the movement became an established congregation in Rio de Janeiro, planting new congregations in Sao Paulo and other states of Brazil. In the United States, the Universal Church of the Kingdom of God has organized congregations in all major cities. In Chicago, Los Angeles, Miami, New York, and Orlando, they offer a multifaceted ministry with counseling (in some cities it is a 24-hour counseling service), healing (primarily exorcism sessions), education, and support to Latin American and Caribbean immigrants. The Hispanic population is the number one target in proselytism, offering recreational activities for the youth and children. One area that is of primary importance is communication through newspapers, bulletins, Internet, radio, and television stations in Portuguese and Spanish. Two predominant themes are displayed in their temples: "Jesucristo es el Senor" (Jesus Christ is Lord) and "Pare de Sufrir" (Stop from Suffering).

The Universal Church of the Kingdom of God reported that in 8 years 195 temples were built in 14 states of Brazil. By the end of 2006 they reported that the Universal Church of the Kingdom of God is established in more than 115 countries (Freston 2001, 198–203).

Some of the doctrines preached and taught by the Universal Church of God are classical Pentecostal principles based on the foursquare gospel formula: Jesus saves, heals, baptizes, and will return. The distinctive emphases of the Universal Church are expressed in symbols and rituals, which include a black heart with a white hallow in the center, flowers, a glass of water (half empty to illustrate the need for Jesus' healing touch toward completion), a Jewish menorah, and a cross. They emphasize that Holy Communion is a feast to celebrate a resurrected life in Christ, and they gather twice a month around the communion table, more frequently than classical Pentecostal churches. The teachings and exhortations stress that trusting in God requires a positive attitude, invoking that Jesus is Lord and the believer should accept the challenge to stop any suffering in daily life. Jesus Christ has come to offer abundant life and freedom from any bondage and promises to restore the life of the believer like it was in Paradise.

The main emphasis of the Universal Church of the Kingdom of God is on building megachurches in urban areas, with an aggressive anti-Roman Catholic stance. Bishop Macedo is a hero-impresario figure more than an evangelist. His clientele is very diverse, including poor, middle, and upper-middle classes. They run several social ministries, including crisis counseling and prayer 24 hours a day for persons in desperate need in many locations.

The identity and mission of the Universal Church of the Kingdom of God are conceived as a transnational religious enterprise with economic power, which includes the role of mass media in evangelism. As a result, they own radio and television networks, publish a national newspaper in Brazil, and encourage active political participation, including having their own political parties, developing their own political affiliations and coalitions, and electing representatives to Congress and other local and national positions. It is known that Bishop Edir Macedo is a personal friend of the president of Brazil, Jose Inacio Da Silva. Mission and unity in this church model are defined by a global expansive dimension in planting megachurches throughout the world.

Carmelo E. Álvarez

References and Further Reading

Corten, André, and Ruth Marshall-Fratani, eds. *Between Babel and Pentecost: Pentecostalism in Africa and Latin America* (Bloomington: Indiana University Press, 2001).

Freston, Paul. "The Transnationalisation of Brazilian Pentecostalism: The Universal Church of the Kingdom of God." *Between Babel and Pentecost: Transnational Pentecostalism in Africa and Latin America,* ed. André Corten and Ruth Marshall-Fratani (Bloomington and Indianapolis: Indiana University Press, 2001).

Mattos, Paulo Ayres. "An Introduction to the Theology of Bishop Edir Macedo (Universal Church of the Kingdom of God): A Case Study of a New Brazilian Pentecostal Church" (MST thesis, Christian Theological Seminary, Indianapolis, 2002).

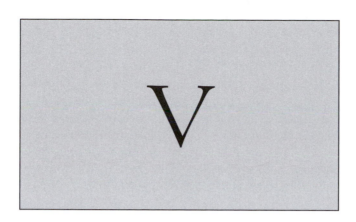

VIRGIN MARY

Mary enters into the faith of the Church through the act of giving birth to Jesus of Nazareth. This single event has given rise to countless studies of Mariology and innumerous Marian devotional practices, shrines, titles, and images. Mary or María, as most Latino/as call her, is many things to many Christians: she is Jesus' mother, Theotokos, mother of the Church, spouse of the Holy Spirit, daughter of the Father, God's handmaiden, the new Eve, our sister in faith, and the first disciple, to name a few. Veneration or respect for the Blessed Virgin Mary goes back to the early Christian community and can be found in different Christian churches around the world today. For this reason, before focusing on María among Latino/as, we will take a brief look at the history of Marian devotion in Christianity, the official doctrines about Mary promulgated by Roman Catholicism. Then we will consider María in the context of Latino/a matriarchy, the Marian patronesses of Spain and Latin America, and in conclusion, we will consider Latino/a Marianism in the United States.

Short History of Marian Devotion

Mary is only directly mentioned 12 times in the New Testament (Galatians 4:4–5; Mark 3:31–35; 6:2–3; Matthew 1:16–25; 12:46–50; Luke 1:26–56; 2:4–33, 41–52; 8:19–21; Acts 1:14; John 2:1–12; 19:26–27) and is alluded to, according to some scholars, once (Revelation 12:1–6). Paul mentions her once as the nameless woman who birthed Jesus, the Synoptic writers give us her name, and Luke raises her to the status of one of the valiant women of the Old Testament. John refers to her as the nameless mother of the Lord, who has some influence on her son and seemingly symbolizes the Church.

The New Testament teaches that Mary is Jesus' mother. When paired with the Old Testament, Patristic writers found several themes that are part and parcel of Christian Marian titles, roles, and doctrines that still influence how Latino/as relate to Mary in the United States. These are focused on Mary's unique relationship to Christ (Christocentric) and on Mary as the best example of what the Church should be (Ecclesiotypical). In her Christocentric dimension, Mary is seen as the daughter of David from whose lineage Jesus comes, bride, sister, and mother of Christ in faith, and Christ's queen mother. Ecclesiotypically, Mary is seen as God's handmaiden, the perfect disciple, the new Eve in relationship to the new Adam, the daughter of the Father, the mother of the Son, and the spouse of the Holy Spirit.

New Testament Mariology fed the early Christian consideration of Mary as the type of the Church. The Church-Mary parallel developed out of the concept of Christ, Jesus as the new Adam; the Church-Mary is the new Eve. The Patristic writers' main interest in Mary seems to have been concerned with her role in salvation history, a role that is extended to the Church. Considerations of her individualized and singular role are few in the Patristic period.

Problems arise when Mary is separated from the Church-Mary parallel. These are centered on maximalist (high) and minimalist (low) Mariologies. In the fourth century, for example, Epiphanius (315–403), Bishop of Cyprus, had to condemn the Collyridians who worshipped her as a goddess. In some extreme cases the maximalist Collyridianism even portrayed Mary as part of the Godhead. Epiphanius also denounced the minimalist Antidicomarianites (opponents of Mary) who saw her as no more than a woman, a vessel from which Jesus came. The leaders of these Christian groups held that Jesus was the son of Joseph and Mary and not the product of a virgin birth. They eventually modified this position to belief in the virgin birth of Jesus, but not Mary's perpetual virginity.

When we look at the relationship that U.S. Hispanic and Latin American Christians have with María, we can see two extremes are still present in the Church. Some Christians exaggerate her importance, coming dangerously close to the point of worship, while other Christians seem to almost despise her. We need to remember that Bishop Epiphanius censured both the Antidicomarianites who refused to honor Mary and the Collyridians who idolatrized her. His orthodox position was that Mary should be held in honor, but only the Father, the Son, and the Holy Spirit should be worshiped and adored. This is still the position expressed in Roman Catholic and Orthodox teachings about Mary today.

Marian Doctrines and Dogmas

Good Mariology follows good Christology, and anything we say about Mary is ultimately Christocentric and Ecclesiotypical. Over the centuries four principal beliefs have developed regarding Mary: her Divine Maternity, Perpetual Virginity, Immaculate Conception, and Assumption. These are especially important for the Latino/a and Latin American understanding of María.

The dogma of Mary's Divine Maternity emphasizes that she is the Mother of the Second Person of the Trinity. However, rather than focus on her virginity, this doctrine is meant to highlight the divine nature of Jesus. The Council of Ephesus (431) while discussing the undivided humanity and divinity of Jesus declared that Mary is more than just

Christokos (Christ-bearer), she is Theo-tokos (God-bearer). The title "Theoto-kos" or "Mother of God" affirms that just as all human mothers give birth not only to the body of their child but to the whole person, so too Mary gave birth to the person, Jesus Christ, who is both human and divine.

Mary's Perpetual Virginity has never officially been proclaimed a dogma. Rather, it seems to be a product of the *sensus fidelium* (consensus of the faith-ful) by which popular religiosity affirms a general Christian belief. In the case of Mary's Perpetual Virginity, Christians affirmed belief in Mary's virginal birth of Jesus, which slowly turned into belief in her having kept her virginity through-out her life. By the fourth century this popular notion had become so wide-spread that it made its way into official Church documents as a given. Compar-ing her to the Ark of the Covenant, Mary is seen as the Ark of the new Covenant in Christ. It is not fitting that her womb would have carried anyone but God.

The doctrine of Mary's Perpetual Vir-ginity is also tied to the devotion that sees her as the New Eve, reflecting on Paul's image of Jesus as the New Adam. Patristic writers recalled that Adam did not bring sin into the world by himself. The virgin Eve also had a definite role in original sin and the fall. Just as the virgin Eve's disobedience paved the way for Adam to sin, the Virgin Mary's obedi-ence made it possible for the Incarnation of the New Adam. The first Eve brought the stain of original sin unto the human soul and the New Eve was made immaculate so that the New Adam could render the faithful immaculate once again.

The dogma of the Immaculate Con-ception of Mary is probably the most misunderstood dogma about Mary. Peo-ple often believe that the dogma is meant to proclaim that Mary did not have sex-ual intercourse to conceive Jesus. And, although the dogma is ultimately about Jesus, it is not about his virgin birth. It is about the strength of his saving grace. The dogma as explained by the Francis-can John Duns Scotus proclaims that in view of the merits of Christ's salvific action, God kept Mary free of the stain of original sin in order that he be born of her.

The dogma of the Immaculate Con-ception is closely tied to the devotion of Mary's Immaculate Heart, a devotion that can be traced back to the Cistercians of the twelfth century. Scripturally based on Mary's pondering the events of her Son's life in her heart (Luke 2:19, 51), this devotion received greater attention only after Mary's apparition to Catherine Laboure of France in 1830 and three Por-tuguese children, Jacinta, Francisco, and Lucia in Fatima (1917). It is not unusual in Latino/a homes to find this image of Mary's burning heart pierced by a sword hanging alongside an image of Jesus' Sacred Heart. The image is meant to pro-mote love of purity, fervor in living the Gospel, and greater apostolic zeal.

While the dogma of Mary's Assump-tion into heaven was promulgated in the middle of the twentieth century, second-century Christians already held that her beloved Son took Mary, body, soul, and spirit into heaven. This doctrine plays on the love a child has for his mother and the divine power of the Son of God. Mary is given a foretaste of the resurrec-tion and glorification in which all the faithful are meant to share.

The Protestant Reformers of the six-teenth century held Mary's perpetual virginity, immaculate nature, and the

COATLAXOPEUH

Coatlaxopeuh, pronounced quatlashupe, is a composite of coatl (serpent), tla (the), and xopeuh (to crush, step on, stamp out). It is the title by which the Virgin Mary referred to herself on the hill of Tepeyac outside Mexico City in December 1531. By it she proclaims herself as "she who crushes or dominates the serpent." To the Spanish Christian mind of the late Middle Ages, this seems to be a reference to Genesis 3:15, which in the Vulgate had been mistranslated as "she (*ipsa*) shall crush your (snake) head," rather than he (*ipsum*) referring to the woman's offspring. To the Nahuatl mind it seems to be a reference to the goddess Coatlicue (skirt of serpents) who as Tonantzin (our mother) used to appear on Tepeyac and who is the virgin mother of the god Quetzalcoatl (feathered serpent) whose return they awaited. Bishop Zumarraga believed that Coatlaxopeuh was a mispronunciation of Guadalupe, a title by which Mary was revered in Extremadura, Spain. As a result, Our Lady of Tepeyac is universally recognized as Guadalupe. It is only recently that many are reclaiming her original title "Coatlaxopueh" as a means of promoting Latina/o identity and as a symbol for Latina feminism.

—GCG

virginal conception of Jesus as being among the great deeds God has done for her (Luke 1:49). Yet, a seemingly anti-Marian position grew in Protestantism in the post-Reformation period as Marian devotion became a sign of Catholic Orthodoxy in the face of Protestant polemics. Protestant insistence on Scripture alone slowly relegated Mary to the remembrance of Christ's nativity. In the centuries that followed while the Catholics encouraged the development of Marian devotion, Protestants all but ignored her. The last quarter of the twentieth century marked an increase of Protestant interest in Mary. Catholic Marian congresses and conferences chose to invite the participation of Orthodox and Protestant theologians in the hope of finding a common ground for healthy Marianism.

All Christians are again looking at the Marian doctrines and dogmas developed during the first 1,500 years of Christian history. For the Latin American Church,

this is important because they give U.S. Latino/as many of the Marian images of the past 500 years. These images are of a mother who is seen as providing help in defining the identity of mainly Catholic Christians, and through her Magnificat (Luke 1:46-55) move the Hispanic community toward liberation.

Four Mothers of Latin America

It has been said that Latino/as are the children of four mothers: la Violada (raped woman), la Llorona, (weeping woman), la Guadalupana (María), and la Soldadera (soldier woman). In her book *Madres y huachos*, Sonia Montecino talks about Latin Americans as the mestizo children of a Spanish father and an indigenous mother. This hybrid identity born of the clash of two civilizations was not readily accepted by either culture.

When the Europeans conquered America, they often raped the native women, leaving them pregnant with unwanted mestizo (mixed blood) children. Often times, they tricked native women into becoming their concubines, by promising a better life in Europe. Often they abandoned these women, and many of them in desperation and grief tried to kill their mestizo children, giving rise to the legend of la Llorona.

Many Latino/as believe that it was into a panorama of violence and despair that the Virgin Mother of God came in 1531 on the hill of Tepeyac. Many of the Spanish wanted to go home. The native people wanted to die. The new mestizo race was unwanted. In this context María appeared to the native Juan Diego as a mestizo woman who sent him to the Spanish bishop. The Guadalupe event gave all three people, the native, the mestizo, and even the Spaniard a chance at rebirth in Christ.

María, Nuestra Señora (Our Lady), is the third mother who, according to Montecino, becomes the great icon and myth of Latin América. It is she who gave meaning to mestizo reality, taking the bastard and vanquished children of the Spanish invasion and making them children of God. In this way María, who is both Virgin and Mother, becomes the primary feminine figure of Latin América.

The fourth mother is la Soldadera who cries out for justice in lands where the children of God are being oppressed. She is the mother who inspires her children in the search for liberation. Even here María can be found as patroness of many Latin American independence movements and liberation spiritualities from the Mexican revolution to César Chávez's farmworker's movement, from the Madre de los Desaparecidos (Mother of the Disappeared) to the contemporary call for immigration reform.

Marian Patronesses of Latin America

In 1847, the Roman Curia officially consecrated the United States to Our Lady of the Immaculate Conception. U.S. Hispanics, however, continue their Marian devotion to the patronesses of their countries of origin. This is especially true of Cubans and Mexicans who have had their patronesses enshrined in the National Shrine of the Immaculate Conception in Washington, D.C. Before considering Latina/o Marianism, it is important to become familiar with the various titles of Mary in Latin America and Spain. The various titles and invocations of Mary revered by different nations have a common heritage and theology.

Argentina: May 8

Nuestra Señora de Lujan originally belonged to an Argentinean matron, Doña Ana Mattos de Siqueyras. In 1674, she had a chapel built for the reportedly miraculous statue of María. However, the following day the image had made its way back to the hermitage of an African slave named Manuel, preferring to be with the humble. This happened several times before Doña Ana opened the chapel to the public and invited Manuel to be its caretaker.

Bolivia: August 5

La Virgen de Copacabana is the patroness of Bolivia. Her image was sculpted by Francisco Tito Yupanqui, a descendant of Inca royalty. Francisco learned how to sculpt in Mexico and practiced his art for many years before he attempted to sculpt an image of María for his town of Copacabana. He did so in 1583 only after praying to the Most Holy Trinity in order that God might guide him in his efforts to honor Jesus' mother. Quechua and Ahimara natives call her La Coyeta. Her shrine is one of the oldest in América.

Brazil: May 11

The patroness of Brazil was discovered in 1716 by three fishermen who caught her image in their nets in the Paraiba River. The 36 centimeter image had been in the water for a long time and had attained the dark color of many Latin Americans. For this reason the Brazilians have taken her as their patroness, giving her the name of Aparecida, which can mean "she who appears" or "she who looks like us."

Chile: July 16

The Chilean people honor the patroness of the Carmelite Friars, Nuestra Señora del Carmen (Mount Carmel) as Maipú. According to tradition, she gave the Carmelite General Simon Stock a scapular with the promise that whoever dies wearing the scapular will go directly to heaven. As a result, the Virgen del Carmen is the patroness of all those who have dangerous jobs, like soldiers, sailors, firefighters, and the police.

Colombia: July 9

Nuestra Señora de Chiquinquirá, patroness of Colombia is called la Chinita by her devotees. Painted by Alonso de Narvaez, it is an image of Our Lady of the Rosary holding the child Jesus and standing between Saint Anthony of Padua and Saint Mark the Apostle. Doña María de Sevilla inherited it from her brother Antonio and, although dark and ruined, she placed it in her private chapel in Chiquinquirá. In 1586, a native woman and her son saw a glow coming from the faces of Jesus and María. They called Doña María, who came to the chapel in time to see the image restore itself with vivid color and brilliancy.

Costa Rica: August 2

Santa María de los Ángeles (Saint Mary of the Angels), patroness of Costa Rica, is said to have been found on August 2 by the mestiza Juana Pereira. The 7.5 centimeter image called "la Negrita" (dear Black woman) kept returning to the place where it was found, so her Church was built there. She is officially named after the patroness of the Franciscans. Francis of Assisi had given birth to his family at the chapel of the Portiuncula dedicated to Mary of the Angels just outside of Assisi.

Cuba: September 8

Nuestra Señora de la Caridad (Charity) was discovered floating at sea by two indigenous youth and an African child in 1600. They are known as los tres Juanes (the three Johns). The image of María and her child was miraculously dry. She is dressed in a triangular shaped cape that is common to many Marian images in Latin America. Also known as la Virgen del Cobre and Chachita, she has been Cuba's patroness for almost a century.

Dominican Republic: January 21

In 1502, Friar Nicolás de Ovando and 11 other friars were sent by the Spanish king to the Dominican Republic to convert the natives "without doing them harm." The missionaries brought with them a painting of María looking at her child in the hay entitled *Our Lady of Altagracia* (Highest Grace). John Paul II crowned her as the first Evangelizer of America in 1979.

El Salvador: November 21

In 1682, some businessmen found an abandoned box on the beach in El

Salvador. Unable to open it, they put in on their mule's back and took it to town. As it passed the Church, the mule stopped and the box opened revealing a statue of María. She came to be known as the Virgen de la Paz (Virgin of Peace) because her first miracle was to reconcile warring factions in El Salvador. For this reason, she holds a palm frond in her hand.

Ecuador: November 21

Nuestra Señora del Quinche was originally painted in 1589 for those colonizing Ecuador. However, when they could not pay for it, the artist Diego de Robles sold it to the Oyacachis. These natives recognized it as a painting of a woman who had rescued some of their children from ferocious bears. By 1604, the Oyacachis had been Christianized, and they gave the image to the bishop of Quinche. She is called "la pequeñita" (the little one) by her devotees.

Guatemala: October 7

In 1592, a Dominican friar had an image of la Virgen del Rosario made. With the growing interest in the Rosary, this image became an important one in the region. In 1821, the Guatemalan independence movement took her as their protectress. Catholic devotion to María is often tied to the Rosary. Popular legend attributes it to the thirteenth-century Spaniard Domingo de Guzman. He and other mendicant friars seem to have had some input in the development of the use of prayer beads by lay people to pray 150 Our Fathers in place of the 150 psalms. However, the Rosary in its present form can only be traced back to 1569 when it was promoted by Pope Pius V as a useful instrument for all Christians to meditate on the mysteries of Christ's joyful incarnation, sorrowful passion, and glorious resurrection. It was then that the Hail Mary also took its present form.

Honduras: February 3

Nuestra Señora de la Concepción de Suyapa (Our Lady of the Conception of Suyapa) commemorates a small wooden image found by a young worker, Alejandro Colindres, and the child Jorge Martínez when they stopped to rest for the night. The 6.5 centimeter image portrays María with the face of a native woman. Her temple was built in 1780, and she was declared patroness of Honduras by Pius XII in 1925.

Mexico: December 12

In 1531, Mary appeared as a mestizo woman to the native convert Juan Diego at Tepeyac. In response to Bishop Zumarraga's request for a sign, she left behind a miraculous image filled with Nahuatl and European symbolism. The Story of Guadalupe is that of flor y canto (flower and song), which the Nahuatl tribes prized as beauty and truth. She referred to herself as Coatlalopeuh (she who crushes serpents), which sounded like "Guadalupe" to the Spanish Franciscans. The original Guadalupe is named after a dark statue of the Madonna and Child carved by Saint Luke and found by the Guadalupe River in Extremadura, Spain. The first Franciscan missionaries that came to America were from that region. A shrine was built on Tepeyac for the new Guadalupe and, in 1945, Pius XII declared her the "Empress of America."

Nicaragua: December 8

The Virgen del Viejo (Virgin of the Old Man) honors an image that once belonged to an old hermit who was traveling with a group of sailors, when their boat refused to go any further. The sailors made him get off the boat and take his image with him. Only then could they continue their journey and la Virgen del Viejo arrived in Nicaragua. The Viejo in question was probably Francisco de Ahumada, brother to Teresa de Ávila, who brought three images of María to the missionaries in Guatemala, Perú, and Nicaragua in 1562 as a means of encouraging the evangelization of América.

Panama: December 8

Panama does not have a national patroness, but it does celebrate the Solemnity of her Immaculate Conception as a national holiday. The lack of a national patroness has led to holding various images of María in high esteem. The more popular of these is Nuestra Señora de la Antigua. This painting of the Madonna and Child is in the Church of Chirivi, Tunja, and has had a large following since 1691.

Paraguay: December 8

Nuestra Señora de Caacupe, also known as La Virgen de los Milagros (Miracles) was carved by a Guarani Christian who implored Maria's intercession for protection from nonconverted natives who were chasing him. In gratitude for his safety, he carved two images of María from the tree trunk that had hidden him. The larger one (50 centimeters) was donated to the church of Tobati. She is also known as La Virgen Azul (Blue Virgin) de Paraguay because she wears a blue cloak over a white tunic.

Peru: September 24

The Mercedarian Friars built the first Christian church in Lima, Peru. They dedicated it to their patroness, the Virgen de la Merced (Mercy). The Mercedarians were founded in the thirteenth century to buy freedom for slaves or offer to take their place. For this reason the Virgen de la Merced is often depicted with bags of money. She is also depicted with broken chains, indicating the desire for liberation that is part and parcel of oppressed and marginalized peoples. In 1730, the Peruvians took her as their patroness.

Puerto Rico: November 19

In 1969, on the anniversary of Puerto Rico's discovery by Europeans, Paul VI declared Nuestra Señora Madre de la Divina Providencia (Mother of Divine Providence) as patroness of the Island. La Providencia is an image of María sitting down with the child Jesus asleep on her lap and was first brought to the Island by Bishop Gil Esteve y Tomás in 1851.

Spain: October 12

On October 12, when Latino/as commemorate el Día de la Raza (Day of the People), Spaniards are celebrating Santa María del Pilar, María's oldest known apparition. It is believed that before her assumption, she made an appearance to the Apostle James (Santiago) in Zaragosa, Spain. She wanted to encourage him not to give up on the people living on the Iberian peninsular. She gave him a small image of herself with the child Jesus standing atop a pillar. Pope Clement XII declared October 12 her feast day in remembrance of the Christianized Hispanic arrival in America.

Spain (Extremadura): September 8

Although this image is not a national patroness, she is of special importance to Latino/a Marianism. She gave her name to María de Tepeyac and her dark skin paves the way for the dark and mestizo images of María venerated by many Latino/as. Her shrine is in the town of Cáceres by the Guadalupe River where the image was found in 1326. Documentation found with this dark image of Mary and the child Jesus states that Saint

Luke carved the evangelist. Through a series of events, the image ended up in Sevilla, Spain, in the latter half of the sixth century. In 711, Christians buried Luke's image of the Madonna and Child near the Guadalupe River to protect it from the Moors. It lay hidden for over 600 years until the Virgin Mary revealed its location to Gil Cordero.

Uruguay: November 4

La Virgen de los Treinta y Tres (of the 33) is a 36-centimeter wood carving of María. This originally Jesuit image wears a rather large crown, which was given to the statue by a military general in honor of Uruguay's independence. She is named after the 33 people who took charge of the war of independence in the early 1800s. In 1962, John XXIII named her patroness of Uruguay.

Venezuela: September 8

Nuestra Señora de Coromoto represents an apparition of Mary to the Cacique natives. The Caciques resisted the evangelization efforts of the missionaries, until Mary appeared to them on the water and invited them to receive baptism. When the Cacique chief continued to resist conversion, she appeared to him in his hut. It is said that he went after her, and when he grabbed her, she disappeared and he found a holy card of her holding Jesus on her lap in his hand. Pius XII named her patroness of Venezuela in 1944.

U.S. Hispanic Marianism

After the crucified Christ, the image of María is the single most important religious symbol among U.S. Hispanics. Among Latino/as, however, María is never just Mary, she is *la madre* (the mother), madre of Jesus, and madre of Hispanics. This is especially important to people who have had to leave their mothers behind in countries south of the border. For many, la madre is Guadalupe.

In the United States, Guadalupe is such a strong cultural symbol among Mexican Americans and other Latino/as that many wanting to reach out to Latino/as are learning to appreciate her importance. Guadalupe/Mary is being considered as helpful to Protestant pastoral ministry and to Hispanic women's liberation. These new considerations are built upon and different from Roman Catholic considerations of Guadalupe/Mary.

Marian devotion is common among most Roman Catholic cultural groups, but in Latino/as, this devotion is closely tied to cultural self-identity. This is especially true of Guadalupe and Mexican identity on both sides of the Rio Grande. In the United States, roughly three out of every five Latina/os are of Mexican origin. This fact, plus the Catholic Church's making Guadalupe the Empress of America has its ramifications on overall Latina/o Marian devotions. The story of the Guadalupan event at Tepeyac seems to be the glue that holds Latino/as of various countries of origin together. In the Mexican mind-set, she came to a land of desolation where death seemed to reign supreme and brought new life.

Mexican American devotion to Guadalupe does not look any different than Mexican devotion does. What is different is Mexican American theological reflection on Guadalupe. Thanks to the work of Virgilio Elizondo, Latino/a theologians begin their considerations of María, especially Guadalupe with contextualization. The image of Guadalupe that reigns supreme in the popular heart is being considered in its historical and mariological contexts.

U.S. Hispanic contribution to Mariology is Mary's option for the poor, and her assistance in the work of evangelization. In Guadalupe of Tepeyac, these two things translate as the dignity of the mestizo and the importance of inculturation to the spread of the Gospel. In Guadalupe, Hispanic theologians find a locus for theological reflection on the new mestizaje continuing among the various generations of Latina/os in the United States. Contextualized studies of the Guadalupan event reveal inculturation as an essential means of evangelization. The contextualized study of the María at Tepeyac has also led theologians to consider Guadalupe a theophany, which is to say a manifestation of God. In Guadalupe, God has revealed God's self as one who loves the marginalized and oppressed and gives them the dignity of the children of God.

Both Latin American and U.S. Hispanic theologians are reconsidering the importance of Mary to our understanding of God and especially of the Holy Spirit. Once again Mary's role as model of the Church is being underscored. She is the model of what it means to be a disciple: children of the Father, mothers, brothers, and sisters of the Son, and spouses of the Holy Spirit. A revisiting of the Lucan Mary reveals a woman in whom the Spirit is at work, a woman who prays and takes action. In both Guadalupe and Luke's Mary, Marianism can be purged of the use of humility and docility to keep women "in their place." Latino/a theologians are discovering that Marianism can and must be liberating if it is to be Spirit filled.

Conclusion

A popular Spanish hymn, "Santa María del Camino" (Saint Mary of the Journey) written in the latter half of the twentieth century puts it very well when it requests "Ven con nosotros al caminar; Santa María ven" (Come and walk with us; Saint Mary come). The song virtually removes Mary from an altar requesting her presence in the *lucha cotidiana* (everyday struggle) for a better world. U.S. Hispanic Marian devotion continues to have the trappings of traditional Marianism: the Rosary, interest in Marian apparitions, and turning to Mary as mother. At the same time, advances in a more liberating understanding of Mary/Guadalupe are beginning to show themselves in popular religiosity as U.S. Hispanic theology reflects on María's importance to mestizaje, inculturation, our understanding of the Holy Spirit, Christian discipleship, and the work of liberation.

Gilberto Cavazos-González

References and Further Reading

Alvarez del Real, María Eloísa. *Santuarios de la Virgen María, Apariciones y Advocaciones* (Panamá: Editorial América, S.A., 1990).

Elizondo, Virgilio. *Guadalupe: Mother of the New Creation* (Maryknoll, NY: Orbis Books, 1997).

Gasventa, Beverly Roberts, and Cynthia L. Rigby. *Blessed One: Protestant Perspectives on Mary* (Louisville, KY: Westminster John Knox Press, 2002).

Lozano-Díaz, Nora. "Ignored Virgen or Unaware Women: A Mexican-American Protestant Reflection on the Virgen of Guadalupe." *A Reader in Latina Feminist Theology: Religión and Justice*, ed. María

Pilar Aquino, Daisy L. Machado, and Jeanette Rodriguez (Austin: University of Texas Press, 2003).

Montecino, Sonia. *Madres y huachos. Alegorías del mestizaje Chileno [4ed.]* (Santiago: Catalonia Editorial, 2007).

Pelikan, Jaroslav. *Mary Through the Centuries: Her Place in the History of Culture* (New Haven, CT: Yale University Press, 1998).

VOODOO

The belief known as Vodou in Haiti is called Voodoo in Georgia, Louisiana, and Mississippi. Originally it was a religion that slaves brought from West Africa. In Haiti, Vodou encountered the Roman Catholic Church, which was part of the colonial structure. In the southeastern United States it was Christian mysticism and folk religion combined with religious practices and beliefs from West Africa that created Hudu or Hoodoo. Hoodoo evolved into a system of magic, herbalism, divination and sorcery, to become more than just an organized religious ritual.

Vodou in Haiti, as well as Santería in Cuba, were influenced by the Roman Catholicism brought by the conquistadores to the Caribbean. The Spanish *Reconquista* of the fifteenth century was strongly shaped by a crusading spirit in European Catholicism. A dominant factor in Spain was a folk Catholicism influenced by local religious beliefs. Vodou in Haiti encountered a French Catholicism that was also an integral part of the colonial system. Through interaction and transformation, Haitian Vodou and Cuban Santería became hybrid religious systems with their own unique rituals, dynamics, and energies, while preserving some of the sacramental and ritualistic dimensions of European Catholicism. The core of their African religious heritage, common to both, was the Yoruba religion. At the heart of their sacrificial, cosmological, spiritual, and ethical principles, they experience a deep sense of the divine in daily life. With these principles, Cubans and Haitians in exile maintain a religious and cultural identity that survives in the challenging realities of people in diaspora, particularly in the United States.

Haitian Vodou developed into a dynamic belief system incorporating and integrating new elements, forming a new synthesis with its own emphasis and rituals. It maintained the core of African beliefs, which consisted of spiritual forces in the universe and how these forces are present both in creation and in human life. God as creator is at the center of the cosmos (*Le Bon Die*) and the *voduns* (spirits) are manifestations of the divine in earthly situations. There is a strong oral tradition based in faith stories and myths shared from generation to generation intended to honor deities and venerate the ancestors.

What is considered today as the Caribbean is the by-product of a colonial enterprise in which slavery and plantation economy (primarily cane sugar), as well as race and class within Creole culture and institutions, forged a Caribbean identity. A major component of that identity is African, introduced to the Caribbean in the seventeenth century via the slave system. An African labor force was created to work the new sugar plantations. The Portuguese established a slave-trading system with Spain and England to bring slaves from Guinea to islands throughout the Caribbean, including Hispaniola. The colonizers and the soon-to-be colonized started a complex process in the formation (*mestizaje*) of new racial, social, ethnic, religious, and cultural entities. The slave trade and the slave-trade system lasted two centuries, deepening both the political and the economic domination in a colonial society.

One of the most important aspects of Afro-Caribbean religions is the faith of a people expressed in popular religiosity that is as complex and diverse as colonial domination itself. On each Caribbean island, religion plays a dominant role. The most dominant Afro-Caribbean religious movements were Santería in Cuba and Vodou in Haiti, the latter being influenced by Rastafarianism, a twentieth-century religious movement founded in Jamaica. These religious movements show a strong element of religious, cultural, and anthropological integration, a distinctive worldview from African religion, and a resistance to colonial domination.

Vodou developed and adapted as part of the liberating process toward independence in Haiti, becoming the religion of former slaves. One key element is that the followers of Vodou were open to innovation and adaptation in an increasing process of synthesis more than syncretism. The interaction between Dahomean spirits and Roman Catholic saints developed new rituals where people's daily experience of the divine was accomplished through dance, symbols, herbs, sacrifices, and customs. These new rituals and ceremonies were highly influenced by components from the Igbo and Yoruba of Nigeria, and the Bakongo of Central Africa. Even Islamic elements influenced the development of these new expressions of worship. Also, the original occupants of the Caribbean—the Taíno and Arawak Indians—who venerated their own deities were influential in the formation of Haitian Vodou. The Kongo component or Kongo rite or Lemba was influential in the northern part of Haiti, while in the southern Haiti the Kongo influence called Petro was more influential.

Vodou is a cultural event as much as it is a religious ceremony. It integrates ethical values and a deep reverence for life, emphasizing honor and respect for God, the spirits, family, society, and one's self. The metaphor of the extended family can be applied to a Vodou house or society that is organized as an independent unit, but many times interacts with other societies. The basic beliefs of Vodou include the centrality of the *houmfort* (temple) and the key role played by religious leaders, specifically the *houngan* (man) and the *mambo* (woman) who are invested with authority and divine knowledge. The *houngan* and the *mambo* are healers with knowledge of herbs and are able to identify diseases and natural medicines that might be applied to specific illnesses. It includes some basic knowledge of human behavior and the role of the community in the healing process. The lay people bring offerings from nature, including the sacrifice of chickens, goats, or bullocks. Human sacrifice was never part of these ceremonies. As *papa* (*houngan*) and *mama* (*mambo*), they mediate with the *loas* or spirits, the gods, and the departed ancestors.

These *loas* are protectors of the communities, receiving the devotion and veneration of believers. The *zaka* and the *guede* (divinities) are invoked in the *rada* ceremony, inducing the possession of spirits, thus revealing the spiritual energy of the *loas*. The spirits are divided into two categories, hot and cool. The cool spirits are under the *Rada* category and are congenial and benevolent, while the hot *Petro* spirits are restless and more aggressive. Their character and behavior is not determined to be good or evil.

Every believer has an *asiento* or "owner of their head" who can possess the devotee. The believer can experience these possessions by dancing, wheeling, or leaping. The hope of the possessed is receiving a blessing. The songs and prayers are important elements in the liturgy, complemented with offerings to the *loas*, praising and honoring them and invoking their manifestation. As the songs continue, the spirits manifest themselves in the dancing individuals who are expecting divine visitation. These spirits act and speak through the one possessed. The ultimate goal of the Vodouisant (believer) is to seek harmony with nature, family life, personal relationships, and the community.

Haitian Vodou provided the roots of resistance to former slaves, the hope for a better future to the Haitian people in building the first African republic in the world (1804), the capacity to dream and struggle for justice to African American ex-slaves in southeastern United States, and spiritual energy and inspiration to the Haitian Diaspora in many parts of the United States. As a religion and cultural expression, Vodou was an integral part of the Haitian population and its colonial heritage. For centuries it operated as a quasi-clandestine practice of the slaves, a faith to resist the oppression and economic exploitation of a brutal slave system. When the independence movement succeeded in establishing a new republic, Vodou continued to be a major force in the spiritual experience of Haitians and a cultural component in the configuration of a new nationality.

François Duvalier (1957–1971), a strong man who knew very well the history of oppression and successive dictatorships in the country, was able to establish a regime in which Vodou played a central role. Duvalier, an astute medical doctor who developed a close relationship with the peasants and studied closely their daily experiences, was able to discern that voodoo was a predominant force both culturally and religiously. He manipulated this experience and combined it with a paternalistic authority expressed in a dictatorial and brutal regime. He became an open believer of Vodou and related to Vodou practices and *houngans*. He created an intelligence network in which many of these *houngans* became torturers and informants in what was known as the *tonton makouts*. Many stories were told about his private practice of magic and sorcery. Duvalier was the president that really put together recognition of Vodou as the dominant religion and a religious experience manipulated for political purposes. He also confronted the Catholic Church, and he humiliated the French clergy by deportation or repression and silence.

For centuries the Catholic Church in Haiti assumed an ambiguous position with regard to voodoo. Many bishops considered Vodou a religion of obscurantism and barbarism, plagued with superstitions and demonic spirits. Very few priests make a serious attempt to discern the meaning and place of voodoo in Haitian history, culture, and society. More recently, Jean-Bertrand Aristide, a Catholic priest elected president of the country, tried to reverse the traditional attitude of the Catholic Church by promising to officially recognize Vodou as a national religious movement, donating land to build temples, and asking Vodou leaders to help in national reconciliation

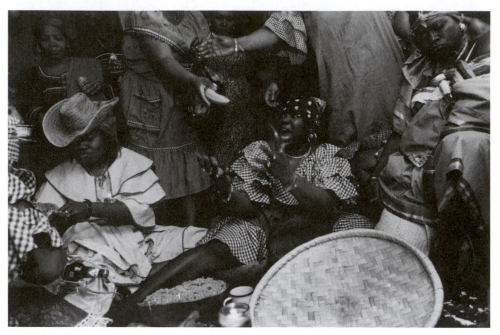

Preparation for a voodoo ceremony in Brooklyn, New York. (Marc Asnin/Corbis Saba)

toward the much needed end to violence in Haitian society. Aristide was also reversing the paternalistic attitude and manipulation observed by François Duvalier in the late 1950s.

The Protestant movements in the Caribbean played an ambiguous role with regard to the religious experiences of the slaves, and particularly that of Vodou. Vodou was often viewed with suspicion as an expression of heathen and infidel people in need of the enlightened and civilizing values of the Protestant faith. In recent decades, neo-Pentecostal and charismatic groups from the United States and Europe have insisted on a prosperity theology and a gospel of success that see Vodou religion as alienating and retrograde. An aggressive evangelistic effort by conservative evangelicals, aiming at converting vodouisants to their brand of Christianity, is extending its influence both in Haiti and among Haitians in the Diaspora. Haitian Vodou continues to play a central role in that society. It continues to be a source of hope and resistance in the midst of instability and uncertainty.

Haitian Vodou was officially recognized in 2003. It has shown a capacity to survive in a continuous process of adaptation to the political, cultural, social, and spiritual challenges in a country torn apart by violence, political turmoil, and extreme poverty. Nonetheless, many Haitians migrated to other parts of the Caribbean, and particularly to the United States. They risk their lives in search of better living conditions and a better future for their families. And they bring their Vodou faith with them. The faith was established in Chicago, Miami, New York, and other major cities in the 1960s and 1970s, as part of the waves of Haitian immigrants coming to the United States. The story of Mama Lola, a

Haitian Vodou priestess in Brooklyn, New York, and her family as immigrants in the United States, their struggles and sufferings, is a good example of Haitian Diaspora and the role of Vodou in their lives. A strong presence at the beginning of the twentieth century of Haitian Vodou in Cuba interacted with Santería and its Yoruba heritage, allowing for the adoption of new *loas* to their system, including the formation of *ogunismo*, a variant of Haitian Vodou in Cuba.

One important dimension of Haitian Vodou and its influence needs to be assessed with regard to the religious culture of the Haitian people. Many autochthonous religious groups, including those Evangelical and Protestant churches planted initially by missionaries from the United States, Canada, and Europe, received the impact and incorporated in their worship dances, symbols, and selective practices inherited from Vodou.

Today, Haitian Vodou, and vodouisants in the Diaspora in other countries, is challenged by the changing face of the Caribbean, and particularly in Haiti, in the context of a globalized world in which religious experience is affected by an expansive religious market competing for the lives and loyalty of traditional religious believers. All religious movements are influenced by this global economy. All religious experiences are pressed to respond to the challenges of new technologies, new information and discoveries, new dimensions of social relationships, and new spiritual dimensions, in which ethical and moral values become crucial in the global era. The teleinformational and technological revolutions have expanded traditional views about religion, providing for international interconnections and interdependence. World economies are more interdependent in this global market, which expands its trading capacity, opens new markets, deregulates prices, promotes competitiveness, and offers the possibility of a free market. Religion plays a crucial role in the market economy. Vodou is one of those religious systems challenged by this global context.

The first challenge has to do with the cultural resistance and faith of the people. How people interact and make transactions with new religious systems and spiritualities is crucial. Second, how to promote peace and reconciliation in societies plagued with sociopolitical conflict and a spiral of violence becomes a priority. Third, extreme poverty is increasingly moving toward levels of misery and exclusion for the majority of the population and creates frustration and desperation. Haiti is one of the poorest countries in the world by any standards. Fourth, the role of religion has the potential of becoming a transforming element, but it can also be used to promote resignation and hopelessness. All religious symbols carry either a liberating power or an alienating inertia.

Some important lessons can be learned by institutional churches about an Afro-Caribbean religious experience like Vodou. Going beyond the prejudices of the past 500 years, acknowledging the African worldview as a valid way of understanding and experiencing the divine is a good place to start. Accepting that there is a spiritual realm not always discernible intellectually and logically in this kind of religious experience is another helpful approach. The interaction between dances, movement, rhythm, and the expressions of the body in worship could be another important dimension, neglected many times in westernized liturgical experiences. Caring for the sick and their daily needs, both material and spiritual, are two dimensions present in the priestly roles of religious leaders in Vodou. For these reasons, a need exists for the Catholic Church and mainline Protestant denominations to rediscover and engage Vodou.

Carmelo E. Álvarez

References and Further Reading

Desmangles, Leslie G. *The Faces of the Gods: Vodou and Roman Catholicism in Haiti* (Chapel Hill: University of North Carolina Press, 1992).

Dixie, Quinton, and Juan Williams. *This Far by Faith* (New York: Harper Collins Publishers, 2003).

Hurbon, Laennec. *Voodoo: Search for the Spirit*, trans. Lory Frankel (New York: Harry N. Abrams, 1995).

Metraux, Alfred. *Voodoo in Haiti*, trans. Hugo Charteris (New York: Oxford University Press, 1959).

Pinn, Anthony B. *Varieties of African American Religious Experience* (Minneapolis: Fortress Press, 1998).

YOUNG LORDS PARTY

The Young Lords Organization (YLO) originated in the streets of Chicago as a turf gang to provide protection from other ethnic gangs in the neighborhood. In the beginning, the Young Lords were composed mainly of first- and second-generation working-class Puerto Rican youth that arrived in Chicago during the migration of the 1950s. Although the Young Lords were mostly composed of Puerto Ricans, the membership of the organization boasted multiethnicity, including Latino/as from diverse national origins and African Americans. The hope of securing better living conditions in the postwar economy led many Puerto Rican families to relocate to Midwestern cities such as Chicago and Detroit. Yet, these dreams rarely turned into reality as their experience was marked by denigration, discrimination, lack of opportunities, urban poverty, and lack of political clout.

In the midst of the acerbic environment, with little or no opportunity for success, and engulfed in the competition for scarce resources with other ethnic minorities, gang membership became a way to seek success, a sense of security, and accomplishments for many youth as they took to the streets. The chairman of the Young Lords, Jose "Cha Cha" Jiménez, was eventually imprisoned for his gang-related activities. It was during his imprisonment that he became radicalized and motivated to engage in political action on behalf of the Hispanic community. His reading of Thomas Merton's *Seven Story Mountain* and *Malcom X's* autobiography served as a catalyst to ignite political action. After his release from jail, Jiménez redirected the gang's energy into a social movement with a Maoist-Marxist orientation. The gang transformed into a social movement that took on the fight against gentrification of the Lincoln Park neighborhood, poor social services, and a lack of political power to effectuate change. From the organization's beginning in Chicago, chapters were organized in other major cities in the United States such as New York (later the Young Lords Party

Members of the Puerto Rican activist group the Young Lords gather in East Harlem, New York City, in June 1970. (Meyer Liebowitz/New York Times Co./Getty Images)

[YLP]), Philadelphia, and Hartford. It should be noted that these various chapters existed with a large degree of independence from the originating body, but they kept the organization's political outlook alive, wore uniforms, and imitated some of its strategies.

The Maoist-Marxist political orientation did not prevent the Young Lords from making alliances with religious communities, but they were difficult and often sparse. Like many other Marxists throughout Latin America, this group found a way to tap into the religious community of the urban setting they inhabited and to seek a common ground of cooperation with religious bodies for improving the living conditions of Latino/as. The ability to tap into the resources of the Latina/o religious community did not necessarily include an

embrace of a Christian worldview. Instead, the engagement was marked by a willingness to recognize the liberatory potential of the faith of the people and the need to find creative ways to join efforts with them. Furthermore, the Young Lords goaded religious communities to live to their full Christian potential.

Of the many Young Lords' activities (both the YLO and the YLP) two should be highlighted as sites where their importance for the study of Hispanic religion lies. Those two moments are the takeover of McCormick Seminary in Chicago in May 1969 and the takeover of the First Spanish Methodist Church in December 1969 (La Primera Iglesia Metodista Hispana) in New York City. These two events make clear the Young Lords' critique of the church as an institution as well as their awareness that the church plays a vital role in the lives of Latino/as that should not be ignored.

Both events trace their root causes to the same reasons: the institutional church as represented by McCormick Seminary and *La Primera Iglesia Metodista Hispana* fell short of living the Christian mission they professed. They posed similar demands in both cases. They called for the development of child-care facilities for working parents, the development of a breakfast program for children, the opportunity to develop a space for political education, and more concerted investment in social services for the community. These actions, as understood by the Young Lords represented a truer interpretation of the Gospels' meaning and Jesus' mission. After all, if during Jesus' earthly ministry he walked among the poor of the earth, so should the church. In both of these cases, McCormick Seminary and the First Spanish Methodist Church had retreated into a comfortable space where the people's spiritual needs were attended to but not their physical or material ones. Furthermore, they provided services only to their members and not to the immediate community. In their estimation, spiritual needs could not be addressed in isolation from physical or material needs.

Through the running of breakfast programs, clothing drives, legal defense, political education, and health clinics from the space of a church or church-affiliated institution, the Young Lords sought to radicalize the extent of the care the church could provide. The care of the people moves beyond their spiritual needs, instead, they seek to move toward a holistic care of the person. The pressing needs of Latino/a communities—subpar education, social services, and political disenfranchisement—moved the Young Lords to carry out a fight for their rights. Urgency for liberation drove the political agenda that motivated the Young Lords' actions.

For the Latina/o religious ethicist, the history of the Young Lords provides material for reflection of an early expression of liberationist thought by Latino/as in the United States. They stand as an example of radical engagement against the social forces oppressing communities of color in the United States and a call for religious institutions to meaningful Gospel practices in their surrounding community.

Elias Ortega-Aponte

References and Further Reading

Browning, Frank. *From Rumble to Revolution: The Young Lords* (Ithaca, NY: Glad Day Press, 1970).

Melendez, Miguel. *We Took the Streets: Fighting for Latino Rights with the Young Lords* (New York: St. Martin's Press, 2003).

Torres, Andrés, and José E. Velazquez. *The Puerto Rican Movement: Voices from the Diaspora* (Philadelphia: Temple University Press, 1998).

Part 2
ESSAYS

CHRISTOLOGY

Luis G. Pedraja

Through almost two millennia, theologians have struggled with the questions raised in our attempts to understand who Jesus of Nazareth was. The questions arise from our attempts to understand not only the significance of his life, ministry, and death but also his relationship to both God and humanity. In essence, both the Trinitarian and Christological controversies that beleaguered the church for centuries stem from our attempts to understand relationships. While the Trinitarian controversy sought to understand the relationship among our different experiences of God—creator, incarnate, and spirit—the Christological controversy hinges our attempts to understand the relationship between divinity and humanity as experienced in the life and work of Jesus of Nazareth. For over four centuries, the church debated the issue, which culminated in the Council of Chalcedon and its dictum that Jesus was both fully human and fully divine. However, this edict did not fully stem the controversies and our continued attempts at understanding who Jesus is and the significance of his life and ministry.

The Person, Work, and States of Christ

Traditionally, Christology, as a theological enterprise, is divided into three themes. The first theme revolves around the person of Christ and traces our attempts to understand who Jesus is—questions that focus on the relationship between Jesus' humanity and divinity. The second, the work of Christ, explores what Jesus does, that is, the significance of his life, ministry, death, and resurrection—in relation to their significance to humanity and to our understanding of Jesus as both human and divine. The third, an ancient and little known approach called the "states of Christ," follows the kenotic passages of Philippians 2:5–11, where Jesus divests himself of divinity, becomes a humble human being, and is then exalted once again. These three approaches are not separate, but overlap and connect with each other. To understand Christology as framed within the Latino/a context, we must first explore and contextualize these themes further.

589

Jesus' contemporaries did not have the perspective of history and centuries of theological interpretations upon which to draw. They encountered and interacted with someone they knew as Jesus of Nazareth, a human being. While they might have thought of him as an extraordinary human being, a prophet, or a miracle worker, it is doubtful that he had a halo or glowed in the dark. If his divine nature had been evident and undisputable, it is doubtful that he would have met the fate he did or that his nature would have been the subject of centuries of debate. In Jesus, his followers found a unique insight into God and God's work, but whether they fully understood from the beginning that Jesus was divine is still subject to debate. It is only in retrospect that people made a connection between Jesus of Nazareth and God—and even then, the nature of that connection is still unclear.

As the decades and centuries passed, Jesus' followers sought to understand the nature of Jesus' relationship to God. Most of our attempts at understanding Jesus were influenced by our philosophical assumptions of both God and humanity, as well as the use of static philosophical categories such as substance and nature. Being was defined primarily in terms of static and fixed categories influenced by human assumptions of perfection, ideals, and deity. Christologies that emphasized Jesus' divinity over his humanity were called "high Christologies," while those that emphasized his humanity over his divinity came to be termed "low Christologies." In a sense, we can imagine a vertical line with divinity at the top and humanity at the bottom of the line.

The work of Christ is also influenced and connected with our understanding of who Jesus is. Thus, the nature and significance of Jesus' work on earth can also be located within this high Christology–low Christology continuum. Traditionally, the work of Christ has been defined in terms of three roles, what John Calvin calls the *triplex munis* (triple offices). These are Christ as king, priest, and prophet. Naturally, these roles with which theologians identify Christ are artificial and problematic theological constructs. While theologians might identify primarily with one of these roles, most would probably include aspects of the others in their understanding of Christ. Most high Christologies tend to identify with Christ's divinity, authority, and power as king.

While some Latino/a theologians might shy away from this particular understanding and its emphasis on power, along with the risks of the identification of Christ as king with oppressive power structures, there is a strong sense among Latina/os that Christ has authority and power. Without power, Jesus' ability to overcome the power structures of sin, to change the status quo, or to liberate humanity become moot. The average Hispanic at least hopes that Jesus is able to overcome evil, transform lives, and act on his or her behalf. Latino/a theologians might vary on their understanding of the nature of this power, and most understand it in terms of empowerment instead of an identification with oppressive power structures.

Others emphasize Jesus' priestly role as an intermediary or intercessor on our behalf. Again, this understanding of the work of Christ is important to Latino/as. It is important in that as a "priest" Jesus not only intercedes and advocates on our behalf but also identifies with us. Our notions of the atonement and salvation tend to be ones not of Jesus paying a price to a vengeful God who has been offended, as in Anselm's understanding of the atonement, but on Jesus' vicarious suffering, not just for us, but as one of us. This does not mean that some Hispanics do not understand Jesus' role as priest as bearing our sin, ransoming us from the power of evil, paying our debt, or even vanquishing the powers of death and sin—many Latina/os understand Christ's work in this way. What it means is that the emphasis tends to be more on Christ's example and identification with our sin, as well as Jesus' love for humanity, all of which resonate more with Peter Abelard's theory of the atonement.

Most Latino/a theologians tend to emphasize Jesus' role as prophet due to the significant influence of Latin American liberation theologies and their shared interest in socioeconomic justice. The understanding of sin in terms of oppression in these theologies, concerns for socioeconomic justice, and emphasis on God's preferential option for the poor tended to place greater emphasis on Jesus' work, particularly in terms of Jesus' preaching and prophetic role. As a result, most Latino/a theologies tend to have "lower Christologies," emphasizing Jesus' humanity, prophetic message, and work. This does not negate or diminish their understanding of Jesus' divinity, but rather, it reveals a radical difference between traditional understandings of divinity and Latino/a theological understanding of divinity.

Christologies tend to fall somewhere along the continuum between high Christologies and low Christologies, depending on how much emphasis is given to Jesus' divinity as opposed to his humanity. If we were to look at this continuum, at the top, we find Docetism, as well as some forms of Gnosticism, that emphasized Jesus' divinity to such an extent that they obscured or denied his humanity. On the other end of the spectrum were theologies such as Adoptionism, the belief that Jesus was merely a good man adopted by God and filled with the Spirit, or theologies that thought Jesus was a prophet. However, regardless of where on the continuum these theologies were, they had a common trait. They contrasted humanity and divinity. Jesus had to be one or the other. The more he was of one, the less he was of the other. The juxtaposition of humanity and divinity is problematic not only in the philosophical and theological sense, where the two might be understood as different essences, natures, or beings, but it is also problematic in the socioeconomic sense of what is implied in the manner we understand each.

Christological Heresies and Latino/a Christology

Latino/a theologians offer unique insights on the polarization of the person of Christ on this continuum of high and low Christologies, including the extreme positions of Docetism and Adoptionism. While both Docetism and Adoptionism would eventually be rejected as heretical, both extremes still persist in the ways that we try to understand the relationship between Jesus' humanity and divinity. To say that Hispanics subscribe to either, both, or neither would be wrong. The ways in which most Latino/as understand who Jesus is and what Jesus did are as diverse as our communities. But for Latina/o theologians, these extremes hold dangers to our community and to our faith, not simply because they go against the orthodoxy of the church, but because they each have cultural, economic, social, and political implications for us all.

In his book, *Mañana*, Justo González argues that each extreme poses a danger to the development of Latino/a Christologies. Christologies that emphasize Jesus' divinity over his humanity tend to view the material world as base and inferior. In these

Christologies, the spiritual overshadows the physical, causing us to trivialize or ignore physical circumstances and needs. The focus of these theologies is otherworldly. According to González, this is problematic for communities that suffer under economic and social oppression. The suffering of this world becomes inconsequential and expected. Rather than seeking social justice and attempting to change oppressive socioeconomic structures, emphasis is given to spiritual conversion. Sin is solely a spiritual problem and our bodily existence is minimized. Our goal is to escape the material world and seek the higher spiritual realities. By spiritualizing Jesus, it is easier to allow the status quo to go unchecked, making it easier to ignore the physical needs of individuals and less likely that we would strive to transform society. Ultimately, this extreme separates the spiritual from the material, increasing the distance between God and humanity. Humanity and divinity are so radically different that it rejects the incarnation, removes Jesus from the messy realities of the world, and makes it impossible for him to identify with human suffering and death.

Adoptionism, on the other hand, emphasizes Jesus' humanity. He is one of us, chosen by God and filled with the Holy Spirit. This makes it possible for Jesus to identify with our humanity, frailty, suffering, and death. However, although God can adopt a human being and coexist with humanity through the Holy Spirit, humanity and divinity are still considered radically different. In addition, adherence to this extreme, according to González, can give credence to the "local boy does good" or "anyone can make it" myths. As a result, it can further oppressive myths that one can succeed simply through hard work, that people of means earned their position in life, and that the poor are lazy.

Both of these extremes share common preconceptions about humanity and divinity, assuming that the two are radically different. Even later attempts at understanding Christology, such as the Antiochene and Alexandrine schools, which allowed for both Jesus' divinity and his humanity, still operated under the assumption that both divinity and humanity were radically different.

Chalcedon, by decreeing that Jesus was both, fully human and fully divine, appeared to settle the matter. Jesus was fully both. Yet, while Chalcedon provided a rule or guide by which our language about Jesus was defined, it did not really clarify the relationship. Chalcedon simply created a paradigm that framed the question as a paradox. In addition, it still retained an essentialist perspective that understood both divinity and humanity as radically different. While the two could fully coexist in the person of Christ, the way they coexisted was not clearly defined, relegating the relationship between divinity and humanity as encountered in Jesus of Nazareth to the realm of mystery.

Chalcedon's resolution, that Jesus is both fully human and fully divine, does not completely resolve the paradox. If one considers that humanity is created in the image of God, it may be better to seek the similarities than to emphasize the differences—to understand how humans bear the image of God. For González, the answer lies not in the contrast between the human and divine, but in the common traits we share, especially love.

Language, Culture, and Borderland Christology

Latino/a Christology, like Latina/os, exists at the borders—not only as defined by the boundary between nations, but also in cultural, bodily, economic, and sociopolitical realities. In the Spanish language we speak of *Jesucristo*, Jesus and Christ are not separate words that speak to a dual reality. The human person, Jesus, and his role as the Christ are inescapably interconnected in the language and minds of the people. In addition, unlike English, where the casual use of the name of Jesus is considered sacrilegious, in Spanish it is invoked in our ordinary existence almost as a prayer, as well as used to name our children. Naming children Jesus and invoking Jesus' name is in part a product of the culture. Spain, for centuries before the conquest of the Americas, was a country where Muslims, Jews, and Christians coexisted with each other—sometimes in a spirit of tolerance, other times at war with one another. During this time, Christians, who lived with people named Mohammad and Moses, would honor their identity by naming children Jesus.

While naming children Jesus might have been a product of history and culture, there is still a certain cultural implication to the way we talk about Jesus. In *Jesus Is my Uncle: Christology from a Hispanic Perspective,* I argue that the language both reflects and affects a more immanent understanding of God. In Hispanic culture, God is more closely identified with humanity and inhabits our world both spiritually and incarnationally. In contrast, the English language tends to evoke a more transcendent understanding of God. In order to respect God's holiness, there is a tendency to invest things associated with the divine with a greater degree of otherness that proscribes the use of certain terms in ordinary language and creates a more effective distance between God and the ordinary language of human existence. In a sense, both linguistically and culturally, Latinos/as reflect a lower or at least more immanent Christology than is expressed in English.

Orlando Costas, for instance, speaks of the incarnation as the ultimate validation of cultural contextualization. Jesus, becoming human, enters into a particular human culture at a unique point in history. This act invests humanity with a sacramental presence and demonstrates that God is revealed not in the abstract as removed and separated from culture and history, but rather God is revealed through culture and history. In contrast to Neibuhr's dichotomies of Christ and culture, for Latino/a theologians, Christ is manifest through culture. If Jesus was indeed a historical figure born into a particular time and place, as well as a culture, then we cannot separate who Jesus is from a cultural interpretation. On the contrary, the incarnation, Latino/a theologians would argue, demonstrates that God is revealed through culture. Albert Schweitzer, in his classic book *The Quest of the Historical Jesus*, makes the argument that our attempts to understand who Jesus was as a historical personage, divested from all the accruements of faith and theological interpretations, still tends to look like the person undertaking the task. In other words, we tend to make Jesus into our image.

Most Latino/as tend to identify with Jesus. Like Latina/os, Jesus was born into an occupied country with political unrest. He lived in a country at the margins, being neither Roman nor Greek. In addition, he identified not with the rich and powerful of his time, but with the poor and the outcast. He was not even part of the religious establishment. As many Hispanics, Jesus was persecuted by the political and religious powers of his time, unjustly imprisoned for his views and actions, tortured, and executed. Jesus suffered and died. Latino/as, like many others who often exist at the margins of culture and society, identify with Jesus because Jesus is one of them. In Jesus, we find someone who understands and who can identify with our plight. Such a God—who experiences human suffering and death—can understand, sanctify, and vindicate our own suffering and pain.

The incarnational, immanent, nature of Latino/a spirituality allows for a stronger identification with Jesus, without necessarily diminishing the understanding of Jesus as divine. While some Latina/os do tend to emphasize Jesus' humanity over his divinity, the contrast between Jesus' humanity and divinity is not as pronounced or dichotomous. In a sense, we can say that God is accessible through Jesus' humanity. Latino/a Christologies for the most part shy away from the more radical polarities drawn between God and humanity. For example, Orlando Espín's Christology focuses on the human Jesus, exploring what we know about Jesus both through the lenses of the historical context and the faith of the church. We understand who Jesus is through his human experiences and understanding of God. Jesus' actions and message reveal an understanding of God as caring, involved with human affairs, and committed to a transformed social order manifest in his message about the kingdom of God. For Espín, we know the divine through Jesus. Jesus' death, vanquishment, and apparent failure provide an alternate view of who God is—located not in the throne of power, but in the midst of suffering, humiliation, and death. Oppressed communities can identify with such a God, who in turn also identifies with them. Thus, there is *antologia entis* that provides us a glimpse into the divine that is different from our own philosophical constructions of perfection, detachment, and absolute power. In turn, it vindicates our suffering and provides for the possibility that God can be found in the suffering of the cross. To use Martin Luther's phrase, Latino/a Christology is a theology of the cross.

Another area that the identification between the Latino/a culture and Christology occurs is through cultural parallels. It is common for theologies that acknowledge their cultural context to draw parallels between their own culture and biblical events. In *Galilean Journey,* one of the seminal books of Latino/a theology, Virgilio Elizondo makes a connection between Jesus' Galilean roots and Hispanic identity. Galilee's geographic location as a remote border province allows Elizondo to draw a comparison between the experience of Latina/os at the borders of the United States and Jesus. Existing at geographic and cultural crossroads, both Jesus and Latino/as are caught between cultures. Whether it is that of a Jewish boy growing up in a Roman-occupied country at a border town or a Mexican American growing up in San Antonio, both live at cultural crossroads. While Chalcedon was not able to resolve how both divinity and humanity could exist in the person of Jesus, the cultural identity of Hispanics allows us to understand how one person can embody two realities. Thus, the Galilean identity of Jesus parallels our own borderland experience, both affirming our own experience and giving us insights into the hypostatic union, how Jesus could be both human and divine.

Beyond our identification with Jesus' Galilean experience in the borderlands of culture, the *mestizo* and *mulato* identity of many Latino/as provides us with additional paradigms for understanding the hypostatic union. First, Hispanics not only exist at the cultural borderlands, able to function to some extent in two or more cultures, they also embody various cultures, races, and languages. Thus, Latino/as know viscerally what it is like to embody the tension of disparate realities that may seem incongruous with one another.

Some might fear that speaking of the hypostatic union in terms of *mestizaje/mulatez* is reminiscent of heresies, such as Eutyches, who claimed that divinity and humanity mixed in Jesus to create a new reality. However, Chalcedon's rejection of Eutyches was due to the fear that such a mixture would lead to Jesus' divinity overshadowing his humanity or diluting both. Underlying Chalcedon's rejection are various assumptions that might not be as relevant today. First, it assumes that there are two static substances or essences, unique to themselves—one human and the other divine. Second, it assumes that these essences are incompatible with each other and that one could overtake the other. These were valid concerns given the philosophical categories available at the time. Today, there are other options for understanding identity and being that use dynamic rather than static understandings of identity, personality, and continuity. Thus, the dangers of different substances dominating or intermingling are no longer rigidly determined. In addition, our understanding of God and humanity do not necessarily lead to radical differentiations that would cause one to negate the other and make their coexistence untenable.

Understanding the hypostatic union in terms of mestizaje/mulatez need not lead to a mixture that diminishes the reality of both or that causes one to overshadow the other. Those of us who embody two or more cultures know that the two do not blend into a melting pot that eradicates the differences and tensions that exist between them. Genetically, our different races can be identified as much as the traits from each race are evident in our futures, skin, and bodies. Latino/as may speak English and Spanish, aware of the differences between the languages even when speaking a mix of the two. We are painfully aware of the tensions between the cultures we inhabit and embody, knowing what aspect of our experience comes from each. We are not an undifferentiated amalgam of cultures and races that melt into each other. Rather, we are both and in a sense more than both by being cognizant of each in ways that others may not be. The embodiment of these cultures not only provides us with a paradigm for understanding the hypostatic union—how divinity and humanity can exist in one person—but also enable us to draw an analogy between our experience and the incarnation.

An added advantage to using the cultural and racial borderland experience to understand Christology comes from the pejorative treatment of those who exist at these crossroads. Being mestizo (a mix of European and indigenous) or mulato (a mix of European and African) also meant embodying a history of domination, subjugation, and rape, as well as not being accepted by either culture or race. It meant being viewed as inferior and treated with disdain. To identify Jesus with those relegated to the margins of society, whether it be through socioeconomic reasons or through racial and cultural discrimination, meant imbuing with value that which was rejected. Jesus identifies with the lowly of society not only through his ministry but through his borderland existence. Like Latino/as who are often viewed with disdain or suffer from various forms of discrimination—economic, cultural, racial, and gender among many —Jesus, too, is marginalized by the elite of his time. Jesus is not only a Jew, a marginal country and sociocultural group in a time dominated by the Greco-Roman ethos, but as a Galilean, Jesus is also marginalized by the centers of Jewish power in Jerusalem. The identification of God's presence on earth with a marginalized person of humble origins speaks volumes about the contrast between our understanding of God and God's reality, as well as the things we value in society. Thus, while the parallels between the Latino/a identity can provide us with a paradigm for understanding Christ, the incarnation also provides Hispanics with empowerment and value. The crucified man from the margins of society as the locus of God's presence on earth certainly captivates our imagination and provides us with a far richer understanding of God than the philosophical categories.

As Orlando Espín notes, Jesus' death, vanquishment, and apparent failure at the cross helps us understand and rethink how we imagine God. Jesus' human experiences, his way of relating to and understanding God, as well as his actions and preaching, provide us with a unique insight into who and how God is. Regardless of how we might understand Jesus' divinity or humanity, he provides us with a unique view into God. No longer is God the detached, immutable, impassible, remote perfection of the philosophical ideal. God, as experienced through Jesus, reveals a God who is caring, who meddles in human affairs, and who identifies with those who suffer more than with those in power. In Jesus, the possibility of human experience revealing God becomes real. Thus, the possibility that the Latino/a experience can also reveal God not only by identification, but as a *locus dei*—a place where God can be found actively present—also becomes real.

Key Paradigm for Latino/a Christology

While Latino/a Christologies provide us with unique insights into Christology as a whole, helping us to better understand the person and the work of Christ, they also gravitate to certain key paradigms and understandings. First, as noted above, Latino/a Christologies draw parallels between the Hispanic experience and Jesus, making it possible to identify with Jesus as one who understands and, to some extent, validates the Latina/o borderland experience and marginalization. Thus, Latino/a theologians tend to identify with Jesus as a mestizo, a mulato, or even as a *sato* (mutt), as Loida Martell-Otero does. This helps locate God's activity in our midst, just as the incarnation places God within human history, God can also be found in the struggle and suffering of humanity at the borderlands, at the margins, at the places where we seldom seek God. In the same manner that Liberation theologians draw an identification between God and the poor, Latino/a theologians extend this identification to cultural and racial dimensions of marginalization. Jesus allows us to see God as present in the barrio, in the junkie dying alone on a rooftop—where Recinos sees Jesus. God is relocated from the luxury and power of palace halls to the grungy dimly lit back alleys of life. As for Martin Luther, Latino/as reject the theology of power in favor of a theology of the cross—and not only extends to but is made possible by our Christology.

Hispanic Christology not only identifies with Jesus' borderland experience, it also identifies with his message. Jesus' prophetic role and message are significant to Latino/as. Inherent in Jesus' preaching is a message of love for everyone, forgiveness, justice for those who suffer at the margins, and the advocacy for a unique understanding of God's reign on earth—the Kingdom of God or, as Ada María Isasi-Díaz argues, the kin-dom—for it is a reign distinguished not by power, but by the equity of love and the valuation of all human life. It is God's family, where we all are God's children. Jesus' message and action not only manifest God's love, but call humanity to act out of love. Justo González, advocates the power of *mañana* in Jesus' message as the vision of God's vision of the future, of what could be, as a judgment on what is and should be changed.

In Elizondo, while the Galilean Principle speaks to Jesus' identity as a mestizo, the Jerusalem Principle addresses Jesus' work in confronting the powers of society, and in doing so risking death. In Jerusalem, Jesus exemplifies God's call to confront injustice and oppression at the risk of one's life. This is a key core of Jesus' message. Love forgives, but love cannot tolerate injustice and oppression either. Love must confront the power of hatred. Finally, it is the Resurrection Principle that empowers Jesus, as well as all of us, to confront the powers of hatred by promising that God will ultimately vindicate and validate our struggle.

Latino/a Christologies place greater emphasis on the work of Christ. We know who Jesus is by what he does. Thus, ultimately the person and work of Christ are collapsed. It is not being divine that allows Jesus to act, but his actions that reveal his humanity. When Latina/os read John 1:1, they do not read "in the beginning was the Word, and the Word was with God, and the Word was God." In the Spanish Bible, the Greek word *logos* is translated as "verb." Thus, rather than in the beginning was the "word," we read, in the beginning was the "verb." In Jesus, God is not merely present as a cognitive content or word. God is present in an active sense. It is God's creative word—God's definitive act and activity that we encounter in Jesus.

Ultimately, Latino/a Christologies reject the harsh dichotomies drawn between humanity and divinity. Rather than arguing that the more divine the less human, there is a drive to identify the parallels between the two. Human beings were created in God's image. While many theologies believe that this image was eradicated by sin, there is nothing in the biblical account that would indicate this is the case. Thus, it is possible for those created in the image of God to bear the image of God. The incarnation is not an anomaly. It is a restoration of what humanity was meant to be. Hispanic theologians directly and indirectly recognize the possibility for God's presence to be found in the midst of humanity. The incarnation attests to this possibility and to its reality. Rather than understanding the person of Christ in a dichotomous sense, Latina/o theology understands it in an active sense. Gonzalez, for instance, argues that virtues such as love, which are shared by both God and humanity, are the key for understanding the juncture between the human and divine. The more we act out of love, the more divinity is revealed through our actions. But the key is ultimately in the actions. The person and the work of Christ are not two separate categories. Jesus is divine by virtue of what he does.

References and Further Reading

De La Torre, Miguel A. *The Quest for the Cuban Christ: A Historical Search* (Gainesville: University Press of Florida, 2002).

Elizondo, Virgilio. *Galilean Journey: The Mexican-American Promise* (Maryknoll, NY: Orbis Books, 1996).

Espín, Orlando O. *The Faith of the People: Theological Reflections on Popular Catholicism* (Maryknoll, NY: Orbis Books, 1997).

Isasi-Díaz, Ada María. *En la Lucha: Elaborating a Mujerista Theology* (Minneapolis: Fortress Press, 1993).

González, Justo. *Mañana: Christian Theology from a Hispanic Perspective* (Nashville: Abingdon Press, 1990).

Pedraja, Luis G. *Jesus Is My Uncle: Christology from a Hispanic Perspective* (Nashville: Abingdon Press, 1999).

Recinos, Harold J. *Who Comes in the Name of the Lord?: Jesus at the Margins* (Nashville: Abingdon Press, 1997).

ECCLESIOLOGY

Nora O. Lozano

Ecclesiology is the study of the church and how the individual Christian lives out his/her life and expresses his/her beliefs within a community of faith. As such, ecclesiology is a rich, challenging, complex, and diverse doctrine that deals with fundamental elements in the life of the Christian churches, as well as with the particular expressions of these elements in different Christian denominations. It is rich because it describes the nature, attributes, mission, government, and sacraments/ordinances of the church, as well as its final hope of an eternal, abundant life with Christ. It is challenging because it reminds Christians daily to live as the body of Christ where each member cares for the other—both spiritually and materially. It is complex because as a concrete, present, corporate expression of the body of believers, it is inextricably tied to issues of culture, identity, power, and control. It is diverse because it embraces a variety of understandings and practices of what church should be—derived from various biblical and denominational perspectives.

In their ecclesiological articulations, Latino/a theologians have embraced the traditional Christian categories or approaches of the study of the church as a way of dealing with this doctrine from their own perspective. They have reflected on the Latina/o church using categories such as the visible and invisible church, or as being one holy, catholic, and apostolic church. Other times, Latino/a theologians ground their reflections in images of the church as the body of Christ, the people of God, or the temple of the Holy Spirit. Still others foreground the mission of the church and consider how that priority shapes or should shape the community of believers. Finally, others reflect on how and why power and control in church governance marginalizes Latinos/as in general from the power structures of their denominations and women in particular from achieving positions of leadership and power.

Given this diversity of approaches, issues, and content, this entry can only introduce some of the major trends in Latina/o ecclesiology. To place these trends in their right context, I will first explore the history of the Latino/a Roman Catholic Church and the major trends and theologians in this type of ecclesiology, and then do the same from a Latina/o Protestant perspective.

Roman Catholic Ecclesiology

The general context of this study of the church is the traditional categories of ecclesiology that have been developed throughout Christian history. The particular context for our purposes is the era of the Latin American conquest during the sixteenth century when the Catholic missionaries and priests came from Spain or Portugal to establish the foundations of the Catholic Church in the Hispanic Americas. Justo González (1990), along with others, affirms that since its beginning the church in Latin America has been divided into two churches: the church of the hierarchy and the popular church or church of the poor. The first one is typically identified with the powers of conquest, colonization, and oppression, and the second with the oppressed and those who opposed such inhumanity.

González (1990) suggests that this tension of commitments and values within the Catholic Church continues to the present in Latin America as well as in the Latino/a church in the United States. In Latin America, this struggle was particularly evident when the underside church raised its voice in favor of the poor and oppressed at the Latin American bishops' assemblies in Medellín (1968) and Puebla (1979). Within the Latina/o experience, this duality in the Catholic Church is particularly visible in the national hierarchy of the church mainly made up of non-Hispanics, while the popular church is predominantly led by Hispanic priests who better understand the struggles and sufferings of the Hispanic people. The task of the popular church and its leaders has been to respond to the spiritual, material, and justice needs of its parishioners. As a result, this popular church has become a voice for the voiceless, and as its leaders start to penetrate the hierarchical structures of the church, they are offering a new way of doing church that is more consistent with the concerns and perspectives of Latino/a Catholics. An example of this new trend is the three *Encuentros Nacionales Hispanos de Pastoral* (1972, 1977, 1985) in which grassroots Hispanics articulated the mission of the church and participated in planning its ministry. González (1990) describes this development as the dawning of a new and hopeful day for the Roman Catholic Hispanic church. These Encuentros and the documents that came from them have become foundational in the articulation of a Latina/o Catholic ecclesiology.

So as Latino/a Roman Catholic theologians articulated different elements of the doctrine of the church, they have increasingly sided with the popular church in order to nurture, strengthen, and empower it. In light of this shift, Jeanette Rodríguez (2006) has reflected on the composition of the church by asking: Who is the Catholic Church? Whereas in the past many Catholics would have responded by saying the Catholic Church is the hierarchy and the priests, Rodríguez (2006), with the "Encuentros Nacionales Hispanos" in mind, suggests instead that the church is present wherever there is a faith community, no matter how small. These faith communities attempt to live according to the model of church in Acts, and in order to do that they follow the pattern of the small Latin American Base Christian Communities in which church members are encouraged to reflect on people's lives in light of their faith. This reflection involves *to see* reality, *to think* about it in a critical way, *to act* or commit to do something about it, *to evaluate* the meetings, and *to celebrate* or share with each other. Rodríguez (2006) reminds us that this model of church is rooted in the particular context of the oppressed and suffering Latino community, which is now called and empowered to follow Jesus' example in being a voice for the voiceless, in seeking out social justice, in struggling to bring liberation to all areas of people's lives, and in worshiping and celebrating the Reign of God in their lives.

Ana María Pineda (1995) has analyzed the ministry of the Latino/a Catholic church by reflecting on the term *pastoral de conjunto* (organized pastoral effort). She reminds us that although this term was present in the deliberations of the Second Vatican Council and in the documents of Medellín and Puebla, it took on a special significance during the three *Encuentros Nacionales Hispanos de Pastoral* when U.S. Hispanics contextualized it to fit the U.S. Latino reality. Pastoral de conjunto is a harmonious coordination of all the aspects of pastoral ministry in the particular social, cultural, and religious context of the people with the goal of continuing the work of Jesus and making more present the Kingdom of God among them. As a concept rooted in the Gospel values and in the best cultural values of the people, pastoral de conjunto has fostered a particular model of church as a family where fraternal love and community are the norm, and where injustice is challenged. These understandings, which are based on the interdependence of the faithful and genuine respect and regard for all, Pineda (1995) suggests are a significant Hispanic contribution to the church and society at large.

Gary Riebe-Estrella (1999) has looked at Latino/a Catholic ecclesiology through the traditional lens of the church as the people of God. He considers this image to be central because of its constant presence in the documents of the three *Encuentros Nacionales Hispanos de Pastoral*. He argues that even though this biblical image has been used in many different ecclesiological articulations, each of these articulations takes on a particular meaning depending on the context and experiences of the group that is defined as "the people of God." Thus, he suggests that for a Latina/o Catholic ecclesiology it is important to define Latino/as as a group that struggles not only with poverty but also with cultural oppression and marginalization that restricts their achievements in educational, employment, and economic areas. Such experiences inevitably shape their understanding of the church as the people of God.

Language is another key factor in understanding this image of the church as the people of God. Latino/as will typically think about it in Spanish as *el pueblo de Dios*, and this notion has particular connotations in the Latina/o mind. The configuration of a *pueblo* is delineated by Latino/as' understanding of who its members are. Furthermore, "pueblo" may denote a geographical town or the people who live in this town. Thus, the pueblo is formed by groups of individual *familias* (families) that through different relationships in the community form the pueblo (the community of a particular town). Of course, these families include not only the nuclear family but the extended family (cousins, aunts, uncles, and grandparents), as well as those added to the family due to significant relationships such as the *compadres* (co-parents) who enter the family when they become a child's *padrino/madrina* (godparent). This sociocentric organic culture, Riebe-Estrella (1999) affirms, is still very predominant among Latino/as and it defines how they understand themselves as *el pueblo de Dios*.

Good Friday passion reenactment in the Pilsen neighborhood of Chicago, Illinois. The reenactment has been a Good Friday fixture in the predominately Mexican community for 31 years. (Getty Images)

Having defined the particular cultural context and web of relationships of Latino/as, Riebe-Estrella (1999) analyzes this image of the people of God and its implications for the Latina/o Catholic Church. He argues that in the Old Testament, Israel was called to be the people of God in order to become a blessing to the nations. In this sense, the Latino/a Catholic Church also has been called to be a blessing to others. Yet the Latina/o Catholic Church also resembles the people of Israel in less desirable characteristics, such as an egocentrism that does not allow them to stop thinking about themselves as the needy ones who are on the receiving end. Riebe-Estrella suggests instead that the Latino/a Catholic Church has much to give to the dominant Anglo culture by living a model of church that moves away from an individualistic life-style to a more social, collective one that lives for the common good. And this is a challenge, for oftentimes in the U.S. Latina/o Catholic landscape this sense of *el pueblo de Dios* is understood narrowly as being restricted to "my local parish" where "my family" worships and serves. This narrow understanding has brought divisions within the parishes of individual cities and has prevented them from working together for the common good. Riebe-Estrella (1999) concludes by inviting Latinos/as to consider that in the New Testament Jesus expanded the notion of el pueblo de Dios to include all of the people who responded positively to his calling, all who were willing to live now in his love, by forming a true sisterhood and brotherhood. This new understanding of el pueblo de

ANTONIO JOSÉ MARTÍNEZ (1793–1867)

Antonio José Martínez was the leading figure among nineteenth-century New Mexican Catholic priests. His numerous accomplishments include a distinguished academic career as a seminarian in Durango, the establishment of a primary school and seminary preparatory school in his hometown of Taos (from which some 30 students went on to be ordained for the priesthood), the operation of the first printing press in what is now the western United States, authorship of numerous books and pamphlets, formal certification as an attorney, and extensive service as an elected New Mexican representative in legislative bodies under the Mexican and later the U.S. governments. In 1854, Frenchman Jean Baptiste Lamy, the newly arrived first bishop of Santa Fe, instituted mandatory tithing and decreed that heads of families who failed to comply be denied the sacraments. Martínez's public contestation of this action eventually led Lamy to excommunicate him from the Catholic Church, which in turn caused a schism between Martínez's supporters and the leaders of the Santa Fe diocese. A controversial figure whom Willa Cather presented in a highly negative light in her infamous novel *Death Comes for the Archbishop*, Martínez and his legacy were defended by contemporary Latino/a writers like Juan Romero who documented his numerous accomplishments.

—TM

Dios calls Latino/a Catholics to live out their Christianity beyond their families and local parishes, embracing the people outside their primary circle of relationships.

Orlando Espín (1995) offers a different and provocative perspective on this doctrine. By dealing with issues of revelation and theological authority within the Catholic Church, he empowers the Latino Catholic Church by affirming the importance of its popular religious expressions as valid and appropriate ways to witness to the revelation of Christian tradition. He thus provides a theological voice to a sector of the church that has often been voiceless. He argues that by the sense of the faithful (*Sensus Fidelium*) is meant the faithful intuitions of the Christian people as they are moved by the Spirit through their interpretation and experience of the Word of God. In order to protect the validity and authenticity of these popular intuitions as an appropriate witness of the revelation, Espín (1995) argues that these expressions need to be confronted with the Bible, the written texts of tradition, and the particular lenses that the theologian may be using as he/she studies them.

One of these Latina/o Catholic popular religious expressions is the celebration of Good Friday. This is the day that Latino/as get together to relive and meditate on the passion of Jesus. This celebration has a special meaning to Latino/as because often they can relate to Jesus' suffering through their own experiences of racism, discrimination, and marginalization. Another popular devotion among Catholic Latino/as is the veneration of the Virgin Mary as the Virgin of Guadalupe, the Virgin del Cobre, or the Virgin of La Caridad. Catholic Latina/os, especially in the Southwest, observe *Las Posadas*, a Christmas celebration that reenacts Joseph's and Mary's search for shelter, as well as *quinceañeras*, a rite of passage that celebrates girls moving from childhood to adulthood.

Protestant Latino/a Ecclesiology

Protestant Latina/o ecclesiology generally includes the traditional categories of ecclesiology that have been developed worldwide in the course of Christian history. Yet the particular context of this Latina/o ecclesiology is that it developed within a Catholic environment and culture that became well established in the Americas after the Conquest, surrounding Latino/a Protestants with Catholic symbols and understandings that inevitably affected their lives. As a way of differentiating themselves from this pervasive Catholicism, Hispanic Protestants have long harbored a radical anti-Catholic feeling that led them to disassociate themselves from the existent culture. Justo González (1990) describes his experience with these dynamics. He grew up in Cuba as a religious minority questioning the values of his own culture. However, when he moved to the United States he experienced what many Protestant Latino/as have also experienced: even though he no longer belonged to a religious minority, he continued to be a minority—though now in the cultural sense. Many of these Protestant Hispanics learned to criticize their original cultures in their countries, and continue this dynamic by questioning and criticizing the dominant Anglo culture that marginalizes them.

Justo González (1990) continues by describing the roots of Hispanic Protestantism in both Latin America and the United States. In Latin America, Protestantism was the result of the missionary work of the nineteenth century as well as of the faith that Protestant immigrants brought with them. Some of these migrants came from northern Europe with their Protestant beliefs and established churches in South America. Others were Latin American migrants who for diverse reasons had been in the United States. They came back to their original lands and brought Protestantism with them. Finally, some churches were formed due to schisms within the Roman Catholic Church.

In the case of the United States, many churches there have been formed by Protestant immigrants from Latin America, and many others by new converts who are looking for an alternative to Catholicism. In general, these Protestant churches are churches of the poor in the sense that they are formed by poor people and are committed to help the poor ones in their communities.

Protestant theologians agree that the articulation of a Protestant Latina/o ecclesiology is a challenge. Juan Francisco Martínez (2006) argues that its difficulty is due to the diversity of views of the church within Protestantism. Justo González (1997) suggests that traditionally this doctrine has played a secondary position in relation to other doctrines due to the following factors: First, the Protestantism that was introduced in Latin America as well as in much of the United States was one centered in the faith of the individual believer, and not in the faith of the community. Consequently, the church was perceived primarily as a vehicle to preach salvation and to nurture those who were saved. A second factor was that this Protestant preaching was done in a predominantly Catholic environment; preachers would often point out the contradictions that they perceived in the Catholic Church, thus provoking an antichurch feeling. Third, as a further challenge to this Catholic environment, the preachers affirmed the authority of the individual in matters of biblical interpretation and questioned the Catholic view of the authority of the community of faith on matters of faith and doctrine. Fourth, during those days of the pre-Vatican II era, the church was understood to be composed of the members of the hierarchy and priests, and not of the common people. People did not see themselves as the church. Fifth, after the Vatican II days, the rise of Pentecostalism among Latino/as in both Latin America and the United States brought a similar challenge to the church, but from a different perspective: the Pentecostals challenged the structure, traditions, and expectations of the churches by emphasizing the freedom of the Spirit. González (1997) suggests that a final challenging factor is that in the United States many Hispanic churches belong to larger White denominations that have marginalized them. Since the Hispanic pastors of these churches tend to have less theological education than their White counterparts, and the lay members tend to be poor and uneducated, they are deprived of positions of leadership within the larger body of the denomination, and in consequence they developed a functioning congregational ecclesiology. All of these factors have hindered the development of a Latino/a Protestant ecclesiology.

In his Latina/o Protestant ecclesiological articulations, Justo González (1997) decided to use biblical metaphors to reinterpret the four traditional and foundational marks of the church: that the church is one, holy, catholic, and apostolic. Gonzálcz (1997) stresses that since the current Latina/o perspective of the church is more missional (what is the church for?), than definitional (what is the church? or who is the church?), in his study he inverts the order of these distinguishing marks. Thus, he begins by defining the apostolic mark of the Latino/a Protestant church. The traditional interpretation of this mark in Protestant circles is conformity to the doctrines and practices of apostolic time. However, González (1997) decides to approach this apostolic mark by analyzing its etymology; "apostle" means to be sent, to have a sense of mission. Considered from this perspective, the Latina/o Protestant church is highly apostolic. In this community the Gospel or the people's need of salvation is presented with a sense of urgency. To be sent to share this salvation is the mission of the church. But this mission is lived from the perspective of a pilgrim people who have not experienced a sense of belonging in the United States, even though some of these people have been here for centuries. Thus, the Latina/o Protestant church is formed by people who are sent, on the march, on a pilgrimage full of joy as well as pain. This pilgrimage is done as a group, and it welcomes whoever wants to join in the marching toward a promised future, to a great *fiesta*.

In much the same way, González (1997) then proceeds to analyze the catholic mark of the Latino/a Protestant church. Traditionally, the term "catholic" has been understood to mean universal, and this meaning has been difficult for the Latina/o churches to embrace. It implies that there is a universal, valid way to be a Christian that excludes the contributions of those who are on the margins, such as Latino/as. González (1997) argues that the true meaning of the word is "according to the whole," which implies a unity where variety is necessary for the group and thus welcome. The best image to convey this idea is the body of Christ where there is room for every person regardless of his/her color, language, or social status. This body is completely interdependent, so if one member suffers, all suffer, and if one member rejoices, all rejoice. Furthermore, this image stresses that in order to have a whole, healthy body, the presence of all of its different members and their contributions are necessary and valuable.

But González (1997) is not quite done. He insists that the notion of the holiness of the church be reinterpreted too. The traditional understanding of this term is derived from the missionaries who evangelized the Hispanic Americas, and who had the tendency to associate holiness with the worthiness or unworthiness of particular persons. This understanding led the Latino/a Protestants to perceive the church as the guardian of morality, and to be extremely judgmental of each other. These dynamics, González affirms (1997), have been very damaging and tragic for the Latino/a church. In his reinterpretation of this mark of the church, he therefore stresses that the church is holy because of its connection to God and Christ, not because of its members' worthiness. Accordingly, its members are able to experience the holiness of the church when they, as children of the Holy, encounter and worship this Holy God.

Finally, regarding the church as being one, González (1997) explains that this mark has been expressed through the word "unity." Unfortunately, Latino/a Protestants perceive this unity as something undesirable because it reminds them of the traditional Roman Catholic understanding that to be "one" all Christians need to be subject to a particular authority—leaving no room for Protestants. Also, the word "unity" makes Latino/a Protestants feel uncomfortable because often the Anglo White denominations speak of a unity that seems to imply uniformity in which Latino/as' perspectives and values are not appreciated or accepted. González affirms that in spite of their uneasiness with this concept, Latino/a Protestants experience it in a particular way as they live as the family of God. Here González (1997), in agreement with other Hispanic theologians such as Riebe-Estrella (1990), explains that the family, in the Latina/o context, is not only the nuclear family but the extended family that includes all sorts of blood relatives as well as relatives by marriage and by baptism (*compadres/comadres*). In the U.S. context where many immigrants have had to leave their families behind, this extended family of God, the church, becomes an opportunity to enjoy again the warmth of a true family. Through this extended family of faith, Latino/a Protestants are able to experience the unity of the church as they live like a blood family that, though it experiences tensions and conflicts from within, knows that its members cannot just break away from it. Another expression of this unity is the sharing involved in the Latino/a Protestant church. This solidarity is such that members in very intimate ways share their problems—and the resources to solve these problems. Finally, seen as an extended family, the boundaries of the Latina/o church are not totally defined, meaning that there is always room for more relatives/members who may be different, but who still belong in the unity of the family.

Other Protestant theologians have decided to study the church by analyzing particular bodies within the Protestant traditions. In his articulations about a Latina/o Protestant ecclesiology, Juan Francisco Martínez (2006) reflects on the believer's church perspective as represented mainly by Pentecostals, Baptists, Mennonites, and Disciples of Christ. From this perspective, the church is a community of people who have made a voluntary commitment of faith and have been baptized by immersion as a public expression of this commitment. He affirms that for these Protestant Latino/as, the local church occupies a central place in their lives because this is where they experience God in worship, as well as the support and affirmation of the community that functions as an extended family. These churches tend to give much importance to the

HERMANO/A

While commonly used as a term of endearment among Latino/as, the concept of *hermano/a* preponderates the language of faith in Spanish-speaking communities. Members of religious orders within the Roman Catholic tradition are referred to as "hermano" or "hermana" in some generic way in lieu of a vocational title. Within the Hispanic Protestant tradition it is the common greeting used by members of the faith community. The term is utilized both in the context of worship as well as in the daily interactions of Protestant Christians as a form of public identification. To be called "hermana/o" implies a level of intimacy among people who share a common perspective on life and faith and carries with it an inherent responsibility for ethical behavior, interpersonal commitments, and reciprocity. In religious practices like Santería the term is also used by participants in the context of rituals. In the religious practice of Espiritismo, the term is frequently used in reference to the person who officiates the rituals and serves as the medium for channeling the manifestations of the spiritual world. In all of these uses, however, the term implies a symmetrical relation among religious practitioners and their leaders rather than a hierarchical understanding defined by relational authority and detachment.

—*JI*

Bible and to the life of prayer. In terms of the governance of the church, they affirm a congregational government with autonomy to deal with its own affairs. A key principle in this government and in the life of the church in general is the "priesthood of all believers." This notion is empowering because it allows all of the members of the church, regardless of their education, occupation, or legal status, to have a role and a responsibility in the church. As they experience increased responsibilities, these lay leaders may move to key leadership positions in the church, perhaps including the pastorate. This kind of organization allows for Latino/as who are marginalized in the White denominations and in society at large the rare opportunity to be leaders and owners of their own local organizations.

Martínez (2006) suggests that in terms of Latino/a identity, these churches have been a vehicle to transmit and maintain values of the Latina/o community, such as the Spanish language and diverse cultural traditions. This maintenance of Latina/o values has been difficult on two fronts. On the one hand, the White denominations put pressure on these churches to acculturate. On the other hand, these Protestant Latino/as continue to live in a culture impregnated with Catholic beliefs and traditions, and as they leave Catholicism, they are no longer regarded as being fully Latino/a. Martínez (2006) concludes that these churches will continue to attract Latino/as in the future because of the particularly familiar model of church that they offer to the Latino/a community.

Ruben P. Armendáriz (1999) presents a different perspective as he analyzes the characteristics of some Hispanic congregations within the mainline traditions, such as Episcopalian, Lutheran, Methodist, Presbyterian, and United Church of Christ. In agreement with other Hispanic theologians, he affirms that in these Latina/o churches

CULTO

The liturgical experience within the Latino/a Protestant community is referred to as *el culto*. "El culto" is both the way of practicing or rendering worship to God (*rendir culto*) and the place separated for those practices where people go for spiritual (cult)ivation (*ir al culto*). The substitution of the most traditional term for referring to Protestant worship (*Servicio de Adoración*) for *culto* lacks a consistent history. It is possible that the term was claimed by *Evangélica/os* after the Roman Catholic Church began to refer to the emerging Protestant houses of worship as *cultos*, or cults in the most pejorative sense, in order to detract the Catholic faithful from visiting these communities. Another possibility is that Protestant missionaries used the term *culto* as a linguistic equivalent for "worship," since the appropriate word in Spanish, *adoración*, was reminiscent of the Catholic veneration of saints, a practice that Protestant missionaries discouraged. Some common features of "el culto" across the diverse theological traditions is the frequent use of single stanza canticles for praising named *coritos*, the incorporation of musical styles and instruments that are common in the popular culture, unrehearsed public prayer, the sharing of "testimonios" or verbal witnessing to God's work in people's lives, and extended sermons and liturgies.

—*JI*

the people clearly relate to one another as members of an extended family, calling each other *hermano* and *hermana* (brother and sister). Although there is the assumption that in most of these churches Spanish is the predominant language, Armendáriz (1999) discovered in his study that the current trend is bilingualism (Spanish and English). The reason for this is that as an intergenerational group, the older members of these Latina/o churches prefer Spanish, while the younger generations prefer English. Another characteristic of these churches is that their members prefer to be called *evangélicos/as* instead of *Protestantes*. As *evangélicos/as*, they affirm the centrality of the Bible as normative in their faith and practice, and self-disciplined behavior as a *testimonio* (witness) to how they have been transformed by the Gospel. The members of these churches recognize that they are a minority (Protestant) within a minority (Latina/o), and that is how they account for the small size of their churches. However, they see this characteristic as something positive that allows them to experience closeness and familiarity within the congregation.

Finally, in terms of the worship experience, Armendáriz (1999) argues that even though these congregations have for the most part copied the worship services of their Anglo Protestant counterparts, they also have their own cultural expressions within the service, such as the decorations, and some traditional celebrations such as *quinceañeras* and *las posadas*.

In terms of popular religiosity, the Latina/o Protestant churches also have their own particular expressions such as *los coritos*, which are informal songs often written by ordinary people in the churches. They are used in casual gatherings such as youth meetings or less conventional services where the whole church participates. Another expression of popular religiosity is *testimonios*, which according to Juan Francisco Martínez (2006) are spiritual narratives told by a particular member of the church, narratives of how God blessed or helped him/her in a particular problem or struggle. In many Latina/o Protestant churches, these testimonios are a major part of the service and function as a way of nurturing the spiritual life of the congregation as well as being an opportunity to evangelize the visitors by sharing God's power with them.

Final Remarks

To conclude this survey of ecclesiological articulations from the Latino/a perspective, it is important to present some observations related to both traditions: Catholic and Protestant. First, regarding the popular expressions of these traditions, they seem to be very fluid, as they move from one group to the other. For instance, *los coritos* are very popular in Latina/o Protestant circles, but every day they become more common and present also in Catholic worship experiences. *Las Posadas* are a Catholic tradition, but they have made their way into the Latina/o Protestant churches. The same can be said about the celebration of *la quinceañera*.

In terms of challenges, both of these traditions will continue to experience challenges by their own women (and some supportive men), as they recognize more and more that women are also called to ordained ministries. A second challenge for both traditions will be the issue of ecumenical relationships as both groups attempt to work on issues of social justice. Since both Latino/a Catholic and Protestant people have been oppressed by issues of racism and discrimination, it would make sense for both parties to join together to confront these evils. The theologians of both sides have experienced the issue of being Latino/a as a uniting force, and thus they have set apart their theological differences in order to work together for the common good of the Latina/o community. Hopefully the example of these theologians will move the local churches of both traditions to start working together, without compromising their theological beliefs, to bring God's justice and peace to the Latino/a community. Furthermore, as Latino/a theologians explore this doctrine of the church from their own perspectives, their articulations will continue to enrich the lives of their respective churches, as well as the life of the Christian church as a whole.

References and Further Reading

Armendáriz, Ruben P. "The Protestant Hispanic Congregation: Identity." *Protestantes/Protestants: Hispanic Christianity within Mainline Traditions*, ed. David Maldonado Jr. (Nashville: Abingdon Press, 1999).

Espín, Orlando. "Tradition and Popular Religion: An Understanding of the Sensus Fidelium." *Mestizo Christianity: Theology from the Latino Perspective*, ed. Arturo J. Bañuelas (Maryknoll, NY: Orbis Books, 1995).

González, Justo. "In Quest of a Protestant Hispanic Ecclesiology." *Teología en Conjunto: A Collaborative Hispanic Protestant Theology*, ed. Jose David Rodríguez and Loida I. Martell-Otero (Louisville, KY: Westminster John Knox Press, 1997).

———. *Mañana: Christian Theology from a Hispanic Perspective* (Nashville: Abingdon Press, 1990).

Martínez, Juan Francisco. "Church: A Latino/a Protestant Perspective." *Handbook of Latina/o Theologies*, ed. Edwin David Aponte and Miguel A. De La Torre (St. Louis: Chalice Press, 2006).

Pineda, Ana María. "Pastoral de Conjunto." *Mestizo Christianity: Theology from the Latino Perspective*, ed Arturo J. Bañuelas (Maryknoll, NY: Orbis Books, 1995).

Riebe-Estrella, Gary. "Pueblo and Church." *From the Heart of Our People: Latino/a Explorations in Catholic Systematic Theology*, ed. Orlando E. Espín and Miguel H. Díaz (Maryknoll, NY: Orbis Books, 1999).

Rodríguez, Jeanette. "Church: A Roman Catholic Perspective." *Handbook of Latina/o Theologies*, ed. Edwin David Aponte and Miguel A. De La Torre (St. Louis: Chalice Press, 2006).

EPISTEMOLOGY

Elias Ortega-Aponte

How do we come to know the world? Can the world be known? What is the nature of knowledge? What role do our senses play in obtaining knowledge? Is the world out there to be known; is it internal to the subject; what are the relationships between the two? Answering these and related questions constitute the goal of Epistemology. In its most simple formulation, epistemology is the study of knowledge. It attempts to clarify the basis upon which we can claim to know the world and gain true beliefs. As a philosophical discipline, epistemology searches to account for how beliefs may be true and for justification in relation to knowledge of the objects in the natural world and/or in the world of the knowing subject. Traditionally, philosophical epistemology privilege knowledge of propositions (that a subject possesses knowledge of *P* as a proposition) over other kinds of knowledge, like the knowledge of how to do *X*.

As a theological approach, epistemology seeks to answer the question of the possibility of gaining knowledge of God. It attempts to give an account of the nature of knowledge of the divine. Is knowledge of God *true* in the same way that mathematical knowledge is considered truth? How about proofs for the existence of God; do they share the same warrant of scientific proofs?

A clear view of what knowledge might be bears significant impact in disciplines other than philosophy and theology. A solid theory of knowledge will weigh ethics, politics, sociology, the natural sciences, and other areas of inquiry, making the discipline of epistemology a prime candidate for interdisciplinary endeavors. An understanding of knowledge gathering and transmission is basic to any human anthropology; human societies are organized around vast reservoirs of knowledge (to which new materials are always added) that enable social, political, economic, cultural, and religious activities.

Latino/a theology and religious thought emphasize experience, but experience with a particular focus, that of *lo cotidiano*. Lo cotidiano, that which happens in everyday life, is at the center of Latino/a theological analysis. The substance of epistemological reflection within the Latino/a scholar, rather than an abstract, denatured experience akin to Cartesian reflections, is embodied in the lives of the people. Everyday experience provides the material of thinking about faith and life. Everyday practices, rituals, devotions, artistic expression, culinary creations, *remedios*, and popular wisdom are knowledge incarnate. A careful and methodological analysis of these activities reveals important lessons of how God's revelations are interpreted and subsequently practiced in our communities. This is the first contribution that U.S. Latino/a religious thought makes to the study of epistemology.

A second contribution to the field of epistemology from Latino/a theology takes the form of reading the Christian tradition *latinamente*. This latinidad scrutinizing unmasks racism and prejudice of views seeking dominance of the ways to interpret Christian tradition; it also moves beyond this necessary critical moment to separate the wheat from the chaff, searching for how the truth of the gospel and God's revelation speak to the Latino/a communities. By gathering the wheat, Latino/a scholars have availed themselves of the grain of tradition, grinding the grain and leavening the flour to make bread to nourish our peoples; at the end, burning the chaff or letting the wind blow it away, we open ways for our communities to heal. Thus, reading tradition latinamente enables new and creative ways of *traditioning*.

Traditioning is the activity of passing down a tradition. This activity should be understood as a knowledge-disseminating practice. Traditioning as a way of gathering knowledge understands that divine revelation takes place in the midst of our daily lives, in struggles, victories, survival strategies, and sinfulness. It is here that divine reality is most present, not in abstract formulation of armchair theologians. The act of handing down a tradition passes on the kernel of it, but also adds to it from the experiences of those who hand down the tradition.

U.S. Latina theological feminist contributions to the field of epistemology are numerous. Among them, they have the centrality of the experiences of women of color as a starting point of theoretical and methodological reflection. The starting point of Latina theological feminism in the experience of Latina women has enabled a reconceptualization of divine reality in which aspects of Latinas culture and histories have enriched and challenged traditional conceptions of the divine. It has also taken recourse in extensive literary and artistic productions of Latinas seeking new sites of divine revelatory activity; this has become particularly useful in challenging the patriarchal nature of Hispanic culture and set sexual politics. A third contribution of Latinas to epistemology has been in the field of ethics.

Although common among the scholarly work of Latino/as as a whole, Latina theologians have led the way in exploring the ethical connections of sexuality and race through the development of concepts like *mulataz*, *mujerismo*, and *lo cotidiano*. Their work has opened new ways of thinking about appropriate ethical behavior, the relation between religious practices and ethics, and more importantly, the role of the theologian for the Latino/a community.

Another significant contribution of U.S. Latino/as to epistemology has been the expansion of the field to incorporate issues of aesthetics and justice into ways of knowing. Knowing is gaining knowledge of what is beautiful and shedding a different light on traditional ways of justifying knowledge. The demand is not placed to give appropriate and sufficient evidence in favor of a belief. Instead, the emphasis lies in the beauty and intent of the world. What the bases are for beauty in creation in connection with the divine plan takes the shape of humanizing activity. Justice is primary in securing and preserving human dignity and the flourishing of human beings.

Finally, U.S. Latino/a religious epistemology takes the standpoint of the poor, oppressed, and downtrodden. By giving epistemic privilege to the experience of the poor, the end goal of a Latino/a religious is one of liberatory knowledge, knowledge of the divine that informs and calls for a practical expression in liberation. Liberatory knowledge for the Latino/a theologian leads to liberating praxis. This emphasis reveals an often ignored form of knowledge, the knowing how to do an activity. For the Latino/a theologian, knowing the divine occurs in the midst of daily life, during the search for humanizing and liberatory practices.

References and Further Reading

Aquino, María Pilar, Daisy L. Machado, and Jeanette Rodríguez. *A Reader in Latina Feminist Theology: Religion and Justice* (Austin: University of Texas Press, 2002).

Espín, Orlando, and Gary Macy. *Futuring Our Past: Explorations in the Theology of Tradition* (Maryknoll, NY: Orbis Books, 2006).

Maduro, Otto. *Mapas Para La Fiesta: Reflexiones Sobre la Crisis y el Conocimiento* (Atlanta: AETH, 1998).

ESCHATOLOGY

Luis E. Benavides

The Greek word "eschatology" means "last things." The fields of philosophy, theology, religion, and psychology appropriated this meaning to explain: (1) how humankind and the universe will end, and (2) the hope for a radical transformation of both of them in the future. In this sense, eschatology became known as both the doctrine of the last things and the doctrine of the beginning of eternity. Eschatology chronicles the end of the beginning and the eternal beginning of the endless end; as such, we can conceive of eschatology as the creation's journeying back into its Creator.

In Christianity, history has a linear movement toward a destiny: God (eternity)-creation and fall-redemption-transformation-God (eternity). Because God's destiny is God-self, the destiny of God's creation is also God-self. Eschatology cares for providing the truth claims necessary for understanding the destiny of the individual (death, judgment, heaven, and hell) and the final stages of the physical universe. However, as the history of the church and theology advance, Latino/a theologies have enlarged the meaning of eschatology held for many years by Western theology in contemporary theological discourse.

The question of eschatology, its meaning and content, has been handled in Latina/o scholarship by reviewing the vicissitudes of history faced by the Latino/a community in the United States. Latino/a eschatology emphatically has the status of a verifiable objective for social justice today, in which hope for the future becomes, retrospectively, hope for the present. Since the driving religious element in eschatology is essentially the expectation of a new state of things, Latina/o eschatology stands for liberation from a particular social, economic, and political situation toward a more just situation in the society of the United States. Such betterment is inextricably bound up with the understanding of the Kingdom of God, in which traditional eschatology is transformed into sociopolitical action, theology into sociology, and idealism into materialism. Western theology's eschatology, understood as proclaiming a "pie in the sky when you die," is seen as suspicious by Latino/a eschatology, which is striving for recognition, acceptance, and participation of the Latina/o community in the U.S. society. If there is a "pie," then let us share it here and now on earth.

Latino/a eschatology's truth claims hold that hope for the future must not distract but, instead, foster the Church's responsibility for preaching a gospel of social justice, economic equality, and political change. With these three elements, Latina/o eschatology aims to substantiate the rest of Latino/a statements of faith about God and God's relationship with God's creation. Latina/o eschatology is not a chapter at the end of a theological system, as happens in traditional Western theology, but an omnipresent theme. This is why eschatology pervasively penetrates the truth claims of Latina/o theologies in every theme. In Latino/a eschatology the truth is both contextually bound and realized in history.

Truth as Contextually Bound

In Latino/a eschatology, the claim that truth is contextually bound conveys a preferential option for a culture, implying that a minority culture lives within a dominant culture. In Latin America, the focus is economic, but in the United States, the focus is cultural pluralism, which is totally antithetical to the well-known melting pot. Latina/o eschatology does not advocate for assimilation that produces Americanization nor for rejecting assimilation that produces tolerance, but for cultural pluralism that produces differentiation. This differentiation suggests neither superiority nor cultural insulation, but cultural distinctiveness in the United States. Cultural distinctiveness is identical to the Latino/a awareness of being in the world. In the last analysis, cultural distinctiveness, or otherness, makes Latina/os the subject or the object (participant or oppressed) in any context.

Liberation theologians have long held that all types of indigenous or contextual theologies are inimical to those systematic theological reflections practiced for centuries by Western theology. Since Latino/a theologies are daughters of Liberation Theology, this inimical aspect has conditioned the whole of Latina/o eschatology. Such a sense of distance between various forms of contextual theologies and Western theology becomes evident when viewed through the lens of the three models of contemporary theology outlined by David Tracy (1982). Tracy suggests that contemporary theology can be divided or categorized among three basic ideal types: foundational or philosophic theology, systematic or church-based dogmatic theology, and praxis or contextual theological systems. Each form of theological discourse has its own canon of interpretation, audience, authority, and warrants of rationality and argumentation.

Contextual theologies, such as African (e.g., John S. Mbiti and John S. Pobee), Latin American (e.g., Gustavo Gutiérrez and Leonardo Boff), Asian (e.g., Nam Dong Suh and Choan Sen Song), and more recently Latino/a theologies (e.g., Justo González and Virgilio Elizondo), are neither agreeable with nor analogous to the style of reflection indigenous to Western theology. For contextual indigenous theologians, theology is mostly a passion, and theology is to be lived in a given local situation. Experiencing God in a given oppressed situation or structure is the foundation of theological reflections of God. While systematic or unsystematic reflections intellectually help others to understand God and God's relationship with the creation, contextual indigenous theologians reflect, and try to live their beliefs, in a particular context that could be Asian,

African, Latino/a, or North American. In this way, contextual theologies evolve from the practical living in a particular context.

Contextualization means the application of the understanding of the Christian faith in a concrete location within a specific situation. Concrete location means a geographical scene that could be Latin America, Asia, Africa, or the United States. And the situation refers to that historic-existential condition from which Latina/o eschatology abstracts its truth claims. Contextual theologies such as Latino/a, Korean, Black, and Haitian are characterized and limited by having their own perspective and situation. This characterization is relevant because some issues and symbols that are significant in one culture are irrelevant in another culture. Also, by attempting to make the gospel relevant in a contemporary culture, we do not have to confuse or identify contextualization with implementation. Contextualization does not ascribe superiority to Western theology. But because the gospel is pliant, the context actively assumes an important role in interpreting the gospel and Jesus Christ as unique, in order to solve different cultural plights. Latina/o eschatology embraces this view as part of its truth claims.

For Latino/a theologies, and particularly for Latina/o eschatology, context is fraught with three existential meanings: location, rejection of ethnocentrism, and knowledge of the culture. All of them expect a new state of things. Regarding location, Latino/a eschatology asks the question: What is the existential meaning of the place in which Latina/os live, namely, North America? The label "North America" bears two meanings, a literal one and a figurative one. Literally speaking, "North America" entails the whole of the geographic, social, economic, institutional, and political structures of the continental United States. It refers to the physical scene or historical arena in which the Latino/a experience is currently taking place and has also been shaped and developed.

Figuratively speaking, "North America" implies more than a geographic place. For Latina/os, it has an existential meaning without a single focus, but with several locations. For instance, Latino/a theologians have identified "North America" with the following ideas: (1) the land where Latino/as forcefully experience a change in social status; (2) a place of desolation; (3) the land of oppression for Latinas; (4) a place for a new social location or immigration; (5) a land for becoming a Chicano/a after experiencing two-times mestizaje; (6) a place to live an imposed exile; (7) a place for being invisible; and lastly, (8) a place for an ambivalent identity in which Puerto Ricans, for instance, have been conquered in 1492 and colonized in 1898; Puerto Ricans are Latino/as, belonging to the United States involuntarily.

In summary, "North America" is the place in which Latina/os have found cultural, sociological, and existential reasons for raising up new theological voices, striving for liberation. These voices have been nurtured by an existential engagement with the daily life of the Latino/a community in the United States. These voices are also unique in the sense that they are self-consciously non–North American. Ontologically speaking, Latina/o eschatology theologizes for moving the Latino/a community from nonbeing to a new being in the United States. This movement has not yet been achieved. Nonbeing is understood here as a by-product of Latina/o existential anxiety and, therefore, part of the Latino/a condition. In the Latina/o culture, awareness of nonbeing is heightened when Latino/as realize they are a minority group struggling for cultural distinctiveness while resisting cultural and theological assimilation.

In this regard, Latino/a eschatology asks the question, what does it mean to be Latina/o in the United States? Interestingly, in the United States, and not in their former homeland, Latino/as realize they are a mixture of being and nonbeing, and that the immediate existential situation is leading them to seek a new being. Latino/a eschatology functions here to bring hope today. Latina/o eschatology recognizes that cultural diversity is a constitutive element of ecclesiology. For this reason alone, Latino/as reject ethnocentrism: the assumption that the worldview of one's own culture is central to all realities. The American way is not the only way. In the New Testament, for instance, Pauline churches function as an example of cultural diversity for us today. Such churches were not formed with a single homogeneous group, but with heterogeneous groups. The first Christians were not exclusively or even predominantly poor, and the Pauline churches gathered people from many of the social strata of the society. They came from high as well as low social classes.

Many Latino/as are in the United States because of the problems they left behind, not because they want to stay here voluntarily. Part of this immigration is due to the U.S. political interventions in Latin America. Immigrations into the United States are a symbolic price that the United States is paying for being the police force of the world. In one way or another, Latina/o existential situations have pushed them to abandon their homeland to come to the United States, which supposedly is the land of social, political, and economic stability, in order to build a better life. In so doing, voluntary, along with involuntary, immigrants have to pay an existential price, being read by the society as merely "Latino/as." Because many Latino/as have to work two or three part-time jobs to meet their material needs, "the American dream" has become the sleeping time one can get from midnight to five o'clock in the morning. The American dream is, in reality, a nightmare.

Truth as Realized in History

The interpretation of history has had many participants who have assisted in the construction of a universal historical consciousness from different approaches. For instance, Augustine of Hippo reads human history as an ongoing struggle between two kingdoms: the city of God and the city of man. Georg W. F. Hegel reads human history as the place where God is at work in the world by unfolding the Spirit's self-conscious, which is the self-realization of God in human history. John Wesley reads history as the arena of God's saving work. Karl Marx and Friedrich Engels read history as the product of economic class struggle. Paul Tillich reads history as the arena from which the human being is translated from the temporal to the eternal. More instances can be added to the list, but these illustrate how Western thinkers have approached history, providing an enormous contribution for the expansion and enrichment of historical consciousness. But, the contents of historical consciousness must serve a function, namely, to lead us to reason.

Western thinkers have always seen reality as ontological; they attach to the fact that the human plight and its destructive nature appeared as a result of the fall of humankind. This fact is understood and widely accepted in Christianity as the original sin incorporated into human nature since Adam and Eve's times. But, the conviction that human beings can assist in God's redemption plan, and in the construction of a more just society, have also been clearly understood and widely accepted in Christianity. Latina/o eschatology claims that ontology must be transformed into social action. The understanding of individual salvation must reverberate in community life today, not just tomorrow.

Latino/a eschatology recognizes that perfect social conditions are utopian; on the other hand, it also recognizes that only a transformed individual can create new social actions. In this respect, Latina/o eschatological interpretations of history strive for both the transformation of the individual with regard to individual salvation (ontology), and for the transformation of society with regard to the search for a more just society (social action). Latino/a eschatology focuses on the natural rather than focusing on the supernatural.

Approaching history from a Latina/o eschatological point of view suggests that history and historical consciousness are more than simple accounts of the past. History should function to define the future by changing the present. History has been read with an East-to-West orientation, misrepresenting the contents of the long history of injustice and pain with regard to Latino/a emigrations from all over Latin America to the United States. For this reason, Latina/o historical consciousness demands that history should also be read with a South-to-North orientation.

Immigrants from the Mexican-community group the Tepeyac Association demonstrate on Good Friday in front of Federal Plaza in New York City. The group demanded equal rights for immigrant workers and criticized Bush administration immigration policies. (Ramin Talaie/Corbis)

There are events in place merely by the Latino/a presence in U.S. history and society that have gained significance, but are eschewed by or not contained at all in, Western historical consciousness. This significance warrants that Latina/os be considered as an historical group. Latino/as should be responsible for interpretation. In this interpretation, Latina/os are aware that their history is embedded within the U.S. history, having invisible ties to their country of origin. The selection of events that are to be established as historically significant, before starting to think eschatologically, is the most important task for Latino/as to make such events visible. This selection will depend on the evaluations of its own importance for the establishment of the Latino/a culture and identity as an historical group, and for their contribution to expanding and enriching historical consciousness, but in a Latino/a way or *Latinoly*. Most of the Latina/os who dwell in the United States have been reading history and their plight from social, economic, and political points of view. Latino/a eschatology, therefore, serves a function, which is to care for the present Latina/o plight and not for "a pie in the sky when you die."

Latino/a eschatology is committed to claiming social, economic, and political rights. This struggle is fundamentally in search of equality, despite the inequalities imposed by what the majority culture perceive as its natural privileges. Latina/o eschatology is not tangential to this struggle; it acknowledges that the struggle is here and now, not just in the afterlife.

The Contents of Latino/a Eschatology

There is a scarcity of writings about Latina/o eschatology. The subject is held in great abeyance in Latino/a scholarship. There is neither a specialized scholar nor a book on Latina/o eschatology that explains the contents fully. Ada María Isasi-Díaz, Virgilio Elizondo, and Justo González have made brief incursions into the study of Latino/a eschatology. In advancing the study on eschatology, these three scholars do not accept those eschatologies that jeopardize sociopolitical action undertaken by Latino/as. That is to say, Latina/o eschatology's present discourse is focused on historical praxis, with the intention of changing history as it unfolds, rather than focusing on an explication of the conclusion of history, or the supernatural afterlife. Three characteristics delineate the contents of Latino/a eschatology in these three writers: Latina/o eschatology is (1) teleological in nature, (2) focused on sociopolitical action, and (3) based on a common vision of struggle.

Latino/a Eschatology as Teleological

Latino/a scholars believe that an overall design or purpose in nature guides human history in which God alone has established the purpose. For example, Isasi-Díaz (1993) believes in one human history that has at its very heart the history of salvation, dismissing in this way the idea of two separated histories, i.e., the secular and the sacred. What really counts for Isasi-Díaz is not human history as history, but what is inherently tied to the salvation of humankind. More to the point, what really counts is the salvation of Latina women. She claims that by history of salvation, Latinas refer to what they believe are divine actions—creation, incarnation, and redemption—as well as human responses to this, whether positive or negative. For Isasi-Díaz, human history and salvation history are identical, having at the center the incarnation. Also, human history must be seen against the framework of God's divine actions in three objective movements in history: creation, incarnation, and redemption.

González (1992) sees history quite differently from Isasi-Díaz. Following the scriptural narratives, he thinks that biblical history, along with church history, functions to illustrate what is happening today. He does not use history to elaborate a future eschatology, but to explain the contents of the present in order to insert Latino/a history into the context of general history. For him, biblical history is a history beyond innocence. Its only real heroes are the God of history and history itself, which somehow continues moving forward in spite of the failure of its great protagonists. In this definition, González holds that the Scriptures describe how great biblical heroes failed God. God then becomes the only true hero.

He also sees history as a linear movement mostly characterized by failing people rather than full of novelistic idealizations. González claims that those who think of their own history in terms of high ideals and purity detract from the power and inspiration of Scriptures. This, however, is not the case with Latina/os. Because of the brutal conquest of Latin America by the Spaniards, Latino/as know that they are born out of an act of violence. He interprets Latina/o history not with idealistic assumptions, but by vicissitudes of contingency. His view of history is objective in which the brutal Spanish conquest and history itself function as verifiable truths. Through this method of reading history, González thinks that by looking only at the ideal heroes, we are falling into an innocent reading of history that must be surpassed. The reality is that history is fraught with pain, as Latino/a history demonstrates, and this pain functions as the starting point in Latina/o eschatology.

Latino/a Eschatology as Sociopolitical Action

Latina/o scholars are concerned with their present predicament, but they are not concerned with an eschatological otherworldly view of reality. Specifically, Latino/a scholars are concerned for salvation as liberation in which they think God is particularly concerned to remove the restraints on the self-determination of Latino/as. Isasi-Díaz, who is the feminist voice in Latina/o scholarship, rejects any concept of salvation that does not affect present and future reality of Latina women. Salvation occurs in history and is intrinsically connected to their liberation. In other words, liberation of Latinas and salvation are identical; if Latinas do not reach liberation, they are not going to be saved. For Latinas to talk about salvation, liberation, and the coming of the "kin-dom" of God are one and the same thing. Therefore, eschatology becomes sociopolitical action. If Latinas are not liberated, then the Kingdom is not here yet and salvation is only in the process of becoming a historical reality.

González rejects all eschatologies that avoid social and political concerns today. For liberal theologians, both enlightened and sophisticated, eschatological expectation undercuts the social and political action of Christians. This is true only on the basis of a particular understanding of eschatology or of a particular understanding of social and political action. He also blames those "spiritualist" eschatologies that prevent Christians from taking social or political action. There have been abusive eschatologies with strong political emphasis such as the Anabaptists. He then announces what he considers an eschatological alternative for Latino/as today: Mañana (tomorrow). As eschatological hope, "mañana" is much more than tomorrow, it is the radical questioning of today. By this he means a critical confrontation and evaluation of the Latino/a predicament against the social and political structures of the U.S. society. Therefore, liberation is for today; thus transforming eschatology into sociopolitical action. This is a clear postulation of "sociopolitical action" as an a priori realm, which González exploits to explain the plausibility for freedom. Such a postulate seems to be valid for González, who sees sociopolitical action as necessary and applicable to all circumstances without an a posteriori verification. Latina/o eschatology is then sociopolitical —a radical questioning of today.

González reinterprets the expression "a pie in the sky when you die" by claiming that if God's intended order is that we have a pie, how come others get all the pies and Latino/as get all the pain? This question reflects González's concern for social justice today. González sees the future sociopolitically and retrospectively. For him, anyone who believes that the future God promises has nothing to do with physical life, and with the social order, will hardly be overly interested in the political struggles of our day. In addition to González's thinking, we need to include that God's intended order is also to give justice in the eschaton, in the second coming of Jesus the Christ, or at the time we pass away. This is illustrated in the narrative of Luke 16:19–31 with the story of Lazarus and the rich man. But, how is it that Lazarus gets all the pain and the rich man all the pies? Latina/o eschatology would advocate for making justice for Lazarus while he was alive. In this case, Latino/a eschatology will hold as untenable the fact that Lazarus, in his earthly life, had all the pain and the rich man all the pies.

Latina/o Eschatology as Common Vision for Struggle

Latino/a scholars, both Catholics and Protestants, share a common eschatological vision for struggle. They have transformed the future eschatological hope into a present sociopolitical hope, which is reflected in their common struggle for liberation. Each Latina/o scholar has taken a particular stance in order to struggle with a particular aspect of the present Latino/a predicament. In this way, mujerista theology adopts to struggle for the Latinas' economic situation (Isasi-Díaz 1993); barrio theology adopts to struggle for the Puerto Rican's housing situation (Recinos 1989); sufferer theology adopts to struggle for the Puerto Rican Pentecostals' suffering condition (Solivan 1993); and mestizo theology adopts to struggle for the Chicano's socioeconomic condition (Elizondo 1983). The truth claims that lie behind this common vision for struggle is that Latina/o eschatology acknowledges there is something wrong in all of us and in society; and we need to be liberated from that sense of wrongness. In Latino/a eschatology, the theologian's personal journey functions as a starting point for doing theology. Latina/o theologians are not detached from the realities of their own communities, they are fully engaged in the realities about which they theologize, and they, in themselves, are a source for theological reflection.

Issues Requiring Further Discussion

Latino/a eschatology is still in the stage of chrysalis. It is a new theological voice just starting to have presence, and it must be credited for the remarkable success it has had in the short term. But the virtue to success is also a temptation to weakness. The following aspects require further reflection in Latina/o eschatology:

First, Latino/a eschatology is driven by historical facts that are, in turn, conditioned by the Latina/o situation in the U.S. society. Latino/a scholars are concerned with the social, political, and economic situation today. For this reason, the notion of "a pie in the sky when you die" is approached with suspicion, because it distracts from the significance of history today. This is precisely why Nietzsche attacked Christianity; he did so because Christianity cared more for the next world and forgot about the beauty of the present world.

When the "pie in the sky" notion is employed to legitimate oppression, it becomes sociopolitically suspect. From this point of view, eschatology is a changing or improving of Latina/o life conditions, becoming a representative of class struggle. But, since Marx is not a Latino/a discovery, but a European one, and since Latino/a eschatology belongs to the contextual theologies paradigm, then the questions arise: How much and why is Marx present in Latina/o eschatology? And, does Latino/a eschatology have a classless society as the aim of history? God understands the oppressed situation and needs to be portrayed as one who understands all conditions: the Latina/o condition and the non-Latina/o condition. All people need to know that God understands every single culture. This does not mean that God is a proponent of wealth and cultural domination; it means that God cares for all peoples equally as God does for the oppressed minority populations.

Second, Latina/o eschatology is written with particular biases. Eschatology is being read with particular proclivities that consciously affect the view of eschatology. Mujerista theology reads eschatology through the lens of Latinas; barrio theology reads eschatology through the lens of Puerto Ricans' poverty; and mestizo theology reads eschatology through the lens of Chicanos' poverty. In Latina/o eschatology, the theologian is, in himself or herself, a source for theological reflection; his or her cultural and existential pedigree matters. Then the question arises: Is Latino/a eschatology a theology of introspection or internalization? Saint Augustine was criticized for grounding much of his theology in introspection, producing a theology based on personal experience. We cannot equate others' experiences with our own.

Other Latina/o scholars employ their personal backgrounds to highlight what they consider is the Latino/a predicament. Elizondo, a Chicano, is identified with the Chicanos; Solivan, a Puerto Rican, is identified with Puerto Ricans; Villafañe, a Puerto Rican, is identified with Puerto Ricans; Isasi-Díaz, a Catholic Cuban, is identified with oppressed Catholic Latinas; and so forth. These biases are a virtue, but also a danger. It is a virtue because they are writing with passion, directly from the heart; but the danger lies in the fact that theology serves a particular function, and thus is deprived of the purity of impartial analysis. Latina/o eschatology fails to explain how eschatology, in a general sense, connects with those who are not Latina/os.

Third, Latino/a eschatology is written from the side of the victims. This aspect encourages some limitations via the plausibility of Latina/o scholarship. When the past, present, and future is centered on a particular plight of a particular Latino/a group, this creates a problem. History is reduced from its universal characteristic to a narrow point of view. The meaning, relevance, and characteristic of universal history (creation, incarnation, and redemption) cannot be derived from one small segment of the historical matrix, namely Latina/o history. History is meaningful and relevant when past and present history are related to the future, knowing what is at the end of history. Present history is incomplete if we do not make an effort to establish how history will be completed. In this way, eschatology becomes a necessary element for hope in the present. We can absolutize neither history nor eschatology as a function of the Latino/a predicament. This is especially true when we discover that Latina/o theologies do not appear open to the future in the light of present historical decisions. Establishing a communal hope of deliverance from oppression does not prevent one from having a personal hope for the future. Latino/as need both sociopolitical action today and a hope for the future. Latina/os die one by one, as individuals; they do not die in groups. General eschatologies are concerned with the future of every human being as an individual, including the cosmos. This does not suspend the fact that Latino/as, as a community, can develop a hope for the group. Koreans, Haitians, and African Americans are also history bearing groups, and they also have the right to social action and a hope for the future. Then the question arises: Is Latina/o eschatology exclusivist?

Finally, Latino/a eschatology lacks ontological content. Eschatology is not only related to the ultimate end of humankind and the renewal of the cosmos, but it is also related to our inner being, as well as to the divine being. Latina/o scholars do not seem interested in developing an "enlightened" or "spiritual" eschatology, but a concrete eschatology. They want improvement in their standard of living now, but not in the afterlife. They are approaching the meaning of life with social justice as an agenda and not accepting life in the U.S. society as it exists. This is similar to what Latin American liberation scholars are doing. But neither Isasi-Díaz, nor Elizondo, nor González defines eternal life and how Latino/as are related to it. This eschatology should be complemented with an adequate eschatology, in which both divine and human lives are successfully united, to the extent that in the present life human beings can participate partly in such divine life; and with a theory of how history will end by interpreting the destiny of humankind as a whole. This is a void left in Latina/o eschatology, since Latino/as are in one way or another related to the Catholic or Protestant tradition. Historically, they are in their inner being evangelicals by birth (believers of the Scriptures) and, as such, they still believe in the afterlife.

References and Further Reading

Benavides, Luis E. *Latino Christianity* (Madison, NJ: United Methodist Church, General Commission on Archives and History, 2005).

Elizondo, Virgilio. *Galilean Journey* (Maryknoll, NY: Orbis Books, 1991).

Gonzalez, Justo. *Mañana: Christian Theology from a Hispanic Perspective* (Nashville: Abingdon Press, 1990).

Isasi-Díaz, Ada María. *En la Lucha [In the Struggle]* (Minneapolis: Fortress Press, 1993).

Solivan, Samuel. *The Spirit, Pathos, and Liberation* (Sheffield, England: Sheffield Academy Press, 1998).

Recinos, Harold J. *Hear the Cry* (Louisville, KY: Westminster/John Knox Press, 1989).

Tracy, David. *The Analogical Imagination: Christian Theology and the Culture of Pluralism* (New York: Crossroads, 1981).

ETHICS

Ismael Garciá

The categories "Hispanic American" and "Latino/a American" are a recent social construction that describe those people from Latin America and the Spanish Caribbean that have made the United States their homeland. These terms are comprehensive and at times ambiguous. Both of these terms make reference to people that represent over 25 countries and embody significant historical, cultural, and political differences. The terms also try to include people who have lived here for many generations as well as those who have recently resettled in the United States. A sign of the pluralism and diversity that exists within this group is indicated by the fact that they do not agree as to which term, "Latina/o" or "Hispanic," best defines their self-identity.

Some prefer the term "Hispanic" because it includes all those people for whom Spanish was the dominant language. This extends the net of inclusion to cover Europeans, particularly people from Spain. It does struggle, however, with the inclusion of Brazilians and indigenous populations within Latin America who resist making Spanish their dominant language. The term is quite prevalent in the southwest region of the United States. Others prefer "Latino/a" to emphasize the Latin American and Caribbean roots of the population. They struggle with the inclusion of non-Latin American Spanish speakers. While the term "Hispanic" tends to focus on cultural identity, in particular the politics of language, the term "Latino/a" tends to focus on questions of political engagement and empowerment.

Both terms, however, do signal a deep desire of all these groups to find a way to define this new identity not by place of national origin but by the social, cultural, and political injustices most Hispanics confront within the United States. Both terms have gained political connotations. They signal a commitment to establish and sustain bonds of solidarity among the many different Latino/a groups, as well as a commitment to processes of social and political change aiming at greater social inclusion and political and economic equality. They signal that, in spite of many differences, there is a growing agreement that the preservation and enhancement of cultural identity is essential to bring the diverse Hispanic groups together, to achieve greater justice, and for members of the Hispanic community to flourish and enjoy a meaningful and good life.

It should be clear by now that Latino/as are not a monolithic group. This is also true morally and ethically speaking. One finds both commonalities and differences among Latina/os themselves and among Hispanics and other North American racial ethnic groups. That Latino/as share with other racial ethnic groups many of the same ethical commitments, principles, and modes of making ethical decisions should come as no surprise given that they dwell within and share the same religious, social, political and cultural milieu. Sharing life together does shape one's moral point of view. That they harbor different views about abortion, stem cell research, gay marriage, the death penalty, the legitimacy of war and other such moral concerns should also come as no surprise. They belong to a pluralistic society with its competing social and moral values. Their moral and ethical diversity is also the result of the way different Latino/as prioritize competing moral principles and have been influenced by existential realities such as social class, experience of migration, gender, race, and political and religious commitments.

Like other ethnic groups, Hispanics also have different conceptions of how to arrive at sound moral judgments and actions. For some, morality and ethics have to do mostly with duties and obligations that are in themselves binding. When asked "What should I do?" they reply, "Do those things which are in themselves right (truth telling, honesty, promise keeping) and avoid those things which are in themselves wrong (killing, lying, taking undue advantage)." Ethics, in this perspective, is mostly about respecting those laws, rules, and regulations that limit the ways we treat and relate to others.

Folk art depiction of Purgatory, Las Trampas, New Mexico. (Craig Aurness/ Corbis)

For others, morality is focused not so much on laws and regulations but on the consequences or goals of our actions. What goods are worthy of our pursuits and for whose benefit are these actions taken become the dominant moral questions. Morality and ethics, from this point of view, consist of the art of effectively choosing the right means to achieve the ends we pursue, not in the sense that the goal justifies the means but in the sense that worthy goals require fitting means. What matters morally is that we commit ourselves to contribute to enhancing the good that we are able to bring about and that our actions either maximize the good or minimize harm for the many.

Finally, some claim that morality is not so much about formulating principles or external guidelines to rule our actions and decisions. Nor is ethics mostly about achieving particular goals. The dominant ethical concern relates to cultivating and internalizing those virtues, settled dispositions, and motives that define our character. Ethics is about formation of becoming a certain kind of person. From this point of view, being a moral person takes precedence over obeying rules and obtaining goals. More significant than doing a just act or telling the truth or acting courageously is forming moral agents who have the unshakable inclination and disposition to be just, truthful, and courageous. Good action flows from good character. Virtue ethics is equally concerned with the nature of the community that nurtures the agent and shapes his/her being. An essential part of moral formation is the creation of communities whose members can both teach and model the virtues we want to cultivate.

Striking janitors receive communion during a mass led by Cardinal Roger Mahony at Our Lady Queen of Angels Church in Los Angeles, California. Cardinal Mahony, head of the largest diocese in the nation, has called for a mediator to help in negotiations. (Getty Images)

Religion matters to most Hispanics and does so for many reasons. Thus, religious organizations have a formative influence at the personal, communal, and even political levels. First, churches and other religious organizations have the capacity to congregate many members of the Hispanic community. They provide a public forum where many Hispanics gather information on what matters to them. They also provide the only public space where Hispanics feel they are heard and their views are respected. Churches and other religious organizations also provide multiple opportunities for Hispanics to serve their communities and to learn and develop leadership skills.

Second, as they consider what moral principles ought to guide their actions, what goals are worthy of being pursued, and which virtues to nurture, many Hispanics seek guidance from their faith traditions, from their church leaders, from their congregations, and from the Scriptures. Religious beliefs and organizations provide and nurture their sense of meaning. They also play a formative role in their moral point of view. For some the Scriptures provide particular commands and laws that, having been given by God, define the values and moral obligations by which they ought to be bound. For others, more significant than laws the Scriptures provide narratives that make them aware of how God acts in the world and how the faithful should respond. The

Scriptures provide us with examples of how to read the sign of the times and respond in a way fitting God's Kingdom of peace and justice. Others find in Scripture narratives that describe the life and deeds of Jesus, of the Prophets, of the disciples, and of other heroes and saints that serve as examples of what it means to live a faithful and morally authentic life. These stories inspire and encourage us to imitate these saints and heroes. Imitation that, properly understood, consists not so much in mimicking what the saints and heroes did but rather in how to cultivate those virtues and habits that sustain our desire to be faithful to God's purpose.

The moral visions of Latina/os reveal significant diversity. Still, in spite of their diversity, one can identify common and widely shared motifs that dominate the Latino/as moral conversation. One common motif is the way Hispanics understand the relationship between ethics and morality. Many moralists make a distinction between ethics and morality. Morality, in their view, has to do with those practices a particular community identifies and claims leads to and sustains the good life. Thus morality is the practice of the good that a particular community has come to accept and is habituated to. Ethics, on the other hand, is more reflective and theoretical in nature. Ethics makes morality its subject matter. Its task is to question the customs and habits the community takes for granted as being good and critically analyze and evaluate them to see if they can, in fact, be justified as being the best moral practices.

Latino/as do not establish such a sharp distinction and differentiation between the moral and the ethical. In their view, it is important that one keep theory and practice together, both informing and transforming each other. The doing of the good and the thinking of the good is part of a single process that ought not to be separated. Ethical theory and moral reflection are both at the service of sustaining moral practices and cultivating moral habits. Theory and practice constitute a single unity with practice being the beginning and end of this never-ending process. In this entry we shall honor this propensity and will not distinguish between these two terms.

Another strong motif among Hispanics is the commitment and the belief in the importance of keeping an ongoing moral conversation within the community. It is particularly important to keep conversing with those members of the community with whom one has significant disagreements on key issues. What is at stake in this conversation is the quality of life and the sustainability of the community itself. When one stops speaking, one signals that one no longer belongs to or cares for the community. Latino/as emphasize this concern through their notion of doing ethics *in conjunto*. Morality and ethics is always to be done in the context of a covenant community that, while diverse in its value commitments, remains committed to wrestling with one another regarding those issues that matter to them.

At a more substantive level, a motif that dominates Hispanic moral reflection is grounded in their experience of being victimized. The experience shared by many Hispanics of being economically exploited, unemployed or underemployed, limited to boring and underpaid jobs, politically powerless, socially marginal and lacking in recognition, and defined by negative stereotypes developed by dominant groups provides the core content of the ethical concerns of Latina/os. This is why one finds Hispanics primordially concerned with social ethical issues dealing with justice, human rights, and human dignity. The quest for justice has become a central moral concern of the

Hispanic vision of the good life. There are, however, other ethical concerns that domi-nate the point of view of many Hispanics. At the personal level matters of responsibil-ity for family, for one's own self-development, for issues of self-discipline, and for responsibility to one's neighbor also become important.

Another characteristic of the Hispanic moral point of view is the centrality they give to the communal dimension of existence. Part of the trauma and maladjustment that many Hispanics experience when they come to the United States is due precisely to the shock they experience of moving from a culture that values extended family and intimate and broad-based communal relationships to a culture that is dominantly rights oriented, impersonal, individualistic, and radically private.

Two dominant responses have emerged that seek to address the multiple challenges Hispanics confront: the ethics of identity and the ethics of the common good. These two moral points of view are shaping much of the moral discourse that is presently tak-ing place within the Hispanic community.

Those who abide by the ethics of identity argue that for Hispanic Americans to sur-vive and flourish within North America they must create bonds of solidarity among the different Latino/a national groups. Their shared language and key cultural affinities, as well as their shared social and political challenges provide the context for this solidar-ity movement to take place. The ethics of identity focuses on the promotion of group loyalty and fraternal commitment toward those who share similar cultural traits. It is an ethics that emphasizes the centrality of recognition and respect of what is culturally unique to Latina/os as a history bearing group. This ethics rejects the dominant melt-ing pot model of assimilation. It argues instead for social integration on the basis of shared power and recognition and preservation of differences.

From a religious and theological point of view the ethics of identity uplifts biblical narratives of diasporas that depict the struggles of God's chosen people to preserve their cultural and religious identity when, due to either migration or conquest, they find themselves living within a foreign nation. These stories provide analogies by which many Hispanics understand their present state of affairs. Biblical narratives and princi-ples that affirm the diversity and the goodness of all cultural and ethnic particularity within creation are also appealed to as a source of inspiration to struggle for the pres-ervation of identity and for the affirmation of cultural value and recognition.

The ethics of identity, consistent with deeply ingrained values of Hispanic culture, calls on all members of this community to behave toward each other as if they were members of an extended family. This sense of extended family defines in a distinct way the nature of their basic moral actions and obligations. Family relationships do not follow the contractual model through which individuals relate to one another as autonomous and free agents who establish in clear and specific terms their mutual obli-gations aiming to satisfy their self-interest. Within the family, the language of individual rights is not normative, moral obligations are not expressed through impersonal univer-sal rules or principles, much less are they impartially applied. Family ethics is covenan-tal in nature. The family is a given and so are the obligations we have within it. Our duties and obligations are defined by roles we do not choose, but in which we are born. As the language of rights, abstract principles and impartial judgments help and fit rela-tionships between strangers. Within the family these are replaced by a normative sense of obligations and affective responsibilities toward those who depend on us, who have cared for us, and who have helped us become the particular persons we are today. Not self-interest but a sense of sacrifice, forgiveness, and service is what keeps us bonded to each other. Most importantly, family ethics assumes and affirms the preferential treatment we owe to our kin and to those with whom we have special bonds.

Identity ethics claims that the preferential treatment owed those who have cared for us and who have defined our identity is a legitimate expectation and norm of human interaction. To disregard this commitment of preferential treatment toward kin would violate something basic to the human condition. Impersonal fairness and impartiality in the application of principles that dominate much of ethical theories within North American culture, far from being a virtue, is perceived as a vice. It not only fails to acknowledge the special obligations and the responsibility we owe to those who have cared for us, it also is a sign of lack of loyalty and gratitude. What is politically more significant, for Hispanics not to abide by the principle of preferential treatment towards kin, could very well undermine essential social relationships to our detriment. It can alienate those social groups essential for the protection of our survival and well-being. It would be an act of political suicide that can only undermine the possibility for Hispanics to gain and sustain the power they need to secure justice.

The ethics of identity gives priority to virtues and character formation over universal principles. Among the virtues that are predominate are trustworthiness, friendship and loyalty, all of which sustain concrete forms of solidarity. Emotive empathy, attaching attentiveness to the needs of the oppressed and exploited, and feeling their pain also are central virtues. This particular care, obligation and empathy due to the oppressed or most vulnerable Hispanics, is expressed through the phrase "the preferential option of the poor."

There are a number of shortcomings that plague the ethics of identity. First, it cannot fully solve the tension that exists between its commitment to justice for the poor and the need for some dimension of impartiality and fairness that seems basic to any understanding of justice. Second, it has difficulty addressing the tension that exists between its commitment to the preservation of Hispanic identity and difference and the commitment to promote the common good that is foundational to achieve the economic, political, and cultural justice it seeks. Third, it tends to undervalue the appeal to universal moral principles and individual rights, and its strong sense of covenant and virtues is also a drawback. Public life always entails encounters between strangers. We inevitably must appeal to shared moral principles to motivate people to commit themselves to justice struggles, and we need principles to establish and regulate our mutual responsibilities and expectations.

An alternative moral vision within the Latino/a community, that I will call the ethics of the common good, attempts to respond to some of the above-mentioned challenges and shortcomings of the ethics of identity. These two ethical visions share many of the same value commitments central to Hispanic culture and its moral point of view. For example, they both share a similar communitarian ethos. For both of these ethical visions, what is fundamental in ethics derives from communal values, from shared social goals, and from seeking to promote cooperative virtues. They also emphasize the social character of a life worthy of the name "good." And they are both equally critical of the individualism and the private ethos that dominates life in the United States. They are equally committed to preserve the cultural identity of Latina/o Americans as one of their enduring contributions to this society.

For the ethics of the common good, however, the good life requires more than promoting the well-being of racial ethnic groups. What we need to attend to is the quality and nature of our shared public life. Thus, not the ethnic group but the larger public realm constitutes the main community that needs to be addressed. In this view, it is not enough to substitute radical autonomous individuals left alone to pursue their self-interests, with radically autonomous small groups left alone to nurture their identity. Human flourishing and well-being require that all social groups cultivate a vision and understanding of society that depicts our shared public sphere as much more that the sum of its individual members or a sum of its different social groups. What is crucially needed is that it generates the kind of public spiritedness and citizenship that recognizes that the political community must be addressed as an integrated whole.

The ethics of the common good does not deny that we need a new vision of the public sphere that affirms pluralism and differences. But in affirming pluralism and differences, it must also encourage a vision of social life that is both concerned and inclusive of all social and cultural groups, and that affirms our sense of belonging and of being bonded to each other within a shared body politics. We need the kind of political vision and a public disposition that stresses the fact that our lives are intrinsically intertwined and that we inevitably share a common destiny. A new vision that promotes the conviction that the value of our shared social life resides not in its being useful but rather in its being a constitutive part of what it means to be fully human. This vision and the practices that will make it come through is what must be nurtured among all citizens.

Theologically speaking, this alternative emphasizes those Scriptural narratives that depict God's universal love and care for all of humanity. It stresses the conviction that we are all children of God, thus, brothers and sisters, and very much each other's keeper. Biblical narratives that depict visions of a natural law or order of creation structured within the fabric of creation are uplifted as foundational for the conviction that as humans we are more alike to each other than we are different. In terms of church life, concerns with confessional identity, while important, are given a secondary role to the need to promote ecumenical and interreligious dialogue, and dialogue and alliances with all people of goodwill committed to serve those in need within a context of our shared life. The promotion of personal virtues among church members and citizens must also be accompanied by the commitment to change those social structures that affect our life possibilities. Social structures must attend to the promotion of communal virtues and values.

For the ethics of the common good, the injustices that plague Hispanics—poverty, powerlessness, the sense of not being members or not belonging, and the lack of hope and meaning—are also experienced by other social groups. Particular injustices experienced by one racial ethnic group must be framed and addressed in ways that are inclusive of the interests of other racial ethnic groups. In this view, whatever becomes an obstacle to the flourishing of one social group will also have a negative impact on the well-being of other social groups. The basic moral task, therefore, is not just to contribute to the empowerment of a given oppressed group, which must be done, but to do so in ways that also inspire and motivate other social groups to engage in the historical task of changing the basic institutions of society that shape and affect our lives together. More concretely, in minimizing poverty, racial discrimination, political powerlessness, and social marginalization, we contribute to expanding the possibilities of democratic participation for more people within more spheres of life.

For the ethics of the common good, the need for intergroup solidarity is a pragmatic requirement for the promotion of justice and well-being. From a pragmatic point of view, given the pluralistic nature of our society, it is politically impossible for any one social group to enhance its well-being without the cooperation of others outside the group. Justice cannot be achieved, much less sustained, if we do not address the challenges we normally refer to as the common good. This is precisely the main danger of identity politics, that, in spite of itself, it contributes to the fragmentation that already exists within our society that constitutes one of the main reasons justice is denied to most citizens.

The ethics of the common good, while not necessarily rejecting the free market, does take a strong critical stand against many of its negative consequences. It considers that the dominance of the free market in our society has too many significant negative effects. The dynamics of the free market, for example, perpetuates significant social inequality among the members of society that makes it possible for them to share life together and to participate fully in the opportunities granted by this society. The dynamics of the free market also force many of its citizens to accept social and geographic mobility that undermines family togetherness and the sustenance of strong neighborhoods. Market mechanism encourages the commodification and thus the promotion of impersonal relationships. It stresses individual achievement many times at the expense of cultivating the virtues of public care and service.

At the political level, the promotion of individualistic concerns and self-interest, over and against social and political commitment, has led to a weakening of genuine and meaningful democracy. This move toward greater privatization of more and more dimensions of our life contributes to the deterioration of social life at the same time that we are losing the collective will to provide effective communal programs to address critical social ills. For all of these reasons, the ethics of the common good claim that what we urgently need to promote is education in citizenship and a commitment to the general welfare.

For the ethics of the common good, what makes it imperative for a just society to strive for a wide distribution of its resources and its services is not primordially to encourage people to have more but to allow people to become citizens or active agents committed to a better quality of life for all citizens. The good life demands that we cultivate the Pauline virtues now redefined in terms of public spiritedness: love as emancipatory service to others, hope as a shared commitment to long-term goals greater than our personal interest and faith or belief that our commitments to each other are worthwhile and intrinsic to what it means to live a good life and as such will endure.

Because we are citizens, and not family or kin, the ethics of the common good affirms the value of well-formulated universal ethical principles as these have been embodied within a particular political community. Principles such as justice, equality, freedom, and human rights can play a significant role in the process of Hispanic liberation. When these principles are defined in a concrete and inclusive manner, they can inspire diverse social groups to join together in the pursuit of common interest. They facilitate and encourage the kind of alliances and ties of solidarity with those outside of one's main racial or ethnic group, which alone can bring about the empowerment identity ethics seeks. Well-defined political and moral principles enable us to articulate shared aspirations and hopes, and can motivate us to struggle in common for social justice. They support the kind of coalition activism that is indispensable for obtaining shared common goals.

While strongly communitarian, the ethics of the common good also affirms the values of individual human rights. In its view, individual rights are an indispensable requirement for citizens to realize themselves as imaginative political actors committed and able to enhance the common good. In fact, from their perspective rights need be neither individualistic nor self-centered. On the contrary, communities that guarantee the protection of basic rights protect its citizens against the unscrupulous behavior of the state and other social groups. They also enable the sustenance of public spaces where citizens can gather to consider collectively new ideas and social possibilities of change. In so doing, rights can promote progressive change and do so in an orderly fashion. Rights also allow diverse communities and social groups to coexist peacefully within a single political state.

From the perspective of the ethic of the common good, the signs of the times call for us to identify and address those challenges that affect all of us as citizens. It calls for a transcending ethics that, in affirming group difference, also encourages us to see ourselves as part of a broader social whole or body politics. It calls us to commit ourselves to improve the social character of the public sphere or the political community and encourage those communal values and relationships that better fit the social character of our being.

At present, many of the ethical concerns and debates within the Hispanic community are framed within the parameters of these two dominant moral points of view: the ethics of identity that stresses the importance of loyalty to kin and group empowerment, and the ethics of the common good that promotes a vision that genuine empowerment and authenticity calls for changes in the attitudes of citizens and in the institutions that regulate our common life. It is not clear that these two views can be reconciled in a facile way, nor is it clear that we can readily say that one is preferable to the other. Latino/as are struggling to find ways to live in the tension of being loyal to kin and being responsible citizens.

References and Further Reading

De La Torre, Miguel. *Doing Christian Ethics from the Margins* (Maryknoll, NY: Orbis Books, 2004).

García, Ismael. *Dignidad: Ethics Through Hispanic Eyes* (Nashville: Abingdon Press, 1997).

Isasi-Díaz, Ada María. *En la Lucha: Elaborating a Mujerista Theology* (Minneapolis: Fortress Press, 1993).

Valentin, Benjamín. *Mapping Public Theology: Beyond Culture, Identity and Differences* (Harrisburg, PA: Trinity Press International, 2002).

GOD

Miguel H. Díaz

The revelation of the divine name to Moses (Exodus 3:14) provides one of the most important biblical sources into the nature of God. Translations of the divine name into English as "I am Who Am" have often failed to evoke the dynamic and historically transformative nature of God. Given the centrality of the covenant in the Hebrew Scriptures and the emphasis given to God's self-revelation in historical figures and events, the divine name cannot amount to anything less than a promise of divine presence. The answer that God gives when Moses questions the name of the one who has sent him to be the liberator of Israel best translates to: "I am the one who will be present in power (*'ehyeh*) with my people." One might grasp better the theological significance of the divine name if we consider the Spanish rather than the English translation. In Spanish, the English verb "to be" can be translated as *ser* or as *estar*. *Ser* refers to what something is (essence) while *estar* conveys how something is (condition). To affirm God as *Yo soy el que está* (I am the one who is there with you), rather than as *Yo soy el que es* (I am who am) comes closer to the Old Testament understanding of God as a God who is revealed through mighty deeds on behalf of the marginalized and oppressed.

For Christians, Jesus Christ and the Spirit offer two distinct and interrelated ways of understanding God's self-revelation in history. Jesus who was conceived and empowered by the Holy Spirit contextualizes in a particular human way the reality of God. In his life-giving words and actions, especially on behalf of the poor and marginalized, Jesus makes known God's divine name. The breathing of God's Spirit unto all of creation continues to fulfill this promise of divine presence.

Methodological Presuppositions

To consider U.S. Hispanic theological method is to consider the sources that undergird U.S. Hispanic theological reflections on God. Beyond the influence of biblical traditions and various theological contributions within Catholic and Protestant theological traditions, Latino/a theologies of God draw on a number of sociocultural and religious experiences. Among these experiences, *mestizaje* and *mulataje* have been two distinct

cornerstones of Latino/a theology. "Mestizaje" refers to the specific way of being La-
tino/a (in particular with respect to Latino/a communities that have Mesoamerican
descent) that emerged from intercultural and interreligious asymmetric relations
among Spanish and indigenous communities in the Americas. "Mulataje" refers to
the specific way of being Latino/a that came about as a result of asymmetric
Spanish-African interracial and interreligious relations. Because at the time of a conquest Spain had experienced its own mestizaje with respect to Spanish-Jewish and
Spanish-Muslim relations, there is an often forgotten intercultural and interreligious
aspect that precedes and accompanies the Spanish conquest of the new world. This history is also a source in contemporary Latino/a reflections on the reality of God.

Theologians seeking to draw from "interreligious" sources can also turn to the
ongoing resilience of religious practices associated with indigenous (e.g., *curanderismo*) and African communities (e.g., Lukumí-Candomblé and Vódoun). But perhaps
the central source for envisioning the reality of God from Latino/a perspectives is
popular religion, whether related to Catholic or Protestant expressions. Among the
many particular expressions that can be noted as central theological sources are the
following: (1) popular and often public celebrations of faith (e.g., dramatic reenactments of the way of the Cross during Holy Week and the celebration of *Las posadas*
during Christmas), (2) popular wisdom sayings (e.g., *A Dios rogando y con el mazo
dando*, "Pray to God while hammering away"), (3) popular songs or *coritos* (e.g., *Pes-
cador de Hombres*), and (4) ordinary sacred spaces such as home altars.

Among the most salient methodological affirmations of U.S. Hispanic theology is
that God reveals God's self in *lo cotidiano*. Revelation is not concerned with proposi-
tional statements but with the personal self-manifestation of God in the ordinary affairs
of human beings. As a critical hermeneutical category, lo cotidiano underscores the
theological importance of ordinary life experiences for naming and understanding
the reality of God. Lo cotidiano embraces an integral understanding of daily life that
bridges private and public relationships. Seen from a theological perspective, lo cotidiano offers a locus for tapping into what might be characterized as the Latino/a mysticism of everyday life. This mysticism situates God's life-giving presence within
ordinary struggles of Latino/a communities. What is "ordinary" in Latino/a theology
is often associated with the marginalization that accompanies persons (undocumented
immigrant, women, and children), places (home), relations (familial), and popular religious expressions.

The failure to recognize particular persons, places, relations, and religious expressions is to some extent connected to the loss of aesthetic sensitivity. As a number of
Latino/a theologians have pointed out, many enlightened persons who are heirs to
modernity have privileged the "what" of God's self-revelation (theological content)
to the detriment of sufficiently attending to the "how" of God's self-revelation (theological forms). Latino/a theology overcomes this dualism between theological content
and theological form in the following two ways: (1) It critically recognizes as indispensible the forms of popular faith expressions (e.g., the crucified Christ, the Marys of
U.S. Hispanic popular Catholicism, and popular *coritos*). (2) It embraces a preferential
option, or perhaps to be more aesthetically precise, a preferential optic that highlights

seeing and knowing God in the face of the crucified, oppressed, and marginalized of history (Matthew 25).

Naming and Understanding God from Latina/o Perspectives

Nosotros is a word that has been used to describe U.S. Hispanic anthropology. It is a word that names the reality of God from Latino/a perspectives. The literal English translation of *nosotros* is "we-others." To name God as the divine We-other is to continue the long-standing Christian tradition that affirms God does not exist and cannot be conceived apart from interpersonal relations, that is, apart from the divine community of distinct others (Father/Mother, Wisdom/Word, and Holy Spirit). This focus on communal otherness offers a theological foundation for affirming that in Latino/a theology God must be understood apart from the distinct sociocultural and racial relations that have humanly mediated divine life to Latino/a communities. To name God as *el Dios de nosotros* conveys the sense that issues of naming and understanding God are profoundly connected to specific communal experiences. Indeed, God always turns God's face and reveals God-self according to "our" particular communal needs and experiences. Five ways of understanding God within Latino/a communities follows. This discussion is not intended to exclude other ways of understanding the reality of God from Latino/a perspectives. It is simply one way of systematically correlating Latino/a experiences and the reality of God.

The God of the Galileans

The image of God as a Galilean lies at the heart of Latino/a Protestant and Catholic theologies. For Latino/a theologians, the Incarnation is not merely an affirmation that God became flesh. Rather, the Incarnation is ultimately a doctrine that affirms the profound theological significance of the scandal of particularity: God assumed the existence of a marginalized Galilean Jew. It is from within the Galilean landscape (a place defined by its cultural, religious, geographical, and linguistic diversity and the home to outsiders and rebels) that God's offer of universal salvation takes shape.

Numerous implications flow from God's Galilean face. The "incarnational" presence of God among rural and agricultural villagers of Nazareth means that God has assumed "insignificant" human realities and "insignificant" ordinary places. The question that the Gospel raises with respect to insignificant persons and places is the following: Can anything good come from Nazareth (John 1:43–51)? Latino/a theology answers this question in the affirmative: The faces of past and contemporary "Galileans" make known the goodness of God.

The vanquished Jesus is a central signpost for understanding the God of the vanquished and vanquishment of God. Popular symbols of faith such as artistic depictions of the crucified Christ and rituals such as the practice of accompanying Jesus during the celebration of the *Triduum* offer glimpses into this Latino/a understanding of God. The wide appeal of these popular faith expressions among undocumented immigrants and documented exiles and immigrants of various socioeconomic backgrounds suggests the strong correlation that Latino/a communities embrace between their lives and God's paschal mystery.

Latina/o Protestant and Catholic theologies creatively appropriate the classical attributes of God as omnipresent, omnipotent, and omniscient. Clearly, Latino/a popular faith expressions strongly affirm the "always and everywhere" presence of God, the power of God to prevail over all injustices and human sufferings, and the God who knows and hears the cry of the poor. But the preferential optic preferred by these popular faith expressions also offers a powerful critique of the idols that comprise contemporary human experiences. To recognize God's presence in the Galilean and in the "Galileans" who live among us is to embrace a different logic with respect to power relations. For instance, this logic challenges transnational corporations, communication overlords, and neocolonial national powers that have become god-like modern expressions of omnipresence, omnipotence, and omniscience.

Galilee's reputation as a crossroads of peoples, religious experiences, cultures, and languages offers an opportunity to reflect upon the soteriological significance of human diversity. As many contemporary theological voices have pointed out, the doctrine of God is fundamentally a doctrine of salvation, otherwise it would not have been revealed (Rahner). Jesus' inclusive sociocultural relations lays open the possibility for understanding that beyond personal sin and sociopolitical liberation, God's salvation must be concerned with the survival of communal identities. In other words, reflection upon God's offer of salvation must include reflection on how God wills the preservation and transformation of cultural, religious, gender, and racial human experiences. Since humans are embodied beings, and since it is the salvation of the flesh that God wills, these bodily realities cannot be dismissed from theological consideration. In this sense, the *mestizo* understanding of God as *Teotl-Dios* ("Teotl-Dios" is the name used to identify God in the Nican Mopohua) and the Yoruban notion of God as *Ashé* (the principle of life that grounds divine and human existence) offer fruitful ways of understanding the saving presence of God within embodied cultural and racial experiences particular to Latino/as of being human.

The God of Ordinary Accompaniment

¡Caminemos con Jesús! (Let us walk with Jesus!). This often is the communal and public cry of Latino/a communities who gather in streets during Holy Week to proclaim that Jesus Christ is not an abstract notion or an individual but someone who walks and lives among persons in community. Evidence for this embodied and personal understanding of God can be found in the practice of gathering to pray to the saints in front of home altars or before the Word of God. These popular and domestic devotions suggest that God is someone who draws near to us in ordinary accompaniment. Common ways of addressing God as *Papa Dio*, *Dios mio*, and *Diosito* all suggest this intimate way of relating to God. Such Latino/a ways of addressing God correspond to Jesus' familial address of God as Abba.

U.S. Hispanic theology understands accompaniment as the *act* that constitutes persons. Accompaniment presupposes a dynamic, directional, and concrete orientation of one person to another. Relative to God, accompaniment can be understood as the

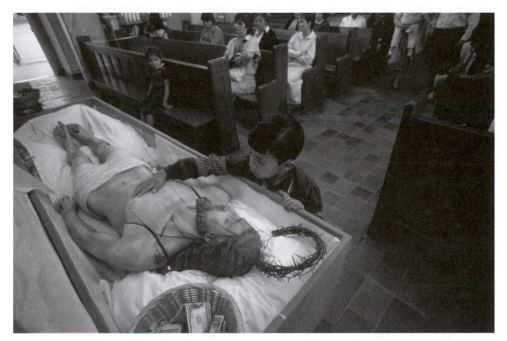

Good Friday services at Our Lady of Guadalupe Church in San Diego. This Catholic Church serves a large segment of the Chicano community in San Diego. On Good Friday, they bring Jesus off the cross and they place him in a coffin for the parishioners to give reverence to him. (Karen Kasmauski/Science Faction/Corbis)

divine act that constitutes the communal life of God. But God's communal life does not remain locked up unto itself. In other words, God does not only will to simply accompany God-self, God wills to share God-self with and accompany human beings. The Incarnation is "proof" that God, whom Christians proclaim to be love (1 John 4.8), out of love necessarily desires to accompany human persons, and in particular, as I have already pointed out, God desires to accompany oppressed and suffering human persons.

One of the most salient characteristics of Latino/a Christianity is the celebration of Holy Week. In reenacting the way of the cross and accompanying Jesus, Latino/a communities proclaim their solidarity with the suffering Christ. This accompaniment is a sacramental sign that proclaims just as the crucified Christ is not abandoned by God, so will they not also be abandoned by God in their daily crucifixions.

As Roberto Goizueta points out, beyond being with others and feeling with others, the *act* of accompaniment implies an ethics of doing with others (1995, 206). This focus on doing rather than simply being has implications for a U.S. Hispanic metaphysical understanding of God. Simply stated, God is S/he Who does for another. The "to be" of God and the "to act" of God are intrinsically related. Reading the prologue of John (John 1:1–14) in Spanish suggests this U.S. Hispanic understanding. The Christian biblical tradition holds that from the beginning the *Logos* was with God.

Through the Logos everything came into being. In Spanish the word "Verb" (*Verbo*) is often used to translate this Greek notion. To say that *en le principio era el Verbo, el Verbo estaba frente a Dios, y el Verbo se hizo carne* (In the beginning was the Verb, the verb was with God, and the Verb became flesh) is to argue that from the beginning it was an act (of accompaniment) that was with God and it is this divine activity that becomes flesh among us. As the Gospel makes clear, it is not the reign (a noun) but the reigning (an activity) of God among the sinner, the poor, and the marginalized that Jesus embodies.

The God Pregnant with Life

In the midst of socioeconomic oppressions and cultural marginalization Latin American and Latino/a theologies share a common affirmation: God is the God of life. For U.S. Hispanic Catholics, popular Marian devotions and, more specifically, the popular devotion to Our Lady of Guadalupe who appears pregnant with life, offer a gender inclusive understanding of the God of life. Among other things, the image of Guadalupe evokes the notion of the divine *rachamim*. The root of this Hebrew word lies with *rechem* (mother's breast or womb). Rachamim associates God with mercy and "motherly" protection. The popular understanding of Guadalupe as mother and protector of the marginalized resonates well with this Old Testament depiction of God. Popularly understood as the mother of a new creation, Guadalupe reveals a God who labors to bring forth life (Isaiah 49:15, Isaiah 42:14).

The *Nican Mopohua*, the story of Our Lady of Guadalupe, recounts the interactions between Juan Diego and Our Lady of Guadalupe. The story connects divine self-revelation to social, cultural, geopolitical, and religious survival. From beginning to end the story of Guadalupe provides a distinct "American" intercultural rendition of who God is and how God acts on behalf of the marginalized of history. The meaning of the story is simple: God is the one who reaches out to and raises from the "dead" the Juan Diegos of this world. Indeed, in her intimate way of relating to *Juan Diegito* —and this as noted above is a central characteristic of the way that Latino/as relate to God and everything and everyone comes from God—the virgin of Guadalupe embodies God's life-giving and transformative presence.

The story of Guadalupe underscores the personal conversion and social transformation necessary to birth human communities in the image of God. Guadalupe's desire to build a new Church does not primarily entail the construction of a building but, more fundamentally, the creation of a new way of relating to one's neighbor that images the inclusive and life-giving reality of God. Furthermore, God shares God's life not just with human creatures but as the story suggests with the predominant role that other creatures play in the story, God desires for all creation to be healed and participate in the presence of God's life.

Echoing Mary's song of the anawim (Luke 1:46–55), the story of Our Lady of Guadalupe portrays God as defender of the oppressed and as the one who brings down the powerful from their thrones. Like other U.S. Hispanic Marian narratives (e.g., the Cuban devotion to Our Lady of Charity), the story of Guadalupe provides a profound theological critique of asymmetric power relations that affect humans and all other creatures of God. As a symbol of God's recreation, the Guadalupan tradition challenges the unnatural and sinful notion that God ordains some persons to exist above others. The story of Guadalupe invites us to imagine God pregnant with life, laboring to birth new persons and a new social order that holds in high regard the cultural and religious heritage of all people. As the beloved disciple and Mary stand with Jesus at the climactic hour of life-giving and community-building experiences ("And from that hour, the disciple took her to his own home"), Guadalupe stands with Juan Diego at the hour of his historical crucifixion. At this hour she summons Juan Diego and all other marginalized persons to be agents of a new *ecclesia*, an inclusive way of being human. As a pneumatological and cultural symbol of the Spirit of God, Guadalupe is a woman full of grace (Luke 1:28) sent to communicate to the "Juan Diegos" of this world that God is Lord and the giver of life.

The God of la Lucha

God is life. In principle, Latino/a theology does not reject the metaphysical truth contained in this statement. However, Latino/a theology historicizes this truth when it affirms that life is a struggle (*la vida es una lucha*). God is the life force in all of us that struggles against all oppressive measures that reduce persons to objects of abuse and consumption. God is the life force encountered in *la fiesta*, those life-giving Latino/a celebrations that prophetically build community and resist marginalization and suffering.

It is customary in Christian tradition to affirm that God is the fullness of Being. In turn, as a result of an analogical relationship between God and all of creation, Christian traditions affirm that human beings participate in, are sustained by, and reflect the divine Being. But Absolute Being and Existence, even in the classical Thomistic Catholic approach is not a static Being. Being is pure act, dynamism, and life-giving relationship. Thus, instead of conceiving the reality of God as stasis, *la lucha* opens up a way to conceive God as ectasis, as the divine Being who struggles to birth life and opposes all that denies life.

Latino/a theology contextualizes life in terms of socioeconomic, cultural, gender, and racial experiences. Life is a struggle to overcome poverty. Life is a struggle to affirm cultural identity. Life is a struggle to reject sexism and racism. In these and other human struggles, Latino/a theology affirms that being human cannot be divorced from the everyday and concrete realities that engender or suppress life. Because of the communion between human and divine life that has been brought about through Jesus Christ, these ordinary concerns become God's concerns. In this sense, God can be faithfully sensed (*sensus fidelium*) in the everyday struggles to survive and live fully as a human.

Together with Irenaeus, the second-century theologian, Latino/a theology proclaims that the glory of God is the human being fully alive. Faced with homogenization and globalization—these are powerful social, cultural, and economic forces that strive to melt away and suppress particular expressions of human life—our challenge is the struggle to affirm the particular that glorifies God today. This struggle to affirm particularity in the midst of communal diversity is not foreign to God's life. If one understands *la lucha* in terms of creative and life-giving relations, then God's life is lucha. God's struggle involves the ongoing creative and life-giving relations of one divine person to another so that the divine community can eternally emerge *from* and be sustained *in* distinct familial relations (Mother/Father, Child, Spirit). The challenge today for us who seek to create human communities in the image of God ethically requires opposing the subordination and/or suppression of human differences. To struggle with God and in God's image involves the struggle against all forces that undermine human diversity.

The God of Life-Giving Migrations

The Old Testament paints a vivid picture of Israel as a migrating people searching for life. As pointed out at the beginning of this entry, the revelation of the divine name to Moses, which amounts to a promise of divine presence, anticipates the Exodus. In the Exodus God leads the people of Israel on a life-giving migration. God offers God's life-giving (salvific) presence in the liberating migration of Israel from Egypt to the promised land. The memory of this event remains formative for the people of Israel, leading to various divine prescriptions that call upon Israel to act justly toward migrating foreigners who abide within its midst. Just as God remembered the Israelites when they were strangers in the land of Egypt so does God call them to remember those who pass through their deserts (e.g., Deuteronomy 5:15, 10:19).

Relative to the Christian doctrine of God, Genesis 18, commonly referred to as the hospitality of Abraham and Sarah, offers a window into understanding how the human experience of migration can be iconic of the life of God. Upon being visited by three passing strangers, Abraham and Sarah hasten to prepare a meal. In the process of opening their home and sharing life's necessities with migrating strangers, they discover that these strangers are messengers of God. Following the biblical motif of role reversals between guest and host relations, this biblical story ends with the stunning announcement that Sarah is pregnant with life. In the migrating strangers, Abraham and Sarah discover the presence of God. The story of the hospitality of Abraham and Sarah crystallizes the meaning of the biblical injunction: "Do not neglect hospitality, for through it some have unknowingly entertained angels" (Hebrews 13:2).

The ongoing migration of documented and undocumented strangers across an arid desert or a shark-infested sea continues to evoke the memory of the hospitality of Abraham and Sarah. Liturgically speaking, the popular religious celebration of *las posadas* recalls a God who is hospitable and beckons hospitality. Based on Mary's and Joseph's search for an inn to birth Jesus (Luke 2:1–7), this ritual symbolizes the risk-taking and life-seeking migrations that marginalized families often undertake. The ritual taps into the most basic Christian understanding of God: The God of Jesus Christ is the God of life-giving migrations whose offer of life crosses over into human reality and stands in solidarity with life-deprived persons.

Risk-taking, life-seeking, and life-giving migrations provide fruitful sources to re-vision God as the God of life-giving migrations. God "ex-ists" because of personal migrations and as a migrating community of distinct others. More specifically, within the context of Latino/a theology, Jesus Christ can be conceived of as God's migrant worker and the Spirit as the divine immigrant who permanently resides among us. Similar to migrants who often come to the United States to work the fields, Jesus comes into the world to labor in the fields on behalf of God. Like many migrants who endure risk-taking labors and often return to their homeland once their seasonal work is done, Jesus risks his life and returns to the Father upon completion of his earthly human labors. Jesus' prophetic exile from this world, however, ushers the life-giving migration of the Spirit. As the one who crosses unto the human realm to permanently remain an advocate of the marginalized, the Spirit can be *latinamente* characterized as the divine immigrant among us.

Conclusion

This brief exploration into the reality of God has shown how Latina/o theology envisions the ongoing revelation of the divine name. As I noted at the beginning of these reflections, the divine name connotes divine presence and the historical experiences under which this presence can be encountered. This exploration has offered various ways in which some communal experiences of Latino/as can anchor reflections on God. The human experiences of sociocultural identity (Galilean identity), ordinary accompaniment, pregnancy, *la lucha*, and human migrations offer new sources to name and understand who God is. And who God is can never be divorced from who God is *pro nobis*. Indeed, God is always *el Dios de nosotros*. In our methodological option to reflect on God *latinamente*, we Latino/a theologians mirror contemporary efforts to moor the doctrine of God in ordinary human experiences. The preferential optic that we have for socioculturally marginalized persons provides a distinct and refreshing angle of vision into the mystery of God.

References and Further Reading

Aquino, Pilar. *Our Cry For Life: Feminist Theology from Latin America* (Maryknoll, NY: Orbis Books, 1993).

Costas, Orlando E. "Evangelism from the Periphery: A Galilean Model." *Apuntes: Reflexiones Teológicas desde el Margen Hispano* 2, no. 3 (1982): 53–59.

Díaz, Miguel. "Life-Giving Migrations: Re-visioning the Mystery of God through U.S. Hispanic Eyes." *E-Journal of Hispanic Latino Theology*, http://www.latinotheology.org (accessed March 15, 2007).

Díaz, Miguel. "Outside the Survival of Community there is no Salvation." *E-Journal of Hispanic Latino Theology*, http://www.latinotheology.org (accessed March 15, 2007).

Elizondo, Virgilio. *Guadalupe: Mother of New Creation* (Maryknoll, NY: Orbis Books, 1997).

Elizondo, Virgilio. *Galilean Journey: The Mexican-American Promise, 2nd ed.* (Maryknoll, NY: Orbis Books, 2000).

Espín, Orlando. *The Faith of the People: Theological Reflections on Popular Catholicism* (Maryknoll, NY: Orbis Books, 1997).

Espín, Orlando. *Grace and Humanness: Theological Reflections Because of Culture* (Maryknoll, NY: Orbis Books, 2007).

Espín, Orlando, and Miguel H. Díaz. *From the Heart of Our People: Latino/a Explorations in Catholic Systematic Theology* (Maryknoll, NY: Orbis Books, 1999).

Goizueta, Roberto S. *Caminemos con Jesús: Toward a Hispanic/Latino Theology of Accompaniment* (Maryknoll, NY: Orbis Books, 1995).

González, Justo. *Mañana: Christian Theology from a Hispanic Perspective* (Nashville: Abingdon Press, 1990).

Isasi-Díaz, Ada María. *Mujerista Theology* (Maryknoll, NY: Orbis Books, 1996).

Pedraja, Luis. *Teología: An Introduction to Hispanic Theology* (Nashville: Abington Press, 2003).

Rodríguez, Jeanette. "God Is Always Pregnant." *The Divine Mosaic: Woman's Images of the Sacred Other*, ed. Theresa King (St. Paul, MN: International Publishers, 1994).

HERMENEUTICS

Efrain Agosto

U.S. Latino/a biblical hermeneutics is a work in progress. One can look back to the biblical interpretative work that Spanish conquistadores used to justify their conquests of native peoples in North, Central, and South America or to the always present subversive interpretations of conquered peoples as they learned the biblical tools of their masters and found in those tools a message of hope and liberation. However, it is in the past 30 years as Hispanics joined the ranks of biblical scholarship in larger numbers that some of the more fruitful and widespread work has been produced to tell the story of Latina/o biblical hermeneutics, including the interpretation of the Hebrew Scriptures and the New Testament. This essay will examine an overview of this recent movement in Latino/a readings of the Bible.

Some Early Voices

Francisco Garcia-Treto is one of the early voices in the modern era of Latino/a biblical hermeneutics. In an essay written about Protestant Latina/o hermeneutics in particular, Garcia-Treto emphasizes two important points that are fundamental to understanding biblical hermeneutics in the Hispanic tradition. First, biblical hermeneutics is Latino or Latina because "a community of interpretation" is being established. One of the fundamental understandings of how Hispanics read the Bible is their engagement in a community of interpretation. Rather than being "lone rangers" in the task of interpretation, Latino/as read scripture in light of community. Garcia-Treto cites the concept of "interpretative community" in literary studies and concludes that the "emerging emphasis on contextual or 'social location' readings of the Bible converge" with "the *teología de conjunto* being developed in U.S. Hispanic churches." That is, theology as a function of community, implies that "new hermeneutical strategies and standpoints are being put in place" (1999, 161).

A second aspect that Garcia-Treto celebrates about Hispanic biblical hermeneutics is its ecumenicity. In fact, the recent emergence of biblical Latina/o hermeneutics is due in part, argues Garcia-Treto, to the growing ecumenicity of Hispanic Protestant and Roman Catholic biblical scholarship, collaboration that transcends any separation based on Reformation principles. He writes, "Today, within the U.S. Hispano/Latino churches, and specifically at the academic-theological professional level, a new ecumenical openness to cooperation, dialogue, and mutual acceptance has developed between mainline and other Protestant and Roman Catholic biblical scholars, to the extent that a true interpretative community . . . may already be identified" (1999, 164).

Rather than doctrinal principles, the focus is on community and the cultural/social nature of that community. Thus, Garcia-Treto concludes that "just as a transnational Latina/o consciousness of being a people is emerging and setting a sociocultural agenda in the United States, so a transdenominational consciousness of being an interpretive community reading the Bible from the social location of our people has arisen and is beginning to bear noticeable fruit" (1999). Thus, an ecumenical Hispanic biblical interpretation has emerged, at least in the academic circles of biblical and theological scholarship, across the Catholic and Protestant "divide." Biblical scholars have led that surge in sharing joint understandings of biblical hermeneutics in the Latino/a tradition.

Biblical Hermeneutics by Latino/a Theologians

Some of those leading the early charge for a Hispanic-specific biblical hermeneutic have been Latino and Latina theologians engaged in interpreting the biblical text for the construction of a U.S. Latino/a theology. For example, the Mexican American priest and scholar Virgilio Elizondo writes about the "mestizo," Galilean Christ, one who, like Mexican Americans, comes from the borderlands of mainstream religion and culture in ancient Israel (i.e., Galilee) to challenge the powers that be at the center of Jewish life and Roman domination in Jerusalem (1983). Elizondo interprets the historical Jesus, as recorded in the Synoptic Gospels, as an outsider challenging the center. In this way, Elizondo demonstrates how to read the Bible from the perspective of "the margins," as does Miguel A. De La Torre, another Latino theologian and ethicist, who reflects from a theological perspective on the function of scripture in Latino and other marginalized circles (2002).

A similar hermeneutic is offered by a third Latino theologian, Harold Recinos, who writes about the "hard-hitting," "barrio" Christ, thus engaging a hermeneutic that highlights the historical Jesus as depicted in the gospel record as one who challenges the "established leadership" of his day, both religious and political (1997). For Recinos, the fundamental fact of Scripture is this challenge from the margins to the center, and thus a hermeneutic that does not engage the political questions of power and privilege is a truncated hermeneutic and not Latino or Latina in orientation. Ada María Isasi-Díaz adds an important dimension to these questions of power, privilege, and the underprivileged or powerless, and that is the dimension of gender in the Hispanic context. Her "mujerista theology" focuses on the religious, theological, and cultural experiences and vision of Latinas, some with a complicated relationship to their faith communities, but who, nonetheless, engage the Bible from the perspective of liberation and antisexism, especially in light of their everyday struggles, what Isasi-Díaz calls "lo cotidiano," that which entails everyday life (1990). For Isasi-Díaz and the women she works with in grassroots urban communities, the Bible is a tool for liberation because of the struggles of marginalized women and men depicted in the stories of the various books of the Bible. However, there are also oppressive sections that have been used to marginalize women. No biblical interpretation that recognizes the sexist portions of the Bible as equally authoritative as the liberating portions, especially as it pertains to women, can be considered authentic biblical hermeneutics. Thus the lives of Latinas become the key to unlocking the authority of the biblical text.

These theological readings of the Bible, therefore, what one might call a Latino/a theological hermeneutics, demonstrate what Fernando Segovia calls "a canon within a canon" approach to hermeneutics, which characterizes much of Latino/a biblical hermeneutics. That which is truly liberating in the scriptural traditions becomes the building blocks of a Hispanic theological, biblical, and hermeneutical tradition (Segovia 1994).

Segovia and the Critique of the Historical-Critical Methodologies

Fernando Segovia critiques more traditional biblical hermeneutics, especially those that espouse a purely historical approach to the Bible, assuming that hermeneutics can be completely objective and divorced from social location, or those that hold the Bible in its entirety as authoritative without questioning the oppressive affirmations of scripture. In a seminal essay on biblical hermeneutics, one that is groundbreaking not only for Latino/a biblical hermeneutics, but for the entire enterprise, Segovia (1995a) argues that giving precedence solely to a historical exercise is not possible or advisable, given the interlocking relationships between reading texts and reading ourselves.

Segovia offers a fundamental critique of the historical critical approach to biblical interpretation because the "text as means," that is, as a source of history, usually does not incorporate the concerns or perspectives of the modern "flesh and blood" reader, including the Latino/a reader. Without awareness of the reader's social context, his or her own social location will still predominate, albeit unconsciously. In reality, historical critical methods offer a scientific basis for what is fundamentally a personal, social, and theological exercise. Without concern for the social location of the reader, historical critical methodologies are often Eurocentric in their orientation, even as they seek to be "objective." Latino/a biblical critics, like Segovia, have led the way, along with African American and Asian interpreters, in challenging a Eurocentric approach to biblical hermeneutics.

Whether it is literary criticism—the "text as medium"—that is a communication between sender and recipient that becomes a literary and rhetorical argument on its own right, regardless of historical background, or the "text as means and medium," which refers to approaches that look at issues of social and cultural context, particularly in light of both ancient and modern social theory, Segovia challenges any hermeneutical method that excludes the role of the reader and his or her social context as a tool of interpretation. The influence of Latina/o biblical hermeneutics and its concern for a robust meaning of Scripture that engages both the ancient and modern context influences these contributions by Segovia. For example, in literary criticism, the communication (a "text") takes on a life of its own beyond the immediate historical context. Yet, literary methods do not lack their own search for objectivity or a "canon" of truth beyond the interplay between reader and text. An implied author or implied reader is considered, but more abstractly, not the "flesh and blood" reader, by which Segovia means a consideration of the contemporary reader and his or her own social location, including the Latino/a reader. Even social scientific criticism, which Segovia calls "cultural criticism," in which the biblical critic reads modern social theory back into the ancient biblical texts and contexts, but also uses cross-cultural and transhistorical anthropological theory to study ancient society and the texts it produced, as well as the people who produced them, is still couched in terms of the search for objectivity, this time through even *more* scientific means. For readers who engage these methods, "the economic, social or cultural dimensions of the biblical texts proved far more attractive than its theological or religious character" (Segovia 1995a, 22). Yet, Segovia points out that in this realm of cultural criticism only Marxist biblical criticism expressed concern for the modern reader, in particular the socially and economically marginalized, including the U.S. Latino/a readers of the Bible.

González and "Reading through Hispanic Eyes"

What is it about the Latino/a reader that evokes these critiques of traditional methodology and calls for a more "intercultural" approach toward reading the Bible? Justo González suggests five hermeneutical points of departure that motivate Latino/a readings of scripture (1996). These include the paradigms of marginality, poverty, *mestizaje* and *mulatez*, exiles and aliens, and solidarity, all of which correspond in one way or another to the experience of Hispanics today. By marginality, González posits that those on the margins of society can often see things in the biblical text that those in power, or at the center of a society, cannot. For example, in the Gospels and Acts we read stories about Jesus, the Apostles, and those who opposed them, oftentimes referred to in the text as "the Jews." Those who stand outside the center of power today can understand how such references do not somehow indict a whole race, but rather refer to the problems people on the margins of a society (Jesus and the peasant population he served; the earliest Christians) often face with those who hold power, such as the Jewish and Roman leadership in Jerusalem.

With regard to poverty, González emphasizes that a Latina/o reading of the Bible, given the economic status of so many Hispanics in the United States, is not just about what the Bible says about the poor, but more about what the poor have to say about the Bible. Therefore, the question is, "What does the Bible say when read from the perspective of the poor?" or "What do the poor find in the Bible that the nonpoor miss?" Ultimately, it is not just a question of helping the poor by telling them what the Bible says about them, but realizing that the reading of the Bible by the poor can contribute to the whole church. Thus Latino/a biblical hermeneutics argues for wide-ranging opportunities in terms of who can read the text and give viable interpretative guidelines to a text.

González also explores "mestizaje" and "mulatez." These key terms in Latino theology refer to the status of many Latino/a groups as mixed races. For example, Mexicans and Mexican- Americans are considered "mestizos" because of their mixture with native peoples and the conquering Spaniards, and later with the North American populations of the United States. In the Caribbean Latin American culture, the phenomenon of "mulatez" represents the mixture of African Black and European White races. Initially these were pejorative terms used by the dominate White culture against these "mixed races." However, both terms have become points of pride. In fact, with increasing mestizajes all over the world, including the United States, the Mexican American and Caribbean experience can be models to lead the way toward mutual understanding and just, joint living.

Living as a mestizo or "mulatto" is not easy. Struggles with identity abound. With what group does one most identify, especially in light of the pressures of the dominant cultures in which one finds oneself, which draws us into belonging, yet we never quite "belong"? With these struggles for identity, the Latino/a reader of the Bible looks for answers, solace, and a historical and theological understanding in the Scriptures. González cites the example of the Apostle Paul as depicted in the Book of Acts. He calls Paul a "cultural mestizo," because of his two names, "Saul," reflecting his Jewish heritage, and the other, "Paul," the name he used when relating to Greco-Roman culture. In the Book of Acts, when the Pauline mission turns to the Gentiles, "Saul" becomes "Paul." Cultural mestizaje as a Hellenistic Jew helps the Apostle Paul accomplish his mission in the diverse world of the first century CE. Latino/a readers of the Bible often interpret these instances of multiculturalism quite well because of their experience with them.

Being "exile and aliens," González's fourth set of interpretive lenses, also fits naturally in the lived experience of Hispanics today. Often cited with regard to Israel's Babylonian exile, these terms speak to the fact and feeling of leaving one's center to enter somebody else's center. Thus, closely related to marginality, the state of being in exile and called "aliens" represents "a strange sort of marginalization" precisely because one leaves a center to enter the periphery. Among Latina/os such a move often implies that one's beloved center, a homeland, has deteriorated due to external intervention, civil strife, economic decline, and political oppression. Thus our homeland no longer enjoys the peace and joy that God intends for all of us. We must leave it for somebody's center. Latino/as understand when the prophets and poets of Israel lament these experiences among their people. In the New Testament writings, the author of 1 Peter describes the experience of Christian "exiles and aliens" in Northern Asia Minor as those who no longer feel like a people until God intervenes on their behalf and creates a "holy nation" (1 Peter 2:9–11). Such passages resonate with the biblical hermeneutics of a Latino/a immigrant community in the United States.

Being an exile and an alien implies, therefore, that difficult experiences await those in this state, as expressed in the Psalmist's lament over the Babylonian exile: "By the rivers of Babylon—there we sat down and there we wept . . ." (Psalm 137:1ff). Yet, the Bible also emphasizes several positive aspects and challenges with regard to exile. First, the notion of caring for the "stranger" is important in the Bible, especially because, in a sense, we are all "exiles and aliens" in one form or another. Israel, formed out of a band of nomads, needed to constantly remember that history by just treatment of the immigrant, the "stranger."

Second, the Bible encourages the exile to make the best of his or her new situation, as noted in the words of the prophet Jeremiah to the exiles in Babylon: "Build houses and live in them; plant gardens and eat what they produce . . . But seek the welfare of the city where I have sent you into, and pray to the Lord on its behalf, for in its welfare you will find your welfare" (Jeremiah 29:5, 7). This is a challenge to Latino/a immigrants as well, to make their new home a safe and just one, confronting those in power to make the changes necessary to ensure the well-being of the new immigrant. The Bible, as read and understood by Latino/a interpreters, supports such action.

Third, the Bible teaches that the center must understand the opportunity they now have with the new influx of new peoples who can help bless the land and improve on it, rather than consider these outsiders as a burden. The story of Ruth and Naomi is a narrative about a woman who becomes a stranger in another land for the sake of her husband, and then another woman who leaves her homeland for the sake of her mother-in-law. Out of such exile, painful though it may have been, arises a great king of Israel several generations later (David). Given such a reading of the biblical text, the Latino/a interpreter insists that the dominant culture take into account the contributions of the immigrant community that is now present in "their" land. A Latino/a biblical hermeneutic uses present experience to help interpret the ancient text, and ancient experience to help affirm present-day, liberative praxis.

Solidarity is the last of González's hermeneutical paradigms for reading the Bible through Latino/a eyes. Unlike the other terms that reflect in many ways the negative experiences of Hispanics in the United States, solidarity lies at the heart of the message of good news in the Bible. The companion terms of "family" and "community" constitute ways in which both the Bible and Hispanics also express solidarity. Unity is another related term. For example, the Apostle Paul seeks solidarity and unity for his congregations, including the troubled context of 1 and 2 Corinthians.

The theme of family is prevalent throughout the Scriptures. It is an important theme for Hispanics as well, especially for many who have immigrated from abroad and lost the sense of *extended* family that is so important. For many Latino/as, the church becomes the extended family that was lost by coming to the United States, with its focus on the nuclear family. Citizenship is another related theme. González reminds us that in the Roman world of the early Christians, citizenship was no easy matter. It required not only legal residence, but a certain amount of social and economic status. Not many, therefore, were citizens of a local city, or Roman citizens, empire-wide. Most depended on slave or client relations with citizens in order to acquire some sense of belonging in a particular social setting. Those who were "strangers" (*xenoi*), with no such ties, were worse off than any other noncitizens. The Apostle Paul's citizenship status, according to the Book of Acts, gave him an enormous amount of freedom to carry out his gospel mission across the Greco-Roman world. However, not everyone in his churches had this status. In Corinth, for example, conflict between persons of different citizenship status may have caused divisiveness as well as an elite, patronal attitude of some over against others (Agosto 2005).

Yet, the Christian assembly should be a home and a family for many who otherwise do not have a place that gives them a measure of status and community. It is this sense of community solidarity that Paul tries to build in Corinth, but experiences serious obstacles in doing so, according to both 1 and 2 Corinthians. Nonetheless, González describes the church, as understood especially by Latino/a participants today, as an integral part of the gospel; it is not a mere "instrument" or "vehicle" or an add-on. For many Latina/os it is the "extended family" that is missed so much as a result of our immigrant status, as "aliens" in a new land. Latino/a hermeneutics open up to this whole theme of solidarity and the search for unity and family in the Bible because of the Latino/a experience of alienation and the search for identity.

Intercultural Studies

With a critique of traditional biblical hermeneutics and an examination of the motifs that motivate such rich Latino/a readings of the Bible, the call for intercultural studies in biblical interpretation seems a natural next step in the development of a Hispanic biblical hermeneutic. Latino/a biblical hermeneutics provides an ongoing conversation between the experience of the first believers and the experience of the modern-day reader around themes parallel in both the biblical text and the lives of Latino/as today. Both sides of the continuum feed off each other in the quest for meaning. Segovia calls such a dialogue "intercultural studies" (1995b). Segovia suggests that authentic biblical interpretation takes into consideration not just the cultural and historical situation of the original text, but the cultural and historical situation— the social location— of the reader. By taking fully into account the context of the modern reader, including the Latino/a reader, for the task of biblical hermeneutics, an interpreter thereby allows for the contextualization of culture and experience, both with regard to the ancient text and to the readers of such texts.

Segovia, like all Latino/a biblical interpreters, agrees that historical critical analysis is a tool in biblical interpretation. It is not sufficient by itself for the hermeneutical task. In particular, a Latina/o reader represents not just an independent reader but also a member of a distinct community, a reader with an identifiable and meaningful social location. Latino/as in the United States, as bilingual, bicultural persons have the experience of being "the other" in whatever situation they are thrust into in this society. Many, whether Mexican Americans, Puerto Ricans, or Cubans (for example) are never fully comfortable, either in this world or the world in which they or their parents were raised. Such a phenomenon and the interpretative lenses that emerge from it must be deemed, Segovia suggests, as "a Hispanic-American hermeneutics of otherness and engagement, whose fundamental purpose is to read the biblical text as an other" (1995b, 58). In fact, as bilingual-bicultural persons, the Latino/a reader of the Bible is in an excellent position to interpret texts that come from a variety of complex social and cultural situations. The complexity and historical distance of the biblical text makes it an "other," which compares well to the diasporic situation of a U.S. Latino/a. In short, the Hispanic reader, who navigates a complicated existence as a bilingual/bicultural person, one who straddles two or more worlds—the First and the Third, at least—is well situated to confront biblical interpretation.

Thus Hispanic biblical hermeneutics entails intercultural studies. How does that encounter take place? Several steps may be cited. For Segovia, the first step in a reading strategy of intercultural criticism is to acknowledge the contextualization of our "texts," both the text being read and the reader of the text. In both instances, we are engaging in the exchange of "others." Both reader and text are contextual, and we must do interpretation of each in the hermeneutical task, renouncing the notion of a universal reading, where only the text is an "other," and not the reader him/herself. Ultimately, meaning lies in the interaction between reader and text. Latino/a biblical interpreters like Segovia emphasize the reader's social location in this engagement between "texts" because of the long-held tradition of focusing on the text as the object, rather than the interplay between the otherness of two equally engaged "texts"—ancient text and modern reader.

Given this Latino/a hermeneutic of textual engagement that involves recognizing contextualization on both ends of the spectrum, interaction between reader and text, and meaning making as the result of this "bicultural" interaction, Segovia posits three specific dimensions of intercultural biblical criticism. First, the reader must recognize the ancient text "as a socially and culturally conditioned other," just like Latino/as, or any other social group must be recognized as such. This dimension recognizes that the biblical text, like all "texts," is a product of a particular social context. Because the biblical text arose from a very different historical situation and cultural setting than Hispanics, it has its own character, it has its own agenda, and it must be understood on its own terms. It is not "atemporal, asocial, ahistorical, speaking uniformly across time and culture" (Segovia 1995b, 68). As a product of its own time, the biblical text must be viewed as an "other" to the modern reader and must be allowed to speak on its own terms. This, of course, is not too different from what a traditional historical critic might say about historical critical biblical exegesis. In fact, we must use a variety of historical, literary, social, and cultural methods to get at the multifaceted dimension of the biblical text. However, the Latino/a biblical critic argues that the other dimensions of a Latino/a hermeneutic are equally as important as the historical dimension.

The second dimension involves the reader, who is also to be viewed as a product of his social and cultural environment, even as he or she engages the biblical text with its distinction dimensions. Both reader and text engage each other as "others." Thus the reader's strategy in engaging this "other" must be brought to the fore, just like the text's rhetorical and ideological strategy must be investigated. No reader is immune to personal, social, theological, and ideological perspectives in the pursuit of biblical meaning. Readers are products of a specific context that has a particular social reality that influences the process of reading and interpretation. No reader can be "atemporal, asocial, or ahistorical" and thus speak "uniformly for all times and all cultures" (Segovia 1995b, 70). Thus what we have is an encounter, an intercultural engagement between two "texts," an ancient one and a modern one.

What makes this reading particularly Hispanic is first the acknowledgement of distinct cultural and social realities in conversation with each other across time, and second the lessons learned from U.S. Latino/a bicultural experience toward that end. For a Latino/a critic, reality is constructed from a variety of cultural and historical experiences in a bicultural context. Moreover, Latina/os know that it is possible to function well in two worlds, moving from one to the other with ease. Thus we learn to appreciate and appropriate difference and diversity, as well as engage the other in ways that permit their voices to be heard. As a result of this posture, Latino/a biblical interpretation emerges with a hermeneutic of otherness and engagement that is committed to all readers and all readings, providing a rich diversity. The Latina/o reader interprets reality with more than one lens. Latino/a biblical hermeneutics should be a robust engagement of many readings, from both antiquity and the present, each with equal value in the quest for meaning making. Hispanic biblical hermeneutics understands that the factors that help identify the social location of readers and texts alike include religious tradition, sociopolitical and economic status, class, gender, racial or ethnic background, and educational attainment, among others. The reader, like the text, becomes understood on his or her own terms, in his or her own world, as a product or "construct" of his or her own context.

The third and final element toward a Latino/a hermeneutic of intercultural engagement between readers and texts (context of text; context of reader) is that such interaction is not neutral. Rather, "an unavoidable filtering of the one world or entity by and through the other" occurs between reader and text (Segovia 1995b, 70). Thus the construction of a new "text" takes place rather than simply the reconstruction of an existing text (normally in traditional hermeneutics, the ancient text is the focus of historical reconstruction). Construction of a new text in Latina/o biblical hermeneutics takes place because both "texts" are influenced by each other in the encounter. Interpretation in this model is not a one-way encounter—a detached, ideal reader engaging a text to find ancient meaning without acknowledging his or her strategy, agenda, or social location. Rather, "the hermeneutics of otherness and engagement," influenced by the Latino/a experience of otherness and engagement in an alien, multicultural context, "argues that the historical and cultural remoteness of the text as an other is in itself not a reconstruction but a construction of the past on the part of the reader" (Segovia 1995b, 71). Moreover, the reader, especially the Latina/o reader who is not neutral in her or his interpretative efforts carries an agenda, whether conscious or not. In the case of the Latino/a reader, a construction that facilitates liberation from oppressed situations is of utmost important. This is the ultimate goal of a Hispanic biblical hermeneutic.

Such an agenda does not preclude historical research into the life and times of a text, but is one more element in the encounter between readers and texts as engaged others in the search for a liberative praxis. Such engagement is not without resistance, especially by those who experience the United States as "monocultural," even though they are surrounded by the bicultural reality of Latino/as. Nonetheless, interpreters of texts, both past and present, become conversation partners in the construction of new "texts," hopefully texts of liberation, as Hispanics experience the mixing of the biblical text, their social location as Latino/as, and the history of interpretation of said text.

The key to Latino/a biblical hermeneutics lies in the process of engagement. We engage texts as constructs of their own reality, in whatever time period and with whatever ideological strategy they employ. We will construct a new reality of that ancient reading, using the tools of history, using the social sciences, and engaging the readings of others, including an investigation of *their* social location, ideological agendas, and otherness. Segovia calls such a hermeneutic a "humanization," an acknowledgement of human reality as it stands under a variety of categories and emphases, rather than trying to "dehumanize" without recognizing the variety of forces and diversities of the human condition, or "rehumanize," such that some universal, all-encompassing categories are invoked, that preclude the reality of otherness.

Such a vision of Hispanic biblical hermeneutics challenges the Latino/a interpreter, as well as like-minded partners, to address specific biblical texts from the perspective of intercultural studies, engagement of the other, and an agenda of liberation and humanization. In this way, Latino/a biblical hermeneutics will continue to be a contributor to the enterprise of biblical interpretation, theological construction, and liberative praxis.

References and Further Reading

Agosto, Efrain. *Servant Leadership: Jesus and Paul* (St. Louis: Chalice Press, 2005).

De La Torre, Miguel A. *Reading the Bible from the Margins* (Maryknoll, NY: Orbis Books, 2002).

Elizondo, Virgilio. *Galilean Journey: The Mexican American Promise* (Maryknoll, NY: Orbis Books, 1983).

Garcia-Treto, Francisco. "Reading the Hyphens: An Emerging Biblical Hermeneutics for Latino/Hispanic U.S. Protestants." *Protestantes/Protestants: Hispanic Christianity Within Mainline Traditions*, ed. David Maldonado Jr. (Nashville: Abingdon Press, 1999).

González, Justo. *La Santa Biblia: The Bible Through Hispanic Eyes* (Nashville: Abingdon Press, 1996).

Isasi-Díaz, Ada María. "The Bible and *Mujerista* Theology." *Lift Every Voice: Constructing Theologies from the Underside*, ed. Susan Brooks Thistlewaite and Mary Potter Engel (San Francisco: Harper & Row, 1990).

Recinos, Harold. *Who Comes in the Name of the Lord: Jesus at the Margins* (Nashville: Abingdon Press, 1997).

Segovia, Fernando. "Reading the Bible as Hispanic Americans." *New Interpreter's Bible*, Volume 1 (Nashville: Abingdon Press, 1994).

Segovia, Fernando. "'And They Began to Speak in Other Tongues': Competing Modes of Discourse in Contemporary Biblical Criticism." *Reading from This Place, Volume I: Social Location and Biblical Interpretation in the United States*, ed. Fernando F. Segovia and Mary Ann Tolbert (Minneapolis: Fortress Press, 1995).

Segovia, Fernando. "Toward a Hermeneutics of the Diaspora: A Hermeneutics of Otherness and Engagement." *Reading from This Place, Volume I: Social Location and Biblical Interpretation in the United States.*, ed. Fernando F. Segovia and Mary Ann Tolbert (Minneapolis: Fortress Press, 1995).

LATINO/A THEOLOGY

Rodolfo J. Hernández-Díaz

U.S. Latino/a theology (alternatively called Hispanic or Latina/o theology) consists of reflections on the practices and faith of the U.S. Latino/a community in light of the sociohistorical context of Hispanics. It stems from the need to articulate a theology reflective of and significant for the Latino/a faith community. While Hispanic theology owes a great deal to Latin American liberation theology, it also contrasts with it. Like liberation theology, Latino/a theology begins with concrete injustices, uses social analysis, and rereads the biblical narrative from the perspective of the oppressed. Unlike Latin American liberation theologians who define oppression in largely political and economic terms, Latino/a theology has expanded the notions of oppression to include social exclusion and cultural marginalization. Thus, Hispanic theology is its own theological enterprise committed to analyzing Hispanic American life and shaping Christian and Latino/a symbols in new ways for the betterment of Latino/as and the wider society.

Far from being homogeneous, Hispanic communities are enormously diverse. Latino/as come from different racial, ethnic, cultural, and national backgrounds. Historically, some Hispanic families trace their origins in North America back centuries before parts of it became the United States, while other Hispanics are recent immigrants. Hispanics are also religiously diverse. The majority of Latino/as practice a form of Catholicism, though Protestantism, particularly in its Pentecostal/Charismatic manifestations, is growing at a phenomenal rate among Hispanics. U.S. Hispanics are not exclusively Christian; indigenous and African-inspired religious traditions also influenced the popular faith practices. There is diversity among Latino/as in terms of education and economic status as well. Though some Latino/as are highly educated and economically successful, most struggle financially and do not reach the necessary levels of education to effectively compete in the job market. Geographically, many Latino/as make their homes on the borderlands of the Southwest while others live in the barrios of the Northeast or in other major urban centers. Since Hispanic theology draws from the experiences of Latino/a communities, it reflects their diverse character. Despite the enormous diversity among Hispanics, they share enough cultural,

JUSTO GONZALEZ (1937–)

Justo L. González is a celebrated Cuban American historian, theologian, and United Methodist scholar with over 70 books published in English and Spanish on the history of Christianity, Hispanic biblical hermeneutics, and Latino/a theological studies. González was born in Cuba in 1937, and earned his PhD in historical theology from Yale University when he was just 23 years old. He taught at Emory University's Candler School of Theology in Atlanta, Georgia, for eight years, and later at Columbia Theological Seminary and the Interdenominational Theological Center. In 1984 Gonzalez published *The Story of Christianity*, a best-selling and highly readable two-volume survey of church history, which has been translated into several languages around the world. He is the founding editor of *Apuntes*, the first scholarly journal on U.S. Hispanic religious studies. During the 1990s González founded three institutions for promoting the presence of Latino/as in North American theological education. Among these are the Association for Hispanic Theological Education (AETH); the Hispanic Theological Initiative (HTI), funding graduate study and academic mentoring for Latina/os across North America and now housed at Princeton Theological Seminary; and the Hispanic Summer Program (HSP), which brings together theological faculty with graduate students for two weeks of learning and fellowship every year during the summer.

—AH

historical, and especially religious experiences to make possible an examination of a shared Latino/a theology.

While Latino/a theology often mirrors and parallels the range of beliefs in mainstream (or traditional) theology, it also significantly contrasts and objects to mainstream theology. For example, Hispanic theology challenges the tendency in traditional theology to insist that its reflection is objective and value-free. In contrast to this discourse of theoretical abstraction and supposed objectivity, Latino/a theology highlights the importance of social and cultural context in shaping ways of thinking. Rather than focusing on the commonalties with mainstream U.S. theologies, the description here centers on the distinctive theological contributions of Latino/a theology to the wider theological enterprise.

Historical Development

Though the history of Hispanics in what is now the United States is centuries old, only in the early 1970s did a distinct theological voice begin to emerge that can be called Latino/a theology. Hispanic theology emerged in the wake of Latin American liberation theology's emphasis on the importance of perspective and social location. Liberation theology stressed that the view from a place of privilege is fundamentally different than from a place of poverty. Theological constructions developed from a place of privilege masks patriarchal, sexist, racist, and classist assumptions and denies the history of domination and oppression. Latino/a theology arose from the need to unmask cultural, social, and economic structures of oppression by articulating a theology from

VIRGILIO ELIZONDO (1935–)

Virgilio Elizondo is internationally renowned as a theologian, speaker, and pastor, particularly for his visionary work on the Mexican American religious experience. A native of San Antonio, Texas, and a Roman Catholic priest of the San Antonio archdiocese, his numerous leadership positions include his service from 1972 to 1987 as the founding president of the Mexican American Cultural Center and his tenure as rector of San Fernando Cathedral from 1983 to 1995. Widely acclaimed as the founder of U.S. Latino theologies, he is the author of 15 books and over 100 scholarly and popular articles. He also co-edited 15 volumes of the prestigious international theological journal "Concilium." The documents and vision of Roman Catholic leaders at the Second Vatican Council (1962–1965) profoundly influenced Elizondo's theology. Following the Council's call for a return to the sources of faith, Elizondo's writings and pastoral ministry are rooted in his creative reexamination of two foundational faith sources: the Jesus stories of the Gospels and the image and narrative of Our Lady of Guadalupe. In both of these sources he finds rich treasures for theological reflection on the life and mission of a mestizo people, more specifically his fellow Mexican Americans of the U.S.-Mexico borderlands.

—TM

the perspective of and meaningful for a community mired in poverty, discrimination, and marginalization.

The initial stage of development of Latino/a theology took place between 1972 and 1990. During this time, three events loom large in understanding the growth and development of Hispanic theology: the founding of the Mexican American Cultural Center in 1972 by Virgilio Elizondo; the publication of *Apuntes*, the first professional journal dedicated to the elaboration of Hispanic theology in 1980; and the formation in 1989 of the Academy of Catholic Hispanic Theologians of the United States (ACHTUS), founded in order to promote theological reflection within the U.S. Hispanic experience. Aside from Elizondo and Justo González, the key figures during this time were Allan Figueroa Deck, Ada María Isasi-Díaz, and Roberto S. Goizueta (among Roman Catholics) and Orlando Costas (among Protestants).

In the period since 1991 Latino/a theology has experienced enormous growth, leading some to refer to the 1990s as a "boom" of Hispanic theology. A number of developments in this period have significantly advanced the study of Hispanic theology: the founding of the Association for Hispanic Theological Education (AETH) in 1991; the 1992 appearance of a second professional theological journal, the *Journal of Hispanic/Latino Theology*; and the inauguration of the Hispanic Theological Initiative in 1996. Alongside these developments, there has been an explosion of theological publications, including over a dozen anthologies, a four-volume study of Latino/a religion by the Program for the Analysis of Religion among Latinos (PARAL), and numerous monographs by individual authors. While most of first generation Hispanic theologians continue to contribute to the field, a host of new Latino/a theologians have

---

ORLANDO COSTAS (1942–1987)

Orlando Enrique Costas was born on June 15, 1942 in Ponce, Puerto Rico. He obtained masters degrees in pastoral, biblical, and systematic theology as well as a master of divinity degree. His doctoral work was in missions and evangelism from the Free University of Amsterdam, Holland.

Costas pastored in the United States and Puerto Rico. Among other things, he served on the Commission for Social Development of Milwaukee, was a founding member of the committee of Latin American Political Education, and was founder of a Hispanic community newspaper, *La Guardia*. He also founded the Latin American Civil Union for Civil Rights and the Universidad del Barrio. The governor of Wisconsin named him to the State Commission on Human Rights in the Division of Industry, Work, and Human Relations. As missionary to Latin America, he served as professor of communication and missiology, secretary of publications, and director of the Evangelical Center for Pastoral Studies (CELEP). In 1980 Costas became the Thornley B. Wood professor of missiology at Eastern Baptist Seminary and in 1984 the academic dean of the Andover Newton Theological School. He authored 15 books along with numerous chapters and articles. His work and life are the topic of five dissertations, two books, and a variety of articles. He died in November 1987.

—ECF

---

appeared. Among them are María Pilar Aquino, Orlando O. Espín, Ismael García, Harold Recinos, Jeanette Rodríguez, Fernando Segovia, and Eldin Villafañe. Along with the growth in numbers of Latino/a scholars has come a proliferation in the richness and maturity of theological explorations of the complex U.S. Hispanic reality.

Methodological Foundations

Because of the widespread marginalization, oppression, exploitation, and domination of Hispanics, Latino/a theology's methodology largely coincides with liberation theology. Three methodological constructs give cohesion to the discussion of Latino/a theology: (1) social location, popular expressions and symbols of the faith, and the daily-lived experience of the people (*lo cotidano*); (2) a preferential option for the poor, understood broadly to include the culturally oppressed and socially marginalized; (3) liberating praxis, the confrontation of oppressive institutions and structures that give rise to colonialism/imperialism, assimilationist tendencies, rampant capitalism, machismo, sexism, and other forces that are antithetical to the reign of God. While the latter two methodological constructs reflect the influence of liberation, Black, and feminist theology, the first methodological move grounds the reflection of Hispanics in the daily struggles and hopes of their own communities.

These three methodological constructs, honed by the extensive use of social analysis (whether from sociology, anthropology, history, linguistics, or otherwise) ensure continued connection to concrete Latino/a realities. Latino/a theologians see social

RIVERSIDE MANIFESTO

On March 12–14, 1981, a major gathering on urban ministry dubbed a "National Conference on the City" was held at the historic Riverside Church in New York City. The occasion was the celebration of the 50th anniversary of Riverside Church. While there were a number of participants, a group of Latino/a church leaders believed that a gross oversight and injustice occurred in the exclusion of Hispanics from the official conference program, especially given the then estimated 20 million Hispanics living in the United States in 1981, mostly residing in urban areas, including notably a few blocks from Riverside Church. On March 13th these Hispanic leaders, calling themselves the Coalition of Hispanic Christian Leadership, interrupted the conference proceedings in the sanctuary of Riverside Church, seized the microphone, and read a statement titled "Complaints and Demands Presented to Mainline Protestants, Conservative Fundamentalists and Establishment Evangelicals at the Riverside Church Conference on the City." This document was later published formally and informally in denominational publications, as well as mimeographed copies in both English and Spanish. Although the document has been referred to as the "Shout" or "Cry of Riverside," over the years it also has been referred to as "the Riverside Manifesto."

—EDA

science methodologies as instrumental in the analysis of reality in order to unravel the dynamics of oppression in all its forms.

Major Themes and Characteristics

Latino/a scholars have contributed creative and original insights to such diverse theological topics as aesthetics, catechesis, epistemology, evangelization, hermeneutics, feminist theology, liturgy, missiology, Mariology, pastoral ministry, spirituality, and theological method. Throughout their diverse writings, certain major themes and characteristics have emerged as fundamental dimensions of Hispanic theology: an emphasis on theology as a shared task, known as *teología en conjunto* (collaborative theology); a concern for culture, manifested in the discourses of *mestizaje/mulatez* (racial and cultural mixing) and the borderland; and explorations of identity captured by popular religion and *la lucha* (the struggle to survive). These dimensions are central to Latino/a theology and give it much of its distinct flavor.

The phrase *teología en conjunto* captures the collaborative spirit that characterizes Latino/a theological reflection. This collaborative spirit manifests itself in two distinct but interrelated forms. First, Latino/a theologians, in contrast to the hyper-individualism of dominant North American theologians, are convinced that theology must be done in collaboration with faith communities. This collaboration is exemplified by the methodology of *Hispanic Women: Prophetic Voice in the Church* in which interviews with Hispanic women are interpreted to critically appropriate Hispanic women's religious experiences. Maintaining open dialogue with communities of faith

Worshipers at the Santuario del Señor de Esquipulas at Chimayó, New Mexico. Believed to be the site of miraculous cures, hundreds of faithful visit the Santuario every Easter. (Kevin Fleming/Corbis)

helps to keep Hispanic theologians grounded in the suffering and struggles of the people and avoids the Enlightenment error of doing theology as an abstract observer. Second, over and against the dominant culture's view of the individual reflecting in isolation as the culmination of academic achievement, Latino/a theologians do their work collaboratively, as evidenced by their predilection for anthologies. These anthologies are not merely collections of the writings of individuals working in isolation, but result from intimate and enthusiastic gatherings of mutual sharing of their stories and theological insights from living as diasporic people within the United States.

The concept of culture has been a central theme and characteristic of Hispanic theology from its beginnings. This emphasis on culture manifests itself repeatedly in the form of discussions about *mestizaje/mulatez* (both terms refer to racial mixing), borderland, and more generally constructions of Latino/a social reality. *Mestizaje/mulatez* have been widely adopted by Latino/a theologians to highlight who they are as Hispanics and explain what is different and new about Latino/a identity and emphasize that hybridity, ambiguity, and pluralism are key dimensions in God's revelation. These terms refer to the result of the violent and unequal clash between Native American, African, Spanish, and Euro-American cultures. Elizondo was the first to skillfully articulate mestizaje (1983). He argues that the clash of the particular bloods, faiths, and worldviews at Tepeyac, with the apparition of *Nuestra Señora de Guadalupe* (Our Lady of Guadalupe), forged a mestizaje. As *mestizo/as*, Latino/as live in a fluid state by their participation in and rejection by two different cultures. It is precisely this double rejection that demonstrates God's election (what the world rejects, God chooses as his very own) and offers a basis for their liberating and salvific efforts as agents for a new humanity, not only for themselves, but for others as well.

The cultural concept of borderlands is historically related to but distinct from mestizaje/mulatez. In the Southern portions of the Americas, the Spanish were forced to live with the original inhabitants, creating a mestizaje. However, the colonists in North America, lusting for Native Americans' land rather than their subjugation, pushed them westward, leading to the "frontier" myth of *terra nullis* (empty land). On this

AETH

The Asociación para la Educación Teológica Hispana (AETH), was founded in 1991. Its main purpose is to promote and enhance theological education for Hispanics in the United States, Canada, and Puerto Rico, at all levels. This includes seminaries and universities as well as Bible colleges, Bible institutes, and lay training programs. AETH now has over 900 individual members and 100 affiliated institutions. AETH itself is an affiliated member of the Association of Theological Schools (ATS). From its inception, AETH has specialized in theological education in a very wide sense. This includes the intellectual as well as the spiritual disciplines of ministry, both for those currently enrolled in formal educational programs and those already engaged in pastoral and other forms of ministry. AETH also publishes and distributes books and other resources to support the tasks of theological education and the practices of ministry. Thus, it is particularly well placed to procure, produce, and/or distribute whatever materials may be needed for, or may result from, this project. AETH is a 501(c)3 not-for-profit organization as determined by the Internal Revenue Service. Its Web site is www.aeth.org.

—JDM

side of the frontier was civilization, on the other a void. From the Latino/a perspective, the borderland is much more than a geographical space; it is an epistemological and cultural category defining the reality of their community. In contrast to the dominant perception of the border as unidirectional, Hispanics perceive the border as allowing for movement in two directions. Instead of a line demarcating savagery and civilization, the border is valorized as a place of growth, encounter, and enrichment. As a result of this borderland experience, Latino/as live simultaneously as insiders and outsiders. They exist as a bridge people between the minority and the majority world, between the center and periphery, between North and South America. In a world of increasingly porous and fluid borders, where "globalization" is seen as inevitable, Latino/as embody the possibility of peaceful reconciliation, hope, and life in the place of legitimized violence, rape, and murder.

Strongly tied to the emphasis of Latino/a theologians on the concept of culture is the stress on identity. The concern for identity arises out of the need to defend Hispanic communities against overt racial and ethnic prejudices, the devaluation of Latino/a collective identity, and strong assimilationist tendencies that frequently demand cultural and linguistic repression in order to attain status as full U.S. Americans. Reflections on the popular symbols, myths, rituals, and practices of Hispanics serve as a major wellspring and bulwark for maintaining the integrity of Latino/a self-identity and culture. Orlando Espín understands popular religiosity as a cultural expression of the *sensus fidelium* (literally, the "sense of the faithful"). Conceptions of Mary and Christ are his prime examples of the *sensus fidelium* (Espín and Díaz 1999). Roberto S. Goizueta contends that popular religiosity embodies a unity of reason, beauty, and justice that offer a radical critique of mainstream North American Christianity and offers the latter avenues for transformation and renewal (1995, 18–46). Though it has been discounted by dominant Euro-American theologies as primitive, vestiges of an ignorant past, a product of syncretism, and an ideological tool to manipulate "simple folks," Latino/as have validated popular religion as a legitimate and vital source of identity, liberative values, empowerment, self-determination, and a corrective to dominant values.

The emphasis on identity in Latino/a theology also manifests itself in the recurrence of the struggle to survive. This stress on identity is legitimate given the shared historical experience of conquest, colonization, and cultural subjugation. In this hostile context, Hispanics struggle to survive as a people, to create a viable self-identity, and to enter into a state of self-determination. Ada María Isasi-Díaz refers to this struggle to survive as *la lucha*. La lucha has to do with the multiple facets of the oppression of Hispanic women manifest as economic, cultural, and gender disadvantage (Isasi-Díaz 2004, 11–33). As Latino/as become authors of their own histories, they combat the denial of violent conquest and the justifications that legitimate culturally oppressive and assimilationist policies.

Contributions to the Formulation of Christian Doctrines

Hispanic theologians have reinterpreted and reconstructed the meanings of doctrines of the faith in a manner that is specific to their cultural milieu. In grounding their reconstruction of Christian doctrines in their culture, Latino/as have reimagined these doctrines in ways that are more responsive to the Hispanic social realities. Rather than limiting the significance of their work, Latino/a theologians hold that their critical engagement with culture has yielded beneficial insights that can serve to empower and enrich the wider church. The task of reinterpreting the doctrines of the faith is perhaps best illustrated in the reconstruction of the doctrines of the Trinity, God, Jesus, the Holy Spirit, theological anthropology, the church, and eschatology.

The Trinity

Hispanic Trinitarian systems are less concerned with the ontological nature of God (a matter of philosophical speculation that can never be resolved) than with how God as the Trinity relates to humanity and works through history. Three theologians exemplify the contributions of Hispanics to Trinity thought: J. L. González, Luis Pedraja, and Zaida Maldonado Perez. González insists that people's notions of the Trinity have drastic consequences for the ordering of society and economic relationships within it. When the Triune God was conceptualized in unchanging Platonic terms in the early church formulations, the status quo was sacralized in a way that benefited the ruling classes. In contrast, the nature of God as three in one reveals for Latino/as the centrality of giving and sharing in the life of the Godhead (González 1990, 101–115). Pedraja argues that the communal and relational nature of the Trinity reveals that God seeks out God's people, accompanies them in their struggles, and stands in solidarity with them. Over and against the xenophobic assimilative tendency of the dominant culture, the diversity within the Trinity resists homogenization and celebrates diversity

(Pedraja 2003, 117–120). Maldonado Perez extends the discussion of Trinity as relationship through the metaphor of *La Santa Familia* (the Holy Family). The Trinity is a *familia* because it shares together their essence, but also their work. This coequality serves as a corrective for the sexist view of *el macho de la casa* (the man of the house), whereby the macho sets the "law" of the home. To follow the example of the Trinitarian God is to live as a *familia*, in complete intimacy with one another, loving each other in the midst of struggling together ("The Trinity," in Aponte and De La Torre 2006, 32–39).

What is in common in these Hispanic Trinitarian systems is a concern for practical implications of the Trinity: concern for socioeconomic status of Latino/as for González, relationship and affirmation of diversity for Pedraja, and the perspective of *familia* for Maldonado Perez. They are concerned not with "how" God is three persons in one but in the liberative and subversive sociopolitical and ecclesiastical implications of a God that lives with diversity within unity and unity within diversity.

God among Latino/as

The statement "God is love" is the foundational affirmation of the Hispanic doctrine of God. Hispanics testify to the intimate experience of the active and relational God of love within the Latino/a community. Hispanics refer to God as *Diosito*, a term implying endearment and *Amante*, or lover, of the beloved community. "Diosito" also reflects this loving relationship with God as an affectionate friend or *Amigo* (Alanís, "God," in Aponte and De La Torre 2006, 11–16). God from the perspective of Latino/as is not relegated to the realm of the metaphysical transcendence, changeless, impassible, and immutable, but is understood as an intrinsically relational and intimate God who actively accompanies people on their daily journeys, as made evident in the incarnational love and ministry of Jesus the Galilean (Elizondo 1983). J. L. González contends that the incarnation (much more than merely a Plan B for human sin) should serve as the basis for the Latino/a doctrine of God (1990). To a people who are constantly rejected or ignored, the sense of being loved and chosen is not merely good news but ushers in a whole new life.

God understood as *Amor*, or love, creates in the community of faith the capacity for reciprocal love even as sin mars this love. The intrinsically relational God creates human persons who are in turn intrinsically related to other human beings, the cosmos, and God. The tendency of humanity to divide each other on the basis of differences and to establish hierarchies of one group over the other is opposed to the universality of God's love. From this perspective, the failure to acknowledge relatedness to others, especially the ever-present poor, oppressed, and marginalized, represents a pathological interpretation of reality. Thus God from the perspective of Latino/as is the loving Diosito who intimately calls all into the beloved community and a loving relationship with others. As Amigo and Amante, God's ongoing and dynamic work challenges the oppressive status quo.

Jesus

Latino/a Christologies stress the concrete historical reality of Jesus and the implications of that reality for understanding the relational and loving character of Jesus and his role as an advocate for the poor. Three dominant images of Jesus permeate Latino/a theology: Jesus as *mestizo*, Jesus as liberator, and Jesus as the one who accompanies (M. A. González, "Jesus," in Aponte and De La Torre 2006, 18). *Mestizaje* serves as a major Christological image within Hispanic theology. Elizondo's landmark work grounds his Christological reflection on the mestizo identity of Jesus as a Galilean Jew. Elizondo insists that Jesus' birth—not in the center of power (Jerusalem), but on the border (Galilee)—is not accidental, but revelatory. Jesus' mestizo experience of being "in between" connects the incarnate Christ with contemporary border reality of Latino/a experience and serves as a call to a new conception of community and church (1983).

Jesus depicted as liberator breaks down the dividing walls among humanity. Foremost, perhaps, is the divide between rich and poor. Pedraja's Christology, by focusing on the earthly incarnation of Christ (as opposed to a preexistent or heavenly resurrected Christ), highlights the liberating work of Jesus in the lives of the poor and oppressed (1999). Jesus' incarnation as a poor person delegitimizes the structures that create unjust distributions of wealth. However, Jesus' incarnation as one of the poor is not merely a means of comforting them, but to enable the poor and powerless to confront and transform the oppressor in society and restore their human dignity.

A third Christological image is that of the crucified Jesus as victim that accompanies the Latino/a community through their struggles. Goizueta stresses that Jesus for Latino/as is foremost a flesh-and-blood person, characterized by the ritual act of accompaniment (1995). The widespread identification with the crucified Jesus among Hispanics does not cancel out the resurrection. Latino/as affirm the resurrection as the ultimate act of confrontation and victory over suffering. As Latino/as accompany Jesus on Good Friday, the emphasis on the hope of new life in the face of suffering empowers the community of faith.

The crucified Jesus best captures the historic experience of Hispanics. Just as Jesus suffered unjustly, so Latino/as are suffering unjustly. From the Latino/a perspective, the dehistoricized Jesus has no place. Instead, Jesus, the mestizo from Galilee, whose concrete concerns for and accompaniment of the suffering poor breaks down the walls dividing humanity, calls Christians to walk in his footsteps in fellowship with the victims of society (M. A. González, in Aponte and De La Torre 2006, 22).

The Holy Spirit

Discussions of the Holy Spirit among Latino/as have focused on the personhood of the Spirit and the presence of the Spirit as a means of affirmation, liberation, and transformation. Hispanics who are constantly at the mercy of forces and powers that dehumanize and objectify them testify, along with scriptures, to the Spirit's personhood. The traditional depersonalization of the Spirit reflects a depersonalization of God that serves to dehumanize people who are created in the *Imago Dei*, the image of God

(Solivan, "Holy Spirit," in Rodriguez and Martell-Otero 1997, 53). The Spirit, as a person, endows Hispanics with the worth and dignity due to all peoples. As a sinful (broken) people and victims, Latino/as look to the person and work of the Holy Spirit as a healer of brokenness and enabler of social transformation. Villafañe emphasizes that God's transforming love gives rise to the Spirit's work in history. It is through the Spirit that Christians are called and empowered to break the chains of hate and injustice within human structures and institutions (1993, 200–202). The Spirit also serves as the guarantor or down payment of the hoped-for liberation and proof that "the one who is in you is greater than the one who is in the world" (1 John 4:4).

The Holy Spirit affirms and empowers the diversity within the Latino/a church and community. The outpouring of the Spirit at Pentecost affirmed diversity and cultural inclusivity as signs of the inbreaking of God's kingdom. Neglect of the Spirit's ministry has led to racism, bigotry, and sexism. The Spirit makes possible the diversity that God intends, but as long as the diversity expressed through language, culture, ethnicity, and gender is denied, the people of God will fail to experience the fullness of the Spirit. Since it was human and not just heavenly tongues spoken among those gathered in Acts 2, the Spirit affirmed the importance of language and culture. Rather than expunge God's gifts of culture and language, the Spirit empowers the Latino/a community of God to use them for the good of all. The identity of Christian Latino/as depends on the personhood and presence of the Spirit. The Spirit's relationship to Hispanics as persons (subjects) and affirmation of diverse languages and cultures empowers Latino/as to free themselves from those who seek to oppress and dehumanize them.

Theological Anthropology

Hispanic theological anthropology seeks liberative answers to the question: what does it mean to be human? Their theological reflections on the relation between the human life and the divine life can be sketched along thematic lines. The doctrine of creation influences the formulation of an other-focused, inclusive, and diverse Hispanic anthropology. Drawing from Genesis 1–3, Hispanic theologians emphasize that human beings were not created to be alone (Genesis 2:18). To be made human in the image of God is to be created for others (J. L. González 1990, 125–138). In a society that tends to exclude and marginalize others, the recovery of the inclusivity emerging from creation offers a prophetic alternative conception of anthropology.

Hispanic theological anthropologies reflect distinctively Hispanic Christologies. The conception of Jesus' identity as a Galilean, the practice of accompanying Jesus, and the way Jesus reveals God's agency in the world are all sources of anthropological thought. To be human after the pattern of the Galilean Jesus is to welcome an intercultural way of life (*mestizaje*) and to cross into the human experiences of others, especially the marginalized (Díaz, "Theological Anthropology," in Aponte and De La Torre 2006, 70–71). To be human is to be *acompañado* (accompanied) by Christ and to imitate Jesus by accompanying our neighbors, especially the marginalized neighbors. The Spanish translation of the Greek Logos as *Verbo* rather than the more static English translation "Word" supports the U.S. Hispanic view of Jesus as revealer of God's agency.

Hispanic anthropologies embrace the communal character of humanity revealed in the communal life of the Triune God. While affirming the distinctive particularities of human individuals, Hispanic anthropologies challenge individualism and individualistic practices. To be human is to be created to live in community and embrace interpersonal dependence.

Ecclesiology

Hispanic views of the church, while varying tremendously, have generally been more with mission ("what is the church for?") than with definition ("what is the church?"). The distinctiveness of Latino/a ecclesiology lies not in its institutional organization, but in its praxis, or way of being church (Goizueta, "United States Hispanic Theology," in Deck 1992, 2).

J. L. González provides three helpful images that describe the Hispanic way of being church ("In Quest of a Protestant Hispanic Ecclesiology" in Rodriguez and Martell-Otero 1997, 85–95). The first is the image of the church as a pilgrim people. As a pilgrim people, Latino/as are a people without a land, either for those who have been here for generations because their land was taken from them or for the recent arrivals because they feel that they do not have any permanent roots. Like the pilgrimage in the wilderness, or the exile and return, it is not a pilgrimage that is undertaken alone. It is a communal pilgrimage for those who share a common suffering, longing, and hope.

Another image for understanding the Hispanic way of being church is that of the body of Christ. This image implies not only that all the members of the body of Christ are different, but also that they are all necessary. As Paul put it, if the whole body were eyes, there would be no hearing (1 Corinthians 12:17). The use of this image in the Latino/a church, however, contrasts with its use in the dominant community. "The church is the hands and feet of Jesus" is a phrase often heard in the dominant churches. Latino/as, who are generally helpless in a society that seeks to take advantage of the powerless, have no use for a Christ without hands or feet.

A third image is that of the church as family. In the dominant culture, family often means nuclear family, and is therefore conceived as narrowly defined and closed. However, in the cultural context of Latino/as in which extended family is the norm, the image of church as family suggests a diffuse, wide, and ever-expandable group of people. This image of church as extended family has a close relationship to the Latino/a experiences of alienation, marginalization, and exile. The church becomes the new community and extended family for those Hispanics who have had to leave their own extended families behind. From the Latino/a perspective, the church provides companions in the pilgrimage of suffering and hope. Though these church companions are different, they are also necessary and accepted as members in the ever-expanding family that is the church.

Eschatology

For Latino/as, eschatology, as the doctrine of last things, deals not with the end of life, but the end of sin, suffering, and death as well as the hope of liberation from sinful structures of oppression and marginalization. This hope permeates all of Hispanic theology, from Christology, to pneumatology, to ecclesiology. Thus, though eschatology deals with the last things, it is not relegated to the end in Latino/a theology. Latino/a theologians emphasize that the Lord's Prayer/Our Father states "Your kingdom come" not "let us go into your kingdom" (Matthew 6:10). For Hispanic theologians, eschatology is about looking forward to a future in which God's will is done on earth as it is in heaven (Pedraja, "Eschatology," in Aponte and De La Torre 2006, 116).

The concepts of *fiesta* (celebration), *mañana* (tomorrow), and "kin-dom" offer distinctly Hispanic eschatological visions. Elizondo articulates "fiesta" as a symbol of eschatological celebration of the new mestizo humanity. Elizondo insists that as mestizo/as Latino/as occupy a privileged position to act as bridge people to both North and Latin America. Mestizo/as must reject rejection and exclusion and lead the way toward a new humanity that will participate in the festive table of fellowship among brothers and sisters (1983). J. L. González captures the Hispanic hopes for the coming reign of God from the perspective of mañana. González's eschatological vision of mañana has two implications. First, it represents the hopes for a tomorrow that will be radically different from today. Second, God's future vision of peace not war, of more egalitarian structures, and of the eradication of poverty and hunger places certain demands on the present. Hispanics, as a mañana people, must live out mañana today, in the tension of the already and not yet of the coming reign of God (González 1990, 28–30). As in liberation theology, the reign of God represents hope for the radical transformation of the present. Isasi-Díaz uses the term "kin-dom" to move away from the patriarchal domination evoked by the term "kingdom." Kin-dom as an alternative vision reflects inclusion of family, in which all people are kin to one another. God's eschatological kin-dom offers glimpses of hope and guidance for present actions (Isasi-Díaz 2004). From the experience of marginalization, oppression, and exclusion in the present, U.S. Latino/as maintain hope of a radically different reality in which love and life eclipse hatred and death (Pedraja, "Eschatology," in Aponte and De La Torre 2006, 119).

References and Further Reading

Aponte, Edwin David, and Miguel A. De La Torre, eds. *Handbook of Latino/a Theologies* (St. Louis: Chalice Press, 2006).

Aquino, María Pilar. *Nuestro clamor por la vida: teología latinoamericana desde la perspectiva de la mujer, Colección Mujer latinoamericana* (San José, Costa Rica: Editorial DEI, 1992).

Deck, Allan Figueroa, ed. *Frontiers of Hispanic Theology in the United States* (Maryknoll, NY: Orbis Books, 1992).

De La Torre, Miguel A., and Edwin David Aponte. *Introducing Latino/a Theologies* (Maryknoll, NY: Orbis Books, 2001).

Elizondo, Virgilio P. *Galilean Journey: The Mexican-American Promise* (Maryknoll, NY: Orbis Books, 1983).

Espín, Orlando, and Miguel H. Díaz, eds. *From the Heart of Our People: Latino/a Explorations in Catholic Systematic Theology* (Maryknoll, NY: Orbis Books, 1999).

Goizueta, Roberto S. *Caminemos con Jesús: Toward a Hispanic/Latino Theology of Accompaniment* (Maryknoll, NY: Orbis Books, 1995).

González, Justo L. *Mañana: Christian Theology from a Hispanic Perspective* (Nashville: Abingdon Press, 1990).

Isasi-Díaz, Ada María. *En la lucha = In the struggle: Elaborating a Mujerista Theology*, 10th anniversary ed. (Minneapolis: Fortress Press, 2004).

Isasi-Díaz, Ada María, and Yolanda Tarango. *Hispanic Women Prophetic Voice in the Church: Toward a Hispanic Women's Liberation Theology* [Mujer Hispana voz profética en la iglesia: hacia una teología de liberacíon de la mujer Hispana] (San Francisco: Harper & Row, 1988).

Pedraja, Luis G. *Jesus Is My Uncle: Christology from a Hispanic Perspective* (Nashville: Abingdon Press, 1999).

———. *Teología: An Introduction to Hispanic Theology* (Nashville: Abingdon Press, 2003).

Rodriguez, José David, and Loida I. Martell-Otero, eds. *Teología en conjunto: a Collaborative Hispanic Protestant Theology*, 1st ed. (Louisville, KY: Westminster John Knox Press, 1997).

Valentin, Benjamin. *New Horizons in Hispanic/Latino(a) Theology* (Cleveland: Pilgrim Press, 2003).

Villafañe, Eldin. *The Liberating Spirit: Toward an Hispanic American Pentecostal Social Ethic* (Grand Rapids, MI: W. B. Eerdmans, 1993).

LIBERATION THEOLOGY

Loida I. Martell-Otero

Theologies of liberation are associated so often with Latin American theologies that one could feasibly lose sight of the fact that they have their foundation in biblical texts. Throughout the Bible, narratives such as those about the exodus of the Israelites from Egyptian slavery and Esther's liberative acts on behalf of her people from a planned Persian pogrom reflect underlying themes of salvation as experienced through concrete historical events. Similarly, historical narratives such as those recorded by slaves in colonial United States, the epistolary protests of Antonio Montesinos and Bartelomé de las Casas on behalf of indigenous people, and the cries and prayers of the Civil Rights Movement are also theologies of liberation. They are, by and large, the reflections by those at the margins involved in prophetic movements for justice and freedom that seek the liberation of the oppressed. If such is the goal of these theologies, then one could posit that Jesus Christ is God's ultimate liberative word, an incarnate "theos/logy of liberation."

General Comments

There are many theologies of liberation. They exhibit distinctive as well as common traits, influenced by their particular contexts. Indeed, they are *contextual* theologies. "Contextual" means they are theologies that intentionally incorporate analyses of particular sociohistorical locations of their respective communities. Very often, these sociohistorical, political, and economic locations serve as the *loci theologicus* of reflection. The purpose of these starting points is to ensure that theologians speak from and to the concerns of their communities, and not in response to absolute questions that have no historical relevance to the needs of real "flesh and blood" people. Contextual theologians of liberation eschew any attempt to articulate theologies as "universal truths." Rather they insist on the "scandal of particularity"—that God speaks in particular ways to people within particular contexts. This principle of "particularity" not only implies that all theology is done within a specific social location but also that its scholars are obligated to consider their own perspectives and biases. If it is true that all human experience is interpreted reality (Schillebeeckx 1993, 31–32), then the impact of context upon hermeneutics becomes a crucial methodological step for theologians of liberation. This paradigm shift to contextual hermeneutics is reflected in the number of theologies of liberation articulated in various forums. Asian and Asian American, African American, gay and lesbian, *feminista*, *mujerista*, Native American, Jewish, Latina/o, white feminist, womanist, and political theologies of liberation are but a small sample, each emphasizing particular themes, issues, and methodologies, and each articulating theologies that faithfully reflect the realities of their respective communities while maintaining a healthy dialogue with others.

Theologies of liberation are also *constructive* theologies. They articulate holistic theologies that provide a sense of life and hope to the oppressed in particular, and to the human community as a whole. Its proponents often begin with the deconstruction of traditions that have proven to be detrimental to, or contain elements contributing to the oppression of, marginalized communities. Scholars then reconstruct these traditions from the perspective of the poor and marginalized. The dialectic of deconstruction and reconstruction uncovers the presence of those made invisible throughout history and in the present. Those dehumanized by unjust structures are humanized and the complicity of sinful institutions is made apparent. For example, white feminists have raised significant arguments regarding the Church's complicit role in sustaining sexism, marginalizing women, and failing to legitimize a rich tradition regarding women's leadership and contributions throughout its history. African American and womanist theologians point to societal and ecclesial structures that support racism. Womanist theologians in particular argue that white women are just as complicit in the oppression of African American women as men. As a constructive venture, theologies of liberation not only provide new ways of examining the tradition, they also raise questions about the interpretations of texts. Such hermeneutical methods as postcolonial readings and ideological criticism provide insights into the myriad ways in which God has spoken to, and through, those oftentimes rejected as "other."

Theologies of liberation can also be considered *praxeological* theologies. In his theses on Ludwig Feuerbach, Karl Marx asserted that the purpose of philosophy is not simply to interpret the world but to change it (Marx 1978, 145). Theologians of liberation carry out their task in this spirit: not simply to be embroiled in abstract philosophical debates or obtuse ideological sparring, but rather to engage real human beings who seek God in the midst of concrete human experiences. These theologies often are accused unfairly of simply being a religious expression of Marxism. While it is true that they use a number of resources from social and political sciences, such accusations are a distortion of their purpose. What theologians of liberation seek to do is to understand the religious, biblical, and therefore theological implications of the eschatological Reign of God and understand its implications for human life and society in the present. They seek to be agents of transformation in the world rather than disinterested spectators. They are concerned particularly, though not exclusively, with those who suffer or are silenced in the world. They believe that God is present in a special way among the "least of these." This latter belief has led them to articulate the well-known maxim regarding the "option for the poor"—that God acts very specially in the midst of the hurting of the world. They affirm that the powerless of the world have an "epistemological privilege"—that they have encountered and known God in ways that are closer to the biblical witness about God and God's purpose for creation than those who are in power.

Consequently and above all, theologies of liberation can be considered inherently soteriologies. While "soteriology" may be defined as "the doctrine of salvation," the meaning of "salvation" is not as clear. Theologians of liberation often criticize the tradition for emphasizing a soteriology that addresses solely the transcendent dimension of salvation—as an eschatological or futuristic hope that is divorced from the concrete realities that the oppressed face daily. They have counterbalanced this futuristic tendency by exploring how salvation is experienced in the here and now. It is not their intention to ignore the eschatological dimensions of salvation. Rather, they seek to articulate how the eschatological vision of the Reign of God as communicated through Scripture has implications for current social, political, economic, religious, cultural, and theological arenas. Simply put, how do the demands of God as expressed in the biblical concept of "*basileia*/Reign" commit communities of faith today to struggle for the transformation of a hurting, unjust world to one in which the fundamental elements of life thrive in human history? How can people of faith be faithful in the midst of a sinful world in which the "powers and principalities" of oppression and injustice seem to sway? These soteriological and praxeological foci lead to theologies that eschew the traditional divorce of theological reflection and ethical imperative.

U.S.-Based Latina/o Contextual Theologies

There are various expressions of Latina/o theologies, including *feminista* and *mujerista* theologies. Some, such as *evangélica* theologies, would hesitate applying the nomenclature of "theology of liberation" yet still consider themselves "contextual theologies." Most fulfill the characteristics described in the previous section. Latina/o theologians certainly seek the holistic well-being of their communities, and speak to and for a people who have suffered and continue to suffer. They, like other theologies of liberation, seek to articulate a theology that advocates for the liberation of all people and the transformation of our society. Nevertheless, these theologies are identifiably "Latino/a" based on the following.

Context. Latina/o theologians reflect from, and for, a people whose bicultural roots originate in Latin America and the Caribbean, but who currently reside within the geographical boundaries of the United States of America. The almost 47 million people of Mexican, Puerto Rican, Cuban, and Central and South American descent are usually among the poorest of this nation, living at the margins of many of their communities. Birthed from the ashes of conquest and violence, they deal with issues arising from a continuing history of colonization, discrimination, and exploitation. Many are im/migrants who live invisibly at the margins of a society that professes to not want them as they use them for cheap labor. Latino/as are usually considered "other" by a dominant Eurocentric culture. Poverty, unemployment and underemployment, poor housing in high crime areas, poor educational attainment, lack of access to health care, along with cultural and language discrimination are part of the daily fabric of their lives. Latinas face the added onus of confronting the sexism that exists within and outside of their communities. Yet their context is not solely about the social ills that beset their communities. It is also about the gifts that they contribute to the wider culture. These include a deep religiosity that is inherently part of the culture, a given *joie de vivre* that is expressed through their celebrations/*fiestas*, and a sense of community that is experienced in their generous hospitality—giving of themselves although they may not have much to give.

Methodology. There are various expressions of Latina/o contextual theologies since they do not represent a homogenous group. Their particular contexts, in turn, influence the methods they employ. For example, feminista and mujerista theologians' starting point for reflection is the quadruple oppression of gender, color, class, and culture experienced by Latinas. Some Latino/a scholars have explored "beauty" and cultural symbolism as interpretive lenses within the field of theological aesthetics. Catholic theologians incorporate the faith practices of popular religiosity as an essential foundation for theological reflection. While evangélica/o recognize the importance of human experience in theological reflection, many insist on the priority of Scripture as the authority of faith and praxis. While diversity is a hallmark of Latino/a communities and their respective theologies, there are also some common approaches that identify them. First, these theologies are defined by the use of *mestizaje/mulatez* as a theological paradigm, which constitutes an "anthropological shift" from the Marxist and politico-economic analyses of Latin American theologies of liberation. They are also defined by their use of popular religiosity and *lo cotidiano* as important *loci theologicus*. Finally, they have a distinctive communal worldview that informs a methodological approach known as *teología en conjunto*. When taken into account, these four important elements are what give Latina/o theologies their praxeological impulse: they respond to the needs of real people in real situations of life and death and are thus true "theologies of liberation."

Mestizaje / Mulatez

José Vasconcelos (1882–1959), a Mexican philosopher, politician, and educator, used what had been a pejorative term to develop the concept of *la Raza Cósmica* (the Cosmic Race) within aesthetic philosophy. For Vasconcelos, mestizaje represented a future in which the ongoing fusion of people and cultures led the way to the ultimate goal of history. Within this historical and cultural framework, Virgilio Elizondo developed his concept of mestizaje as a theological category. Defining it as the process by which a new people arise from the encounter of two or more culturally or biologically disparate groups (Elizondo 2000, 5), he conceptualized it as the "border crossings" that Latina/os in general, and Mexican Americans in particular, experience existentially each day. It is not simply an "event" that takes place, but essentially "identity"—who they are, and consequently how they live out their lives. While such a people are rejected for being impure and hated for overcoming the boundaries of difference erected by racist societies, *mestizas/os* are, in fact, the eschatological promise of God's purpose for all of humanity. For Elizondo, this theological assertion is foundationally Christological: Jesus Christ is the mestizo incarnation of God in history. In and through the life and ministry of Jesus, one can detect the purpose of God. What the world rejects as insignificant, impure, and hateful, God declares to be good, pure, and loved. In raising the crucified mestizo Christ, God declares God's intention of life for all whom the world rejects and oppresses.

Elizondo's work became influential in the work of other Latina/o scholars. It represented a methodological shift from the Marxist/sociopolitical approach favored by Latin American theologians to anthropological/cultural analyses. Elizondo's work was soon followed by other Latino/as who developed ancillary concepts. For example, some noted that mestizaje was an incomplete term that excluded African influences in the culture and suggested mulatez as a better term. Others suggested terms such as *nepantla* (Aztec and Amerindian concept that means the place in between) and *sata* (Puerto Rican term meaning "mutt"). This fruitful avenue of exploration has led scholars to reflect on the theological importance of "in-between-ness"—the liminal space that is the existential matrix of Latino/a life.

Popular Religiosity

Latina/o scholars repeatedly have pointed out the essential religious nature of their culture. Latino/a religiosity transcends religious practice: it is not about calculating church attendance or denominational affiliations. Most Latina/os practice a form of "popular religion"—religious traditions held primarily by marginalized groups to articulate their understanding of life and death through particular symbols, language, and forms of worship. It is a religion "of the people" rather than of any given institution. Among Latina/os, popular religious practices developed within a historical context, in which missionary enterprises partnered with agencies bent on conquest and colonization of the Americas. The cry of *entre la espada y la cruz* epitomized an evangelization that became entwined with the brutal coercion of indigenous and African people. This violent encounter and subsequent union of Amerindian, African, Iberian Catholic, and later North Atlantic Protestant spiritualities produced a worldview peculiar to the Latino/a people. It includes a deep sense of the abiding presence of the divine in all aspects of life, the relationality of all things created and divine, and the sacredness inherent in creation. This "sacramental" worldview (Espín 1995, 27) rejects any division between the sacred and the secular. God is present even in the minutiae of life.

Religion permeates culture to the extent that it is impossible to divorce one from the other. Popular religiosity is, therefore, a defining component of *latinidad* and an important locus for theological reflection. This Latina/o sense of the sacred is expressed in everyday language through *dichos*/sayings as well as through cultural and religious symbols, beliefs, and values. While often rejected by dominant ecclesial institutions as pagan or superstitious, popular religiosity is the means by which the disenfranchised give expression to their suffering as well as their hopes in God as the author of salvation. Latina/o popular religious belief posits that God's purpose will be and is being fulfilled in all aspects of their lives, in spite of the struggles and obstacles that arise. The expressions of popular religious belief among Catholic and *evangélica/o* Latino/as as a foundational *loci theologicus* constitutes an important

defining characteristic of Latina/o contextual theologies and another significant difference from Latin American theologies of liberation.

Lo Cotidiano

Closely related to the concept of popular religiosity, lo cotidiano is the third important
distinctive feature of U.S.-based Latino/a theologies of liberation. Translated as
"daily" or "every day," lo cotidiano is a key epistemological tool as well as a locus
theologicus, particularly for Latina theologies. The majority of the poor and marginalized inhabit these spaces of everyday life where they struggle to make coherent sense
of a world filled with tragedy and death. Here they also experience God's grace-full
presence in visibly palpable ways, large and small. Lo cotidiano is the praxeological
arena where life is lived in its totality. Indeed, life is the means by which God speaks
and moves among "the least of these." It is in these spaces that one can witness God's
"option for the poor." The downtrodden and forgotten of our societies experience and
know God in special ways here. Thus lo cotidiano is a sacred locus of God's grace, liberation, and transformation in the face of the overwhelming structural injustice. As
such it is a space that yields fruitful theological insight.

María Pilar Aquino and Ada María Isasi-Díaz were the earliest proponents of the
use of lo cotidiano as a paradigm in response to the sexism and male-oriented perspectives that predominated in most theologies of liberation, including Latino/a theologies.
As an epistemological tool and a theological paradigm, it exposes the weakness of
male-centric theologies of liberation that rely on sociopolitical, Marxist, and philosophical analyses in their discourse on structural sin while remaining blind to the sin
of sexism and the impact of personal sins. Just as popular religious faith resists any
attempt to dichotomize the sacred and secular, lo cotidiano is the means by which Latinas effectively reject any attempt to separate the so-called public square of theological discourse and the allegedly private/domestic domains of life. The first—which
includes issues related to socioeconomics and politics—was assumed to be of immediate relevance to "real" theological and ethical reflection, while the latter had to do
with "private affairs" often associated with women. Latina scholars challenge such
thinking. They note that it is precisely in the spaces of daily living that the confluence
of the public and the private takes place, and where the impact of macrosystems upon
personal human lives is palpable, particularly among poor women and children of
color who are the ones most often relegated to the margins of "domestic irrelevance."
Latina theologians recognize that lo cotidiano is more than just a paradigm. It is a concrete sociohistorical location where women struggle daily for the survival of their families and communities. These scholars affirm that no theology can truly be
"liberating" in its intent unless it speaks to the full liberation of all people, especially
the most oppressed.

Teología en Conjunto

Latina/o cultures emphasize community and relationality over and above individuality.
Familia/family and community are the basis for a holistic existence. This communal
orientation is expressed in such *refranes*/popular sayings as *mi casa es tu casa* (my

---

CEHILA

The *Comisión de Estudios de Historia de la Iglesia en América Latina y el Caribe* (CEHILA) is an international and interdisciplinary network of scholars committed to recovering the historical dimension of Christianity in Latin America, in the Caribbean, and among U.S. Latinos. It was organized by CELAM (*Consejo Episcopal Latinoamericano*) in 1973 to promote the study of the history of the Church from the perspective of the poor and oppressed. U.S. Latinos became a part of CEHILA in 1975. The scholars are organized by geographic regions, including a continent-wide Protestant section. Over the years it has produced many books, study materials, conferences, and academic seminars on the subject. Enrique Dussel, CEHILA president for 20 years, has written or edited many of the most well-known books, including *The Church in Latin America 1492–1992* (Orbis Books, 1992). Two books about the U.S. Latino Christian experience have been published under the auspices of CEHILA: *Fronteras: A History of the Latin American Church in the USA Since 1513* (MAAC, 1983) and *Iglesias peregrinas en busca de identidad Cuadros del protestantismo latino en los Estados Unidos* (Kairós, 2004).

—JMG

---

house is your house), *dónde come uno comen dos* (where there is food for one there is enough for two), and *dime con quién andas y te dire quién eres* (tell me with whom you walk and I will tell you who you are). This relational emphasis is evident in Latino/a theological discourse. *Teología en conjunto*—literally, a "conjoined" theology—is not simply an intellectual or philosophical exercise, but a truly collaborative dialogue among people of faith who seek to find the answers for the concerns and struggles that they face on a daily basis. This underscores the contextual and praxeological nature of Latina/o theology as a collaborative endeavor that seeks justice and salvation for a marginalized people in a hurting world. It is not isolated from faith, but rather gives expression to the hope of a believing people as they experience the presence of the divine in the spaces of their daily lives. As a collaborative endeavor, Latina/o theology is not limited to an academic setting nor is it the discourse of specialists who use technical jargon understood solely by the members of their guild. Rather, as a teología en conjunto, it is a dialogue carried out among Latina/o scholars, grassroots communities of faith, pastoral leaders, and community activists. Latina/o theologians have no need to "discover" the poor and the marginalized since they emerge from these communities. Furthermore, as active members of their communities of faith, they engage in dialogue not to discredit the popular religious beliefs they have inherited, but rather to articulate and mine them for greater insight.

Teología en conjunto defines the Latina/o theological enterprise in a distinctive fashion. The acceptance of diversity through mestizaje/mulatez allows a greater sense of openness to a varying number of perspectives within the overall Latino/a community. It is therefore not surprising that its theologians approach their task with a truly ecumenical spirit. Religious differences that often prove divisive in other quarters only serve to enrich the dialogue among Latina/o scholars. This collaborative and relational spirit permits Latinas and Latinos to engage in dialogue about sexism and the marginalization of women from ecclesial and theological centers of power. In this spirit, Latina/o scholars actively participate in dialogue with diverse other groups, particularly those engaged in the struggle for justice, thus contributing to the wider theological discourse of the Christian Church.

Conclusion

U.S.-based Latina/o theologies are contextual theologies that seek the well-being of their particular communities and humanity in general. They are not new. However, their existence has not always been acknowledged for a number of reasons. According to Orlando E. Costas, these include the fact that they often were confused with Latin American theologies of liberation, and their use of a bilingual vernacular was rejected as a valid means of theological discourse (Costas 1992, 63). Most mainstream theologies discount Latino/a theologies as founded upon syncretistic or simplistic popular beliefs. Nevertheless, the situation has been changing since the early 1970s. The implications for the use of mestizaje/mulatez in light of globalization and of lo cotidiano as an important paradigm for women scholars are gaining the respect of other theologians. Such concepts have aided in defining with greater clarity the contours of Latina/o theologies. Furthermore, Latina/o theologians have begun to impact the national discourse on a myriad of issues such as im/migration, poverty, biculturalism, and sexism. In doing so, they contribute to theological insights such as the reading of Scripture from the margins, border crossings as the liminal space for reflection, the importance of popular religion and oral histories as a valid locus theologicus, and the importance of communal reflection as expressed through teología en conjunto and *praxis of accompaniment*. They ceased to be irrelevant precisely because they are a collaborative enterprise that, while insisting on their distinction from other theologies of liberation, refuses to be isolated from them. In true conjunto spirit, Latino/a scholars engage others from oppressed communities as well as the larger Church in order to be agents of change as they struggle for the realization of the Reign of God in the midst of human history, especially in the daily lives of people who live in faith and with hope. In so doing, they claim their legitimate place amid the pantheon of theologies of liberation and other Christian theologies.

References and Further Reading

Aquino, María Pilar. "Theological Method in U.S. Latino/a Theology." *From the Heart of Our People: Exploration in Catholic Systematic Theology*, ed. Orlando O. Espín and Miguel H. Díaz (Maryknoll, NY: Orbis Books, 1999).

Costas, Orlando E. "Hispanic Theology in North America." *Struggles for Solidarity: Liberation Theologies in Tension*, ed. Lorine M. Getz and Ruy O. Costa (Minneapolis: Fortress Press, 1992).

De La Torre, Miguel A. *The Hope of Liberation in World Religions* (Waco, TX: Baylor University Press, 2008).

Elizondo, Virgilio. *Galilean Journey: The Mexican-American Promise*, 2nd ed. (Maryknoll, NY: Orbis Books, 2000).

Ellacuría, Ignacio, and Jon Sobrino. *Mysterium Liberationis: Fundamental Concepts of Liberation Theology* (Maryknoll, NY: Orbis Books, 1993).

Espín, Orlando O. "Pentecostalism and Popular Catholicism: The Poor and *Traditio*." *Journal of Hispanic/ Latino Theology* 3, no. 2 (November 1995): 14–43.

Gutiérrez, Gustavo. *A Theology of Liberation: History, Politics, and Salvation*, rev. ed., trans. Sister Caridad Inda and John Eagleson (Maryknoll, NY: Orbis Books, 1993).

Isasi-Díaz, Ada María. *En la Lucha/ In the Struggle: A Hispanic Women's Liberation Theology* (Minneapolis: Fortress Press, 1993).

Marx, Karl. "Theses in Feuerbach." *The Marx-Engels Reader*, ed. Robert C. Tucker, 2nd ed. (New York: W. W. Norton and Company, 1978).

Schillebeeckx, Edward. *Christ: The Experience of Jesus as Lord*, trans. John Bowden (New York: Crossroad, 1993).

LITURGY AND WORSHIP

Eduardo C. Fernández

It has been said that all religions contain three basic elements: creed, code, and cult. Known also as the "three c's," these fundamentals, having to do with a belief system, a code of conduct, and some kind of worship or veneration, present a helpful structure for describing religious beliefs or structures. This entry focuses specifically on the third one, cult or worship, which, in many Christian denominations, in its more official and communal form, is sometimes known as "liturgy." In fact, in many Spanish-speaking Protestant Latino/a congregations, worship or liturgy is described as *culto*. The primary emphasis will be on its Christian manifestations, especially as experienced among Latina/os in the United States. Of course, just as it is incorrect to maintain that all Latino/as are Christian, thereby overlooking a certain, albeit small, population of Jews or Muslims, at the present time, the literature regarding them is rather sketchy. Similarly, the growth of converts among Latinos/as to such newer religious groups as Jehovah's Witnesses, Seventh-day Adventists, and the Mormons (or the Church of Jesus Christ of Latter-day Saints) is drawing attention, but is not yet written about to a significant extent.

Historical Developments and Major Doctrinal Points

In its most fundamental sense, worship is a complex experience, which has been described by Margaret Mary Kelleher as "a response of adoration evoked in one who has encountered the presence of God. It has also been depicted as the grateful rejoicing of those who have experienced God's action in their lives. At times it has been equated with the formal services or rites of a particular religion, and it has also been set out as a way of life" (1987, 105). This definition of worship, a word often used synonymously with cult, one of the three c's mentioned above, nonetheless integrates the other two elements of creed, in this case a belief in a personal God who acts in our lives, as well as code, which has been described as a way of life, a life lived in response to God's gracious self-gift.

Before exploring worship from a Hispanic perspective, it is essential, in order to understand the centrality of the goodness of created matter in Christian perspective, to introduce two terms: one, sacramentality, and two, a derivation of it, cosmic sacramentality (which, incidentally, is making a bold appearance in contemporary writings around Latino/a sacramental theology). In general, "sacramentality" refers to the notion that humans relate to God through material signs, symbols, and gestures. Language, too, whether in written or oral form, is symbolic. Cosmic or creation-centered sacramentality, an inheritance of the Jewish religious heritage of Christianity, embraces the spirituality of Israel in the Hebrew Bible, which is filled with examples of how God becomes present through physical means in creation and the cosmos. Unlike some of the prevailing religious notions of neighboring tribes, the Hebrew Scriptures, beginning with the book of Genesis, point to the goodness of creation. The many *berakoth*, or blessing prayers, witness the goodness of creation as manifested in the material. Early Christians embraced such practices, seeing them as part of the new covenant that Jesus inaugurates. It is through this sacramental presence that Jesus became present in their midst (Luke 24:13–35). Eventually, the larger notion of sacramentality was reduced to the more formal rites surrounding times of initiation, maturity, commitment, healing, and Eucharistic table fellowship.

Unfortunately, however, with the coming of Christendom in 392 CE, Christianity went from being a persecuted or barely tolerated sect of Judaism to the official religion of the Roman Empire. As more and more people became Christian, some whose motivations were more political than religious, the celebration of these sacramental rites underwent enormous changes. No longer were house churches able to accommodate the growing numbers at the Eucharist celebrations. These small, intimate settings were replaced by huge, Roman auditoriums known as basilicas. Lay people were gradually distanced from the Eucharistic table and, in many cases, the rigorous initiation process before Baptism, known as the catechumenate, was abandoned.

As the laity became more separated from the physical celebration of the sacraments and less informed about their meaning because they had not been through the catechumenate of the earlier ages, they looked to other faith practices involving the material to experience the Divine presence in their lives. This growing separation from the material aspects of official sacramentality is one of the main reasons for the rise of popular piety, one that is not clergy centered. Among these practices are the Stations of the Cross, the Rosary, processions, etc. It was not uncommon, for instance, even up to recent times, to have people praying the Rosary quietly during the Sunday Eucharistic celebrations. Within this context, it is not hard to see how some ancient practices such as the celebration of the Eucharist, or the Lord's Supper, became tainted with certain superstitious practices, such as the belief that gazing upon the raised consecrated host (consecrated bread) during the Mass would bring good luck to the person: for example, the birth of a son.

Both the Protestant and Catholic Reformations of the sixteenth century sought to correct these abuses. In many ways, the Protestant Reformation ushered in several changes that only came about in the Roman Catholic Church after Vatican II (convened in the 1960s), such as the importance of the priesthood of the faithful; the language of worship being in the vernacular, the language of the people; and the sharing of the cup at Eucharist, a strong reminder that the assembly is not just there to witness an event as spectators, but to participate in it. One of the greatest contributions of the

SANTOS PATRONES

Patron Saints in the Catholic Catechism are spoken of as models and examples of Christian life, which the baptized are to follow. Often the faithful are given the name of a canonized saint who will be their patron. Church buildings, shrines, and even towns have *santos patrones*. Early Christians usually met in people's homes; however, they eventually began to gather at the tombs of their martyrs. When Christianity became a free religion, many of these meeting places became basilicas, shrines, and churches and were named after the martyr being honored or commemorated at that location. This practice was eventually used to honor the confessors and virgins as well as the martyrs. By the time Christianity came to America in the sixteenth century, the practice of naming churches and towns in honor of saints was common place. As a result many cities in America are named after saints. In the United States we have San Agustin, Florida, Los Angeles, California, and San Antonio, Texas, to name a few. Many regions, towns, and villages celebrate their santos patrones. Patronal feasts are so popular that the small island of Puerto Rico, for example, has 75 fiestas patronales.

—GCG

Protestant Reformation was that it stressed the role of personal faith and active participation in regards to worship. On the other hand, from a more Roman Catholic perspective, it downgraded the role of ritual, at times substituting the reading and reflection on the Bible for sacramental celebration. Many Protestants today, of course, would not see this as a negative development. All in all, even among Protestants, there is a wide range of perspectives in regards to worship and sacraments.

Latino/a Manifestations

To this day, much of the Latino/a discourse around worship and liturgy, as might be expected, focuses on the two main currents: a more traditional, liturgical approach where sacrament and Word are both seen as equally important, and a newer, post-Reformation attitude, one which sees the Word as being primary in the tradition of "Sola scriptura." Another reality, which, in a way, has been around since Christianity first came to the Americas with the Spanish and Portuguese, is that of religious *mestizajes*, or combinations that came about as Catholicism confronted African or indigenous religions, especially in the case where these nonorthodox expressions had to go underground to survive. Finally, more recent phenomena are the alternative religious expressions that are now part of the new religious landscape of Latina/os in the United States such as those who worship as Pentecostals, Evangelicals, Jehovah's Witnesses, or Mormons.

Despite these differences, might there be some general characteristics that describe Hispanic Christian worship? One of the traits of Hispanic worship is its multiplicity. The style of worship, particularly as manifested in music, decoration, or food surrounding church gatherings, reflects certain national origins. Second, the Latino/a

Mexican Americans celebrate Mass, led by San Gabriel Region Auxiliary Bishop Gabino Zavala, at the Cathedral of Our Lady of the Angels on March 31, 2005, in Los Angeles, California. (Getty Images)

religious communities are often divided along generational lines. Because of constant immigration, and the rapidity with which younger generations learn English, within the same pew in church, or within the same family, for that matter, there will be those who are most comfortable in speaking only English or Spanish. Older, first-generation immigrants who often feel isolated in other public places take solace in being able to worship in Spanish, as well as to celebrate their national customs. Unfortunately, in a marked way, the same is no longer true for the younger generations.

Another characteristic of the multiplicity of Hispanics in terms of worship is the denominational loyalties, which can be very destructive at times. Justo González notes that

> Latino Protestantism, both in Latin America and in the United States, has grown mostly on the basis of anti-Catholic preaching and teaching. Among many Hispanics, to be a Protestant means to be anti-Catholic, so often Roman Catholicism is depicted in the worst light possible—they are idolaters who worship the Virgin and the saints, they do not believe in the Bible, they believe that they can save themselves through their own good works, their interpretation of the Eucharist is cannibalistic, priests are tyrannical and immoral, and so on. (1996, 11–12)

At the same time, he points to those Catholics who view Latina/os who leave the Church as being traitors to a common heritage rooted in Catholicism.

Thus, there are many faces to Hispanic worship. Among them, of course, are those Latina/os who, judging by all external means, have assimilated into mainstream U.S.

CORITOS

Coritos literally are "little choruses" (*coros*) used in worship, often biblically based in wording and put to a variety of tunes and instruments. Simply defined, a corito is a short, popular chorus sung widely in Latina/o communal worship, although coritos also may be used in private devotional piety. The very term is instructive in that it is the diminutive of the word coro, a sign in Spanish for affection toward something, and is indicative of its popularity. Coritos are found in both Roman Catholic and Protestant settings, with some of the same coritos appearing in both contexts. While coritos have been collected into songbooks for ready reference, this does not appear to be where they first emerged. Rather than being initially textual creations, coritos arose from the life situations of the people and often the exact origin of specific songs is unknown. These coritos often appear in photocopied collections, in pamphlets, as overhead transparencies, or in slide presentations and in most cases without musical notation. Sometimes a well-known corito is given a new verse that reflects the specific life situation of a particular congregation. Coritos express the concrete manifestations of the supernatural in the everyday for various Latina/o faith communities.

—EDA

culture. Their services, therefore, will all be in English and, particularly in some denominations, they have started to feel not as welcome as newer immigrants. Otherwise stated, Hispanic ministry in many places is basically ministry with and among newly arrived immigrants versus later generation Latino/as.

Even these more assimilated Hispanics, however, in the words of González, probably have had the experience of "worshiping as pilgrims and exiles," or, as otherwise stated, "the experience of belonging, yet not belonging" (1996, 14). Part of a group that is neither completely Latin American nor U.S. American, some have embraced the concept developed by Virgilio Elizondo known as *mestizaje*. Perhaps in the case of those Hispanics who have left their country in pursuit of a better life for themselves and for their children, the notion of being in exile is more acute. González, noting how these realities affect worship, highlights the Christian reality that this perspective embodies: our not quite belonging to the reign of this world, but that of God's, which has been announced but not yet brought to fulfillment (1996, 19).

A description of the various currents of liturgical worship found among Latino/as follows. In the case of those Christians belonging to more liturgical denominations, such as Roman Catholics, Methodists, Episcopalians, Lutherans, and Presbyterians, ecumenism has contributed a great deal toward a liturgical revival, much of it based on historical research about the early church, which surfaced particularly after Vatican II. In some ways, in regards to Roman Catholics who often tended to privilege Sacrament over Word, the mutual enrichment of ecumenical dialogue and occasional shared worship has enhanced the prominence of both. Protestants have become more versed in Sacrament, evidenced by attention paid to more frequent Eucharistic celebrations, the revision of liturgical texts, and the redesign of church architecture to give

VIA CRUCIS

"Way of the Cross," or "Stations of the Cross," is a Catholic devotional practice—sometimes observed within the Anglican and Lutheran traditions—in which participants focus their prayer on representations of 14 scenes or stations of Christ's Passion: (1) Jesus is condemned to death, (2) Jesus carries the cross, (3) Jesus falls the first time, (4) Jesus meets his mother, (5) Jesus is helped by Simon the Cyrenian, (6) Veronica wipes the face of Jesus, (7) Jesus falls the second time, (8) Jesus meets the women of Jerusalem, (9) Jesus falls the third time, (10) Jesus is stripped of his garments, (11) Jesus is nailed to the cross, (12) Jesus dies on the cross, (13) Jesus is taken down from the cross, (14) Jesus is buried. The custom of pausing in prayer at the places associated with the Passion of Jesus goes back to the early pilgrims to Jerusalem. Those who were not able to visit the holy places in person developed the pious custom of making a procession during which they paused to meditate upon the Passion. The tradition as church devotion began with Saint Francis of Assisi. The tradition was brought to the Americas by the first Franciscan missionaries and is practiced by Catholic Latino/as.

—AC

more prominence to the Eucharistic table and baptismal font. At the same time, Roman Catholics have rediscovered the power of the Word through such means as proclamation and study in the language of the people, an inclusion of Scripture passages in all sacramental celebrations, equal reverence paid to the Word at Eucharistic celebrations in terms of gesture and architecture, as when the Lectionary, which contains the readings for the service, is enthroned in a place of dignity and respect. Such groups often have more formal, developed liturgies structured around a liturgical calendar. In the case of Roman Catholics, celebrations of feasts around titles of Christ, Mary, and the saints are an essential part of that calendar.

Much of the literature produced by Latino/a Roman Catholics in the United States, therefore, presents ways of integrating the modern, post–Vatican II liturgy with more traditional, often medieval in origin practices of popular piety or religiosity, stressing that basically there is no contradiction between the two. In fact, according to these authors, these popular practices, often centered in the home where women play key roles, such as those around *altarcitos*, or small, devotional altars, actually enhance official sacramental expressions, particularly because of the sacred sensuality surrounding these manifestations of cosmic sacramentality.

In recent decades, with the increased awareness that creed, code, and cult are not separate from culture, but rather intimately connected to them, there has been an attempt to recapture the cultural diversity that has characterized Christianity throughout the centuries. A word often used to point to this challenge is inculturation. The goal of inculturation is to allow the liturgy or worship to express more clearly the sacred realities that it signifies. Otherwise stated, it is proclaiming the Gospel in ways that the various cultures can understand and feel it.

In giving examples of various forms of inculturation, which are now part of these communities' faith traditions, much of the literature speaks of the "people's faith practices" or the many forms of popular piety, in this case "popular" often having a connotation of being characteristic of the poor, as is more readily seen in the Spanish word *popular*. At times, these manifestations among Latino/a Protestants take the form of Bible study groups, as previously mentioned, testimonies, vigils, singing or corritos, etc. Latina scholar Elizabeth Conde-Frazier, along with others, is paying attention to the connections between social justice and popular piety. *Posadas*, for example, can often be much more than a simple enactment of Joseph and Mary searching for an inn before the birth of Jesus. At a time of increasing homelessness and restrictions to immigration, they remind the participants of the challenge of providing a home for all. Public processions such as the *Via Crucis*, a ritual drama of Jesus' passion, or those held around the feast of Our Lady of Guadalupe, not only speak of the Latino/a community's presence in public areas, especially in the case when much of it is immigrant, but they also strengthen cultural identity, an identity connected to the Divine. This type of worship, which may include indigenous dancing, hymns, or a live marching band, is a reminder that there is more than one way to pray or to enter the sacred realm.

The fastest-growing group of Christians worldwide today are Pentecostals whose style of worship is markedly different from that of the mainline churches described above. According to Arlene Sánchez-Walsh, "Pentecostalism is a movement within evangelical Christianity that stresses the manifestations of the gifts of the Holy Spirit as outlined in the book of Acts and chapters 12–16 of the first letter to the Corinthians" (2006, 199). In Pentecostal worship, *testimonios*, or oral testimonies by believers, play a key role in that they allow a person to testify to the power of God working in their lives and invite communal participation by assenting to the reality that the story conveys. Their overall effect is to accent God's closeness to God's people in the form of constant salvific intervention. Sánchez-Walsh continues by stating, "*Testimonios* bring God's reality and presence into the everyday communications of congregants, who see that God cares about one's health, one's financial situation, and can deal with the most miniscule of concerns" (2006, 200). They can lead to prayer at the altar, which subsequently can provide an opportunity for someone to receive Spirit baptism and have hands laid on them for healing, a healing beneficial not only to them but also to the community. Sánchez-Walsh goes on to quote a Pentecostal theologian, mainly, Samuel Solivá, who stresses the Holy Spirit's active role in bringing about this healing, a healing not unconnected to social transformation. "For Pentecostals, reaching out to the unwed mother, the homeless, the poor and the alcoholic is as politically important as electing a local official. From a Pentecostal perspective, the preaching of the gospel in [*sic*] the most politically and socially radical activity the world has known" (2006, 202).

Pentecostal worship has influenced that of both other Protestants and Roman Catholics. At times, the phrase "Charismatic" denotes a preference among certain such members to integrate a more emotional, healing-centered, participatory, and spontaneous style of worship, one which has been widely received among Hispanics. Among many Roman Catholic Latino/a congregations, for example, "healing Masses" have become very popular. To the extent that Pentecostalism and Evangelicalism are rapidly growing among Hispanics, these forms of Charismatic worship have the potential of being a bridge between Catholics and Protestants, especially to the extent that more spontaneous and indigenous forms of music and speech can welcome the immigrant who is feeling marginalized or disoriented in a new setting. This welcoming of the stranger, a historical example of when the church has been at her best, can provide a focus for liturgy or worship, one where creed, code, and cult take their inspiration from Jesus' commandment to love.

References and Further Reading

Deck, Allan Figueroa. "Hispanic Catholic Prayer and Worship." *Alabadle!: Hispanic Christian Worship*, ed. Justo L. González (Nashville: Abingdon Press, 1996).

Empereur, James, and Eduardo Fernández. *La Vida Sacra: Contemporary Hispanic Sacramental Theology* (Lanham, MD: Rowan and Littlefield, 2006).

González, Justo L. "Hispanic Worship: An Introduction." *Alabadle!: Hispanic Christian Worship*, ed. Justo L. González (Nashville: Abingdon Press, 1996).

Kelleher, Margaret Mary, O.S.U. "Worship." *The New Dictionary of Theology*, ed. Joseph A. Komonchak, Mary Collins, and Dermot A. Lane (Wilmington, DE: Michael Glazier, Inc., 1987).

Sanchez-Walsh, Arlene. "Pentecostals." *Handbook of Latina/o Theologies*, ed. Edwin David Aponte and Miguel A. De La Torre (St. Louis: Chalice Press, 2006).

ORTHOPRAXIS

Fernando A. Cascante-Gómez

The word "orthopraxis" combines two Greek words: *orthós*, which means "right" or "correct," and *praxis*, which means "practical action" as opposed to strictly mental activity. Thus, from the etymology of the word, "orthopraxis" means correct practice or right action. "Orthopraxis" is often compared with the term *orthodoxy*, that is, "right belief" or "correct doctrine," a term more familiar in the English language, in which it is generally assumed that "doctrine" and "theory" preside over "practice." But as a theological term, popularized in some European theological circles during the 1950s and 1960s (e.g., Political Theology), and further developed in Latin American theological circles during the 1960s and 1970s (e.g., Liberation Theology), "orthopraxis" takes a very distinctive meaning. First, it does not endorse the common separation made between theory and practice, between doctrine and practice, between faith and works. Second, it questions the assumption, particularly within Protestant Christian theological traditions, that right doctrine presides over right practice, the ruling of theory over practice.

To understand the conceptual distinctiveness made by Latin American theologians (mainly Catholic, but also Protestant), and its impact in Latina/o theology in the United States, a look at the use and understanding of the term *praxis* is of central importance. Therefore, what follows will focus on two philosophical approaches to the term "praxis," the theological meaning of the term in Liberation Theology and its relevance in the development of a Hispanic theology in the United States.

A Philosophical Approach

The word praxis has its origins in ancient Greek. It referred to the public activity of free men, the only recognized citizens since women—like children and slaves—were excluded from the public realm. In Athens' democracy, citizens were responsible for participating in the political life of the city. The realm of action was mainly the *political* realm, that is, the realm where the affairs of the city, Greek *polis*, were decided and carried out. Hence, Greek philosophers were the first to reflect on the problem of the transformation of reality through intellectual means. Among them, Aristotle (384–322 BCE) was the first who addressed the concept of praxis in a systematic manner.

Important in Aristotle's philosophical system was his conviction that pure reason is not the only trustworthy source of knowledge. The material worlds as well as lived experience, perceived through the senses, are reliable sources of knowledge, even of theoretical knowledge. With Plato, his teacher, Aristotle believed that ideas exist in and by themselves, available for discovery by rational means. But contrary to Plato's belief, he maintained that an ordered study of the material world could bring about better or more complete ideas capable of guiding the political activities of the free men and the productive activities of humans in general. Aristotle, in his *Nicomachean Ethics*, discusses three "ways of life" available to free men (1975, 1–11). Each way of life, or way of being in the world, involves particular forms of intellectual engagement, human action, and knowledge. Together they also reveal how Aristotle understands the relationship between theory and practice.

Theoria refers to the life of rational contemplation exclusively concerned with the discovery of universal ideas, or first principles. This contemplative way of life is almost an exclusive prerogative of philosophers, who serve as its prototype. They are the ones who have the training and who enjoy the socioeconomic conditions that allow them to dedicate themselves to a life of contemplation and exercise their rational capacities. The knowledge that matters in this way of life is about the nonsensible eternal realities, the unchanging truths and first principles that help to explain the world and give meaning and guidance to humanity. Theoretical knowledge becomes an end in itself, as it aims at achieving divine wisdom, which for Aristotle is the greatest source of happiness.

Praxis refers to the life that combines rational reflection and purposeful human activity within the political realm. It is a form of life that is not purely intellectual but relates to human conduct. Therefore, praxis is a form of reflective and ethical living in society, which is open to all citizens. The knowledge that praxis generates is more than intellectual knowledge, although it has its roots in human reason. It is a knowledge that needs to be appropriated by the individual and expressed in real life, in the interaction with others. The aim of praxis is achieving practical knowledge, or practical wisdom, which guides both reflection and the action such reflection requires. It is a knowledge that depends on *phronesis*, which Aristotle defines as a "true and reasoned disposition toward action with regard to things good and bad for men" (1975, 105). In sum, for Aristotle praxis is the Golden Mean between pure reason and pure action. Praxis is a deliberative activity (not just contemplative, not just productive) that requires both reflection and action and for the purpose of advancing knowledge and goodness in society. Praxis functions as a mediator between universal ideals about God, humans, and the world, for the making of a better social reality for all free citizens. This process generates more praxis, that is, more reflection and better actions. Therefore, the goal of praxis is more praxis. Not by accident Aristotle places praxis between a way of life that is strictly theoretical and another that is thought of as strictly practical.

Poiesis is the third and final way of life Aristotle discusses. This way of life involves a form of knowing that is productive and creative in nature, exemplified in the knowledge of an artisan, a poet, or a physician. This knowledge comes from the acquisition and use of skill, *techne*, which allows for the making of objects (e.g., a chair) or the achievement of a product (e.g., a poem or a healthy body). For Aristotle this was the lowest form of social life for a free man and also the least dependable way of knowing.

Aristotle's influence on Western theology was not evident until Thomas Aquinas (1125–1274) tried to reconcile Aristotle's philosophy with Christian doctrines in his *Summa Theologica*. Staying within the Greek philosophical tradition, Aquinas believed there are universal truths, and that God is pure reason. However, grounded in the Christian tradition he believed some universal truths are reached by reason while others are received by divine revelation. He maintained that Christian-revealed truths could be understood and reaffirmed through reason. Under Aristotle's influence, Aquinas sustained we can obtain knowledge, even knowledge about God, through careful rational observation and study of the world. The impact of Aquinas's theological thought was paramount in the development of Roman Catholicism, as well as other forms of Christianity after the Reformation. Paradoxically, his emphasis on the role of reason encouraged a rather rationalized version of faith, understood as the assenting to theological statements and doctrines. Even Reformers like Luther and Calvin, who emphasized God's grace and not reason as the source of faith, popularized the use of catechisms with their rational and rote memorization format of question-and-answer. But Aquinas's convictions about human intellectual capacities, in addition to his faith in Scripture and the authority of the teachings of the Church, gave rise to a method that would become crucial for future theological developments. Thanks to Aristotle, Aquinas helped to plant in Christian theology the seeds of a theological method that promotes reflection on life experience with reference to Scripture and teaching of the Church. The development and impact of this method was particularly evident in the emergence of Liberation Theology, to be considered later.

A Socioeconomic Approach

Karl Marx (1818–1883) was the modern thinker who probably captured best the social and political dimensions of the term "praxis." Marx, like Aristotle, saw public or political life as the realm of praxis and saw in the term the presence of both theory and practice. Nevertheless, they articulate their understandings of praxis with different social frameworks in mind. For his definition of praxis Aristotle had in mind the free men of Athens, a minority when compared with the rest of the population. What Marx had in mind was the exploited working class in England and other industrialized countries, a majority when compared with the rest of the population. In other words, Marx developed his concept of praxis in light of and in reaction to the social and economic effects of the Industrial Revolution taking place in Europe and already spreading to other parts of the world. This critical difference is translated into Marx's understanding of theoria, praxis, and poesis.

Contrary to Aristotle, Marx conferred theoria value inasmuch as it is verified in the material world, especially in the world of human interactions. Pure theory, as abstract elaboration, is not real theory, and it only has value for philosophers. In Thesis II of his short 1845 essay "*Concerning Feuerbach*," Marx affirms that "the dispute over the reality or non-reality of thinking that is isolated from practice is a purely scholastic question" (in Raines 2002, 183). For him, the final truth of philosophy is expressed in political action, as it is summarized in his well-known Thesis XI where he says: "Philosophers have hitherto only interpreted the world in various ways; the point is to change it" (Raines 2002, 184). Therefore, the true realm of philosophy, of theories and ideas, is the material and social world wherein the interaction of people with nature and of people with people takes place. Theoria for Marx begins and ends with humans and their world. Theory as abstract speculation or contemplation is not only theory alienated from the world, but it is theory that alienates people from it.

Again, contrary to Aristotle, Marx gives poesis, human productive and creative activity, a central value and an ontological one. He understands poesis as a "conscious life activity" that proves people are conscious beings. In their labor, and the products that result from it, people express their human spirit. In and through their productive activity people manifest their creativity, but also their agonies and their desire for something new and different. In another essay from 1844, "Estranged Labor," Marx affirms that "man reproduces himself not only intellectually, in his consciousness, but actively and actually, and he can therefore contemplate himself in a world he himself has created" (in Raines 2002, 123). With Marx, for the first time, humans are conceived as agents of social transformation, "historic subjects" capable of affecting reality, which is now seen as more than external and objective, unaffected by human action. He finds ontological value in human activity because in it people claim their role as subjects in history, as actors in the political life. There is no denying that human beings are conditioned by natural and historical circumstances. What is affirmed is that human beings are capable of modifying those conditions, if they understand the laws that explain those conditions and their role in changing them. In Thesis VIII on Feuerbach he says, "all social life is essentially practical. All mysteries which lead to mysticism find their rational solution in human practice and in the comprehension of this practice" (in Raines 2002, 184). This conviction is at the heart of Marx's concept of praxis.

Like Aristotle, Marx also understood praxis as reflective human activity within the realm of public life. But Marx, with his understanding of theoria and poesis, of philosophy and labor, gives praxis new levels of meaning. Praxis is more than the intelligent activity reserved for the ruling class that controls the life of the polis. Praxis is more than a desirable balance between pure theory and pure human activity. Praxis is more than a "reasoned disposition towards action." For Marx, praxis is where all people, in particular the proletariat, exercise their essential condition as conscious beings and their role as subjects of their own history. Praxis is where the true value of theory and practice are united and manifested. Theory is praxis and praxis is concrete action for the transformation of the world. Hence, praxis, as a political activity is the ultimate criteria of truth for both theory and human actions. Finally, praxis is motivated not simply by an individual internal disposition towards good actions but by a concrete social commitment towards the transformation of the social world into a classless society. In regard to transforming nature, praxis is production, work, and technique. In regard to transforming society, it is political action, more concretely, militant, organized, revolutionary action for the abolition of class structures and class exploitation (González 1983, 803–804).

With the advancement of industrial societies, the influence of Marx's revolutionary approach to praxis was questioned and eventually faded in European theological circles. European theological movements became mostly concerned with the Kantian challenge of freeing reason from all dogmatisms, including those coming from Scripture or from culturally enforced religious belief systems. Their theological task focused on demonstrating that the truths of Christianity are at the levels of natural and historical reason encouraged by the Enlightenment, as Aquinas did with Aristotle. Also, theologies produced in Europe and North America have been occupied with providing well-educated Christians with new interpretations of Scripture and Christian doctrines. These interpretations have aimed at responding to the rational and existential challenges presented by the modern world of science, increasing secularization and socioeconomic global realities. Accordingly, the "Marxist Enlightenment," which calls for a liberation not of reason but from the oppressive realities of society, was not given serious consideration as part of their theological task. On the contrary, it was theologians from Latin America, and soon after from other parts of the "Third World," who took up the challenge presented by Marx and his "philosophy of *praxis*" in their development of theologies of liberation (Sobrino 1984, 7ss).

A Liberation Theology Perspective

Latin American Theology of Liberation can be described in part as a response to and a critical appropriation of Marx's philosophy of praxis. On talking about the different factors that have influenced liberation theology, Gustavo Gutiérrez, in his seminal book *A Theology of Liberation*, says:

> Be that as it may, contemporary theology does in fact find itself in direct and fruitful confrontation with Marxism, and it is to a large extent due to Marxism's influence that theological thought, searching for its own sources, has begun to reflect on the meaning of the transformation of this world and the action of man in history. (1973, 9)

Two things are important in this confrontation of Christian faith and practice with Marxism. First, the renewed awareness that human action in history, in particular Christian action, can help with the efforts for better understanding Christian faith. In other words, orthopraxis (the right actions) can help to better understand *orthodoxy* (the right doctrine). Two, in the understanding of Christian faith there is meaning for the transformation of the world. Marxism is not the source for a Christian understanding of praxis. The source is a faith in God who loves us and in Jesus Christ's call to love our neighbor, even our enemies (Matthew 5:38–48). Marxism is no more than a tool that helps Christians better understand the socioeconomic realities of the poor and oppressed in the world wherein Christians need to practice obedience to God's call.

Thus, as Marx did in his time, theologians and Christians in Latin America became painfully aware of the realities of exploitation, exclusion, and oppression of millions of people on the continent. The critical question theologians, priests, pastors, and community lay leaders tried to answer was how Christians should live out their faith precisely in that context. It was a question about the living of faith, not about the meaning of faith. At its root, this question is not an intellectual question but a *pastoral* question because, as José Miguez Bonino explains, it invites a "reflection of what the church—the Christian and the Christian community—is doing and should do [in the world]" (Míguez Bonino 1985, 38). Theologians found in Marxism both a call and an impulse to go back to the biblical roots of the Christian faith to answer this question and to recognize the role of people in the transformation of the world.

It became clear that in the Old Testament, Israel's faith is focused not simply on knowing particular truths about God but especially on obeying God's commandments. The Law, the *Torah*, describes the ways God's people are expected to live in relationship with God, their neighbors, and nature. Central to the role of the prophets was to remind Israel when the Law became simple ritualism separated from the practice of love and justice, particularly towards the poor, the orphan, the widow, and the foreigner (Micah 6:6–8). The social demands and the practical dimension of faith also permeate many of the books in the Writings, the third section of the Hebrew Scriptures. In the New Testament, faith is described as doing God's will in our relationship with others. Jesus is God's Word (*Logos*) becoming real in history and the example of what it means to live by God's word in the world. In the Gospels Jesus proclaims good news to the poor (Luke 4:18–19) and lives among and ministers especially to the poor and the outcasts of his society. In Jesus' eschatological vision, those who enter into God's kingdom are those who *do* his Father's will (Matthew 7:21), those who feed Him, cloth Him, and visit Him in the hungry, naked, imprisoned people of the world (Matthew 25:31–41). The apostle Paul in his letters constantly calls Christians to a faith that works through love (Galatians 5:6), that shows the newness of life in Christ (Romans 12). The Book of James exhorts to be "doers of the word" and affirms that faith without works is dead faith (2:17). Professional theologians and Christians in the poor communities found that the Bible was replete with references to God's actions on behalf of the poor and the oppressed (e.g., the exodus from Egypt) and with multiple visions of new heavens and new earth where justice and peace will reign (Revelation 21). The Bible's emphasis on "doing the truth" and on the new people and new creation God wants, allowed for two critical understandings of the Christian faith: First, that it is in doing the truth that our faith (e.g., what we believe and confess in words) is verified in history. Second, that Christian praxis has a role to play in God's reign to be manifested in the world. In other words, what we do or not do as Christians has an impact in this world and the world God wants to create.

In addition to this biblical rediscovery, liberation theologians found, in the history of the Church in general and the Latin American church in particular, examples of committed Christians who gave their lives for the sake of the poor and the oppressed and for the transformation of realities of injustice, inequality, and exploitation. Therefore, liberation theologians began to understand theology and theological method in a new way. For them, in its most succinct expression, theology is "critical reflection on Christian praxis in the light of the Word." Central in the definition is an understanding of praxis as being *Christian*, that is, a practice of faith in response to the message of Jesus the Christ and God's ultimate vision for the world. Christian praxis is informed by critical reflection both on previous Christian praxis and on the message of Scripture. Gustavo Gutiérrez expands his own definition in the following way:

> Theology as critical reflection on historical praxis is a liberating theology, a theology of the liberating transformation of the history of mankind and also therefore that part of mankind—gathered into *ecclesia*—which openly confesses Christ. This is a theology that does not stop with reflecting on the world, but rather tries to be part of the process through which the world is transformed. (1973, 15)

This broader definition makes it clear that Christian praxis does not refer only to the communal practice of rituals and beliefs, and neither is it limited to the sanctuary of a church nor to individual private spiritual practices. Praxis is the living out of Christian faith in history, in the here and now, in the midst of and over against the oppressive forces of society, in order to change the world into a world of justice and peace, according to the vision of God's reign. From both definitions it is also clear that theology as reflection, both on historical praxis and on the message of the Bible, comes as the second step. Historical praxis becomes the first methodological step for doing theology.

Therefore, liberation theology should be understood more as a method for doing theology in which a living commitment with the poor and oppressed comes first and critical reflection on that commitment comes second. In this sense, as Clodovis Boff puts it,

> Any theory, hence also theology, is concretely subject to the influence of praxis as its vital milieu (*medium in quo*). This subordination is registered on three levels: that of the theologian's social involvement, that of the historical relevance of a theme, and that of the political intent of a theology. (Boff 1987, 229)

This does not mean that "pure *praxis*" without reference to theory could exist, nor that critical reflection is secondary. Without critical reflection on historical reality, the church is in danger of supporting an oppressive social and ecclesial order. For this reason the "sciences of the social" (e.g., economics, politics, history, anthropology, etc.) become central to the task of the theologian. In the same manner, without critical reflection on the message of the Bible, the church faces the danger of holding on to outdated traditions and questionable or irrelevant doctrines and interpretations. Thus the traditional theological disciplines of Bible, theology, church history, and practical theology continue to be important. In other words, critical reflection is indispensable for a Christian praxis that is relevant to present realities of injustice and oppression and for a faithful interpretation of the Scriptures and tradition in light of these realities. The methodological importance of theory as a second step is that theory takes place in the context of practice and refers to it. Therefore, *orthopraxis*, more precisely Christian praxis, becomes more relevant to Christian faith than *orthodoxy*, holding on to right beliefs. Again, in the words of Gustavo Gutiérrez,

The intention, however, is not to deny the meaning of *orthodoxy*, understood as a proclamation of and reflection on statements considered to be true. Rather, the goal is to balance and even to reject the primacy and almost exclusiveness which doctrine has enjoyed in Christian life and above all to modify the emphasis, often obsessive, upon the attainment of an orthodoxy which is often nothing more than fidelity to an obsolete tradition or a debatable interpretation. (1973, 10)

Similar to that of Aristotle and Marx, Christian praxis is political—it touches all the areas of human interaction. Beyond Marx and Aristotle, praxis became the political action of the poor and others on behalf of the poor, which includes not only those who suffer from economic oppression (Marx's proletariat) but all who suffer forms of racial, ethnic, and sexual discrimination as well. Praxis in Liberation Theology is more than an action/reflection process to deliberate on how to apply preestablished universal truths, as in Aristotle. Praxis in Liberation Theology is more than the historical verification of an absolute philosophical formulation about a future new social order that has little or no reward for the present lives of those suffering oppression and injustice, as in Marx. Praxis is the active participation of Christians in God's plan for transforming the world, which has meaning for their present life and for the future. The motivation for Christian praxis goes beyond an ethical individual imperative for doing good (as in Aristotle), or a revolutionary commitment to a socioeconomic world order (as in Marx). The motivation for Christian praxis is love of God and neighbor as a response to God's gratuitous love for the world. Once again, Gustavo Gutiérrez states:

> In the first place *charity* has been fruitfully rediscovered as the center of the Christian life. This has led to a more Biblical view of faith as an act of trust, a going out of one's self, a commitment to God and neighbor, a relationship with others. It is in this sense that St. Paul tells us that faith works through charity: love is the nourishment and the fullness of faith, the gift of one's self to the Other, and invariably to others. This is the foundation of the *praxis* of the Christian, of his active presence in history. According to the Bible, faith is the total response of man to God, who saves through love. (1973, 6–7)

In sum, praxis in Liberation Theology integrates philosophical, sociohistorical, theological, and spiritual meanings. It is *philosophical* because praxis involves a dialectical relationship between theory and practice in which they constantly influence each other, and as they influence each other together they influence the reality praxis is exercised upon. In praxis human beings also exhibit the ethical and teleological nature of their actions and their self-understandings as actors in history. Praxis is *sociohistorical* because it refers to the concrete realities of injustice suffered by the oppressed and marginalized people of the world as well as to the concrete historical actions by people committed to the transformation of those realities. It is *theological* because praxis is the way Christians manifest the signs of the truth of their faith; through their historical actions they show their following of Jesus in the world. And finally, praxis is *spiritual* because it is ultimately in praxis where Christian love for God and neighbor is manifested; praxis becomes the concrete expression of active spirituality or, better, of Christian spirituality in action.

Praxis and Hispanic/Latino Theologies

As a distinctive theological movement within the United States, Hispanic theologies have emerged and been recognized as such since the early 1990s. Not surprising, for these theologies the concept of praxis and what it involves have also become important for their development, since Latino/a theologians and Christians living in the United States confront issues and realities similar to that of Christians in Latin America. Although not all Hispanic theologies work out of a liberation perspective, many of them do. Ada María Isasi-Díaz affirms, "our theology grows out of the needs in our communities, out of the role that religion plays in the daily struggle to survive as a marginalized and oppressed group within one of the richest countries in the world . . . [We] understand doing theology as a liberative praxis" (1996, 369–370).

But Latina/o theologies do not mirror Liberation Theology's understanding of praxis. As Roberto S. Goizueta explains, "a genuine fidelity to this methodology will imply that the content of our theological reflection will differ from its Latin American counterpart" (2001, 62). The particular realities of Hispanic people and church in the United States require different manifestations of historical praxis as well as different understandings of the community of faith and its role in society. These realities refer to the experience of cultural, political, and economic marginality; of statehood, exile, and immigration; of "otherness," self-identity, and racial discrimination; and in the particular situation of women, the added reality of sexism inside and outside the Latino/a community. These realities are also marked by the great diversity among the Hispanic community: as citizens, residents, refugees, or recent immigrants from Latin America and Europe; as direct descendants of Spanish ancestry and culture or as a result of the mixing of Amerindian and European cultures; as Catholic, Protestant, Evangelical, or other religious practices. And yet, in the midst of this rich diversity, there is the basic claim that Hispanic people experience praxis as essentially communal and celebratory. That is what is revealed and expressed in the praxis of Latina/o religiosity and in the Hispanic "way of life." This praxis involves a serious intellectual endeavor for the recovery of, as well as critical reflection upon, that praxis. However, this praxis also involves ethical and political implications. Goizueta says that "by affirming community in the face of oppression, and the beauty of creation in the face of de-creation and destruction, popular religious praxis becomes, indirectly, a crucial source of empowerment and liberation" (2001, 69). In addition to this indirect transformative dimension of praxis, various forms of direct historical praxis nurture Hispanic theological reflection, as rightly acknowledged by Justo González (1990, 74). Christians, from across denominational and church boundaries, have been involved in the struggle for the rights of farming laborers and *maquila* workers, in community organizing in the barrios, in the struggle of Puerto Ricans for independence, in the struggles for effective political participation in society and for access to better education, housing, and health services.

As the Latin American Theology, and other theologies of liberation (e.g., Black, Feminist, Native American, Asian, etc.), Hispanic theologies are, for the most part, praxis-based theologies. This praxis aims at being both pastoral and prophetic. It is *pastoral* because it is a praxis that seeks to empower and liberate the Latino/a people to face and transform the realities that oppressed them. It is *prophetic* because it is a praxis that seeks to engage the dominant theological and cultural paradigms that maintain and promote those oppressive realities. And central to the Hispanic praxis of theological reflection and action is the conviction that both should result out of a collaborative effort (Rodríguez and Otero 1997, 1). This way of doing theology, *en conjunto*, is a distinctive commitment among Latino/a Christians, theologians or not, to a particular way of thinking and acting their faith. More importantly, this way of doing theology, of humbly working together for integrating diverse realities, Christian perspectives, and human practices, is an invitation for emphatic dialogue to other theologians and the larger community to weigh and balance orthodoxy and orthopraxis in the common life all share together, both in light of the good news of God's reign of love, peace, and justice, and in light of the best human values upheld in the constitution and laws of this country.

References and Further Reading

Aristotle. *Nicomachean Ethics* (Boston: D. Reidel Pub. Co., 1975).

Boff, Clodovis. *Theology and Praxis: Epistemological Foundations* (Maryknoll, NY: Orbis Books, 1987).

Goizueta, Roberto. *We Are a People! Initiatives in Hispanic American Theology* (Minneapolis: Augsburg Fortress, 1992).

González, Justo. *Mañana: Christian Theology from a Hispanic Perspective* (Nashville: Abingdon Press, 1990).

Gonzalez Ruiz, J. M. "Praxis." *Conceptos Fundamentales de Pastoral*, ed. Casiano Floristan and Juan-Jose Tamayo (Madrid: Ediciones Cristiandad, 1983).

Gutiérrez, Gustavo. *A Theology of Liberation* (Maryknoll, NY: Orbis Books, 1973).

Isasi-Díaz, Ada Maria, and Fernando Segovia, eds. *Hispanic/Latino Theology: Challenge and Promise* (Minneapolis: Augsburg Fortress, 1996).

Míguez Bonino, José. "Theology as Critical Reflection and Liberating Praxis." *The Vocation of the Theologian*, ed. Theodore W. Jennings, Jr. (Philadelphia: Fortress Press, 1985).

Raines, John, ed. *Marx on Religion* (Philadelphia: Temple University Press, 2002).

Rodríguez, David, and Loida Martell-Otero, eds. *Teología en Conjunto: A Collaborative Hispanic Protestant Theology* (Louisville, KY: Westminster John Knox Press, 1997).

Sobrino, Jon. *The True Church and the Poor* (Maryknoll, NY: Orbis Books, 1984).

PASTORAL CARE AND COUNSELING

Rebeca M. Radillo

The ministry of pastoral care and counseling encompasses all aspects of human life. It is interwoven and congruent with every expression of the ministry of the church and manifests itself in the entire life of the faith community. Healing, liberation, and empowerment form the matrix of pastoral care and counseling ministry. Pastoral care and counseling is theological, biblical, and educational. Because it is contextual, cultural, sociohistorical, religious, and political elements influence its meaning and praxis. Pastoral care and counseling from a Latino/a perspective must, then, reflect the particularities of a polycultural community.

Although this entry is written from a Christian perspective, pastoral care and counseling are not the sole possession of Christendom, but are the expressions of many faith traditions, attempting to bring healing and wholeness to their communities. Pastoral care and counseling are always contextual, as praxis is a direct response to the particularities of individuals and groups at specific times within their unique sociohistorical, religious, and even political circumstances. The history and practice of the pastoral care and counseling ministries and the evolution of its theory and praxis represent the constant development of practitioners in the United States as well as in the international community.

This development is reflected in the ongoing dialogue over the appropriate terminology for the practice of care within a congregational context. Pastoral care and pastoral counseling are typically considered interchangeable or synonymous. In fact, there are marked differences between the two concepts in terms of both methodology and educational requirements as well as the actual praxis of care, which will be addressed later in this essay. In Latin America the two prevalent concepts are *asesoramiento pastoral* and *consejo pastoral*.

The focus of the ministry of pastoral care and counseling is to bring healing and wholeness to persons who are experiencing emotional and spiritual brokenness as the result of distressing physical, social, or psychological circumstances. Pastoral care and counseling is contextual and takes into account the complexities of individual lives, addressing the polarization, isolation, and fragmentation of persons and groups, both within faith communities and in the larger society. Sara Baltonado, a Costa Rican psychologist, states that "pastoral care and Counseling always occur within social, political, economic and religious contexts" (2002, 192).

Relationships are at the core of Hispanic identity, and pastoral care and counseling must take into account the importance of the community in the process of healing. Because of the historical importance of the Church to Latina/o identity, it is not surprising that it continues to be a significant institution for Hispanics. Because the church is the spiritual community where people pray, sing, and speak in their own mother tongue, the fellowship of believers becomes home, a place of comfort and solace. The church sustains the family, cultural traditions, and familiar worldviews, while serving as an educational center for newcomers, and a place for multigenerational socialization, bringing a sense of hope and healing to a marginalized population.

Hierarchy and authority are valued and held in high esteem by Latino/as. This, in part, explains why religious leaders are highly regarded and respected. The church is seen as an extension of the home and a "safe space," regardless of immigration status, social context, or economic location. The church is the space where wholeness is most often experienced. At times of unrest and crisis, the church is the first place Latina/os will go for assistance and guidance, and the pastor is the first person with whom they feel free to share their predicament in confidence.

Given the sociocultural and political realities of the Latino/a population, pastoral care and counseling ministry in the Hispanic churches must address with relevancy and intentionality the needs of individuals and groups that seek guidance and support from a trusted institution and faith community. It is critical that caregivers respond to the tangible and concrete expressions of spiritual-emotional-physical care and avoid the dichotomy between flesh and spirit. This care includes pastoral visitation; assisting the family in economic crisis; attending family celebrations; responding to physical needs, such as food or shelter; translations in courts or hospitals; presence during times of illness, unemployment, or death. In other words, a caregiver is very much involved, attentive, and sensitive to the totality of the entire life of a careseeker.

Pastoral care has evolved, historically, as a responsible and effective response to the needs of people in their particular milieu. Traditionally, this ministry has been viewed through the lenses of Eurocentric theology and psychology. The precursors of this movement were true to their worldview and have with integrity and wisdom given the Christian church invaluable models for the care of people.

Globalization and the enormous immigration patterns in this country and around the world have opened new avenues for understanding and responding to the needs of multicultural and racial or ethnic communities. These communities have contributed to an expanded vision and understanding of individuals in communities, and the need to address the totality of the person rather than one aspect of being. Contextualization has opened the field of pastoral care to include socio-political-economic factors that influence emotional and spiritual well-being.

Religion and healing are inseparable and complementary; each social-religious context has interpreted and formulated its particular expression and practice of pastoral care. Although practical or pastoral theology, ecclesiology, and social-historical context are the underpinnings of this ministry, it is important to point to the contributions of the social sciences. Sociology, anthropology, and, especially, psychology have been extremely valuable in the development of a comprehensive caregiving ministry, reinforcing the relational and focusing on meaning and symbol.

Caregivers in the United States who provide pastoral care and counseling in the Hispanic context must be sensitive to the importance of the extended family and the existing ties and responsibilities to and with families in Latin America. The phenomenon of immigration touches not only first-generation immigrants but second-generation families as well. Some pressing issues common to, but not unique to, immigrants are acculturation, biculturalism, and multigenerational family dynamics, including emotional and financial support of family members abroad. In addition, one must consider the stress produced by culture shock, the grief and sense of loss of "home," and the memory of the land, familiar places, language, music, etc. A pastoral caregiver functions on multiple levels: as spiritual leader, social worker, and advocate for individuals and families. The respect and expectations of a spiritual leader by the community carries an enormous responsibility and positions a pastor in an advantageous position to respond to people in an informed manner.

A caregiver must always be aware of the advantages of power and privilege that this respect creates, as well as the unrealistic expectations and immense burdens that it may demand. Unrealistic expectations placed upon caregivers, and the tendency of careseekers to attribute unrealistic skill and power to caregivers, may create a major obstacle in establishing a healthy and healing relationship. Subsequent transferential issues may result in painful confusion.

Celia Jaes Falicov has done extensive work with Latino/a immigrants, and she believes that "perhaps the most fundamental and disruptive consequence of migration is the uprooting of cultural meaning" (1988, 52). She further notes "that migration involves at least three forms of uprooting of meaning systems: physical, cultural and social, all of which have psychological implications. These uprooting experiences are major contributors to spiritual brokenness. Leaving behind a home, family and familiar images and symbols are major

Father Ruben Rios, a native of Argentina, walks behind altar boys during the concluding procession at Immaculate Heart of Mary Church Sunday in Phoenix. Rios is among a number of Latin American clergy serving the growing Hispanic population in the United States. (AP Photo/Ross D. Franklin)

disruptive experiences that threaten the spiritual and emotional well being of any individual or group."

The practice of pastoral care from a Hispanic perspective in the United States must take into account the particularities of the phenomenon of immigration, including the vast range of cultural, historical, and sociopolitical and religious realities of each country of origin. Besides issues concerning the recent immigrant population, the church has a role to play in the healing of a community that continues to face the explicit and implicit expression of racism, a rapid growth of young Latino/a families, poverty, unemployment, and other socioeconomic realities confronted in a more pronounced way by this population. In addition, attention must be given to the regions where they reside, their educational level, economic status, employment opportunities, and history of migration, all of which impact their lives.

The recent increase of immigrants in the United States presents an opportunity and a challenge to congregations and pastors. Immigration is a theological/spiritual reality as well as a social, political, and economic dilemma. It has been well documented that the process of immigration presents a challenge to the emotional, spiritual, and psychological well-being of a person. In order to do pastoral care with individuals who suffer from multiple stressors, a caregiver needs to be able to listen carefully and be prepared to nurture, guide, and support the development of interpersonal relationships and to communicate a genuine sense of caring for the careseeker.

The understanding of the profound impact of pastoral care in the life of individuals, congregations, and communities is crucial to this unique expression of ministry. Pastoral care has been defined as a dialogue that seeks to delve into a person's psychological and spiritual strengths. The dialogue is a powerful interaction between careseeker and caregiver, where verbal and nonverbal communication convey the depth of physical, social, spiritual, and psychological distress. This dialogical interaction is a "sacred" moment that necessitates a relationship that is centered in trust, mutuality, acceptance, and competence. It is through such interaction that healing and transformation are not only desirable, but also possible.

The Spanish-speaking church can provide an essential space for the Latino community. Sergio Ulloa Castellanos raises a very real dilemma when he states that "the social spaces where the human being is able to find love and companionship are becoming increasingly scarce. Humanity claims for itself, in the midst of crisis, a faith community that will be supportive and guiding." It is imperative that churches become a place of healing, a place of hospitality, and a place for transformation. In order to do so, the church has to be prepared to "welcome" the community. The role of caregiver must be expanded to the congregation, and it may be appropriate to review the image of a caregiver.

Because of the multiple needs of the Latino/a population, faith communities must adopt an appropriate model of care and initiate training programs for mature and caring individuals willing to be a part of a ministry of care in their churches. The *Instituto Latino de Cuidado Pastoral* in New York City offers a number of training events and classes for pastors and laity in the ministry of congregational pastoral care. The training program uses the bio-psycho-social-spiritual model and is taught by pastoral counselors and pastoral psychotherapists. The program uses critical theological reflection and praxis as its methodology. It is a successful model where "shepherds" are given the opportunity to develop pastoral care skills. It also prepares members of the Latina/o community to work alongside their pastors as agents of healing and wholeness within the churches.

Pastoral care ministry as understood by the New Testament community and by contemporary practitioners belongs to the "priesthood of all believers." The church has the responsibility to train, develop, and oversee a cadre of people who may become "caregivers" for the congregation. The function of shepherding is not limited to the pastor, but is shared by the entire faith community. Although the shepherd metaphor suggests that pastors are caregivers, the faith community and the church as a whole are agents of healing.

The term "pastoral care" emerged from the concept of "shepherding," where the central content of shepherding is the shepherd's solicitous concern for the welfare of the sheep. This Old Testament concept is an excellent paradigm for the practice of pastoral care. While it is a somewhat difficult metaphor for a postmodern urban society to appreciate in the fullest, it provides a model of care that is based on the love of a shepherd for his/her flock and the skills required to keep the sheep safe from predators and natural dangers.

The characteristics of a skilled shepherd—caring, concerned, and committed—are not unlike those of a genuine, skilled, caring, and competent pastoral care provider. To this image we may add knowledge of the "terrain" and leadership capability to navigate the flock. A shepherd/pastoral care specialist needs practical knowledge of the context in which he/she serves, a basic understanding of the complexity of the human being, and an awareness of the profound spiritual and emotional impact that any disruptive experience can have on the lives of individuals, as well as the community(s) in which they are embedded.

The extension of pastoral care ministry to include the laity reflects a significant redistribution of power and responsibility. Unfortunately, shared pastoral ministry often gives insufficient consideration to the training and reflection necessary to develop caregivers who understand the internal and external dynamics that impact behavior and the implications of such behavior on the development of a healthy emotional and spiritual life. It is, therefore, of the utmost importance that those persons who engage in the ministry of pastoral care learn the skills necessary to respond to people in distress in an informed and responsible manner.

Properly trained caregivers facilitate the wholeness and health of individuals and their families and also foster the development of healthy congregations. Because of the multiplicity of difficult situations in churches and communities, there is need for the training of the caregivers. This training includes the biblical and theological foundation of pastoral care; pastoral care practical skills such as dealing with crisis; attentive listening; and basic understanding of personality disorders, family dynamics, referrals, etc. Training for this ministry does not require a formal education.

Statistics continue to reflect the rapid, ongoing growth of Hispanic cultural ethnic groups, which provide increasing diversity within this population. Although each group has contributed to the well-being of the larger society, they also present a number of problems for that society. A "diverse" community may threaten the identity of members of the dominant society, producing anxiety expressed in ethnocentrism and racism. Immigrant communities confront poverty, multigenerational family issues, racism, and language limitation, especially among the elderly, which may produce major emotional and spiritual problems. Religious or theological tenets may help foster distrust in mental health practitioners.

Hispanics are known to underutilize mental health services. This is due to, but not limited to, a lack of financial resources, negative experiences with professionals who are not culturally competent, insufficient knowledge of services provided by social agencies, and cultural and religious ambivalence regarding mental health or psychological treatment. It is important to remember that the growth of the Latino/a population does not necessarily translate into the power to effect significant changes in the delivery of services.

Pastoral Care, Pastoral Counseling, and Pastoral Psychotherapy

At this juncture it is appropriate to frame pastoral care and pastoral counseling. Each is distinct from the other and both meet very specific needs. As a movement, pastoral care calls providers to an awareness of the complexities and challenges of a postmodern society. Function and praxis of a caring ministry can never result from the placement of "new wines in old skins," but must be an intentional merging of old and new functions and practices that can bring healing, wholeness, and transformation to today's people. These changes have theological, ecclesiological, sociological, ecological, and psychological implications.

The ministry of pastoral care is often confused with pastoral counseling and pastoral psychotherapy. In Latin America, *psicología pastoral* is compatible with the pastoral psychotherapy in educational requirements, methodology, and practice. The American Association of Pastoral Counseling has a category for Pastoral Care Specialist. This particular category requires the ability to integrate the resources of faith and traditions in the practice of care. Training includes, but is not limited to, guidance regarding supportive pastoral care, crisis intervention, a consultation experience to enhance the pastoral caregivers' skills in grief and loss, knowledge of methods for caring, and appropriate knowledge to make referrals to professionals.

Pastoral care does not have educational requirements, although education is strongly recommended, nor does it necessitate a contract to delineate the nature of the caring process, such as a formal counseling session. Pastoral care happens during a coffee hour, a pastoral visit, and any other supportive, nurturing interpersonal relationship. Pastoral care encompasses all pastoral work inclusive of preaching, teaching, educational events, etc.

Pastoral counseling integrates the disciplines of theology and psychology, and requires a Master's of Divinity (or equivalent) that is approved by an accrediting body such as the Association for Theological Schools (ATS), as well as courses in the behavioral sciences. During the training process, the person must engage in a formal educational program and be supervised by an approved clinical supervisor, as well as undergo personal psychotherapy. Pastoral counseling is a contractual relationship in which the counselee and the counselor establish a time and place to meet and usually involves a fee.

Pastoral psychotherapy demands the completion of a graduate program and evidence of proficiency in the counseling and psychotherapeutic process. In some states a person is not able to offer counseling or psychotherapy unless he or she is licensed by the state and fellow members of an accredited professional association. A pastoral psychotherapist also engages in a contractual relationship with a counselee that involves time, place, and an appropriate fee.

It is important that churches establish boundaries in the understanding and practice of pastoral care, so that caregivers do not exceed the limitations of their skill and training and, with the best of intentions, cause more harm than good. It is also necessary that caregivers be aware of the complex relationship between a caregiver and a care receiver. As has been previously noted, because members of the Latino/a community have a high regard for their religious leaders, they tend to seek guidance from their priest or pastor before seeking out a mental health professional. In light of this, it is important that faith communities and their leaders have the skills necessary to provide care and support, including the ability and willingness to refer and/or encourage careseekers to make use of professionals who are culturally sensitive, willing to complement the initial support of the caregiver, and move the careseeker to the next level of caring. It behooves the caregiver to understand the importance of setting boundaries and to maintain a realistic understanding of her/his own capabilities and limitations.

In order to engage in the ministry of pastoral care with Hispanics in the United States with a sense of integrity, one has to engage in a process of critical thinking based on how each discipline and methodology fosters liberation and empowerment that is inclusive of their spiritual, physical, and social lives, instead of contributing to the oppression and marginalization of the Hispanic community. It has also been noted that in the present expression of this ministry, theology, psychology, and the social sciences serve as foundational disciplines from which understanding, skills, and knowledge are acquired.

A discussion of pastoral care and counseling is incomplete unless one takes note of the exciting developments and expressions of this ministry in Latin America. The continental movements for pastoral care and counseling have made profound contributions to this field, and these efforts continue to expand throughout Latin America.

The next paragraphs will introduce the reader to some of the organizations that have made remarkable contributions to this ministry, the ongoing training events, and the direct services to persons in need of care and counseling.

In 1975, the *Fraternidad Teológica Latinoamericana* (FTL) organized a family conference in Quito, Ecuador. The outcome of that conference brought to the fore the need to establish contextualized theological reflection and action focused on the specific needs of Latin American families suffering from severe social pressures. By 1977, the word *eirene* (signifying peace, reconciliation, and harmony) was coined to describe the effort of the Quito conference. Eventually, eirene became a movement. The objectives of eirene include training and certification of pastoral family facilitators, research, and publications that lead to pastoral reflection and education regarding the family.

In 1977, a pastor and psychologist in Argentina created a *Programa de Enriquecimiento Matrimonial* (PEM) that was soon followed by the formation of another group of professionals in the family field. From these three gatherings, eirene International was created. In 1982, visionaries from seven countries gathered in Costa Rica to establish the *Programa de Entrenamiento y Certificacion de Asesores Familiares* (Certificate Program for Family Facilitators), or PECAF. Literature was produced integrating scientific contributions and a profound Christian commitment to this ministry into a model that incorporated praxis, therapeutic techniques, and pastoral care for families.

Another example of the ongoing development in the area of pastoral psychology and pastoral care and counseling is the work being done in Chile. In 1988, Ricardo Crane, after completing his studies in the United States, recognized the need for work with Chilean families. The demand for support and guidance sought by families prompted the addition of courses on pastoral care and counseling at the Evangelical Institute of Chile of the National Presbyterian Church. A number of other trained practitioners such as Plinio Sepúlveda, Felipe Cortés, Vladimir Rodríguez, and physician Jorge Sorbazo, were the founders of the Programa de Entrenamiento en Psicología (P.E.P.P.), an organization that serves the evangelical community.

Jorge A. León, the director of Psicopastoral–Programa Permanente de Psicología Pastoral, has made a significant contribution to the field of pastoral psychology and pastoral counseling. This program has brought together an ecumenical team of psychologists who have theological training and a vast knowledge of the problems faced by members of faith communities. Recently, León was named the "Father of the Latin American Pastoral Psychology" at a theological gathering in Mexico. He has authored 17 books and continues to lecture extensively at different international conferences.

Other Hispanic academicians and practitioners continue to provide rich intellectual and practical approaches to caring as well as theological and psychological foundations upon which this critical ministry rests. In Latin America, there continues to be a concerted effort to develop indigenous literature. This development has contributed greatly to the practice of pastoral care and pastoral psychology in the United States.

Conclusion

The Hispanic church in the United States is faced with new and growing challenges: families separated due to immigration; undocumented parents fearing deportation and separation from their children; children joining gangs or becoming drug users or addicts; the parenting of bicultural children; and increasing numbers of persons dealing with depression or economic crisis. The church is the first place where parishioners seek guidance and support. This calls for a reformulation of the pastoral functions and ministries that provide educational, practical, and spiritual resources. The ministry of pastoral care makes it possible for the church to be better prepared to respond to its constituencies and to offer leadership beyond its walls.

The church needs to rethink and revisit its mandate as a social and theological institution as it responds to this particular population. The new paradigms for ministry call for an interdependence between the church and social agencies that does not reduce its sense of identity or compromise its functions as a place of worship and ritual. New paradigms include envisioning the "new heaven and the new earth" as an intentional healing community.

Pastoral caregivers have a history of listening to the people in their context. Pastoral care from the Hispanic perspective needs to address such issues as parenting children in a bicultural society, deportation, increasing economic crisis, and depression. The church as a healing community is in a position to respond by incorporating into its ministry an intentional programmatic effort that responds theologically, biblically, socially, and emotionally to this growing community. Such a ministry would assist careseekers in finding hope in the midst of their social dislocation or spiritual pain, within the church that offers a safe place where caregivers and careseekers can be healed, sustained, guided, and reconciled as well as nurtured, liberated, and empowered. Such an integrated ministry could serve as a source of transformation for the fulfillment of God's intentionality for all people.

As this article has shown, there is an expansion of such a ministry of pastoral care, counseling and pastoral psychology in Latin America. Major contributions have been made by academicians, pastors, and church leaders from South America and the Caribbean. Several different training programs are being offered by accredited seminaries in the region. The book *Dimensiones en Cuidado Pastoral en Latinoamerica* is a brilliant resource, authored by 17 leaders in Latin America. It is of great value not only for that geographical area but for work with Latino/as in North America as well.

References and Further Reading

Baltonado, Sara. "Pastoral Care in Latin America." *International Perspectives on Pastoral Counseling* (Philadelphia: The Haworth Press, 2002).

Falicov, Celia J. *Latino Families in Therapy: A Guide to Multicultural Practice* (New York: Guildford Press, 1988).

Maldonado, Jorge. *Even in the Best of Families* (Geneva, Switzerland: World Council of Churches Publications, 1997).

Montilla, R. Esteban, and Medina Ferney. *Pastoral Care and Counseling with Latino/as.* Creative Pastoral Care and Counseling (Nashville: Abingdon Press, 2006).

Radillo, Rebeca. "Pastoral Counseling with Latino/a Americans." *Clinical Handbook of Pastoral Counseling*, Vol. 3, ed. Robert Wicks, Richard D. Parsons, and Donald Capp (Mahwah, NJ: Paulist Press, 2003).

Santos, Hugo, ed. *Dimensiones del Cuidado y Asesoramiento Pastoral* (Eagan, MN: Kairos, 2006).

Ulloa Castellanos, Sergio. "The Church as a Holistic Healing Community." *Dimensiones del Cuidado y Asesoramiento Pastoral*, ed. Hugo Santos (Eagan, MN: Kairos, 2006).

Wicks, Richard D. *Cuidado Pastoral, Contextual e Integral* (Grand Rapids, MI: Libros Desafio, 2007).

PNEUMATOLOGY

Albert Hernández

The English term *pneumatology* is derived from the Greek word *pneuma*, meaning "breath" or "wind," and signifies the theological study of Christian doctrines, teachings, and revelations dealing with the person and work of the Holy Spirit. The equivalent Spanish word, *pneumatologia*, has the same meaning as the English term. The invisible, immaterial, and powerful nature of the Spirit of God was associated by the Hebrews with images like flames in a fire, a mighty wind, or the breath of life by a newborn child. Traditionally and historically, pneumatology functioned as the branch of Christian theology dealing with spirituality, personal piety, divine inspiration of saints and prophets, revelatory visions, spiritual gifts, Spirit baptism, and sanctification.

The Holy Spirit is the relational intermediary between the other two persons of the Holy Trinity, and is often described as the mutual love, or "divine kiss," between the Father and the Son. As the third Person of the Trinity, the Spirit's intermediary function relates the particularities of the earthly and human realm of being to the heavenly realm of the Godhead empowering the people of God to carry out the mission and work of Jesus Christ's earthly church. Theological and doctrinal questions aside, a comprehensive definition of pneumatology requires recognition of the Spirit's dynamic relationship with both human particularity and the potential fullness of all things. The work of the Holy Spirit is best understood by recognizing its creative and empowering manifestations across a wide range of Christian denominations and regional traditions spanning centuries of interaction among different cultures and peoples, including specific manifestations of pneumatological spirituality among Hispanic cultures.

The most significant attributes of the Holy Spirit, as well as the general contours of pneumatology, are based on New and Old Testament scriptural precedents together with the apostolic legacies of the Church Fathers. Given their familiarity with Hellenistic Greek, the early Christian Fathers associated *pneuma* with the birth of humanity since God created Adam by breathing into his nostrils and infusing him with the divine "breath of life" (Genesis 2:7). Jesus promised the Apostles that despite his impending departure following the trial and suffering that awaited him, the Father would send forth the Holy Spirit in his name as both Comforter and Counselor between humanity and the Godhead (John 14:16–28). Among the apologists and writers of early Christianity, pneumatology was closely aligned with ecclesiology (the doctrine of the Church).

On the day of Pentecost the disciples began a new life when the flames of the Holy Spirit burst into the upper room, where all of the members of the apostolic community were prayerfully gathered and waiting, and when a miraculous form of communication as "tongues of fire" brought forth a new creation, the Christian Church (Acts 2:1–34). This foundational moment in the New Testament story of Christianity has been revisited over the past two millennia by Christians throughout the world as a deeply inspiring and powerful text, especially when facing questions of church reform, liberation and empowerment, transformative leadership, and spiritual revitalization. St. Basil's *On the Holy Spirit*, together with St. Augustine's pneumatological formulations, became the classic Early Christian and patristic sources for teachings about the Spirit's presence in the Church, in personal piety, and in the larger world.

After the fall of the Western Roman Empire in 476 CE, and the ensuing centuries of invasion, illiteracy, and turmoil known as the Dark Ages, monastic libraries emerged in the late ninth century as regional centers of learning, in which Classical and Christian texts were preserved for posterity. This climate of monastic textual preservation produced few theological or doctrinal innovations as traditional Christian conceptions of pneumatology, ecclesiology, and Christology coalesced with an increasingly conservative and reactionary hierarchy centered at the Papal Court in Rome by the turn of the first millennium. Later, the University of Paris emerged as a major center of Christian Scholastic teaching and philosophy during the thirteenth century. Most of the great medieval Scholastic theologians deviated little from official Christian pneumatological teachings while amplifying the doctrines the Church inherited from earlier patristic sources like St. Augustine and St. Basil, or from medieval theologians like St. Thomas Aquinas and St. Bonaventure whose pneumatological ideas were supported by the Papacy.

The great innovators of medieval pneumatology, such as the Calabrian Abbot Joachim of Fiore or the Franciscans Spirituals, both of which prophesied the coming of an "Age of the Holy Spirit," were eventually accused of heresy and suppressed by the Papacy. Some of these movements of the Holy Spirit would later influence Catholic clergy in the Spanish colonies on issues of dignity and liberation among the indigenous peoples of the New World. Theologians and church historians have suggested that because of such tensions between pneumatological revelation and ecclesiastical authority, Latin Christianity, later known as the Roman Catholic Church, suffered from a "pneumatological deficit" and a tendency to push its spiritual visionaries and reformers underground. It is worth noting that Eastern Christianity, also known as the Greek Orthodox Church, developed a more open and dynamic pneumatological sensibility that informed both lay piety and monastic practices throughout the medieval era until the fall of the Byzantine Empire to the Ottoman Turks in 1453.

The rise of Spain as a global political, military, economic, and ecclesiastical imperial power in the 1400s and 1500s would have definitive consequences for the religious sensibilities of Spain and its Spanish-speaking colonies around the world. If there is such a thing as a uniquely Hispanic pneumatological heritage, then its roots are to be found in the religious and political movements of early modern Spain and its colonies.

Fifteenth century Spain was a land of religious visionaries and reformers, many of whom had been influenced by centuries of interreligious dialogue with Sephardic Judaism and Muslim mysticism from Islamic Spain (al-Andalus). There were movements across late medieval and early modern Christian Spain, like the Alumbrados of Toledo, who advocated an egalitarian pneumatology together with reflective personal readings of the Holy Scriptures, without the interpretive authority of a bishop or the pope. By the 1520s, many of the Alumbrados were accused by the Spanish Inquisition of having ideas that sounded too much like the ideas of Martin Luther, who, in their opinion, was then stirring up heresy and revolt in the German provinces of the Spanish Empire. Indeed Spain's desire to construct and impose a strictly Roman Catholic and Spanish national identity on its Iberian and colonial subjects led to the diminution of pneumatological themes and concerns among Spain's famous Roman Catholic Reformers: St. John of the Cross, St. Teresa of Avila, and St. Ignatius of Loyola who founded the Jesuit Order. This is not to imply that the Holy Spirit is absent from the lives and works of these three magnificent Catholic religious writers and leaders. However, the general mood of suspicion and political persecution throughout Spain and its colonies at this time required that religious reformers be cautious about their pneumatology, especially if the Holy Spirit had inspired them in the struggle for liberation and justice against the excesses of Spain's nationalistic and imperialist agenda. Among the leading twentieth-century Roman Catholic writers on pneumatology and spiritual experience are the Dominican priest Yves Congar (1904–1995) and the Franciscan Capuchin priest Raniero Cantalamessa, who has served as Preacher to the Papal Household since 1980.

The Holy Spirit is that Person of the Trinity who manifests the presence of the Father and the Son in the particularities of the natural world (Nature) and among the local or contextual spiritualities of particular regions, cultures, and peoples. Despite the rigid social class barriers and religious power structures of the Spanish Empire, the colonial blending of translocal Christian pneumatological ideas and sensibilities with local indigenous beliefs and practices, such as Spiritism, Santería, or "El Dia de Los Muertos" (Day of the Dead), produced the vibrant religious syncretism and hybrid spirituality that accompanied the racial mixing, or *mestizaje*, among the peoples and cultures that centuries later became Latin America and the Hispanic American Southwest. Such contextualized and culture specific pneumatological traditions are still evident today from the cities and countryside of South America to the annual religious festivals celebrated in Santa Fe, New Mexico.

Perhaps the most intriguing development in modern pneumatology has been the recent emergence and recognition of "contextual pneumatologies," which have challenged the dominance of Euro-Western theological categories. Among these new forms of pneumatological thinking and sensibility are African and Latino/a pneumatology, Feminist and ecological pneumatology, and the rapidly growing Catholic Charismatic Renewal movement and the Pentecostal pneumatologies, which represent the fastest growing sector of global Christianity. Although the vast majority of Hispanics living in the United States today self-identify as either Roman Catholic or Protestant, there is a rapidly growing Pentecostal presence throughout Latin America and portions of North America. These demographic and religious trends suggest that Latino/a Pentecostals, and Roman Catholic Charismatics, are poised to reshape the nature and scope of Christian pneumatology in the coming decades.

References and Further Reading

Burgess, Stanley M. *The Holy Spirit, Vol. II: Medieval, Roman Catholic and Reformation Traditions* (Peabody, MA: Hendrickson Publishers, 1997).

Congar, Yves. *I Believe in the Holy Spirit* (New York: Crossroad Herder Publishing, 1997).

Groppe, Elizabeth Teresa. "Yves Congar's Theology of the Holy Spirit." *American Academy of Religion Academy Series* (New York: Oxford University Press, 2004).

Hinze, Bradford E., and D. Lyle Dabney, eds. *Advents of the Spirit: An Introduction to the Current Study of Pneumatology* (Milwaukee: Marquette University Press, 2001).

Kärkkäinen, Veli-Matti. *Pneumatology: The Holy Spirit in Ecumenical, International, and Contextual Perspective* (Grand Rapids, MI: Baker Academic, 2002).

POPULAR RELIGION

Gilberto Cavazos-González

Popular religion is often referred to as folk religion, family traditions, pious exercises, popular Catholicism, faith expressions, popular piety, popular devotion, *sensus fidelium*, or religiosidad popular (popular religiosity). In the not-so-distant past it was seen as belonging to the uneducated masses and was juxtaposed to the true religion of an elitist Christianity. Popular religion, however, is an elusive categorization given to a changing reality that can no longer be ignored or snubbed as superstition, unorthodox, or antiquated. Thanks to recent ecclesial documents and the work of various Latina/o theologians, and social scientists in the latter part of the twentieth century, popular religion is no longer simply tolerated as a cultural eccentricity. Popular religion has gradually become a place of theological and social reflection.

Recognizing that Christian spirituality is nourished not only by the Sacred Liturgy of the universal Church, in its Constitution on the Liturgy (*Sacrosanctum Concilium* 12-13) the Second Vatican Council (1963) encourages the use of what it calls the popular devotions, pious exercises, and religious practices of local churches. These, however, need to be harmonized with the liturgical seasons of the Church year and complement the liturgy as source and summit of all Christian worship.

In their discussion on evangelization and pastoral ministry, the Latin American Bishops in Medellín, Colombia (1968), cautioned that popular religiosity is basically "vows, promises, pilgrimages, countless devotions, based on the reception of the sacraments" that have more to do with social activities than they do with "genuine" Christian life. They felt that popular religiosity needs to be purified and used as a point of departure for evangelization and catechesis.

In 1975 Pope Paul VI wrote the Apostolic Exhortation *Evangelli nuntiandi* in which he espouses the use of popular religiosity as a means to a "true encounter with God in Jesus Christ" (EN 48). He describes popular religiosity as "particular expressions of the search for God and for faith." He acknowledges that these expressions are often considered an inferior form of faith, yet he encourages the rediscovery of popular religiosity as manifesting "a thirst for God which only the simple and poor can know." He claims that popular religiosity can make people generous in their sacrifices for others;

713

PROMESAS

Often promesas (promises) or mandas (to send) are made in hopes that God will take mercy on the petitioner or a loved one. This may appear to be bartering with God, but the petitioners need to remember that God's mercy is a free gift. The manda is not so much to influence God but to show gratitude for the favor requested or what has already been received. Promesas help the petitioner grow freely as a Christian, and a person should not make a promesa requesting something from God that God would not approve. One should never make a manda for someone else to carry out and should always avoid promesas or mandas that would hurt the petitioner or someone else. Catholic Christians will sometimes make a promesa or manda to God, the Virgin Mary, or one of the saints. A person can offer to do extra prayers, go on pilgrimage, or read the Bible. Others might promise to avoid eating certain foods or discontinue watching telenovelas (soap operas). Still others pledge to give alms or help in a soup kitchen. In any case, promesas are meant to help the one making the promise through growth in at least one of the three pillars of Christian practice: prayer, fasting, and charity.

—GCG

it has a profound awareness of God's constant, loving, and providential presence; it engenders patience, detachment, openness to others, as well as a sense of the cross.

Four years later, the Latin American Bishops in Puebla (1979) came to a better understanding of popular religiosity. In it they see a combination of profound beliefs, the seal of God, convictions, and expressions of faith. Popular religiosity is seen as the cultural expression that a particular people give to Christianity. Rather than being seen as an instrument the "official" Church can use to evangelize the masses, they claimed that it is a means by which "people evangelize themselves continually."

In 1992 the Latin American Bishops again spoke to the reality of popular religiosity, calling it the "inculturation of faith" involving faith expressions, values, criteria, behaviors and attitudes that come directly from Christian teaching. Many of these may have limitations and distortions that need to be purified, but they can still enhance local churches and pastoral activity.

Since Vatican II and with the promotion of the Medellín and Puebla documents, Hispanic popular religion and religiosity has become the focus of much discussion and study among Christian leadership and theologians in the United States. As the numbers of Latino/as grow in this country, this study of popular religiosity has become an important topic in the social sciences as well, not simply as religious experience but as the expression of Latina/o resistance to assimilation and central to the formation of Hispanic identity. Popular religiosity is seen by these scholars as significant in Latina/o self-identity. It is at the root and can be a corrective to many Latino/a family practices/ traditions, social customs, and personal ways of being. Popular religiosity is about the process of becoming Christian in an inculturated manner through a process of traditioning.

NUMEROLOGY

Numerology is an interpretation of the meaning of numbers based upon systems from a variety of cultures and traditions, among them Babylonian, Hellenic, Egyptian, Jewish, Chinese, and Mayan. It is prevalent with some Mexican American practitioners of *curanderismo*, wherein the interpretation of tarot cards requires an intuitive understanding of numbers, and Cuban gamblers, wherein dreams are interpreted via a Chinese number system in order to select lottery numbers. In all these cases, numerology is a popular method of discernment. Among Mexican Americans, numerological understandings are based upon the cultures and traditions that formed them, particularly Spanish Catholic, Jewish, Islamic, and Mayan/Nahua influences. Though scholars debate the culture of Andalucian Spain (711–1492), relative tolerance characterized the relationship between Jews, Muslims, and Catholics, as well as members of occult societies that practiced numerology and occult arts. These societies were driven asunder after the *Reconquista* (1492), though the occult arts continued and transmigrated as Spain began colonization, blending with Spanish Catholic, Jewish, Islamic, and, eventually, Mesoamerican cultures. Among Cubans and Cuban Americans, cultures from Spain, Africa, and China contributed to the development of Cuba. Chinese culture, particularly ritual Taoism, emphasized the divining nature of numbers, dreams, and symbols, blending with Spanish Catholicism and African Yoruba religious systems.

—OJN

Summing up the work of U.S. Hispanic theologians, popular religiosity is about the cotidianidad of faith, beauty, suffering, hardship, traditioning, and evangelization. It is the inculturation of the Gospel as found in the cotidiano and in relationships. As a result, popular religiosity is seen as the *locus theologicus* of Latina/o theology in the United States.

What Do We Mean by "Popular"?

"Popular" has connotations of being widely accepted, loved, and appreciated. "Popular" in these cases is contrasted with rejection. Popular also has the connotation of being democratic instead of autocratic. Popular has often been considered as that which attracts the illiterate, uneducated masses as opposed to the refined, which belong to the educated elite. This has usually been the case when attaching the word "popular" to music, art, and religion.

Unfortunately, when attached to the word "religion" by social scientists, it was in order to divide religion into a common, superstitious, familial, low religion at odds with an institutional, orthodox, official, high religion. Normally this dichotomy was seen to run along socioeconomic lines with institutional religion being the realm of the upper class and familial religion being that of the lower classes. This dichotomy often became a geographic one with institutional religion being well established in urban settings and popular Catholicism growing in rural ones. These dichotomies cannot be held in strict opposition to each other as involvement in either institutional or popular religion is also affected by race, ethnicity, education, economics, and personal preferences. In Latin America and the Southwestern United States this often meant that institutional Christianity would be led by an educated male clergy as the "fathers" of the faithful while grassroots Christianity was usually led by pious women, the mothers, aunts, and grandmothers of the faithful.

Today, Latino/a social scientists and theologians are reminding us that "popular" primarily means "of the people." While it is true that "of the people" should be all the people, over the course of the centuries "popular" has become of the general, ordinary, and simple people as opposed to the wealthy and the ruling class. For Hispanic theologians this is not a problem. "Popular" expresses a preferential option for the poor that recalls Jesus' identifying himself with the least and the small. What God has hidden from the wise and the powerful has been given to ordinary everyday people.

What Do We Mean by "Religion"?

Religion is often associated with organized faith, cultic worship, and sacred institutions. It is thought of as consisting of creedal and doctrinal positions, moral and ethical teachings, as well as the structured regulation of belief in a sacred and transcendent being or power. Religion is usually thought of as a stable, well-thought-out, and organized institution. While all of this is true in a variety of ways of all religions, we cannot forget that religion is originally about binding people together with each other and with the sacred.

To Latino/as it should come as no surprise that religion, religiosity, and relationship have the same Latin root, *religere* (to bring together). Religiosity therefore cannot be a stable and private matter; it is about actively building up of familia, compadrazgo, friendship, faith, hope, love, and social justice. It is also about dealing with and overcoming death, infirmity, and evil, both personal and social.

In the latter part of last century, Latina/o scholars in the United States adopted *religiosidad popular* or popular religiosity as the best way to define the religious experience of Hispanic in this country. It is an experience of diaspora, a Galilean journey, a Samaritan reality that is often hard to explain and define.

Roots of Hispana/o Popular Religion

Scholars like Luis Maldonado and Jaime Vidal seem to think that popular religiosity has its roots in the coming together of Roman Catholicism and Amerindian Religion. They do, however, distinguish between syncretism and syncretization. Syncretism is what happens when a religious system takes on the trappings of another in order to survive clandestinely in a hostile environment; such is the case of Santería according to Maldonado. Syncretization or what Vidal calls synthetization is possible only when a religious system retains its core message and identity while taking on complementary elements of another religion. Such is the case of Latin-American popular religiosity, which was born of a biological, spiritual, and cultural mestizaje.

When we speak of Latino/as, we are speaking of people in the United States whose ancestry and origins are Latin American. This is a people of diverse cultures that come

CHANES

Chanes are water spirits who can reveal themselves to members of the Latina/o community. These malevolent spirits reside in bodies of water and can prove hazardous to children. Specifically, they prey upon children who ignore their mother's warning of staying away from water. To protect children from the danger posed by chanes, they can be appeased either by leaving an offering of food at the edge of the body of water or by voiding the chanes' spells by repeating certain chants that incorporate the child's name.

—MAD

from a mestizaje of Amerindian, European (primarily Iberian), and African cultures brought together as a result of the Spanish invasion and conquest of America in the early sixteenth century. The Spanish conquistadores and mendicant friars who first came to Mesoamerica brought with them a medieval Christianity based on a rich religiosidad popular that without ignoring the dogmas or the scholasticism of Roman Catholicism developed local customs and traditions that were more affective and archetypal.

Some of the Amerindians consciously practiced syncretism by which they continued to worship Aztec, Mayan, Incan, and other deities under the guise of Christian saints. This they did so as not to raise the suspicion of the early missionaries. Still it seems that a true Amerindian Christianity was born of a process of syncretization or synthesization by which they took on the Christian faith, bringing to it their own religious expressions rooted in agricultural cycles, kinship relations, and rituals expressing joy, grief, and other deeply felt human emotions as well as a sense of the sacred present in the world and the cotidiano. These things were then transformed by rubbing shoulders with the Spaniards who brought their own culturally nuanced version of these elements. Jaime Vidal claims that in this way, Spanish conquerors, mendicant friars, and Amerindian converts shared a common "emotional and psychological grammar," which helped the native Christian neophytes replace their ancient gods and goddess with the Most Holy Trinity, Mary, and other Christian saints. In this way a true internal theological conversion manifested itself with familiar native religious practices, offering continuity to the religious sentiment of the Amerindian. Processions, sacrifices, and gifts that in the past had been done in honor of a certain native deity become processions, sacrifices, and gifts in worship of Jesus Christ, his Father, and the Holy Spirit or in commemoration of a particular Christian saint.

The liturgical celebrations and processions of medieval Christianity were elaborate and festive enough to compete with the pomp and grandeur of Amerindian religious ceremonies. Solemn Christian ceremonies required that the friars prepare choirs and musicians from among the native peoples. This was done so well that it is noted that Amerindian choirs could rival even Imperial European choirs. The use of music and song apparently was so important that in Mexico City it was noted that good song evangelized better than good preaching.

DUENDES

In many households in northern New Mexico, sometimes the dishes do not get washed nor are the beds made every day. Wherever there is a filthy corner in the house, there is an open invitation for los Duendes to come in and dance. Los Duendes are naughty little imps who love to play jokes on people. If someone helps out a duende, his charity is often repaid with little sacks of gold. However, if they happen not to like someone, duendes can cause that person to get lost in the forest. Sometimes duendes cause woodcutters to chop off a foot or leg if they are getting too close to their treasure. Whenever children do not clean their rooms, los Duendes come at night to pull on their hair or to dance in the filth. In the Hispano culture of northern New Mexico, if an elder comes into a room and asks, "Did los Duendes dance here last night?" this is coded talk for "Clean up your room." Duendes, in the sense of being very little people, have historically been equated with dwarfs or midgets. In the Middle Ages duendes, especially if they were hunchbacked, were rubbed for good luck. In literature, Calderón de la Barca's *La Dama Duende* also mentions that duendes tend to be phantasmagorical.

—LT

While sixteenth-century Europe was dealing with the Reformation and the implementation of the Tridentine liturgy, America was being evangelized and catechized with the use of pre-Tridentine Spanish missals, ritual books, and catechisms that had originally been used in Spain for converted Jews and Muslims. These instruments attempted to use the "emotional and psychological grammar" of recent converts to Christianity.

According to Hispanic scholar Jaime Lara, the most widely used ritual book was that of the Dominican Alberto Castellani who in 1523 published his *Liber Sacerdotalis* in which he adapted medieval monastic practices, prayers, and hymns for the newly converted Jews and Muslims. It eventually became the basis of the *Roman Missal* and in America it became the basis of the *Manual de Adultos* that adapted the liturgy to the Aztec and Maya catechumens including the use of feathers, flowers, and finery for various processions and rituals. It also became the basis of the *Manuale Sacramentorum* or *Mexicanensis*, which included rites from Salamanca, Toledo, and Sevilla.

The use of ritual books became very popular, because ritual gives meaning and shape to the cycles of life and death as well as the cycle of time (days, seasons, years). Ritual also consecrates social constructs like society and its hierarchy. Ritual also focuses attention on the presence of God in the cotidiano by emphasizing special times and places for God's external manifestation, for example, the real presence of Jesus in the consecrated Eucharist. The Catholic insistence on the body and blood of Christ being made present by the priest makes the Mass the highest form of Christian ritual.

However, in many parts of America the lack of ordained priests made weekly celebrations of the Eucharist impossible. The mendicant friars of the sixteenth-century resolved the lack of clergy by training local lay leadership to celebrate dry masses in which an Amerindian leader would vest like a priest and recite the Mass for others to hear. In place of the elevation of the consecrated elements he would raise a crucifix. This practice of dry masses was used in Europe by priests who for some reason were missing either the wine and/or the bread for consecration or on ships where there was a great possibility of spilling the consecrated wine. At a time where visual communion with Christ was more important than actually consuming the consecrated host, the use of a substitute image of Christ was not unusual.

Medieval Christians' desire to see Jesus and the saints led to the practice of processions. There was a proliferation of Corpus Christi processions whereby people were able to gaze upon the real presence of Christ who came out to them in the streets. In some places the consecrated host carried in a monstrance was often replaced by an image of Christ who processed out of the church and onto the streets to the people. Oftentimes this image of Jesus would be accompanied by some or all of the images of the saints in a particular church.

In America, processions became even more important as a means of getting the neophytes involved in their new religion. In the sixteenth century the installation of the image of Guadalupe in her newly built shrine at Tepeyac was accompanied by a procession of Aztec ceremonial costume and dancing of a song called the "Pregón del Atabal" (Song of the Drum), which blended both Christian Mariology with Nahuatl imagery. The event also included an Epiphany play.

Religious drama has been important to popular religiosity as a way of telling the story of God's intervention in human history and as a means of promoting an affective spirituality that moves one to a deeper relationship with God in Jesus Christ and his Saints. The most common religious dramas center on the mysteries of Jesus' Passion and Incarnation. As a result the Via Crucis or Live Stations of the Cross and the Pastorela or Nativity Play are probably the most common types of religious drama still in use today. Other plays revolve around the telling of the story of the Virgen de Guadalupe or other patron saints.

Many of the rituals, processions, and religious plays of popular religiosity can be done without the help or leadership of a priest or consecrated religious. The lack of priests helped Amerindian Christianity to grow as a religion that focused on family and local community more than universality and the institution. As the centuries passed and Tridentine liturgy

Box of Jesús Malverde soap.
(David Agren)

JESÚS MALVERDE

Revered throughout northern Mexico for nearly a century, the icon of Jesús Malverde has become popular in the United States since the start of the twenty-first century, particularly in California and the Southwest. According to folklore, Jesús Malverde was like Robin Hood, who stole from the rich and gave to the poor. He was killed in 1909 by the police. People, not the official church, made him into a saint. They began to believe that his image offered protection from the law and, as such, he became the patron saint of drug dealers. Hence, he is known as the "narco-saint." The poor also venerate the image of Jesús Malverde, praying that he will provide either safe conduct into the United States or money. His image appears in statues, tattoos, and on T-shirts. There is Jesús Malverde cologne, Jesús Malverde beer, and even Jesús Malverde bathroom cleaners.

—MAD

and clericalism became part and parcel of Catholicism, popular religion became more ingrained in the Latin American faithful. Institutional Catholicism was identified as an instrument of European colonialization in Latin America and eventually in the conquered Mexican land now known as Southwestern United States.

With the U.S. conquest and colonialization of Mexican territory, institutionalized U.S. Catholicism clashed with Latin American Catholicism. The new missionaries were determined to root out medieval Spanish Christianity and replace it with a more "enlightened" anglicized form of Christianity. This only served to strengthen the Hispanic ties with popular religiosity.

Elements of Popular Religiosity

Orlando Espín describes popular religion as an epistemology, a way that Latina/os come to know and construct the "real." It is probably the most fundamental bearer of social and cultural identity for Latino/as. Through it Hispanic Christians attempt to "remember, symbolize and live by" their religious experience. Like all social constructs not everything in popular religiosity is consonant with the Christian Gospel. Still there are a lot of elements in popular religiosity that are truly evangelical and orthodox. I would like to consider a few of these here.

(1) *All embracing presence of the sacred.* When looking forward to a future event, be it great or small, Latina/os are often heard to say "Si Dios quiere," "Con el favor de Dios," or "Ojala" ("If God wills it," "With God's blessing," "Allah willing"). An essential component of Latina/o popular religiosity is the all-pervasive presence of God. God's Spirit is all around us and is deeply involved in human life and in the world. Things happen if God desires them or allows them. God is on our side, helping us, molding us, and saving us.

This element of popular religiosity is manifested in a number of ways. Besides dichos (sayings) like the ones mentioned above, Latino/as will usually have religious symbols like crucifixes, images of Mary, an image of a saint, or the name of Jesus

AZABACHE

Azabache, known in English as jet, is an intensely black shining lignite that can have either a soft or a rough texture. A mineraloid, rather than a mineral, jet is derived from decaying wood, hence making it organic. The mimeraloid comes from a tree fossil resin that existed during the Jurassic Period. Large deposits of jet are located in Spain, specifically Asturias and the coast stretching from Villaviciosa to Gijon. The mined material is usually cut and polished so that it can be used for ornaments or jewelry. For thousands of years the azabache has been prized as a talisman to ward off evil, envy, illnesses, and violence. Today, many Hispanic groups have fashioned jet into jewelry, which they call azabache. Usually azabache is made into a small pendant along with wood, gemstone, or semiprecious metals, which is either pinned to the clothing of babies or worn as necklaces by small children as protection from el mal de ojo (the evil eye).

—MAD

hanging on a chain around their necks, or on the walls of their homes and businesses. Sometimes these images will even be tattooed on a Hispanic body.

These images can often be found on an altarcito (home altar) in a visible corner of the home or business. Altarcitos are not meant to be in competition with the altar found in the parish church; rather they are seen as extensions of it. An altarcito is blessed by the local priest whenever possible and usually contains items like holy water, candles, images, palm fronds, prayer books, and a Bible that have been blessed in church. It is a place for prayer and devotion. It is where the family goes to implore the Divine Providence of God.

(2) *Affective spirituality.* The predominant images of Christ in the first Christian millennium were those of the Pantocrator, the glorified master sitting on his throne teaching and judging the world. Whether on his mother's lap or on the cross, Jesus is the divine emperor who dominates all things and rules with a strong arm. It is only in the twelfth century that Cistercian monks begin to stress the humanity of Jesus by writing of his kenotic birth into impoverished and harsh conditions or of his even more kenotic passion and death, stressing the physical and psychological suffering he must have endured for love of sinful humanity. This affective literature was taken by the mendicant friars of the thirteenth century and popularized by imaging the poverty that Jesus was born into in the crèche and stressing the role of suffering through bloody and suffering images of Cristo upon the cross. In Spain the suffering image of the Ecce Homo and the crucifix began to show the horrible suffering of Jesus in very tangible ways, yet these images were known as the Señor del Gran Poder (Lord of Great Power).

This paradox of the suffering Son of Man reigning victorious even in death became a powerful image for the conquered Amerindians. Gone were their deities and in their place was a bloody and beaten man who reigned from a cross. Who could not love such a God? Who could not feel pity for such a God, especially when they felt in their own flesh the sufferings he endured?

Affective spirituality and not a morbid sense of fatalism is what is at the corazón (heart) of practices like the Caribbean jibaros fasting all of Good Friday, the Via Crucis en vivo all over Latin America and the United States, the groups of penitentes of Spain carrying heavy statues atop wooden platforms through the streets in procession, and other sacrificial acts. Affectivity stirs the person to want to share in the cross of the Lord, to "make up for what is lacking in the sufferings of Christ" (Colossians 1:24).

Affective spirituality is what lies behind the Latino/a love of images of the Sacred Heart of Jesus, the Santo Niño, and the Madre Dolorosa. It also takes on linguistic expression in the use of titles like "Diosito" and "Virgencita." "Diosito" is a strange nomenclature whereby Jesus is recognized as the holy yet tender and small God. The addition of "ito" to the very category of God or Mary is one of bringing the Sacred into a relationship. "Ito" is added to names by parents to speak of their little children, by lovers to speak of the tenderness between them, by relatives to speak of the loving ties that bind them to each other, and by many Latina/os to speak of their affective relationship with God.

The crucified Jesus and the Virgin Mary are the two most significant and affective symbols of religiosidad popular Latina. They are the two images that give the most important witness to the power of the Gospel message: God loves us and wants us to have a full and happy life.

(3) *Mary and the communion of the saints.* Another dicho is "Jesús en la cruz; María en la luz" ("Jesus on the Cross; Mary in light"). The light in question is always the light of Jesus; la luz del pesebre, la luz de su misericordia, la luz de la cruz, la luz de su resurrección (light of the manger, light of his mercy, light of the cross, light of his resurrección). Mary is human; granted she is a special human being who has received a singular favor from God the Father. Latina/os affirm that she is human, not divine. It is her humanity that attracts devotees. "She is one of us." "She understands our sufferings."

Mary as representative of humankind is glorified in a sacred exchange between her and her son, between humankind and God. God takes on human flesh in her womb and in turn she is clothed in divinity in heaven. To paraphrase Athanasius: "The divine becomes human so that the human can become divine." God takes on human limitation to share divine majesty with humankind.

Mary as representative of humanity in the process of glorification is only one of many humans to participate in a sacred exchange between God and humankind. The light of Jesus' manger, mercy, cross, and resurrection falls on the saints as well. Latino/as love the saints. These holy intercessors are often sought out for special requests. Among the popular saints we will find Martin Caballero who helped the poor, Francis of Assisi and Anthony of Padua who became poor, and Rosa de Lima and Martin de Porres who lived in Latin American poverty.

Poverty seems to be a constant in the lives of many of the great saints. At the same time, it seems to be a constant in the lives of many who espouse popular religiosity. The communion of saints takes on a special significance when the poor saints on earth turn to the glorified saints in heaven for intercession, help, and testimony of life.

(4) *Relationships.* La comunion de los santos (the communion of the saints) is probably the holiest of relationships to which popular religiosity can aspire. Relationship

JUAN SOLDADO (1914?–1938)

Juan Soldado was born Juan Castillo Morales. In turbulent Tijuana of 1938, eight-year-old Olga Camacho was found raped and murdered. An army private now known as Juan Soldado (John Soldier) was condemned amid mob riots, faulty investigation, and poor judicial practice. Although the Camacho family has always held him responsible, it is uncertain if he was guilty as proper procedures were not followed, and in fact he was shot to death in a cemetery through an extra judicial albeit public execution. Almost immediately miracles were attributed to his gravesite, which has become a shrine. Although never canonized and indeed sometimes opposed by Catholic authorities, his popularity grew, especially among those who believe he was executed to cover the guilt of his military superiors. Most adherents consider him a victim martyr, namely, a victim of injustice visited upon the poor masses by the wealthy and powerful but also a martyr to their cause. Hence, he is able to intercede for those who share his lot as well as denounce the consequences caused by such socioeconomic fault lines in society. His biography is mostly anonymous, his death ambiguous, his saintliness contiguous mainly with Christians who share his social class and likewise have survived through faith as well as resistance.

—FAO & KGD

and religiosity as previously mentioned have the same root word. Hispanics are known for both of these things. Besides popular religiosity, another hallmark of Latina/o identity is a fondness for establishing ever-widening circles of relationships from familia, to extended family, to compadres, comadres, and friends.

Even Jesus is seen in relationship. "Ay Jesús, María y José," a common phrase used by Latino/as to express frustration, exasperation, a quick prayer, and/or fatigue, shows the importance of familia and being in a relationship. In the Anglophone world, this phrase is simply "Jesus!" or "Jesus Christ!" as if Jesus stands alone, over and above relationships. To the Latina/o such a thing is unimaginable; Jesus cannot be removed from his parents, his disciples, his saints, his priests, or the laity.

(5) *Role of the laity.* Despite the fact that the Tridentine period of Church history was dominated by the ordained priesthood, in many parts of America the lack of priests or a sympathetic clergy led to a continuation of the medieval involvement of the laity in the world of the sacred. In many parts of the world it became commonplace to think of the sacred as being the realm of priests and consecrated religious while the secular was the realm of the laity. In the traditional Latino/a worldview, such a distinction between the sacred and the profane, the religious and the secular does not exist. The sacred is everyone's domain, just as everyone lives in a secular world.

The lack of ordained priests in many parts of Latin America and the rejection by non-Hispanic clergy of Latino/a Catholics in the United States has led to a lay-led religiosity that in many ways promotes the priesthood of all believers, especially that of women. This is not to say that Hipanics do not need or want the presence of an ordained clergy. Quite the contrary, the absence of priests over the years has caused lay people to be creative in filling that lacuna in their religious practice, but it has also caused a longing for good priests who will provide the sacraments, especially the Eucharist on a more regular basis. The faithful insist on having houses, cars, Bibles, and religious items blessed by a priest whenever possible. They encourage the participation of priests as chaplains and spiritual directors in the lay-led cofradias and other fraternal societies. In these cases, however, the clergy needs to understand and accept that they are under the direction of a lay leader, and that they are simply there to serve the sacramental needs of the community.

In many of the practices of popular religiosity, the role of leading people in prayer often falls to a woman and not to a priest. Latina scholar Ana María Díaz-Stevens claims this is because "women . . . reminisce about the past, give each other counsel and consolation, discuss the events of the community, and plan for family and community celebrations which most often are also religious celebrations." Unofficial ministries that have been held by Latina laywomen can easily be seen as an extension of the medieval beguines, women who lived a consecrated life at home as either married or single women, forming prayer groups, Bible studies, and charitable organizations. In Hispana/o popular religiosity these women take on the roles of rezadoras, salmeras, beatas, and even curanderas.

The openness of Latina/os to the role of women in ministry is a long one and one that can certainly add to the discussion of women in Church ministry. Sadly, as result of this, many laymen see church involvement as womanish. And even though priests are obviously male, they vest in fancy robes like women and serve at table, which in Latino/a households is traditionally a woman's role. Still, this does not mean that Latino men are not touched by popular religiosity. Men form cofradias to have a place where they can encounter the sacred in a more "masculine" way. They turn to priests, consecrated religious, rezadoras, and other pious women for advice, prayers, blessings, and consolation in times of need or grave danger. In the United States, many men turn to the local church and to religious movements as safe havens that remind them of home and keep them somehow connected to their own culture. This turning to institutional religion is resulting in a growing number of male lay ministers that share with women the responsibility for bringing popular religiosity into U.S. Catholic and Protestant churches.

Pastoral Responses

Representatives of Institutional Catholicism and Mainline Protestantism need not be afraid of Latina/o popular religiosity. It is not a problem to be dealt with, but rather a blessing to be cherished. Many Protestant and Catholic pastors and professional lay ministers have begun adopting and institutionalizing Posadas, Quinceañeras, Passion Plays, and other practices of Hispano/a popular religiosity as a way of attracting and serving Latina/os. Cursillo de Cristiandad, the Charismatic renewal, Pentecostalism, and other renewal/evangelical movements have sprung up in the Latina/o community as new manifestations of the elements of popular religiosity. These movements emphasize several of the elements mentioned above, namely an affective spirituality that sees the omnipresence of the divine in the cotidiano (the everyday). They underscore the importance of relationships, lay leadership, and ministry.

References and Further Reading

Avalos, Hector, ed. *Introduction to the U.S. Latina and Latino Religious Experience* (Boston: Brill Academic Publishers, 2004).

Davis, Kenneth G., ed. *Misa Mesa y Musa: Liturgy in the U.S. Hispanic Church*, 2nd ed. (Schiller Park, IL: World Library Publication, 1991).

De La Torre, Miguel A., and Gastón Espinosa, eds. *Rethinking Latino Religions and Identity* (Cleveland, OH: Pilgrim Press, 2006).

de Luna, Anita. *Faith Formation and Popular Religion: Lessons from the Tejano Experience* (Lanham, MD: Rowman and Littlefield Publisher, 2002).

Espín, Orlando O., and Gary Macy, eds. *Futuring our Past: Explorations in the Theology of Tradition* (Maryknoll, NY: Orbis Books 2006).

Fernández, Eduardo C. *La Cosecha: Harvesting Contemporary United States Hispanic Theology (1972–1998)* (Collegeville, MN: Liturgical Press, 2000).

Stevens-Arroyo, Anthony M., and Ana María Díaz-Stevens, eds. *An Enduring Flame: Studies on Latino Popular Religiosity* (New York: Program for the Analysis of Religion Among Latinos, 1994).

SACRAMENTS AND SACRAMENTALS

Anthony M. Stevens-Arroyo

The sacraments and the sacramentals are closely related to the rituals and symbols composed by Latino/a popular religiosity. In analyzing these elements as "religion" rather than merely as "culture," however, theological precision is required. Sadly, this is not an easy task because there is disagreement about the theological definition of sacraments, how they operate, how many there are, and whether sacramentals contribute to or distract from Christian commitment. Most of these issues can be attributed to denominational differences between Catholics and most other Christians. With its ecumenical spirit, therefore, much of the current Latino/a theological reflection skirts argumentational issues in sacramental theology. However, in order to understand why sacraments are special components of Hispanic religious culture, it is necessary to examine the premise that sacraments are rituals that communicate grace and salvation. In four unequal parts, this entry addresses how sacraments gained a significant role in Latina/o religious experiences.

Historical Development

The apostolic church organized itself around rituals such as the Eucharist, Baptism, the forgiveness of sins, the laying on of hands, and the charismatic experience of the Holy Spirit in the gift of tongues. Yet, except for the forgiveness of sins, these rituals were derived from preexisting Jewish practices such as the Passover meal, the *mikvah* (ritual immersion), and the transfer of tribal authority. Moreover, contact through the Hellenist world with Gentiles provided for other crossover similarities with religious rituals, the design of temples, the use of liturgical music and the like.

Early Christian writers referred to Christian rituals with the terms *mysterion* among those writing in Greek and *sacramentum* among those using Latin. Augustine writes of the Eucharist (De Civ. Dei: x): "The visible sacrifice is the sacrament, i.e. the sacred sign, of the invisible sacrifice." Moreover, although they understood that the sacraments had similarities with the rituals of other religions, these early Christian writers generally considered sacraments to have been derived from Christ's directives to his Church.

The development of the great medieval universities after the first Christian millennium gave impulse to systematic exploration of the nature and effect of sacraments. By then the number of sacraments had become generally accepted as seven: Baptism, Eucharist, Reconciliation, Orders, Anointing of the Sick, Marriage, and Confirmation. (Modern terms are used for references to "Confession" or "Penance" and "Extreme Unction.") Two tendencies can be found in the treatment of sacraments by the Schoolmen. On the one hand, there is an emphasis upon the effect of the sacraments producing grace through the use of material elements, proving sacraments were not merely culture. Taken to an extreme, however, this emphasis would reduce the sacraments to magic. The other emphasis was on the invisible, hidden, spiritual force of the sacraments.

In the Pars Tertia of his Summa Theologica, St. Thomas Aquinas traced a middle ground between these two tendencies and laid the foundations for a sacramental theology, although the treatment of the sacraments was not completed until after the saint's death. Aquinas had begun his sacramental theology relating Augustine's visible/invisible linkage to the Aristotelian categories of body/soul so that, like the human being created by God, sacraments are constituted by joining spirit and matter. In Aquinas's analysis, the words of the ritual constitute the spiritual "form" and the physical elements become the "matter" required for the effective dispensation of the sacrament. Both the matter and the form had to be intelligible and intentional to become sacraments, a requirement that inserted subjectivity into the ritual.

The second contribution of St. Thomas was to interpret the maxim of St. John Damascene that "In Christ, human nature was like the instrument of the divinity." Aquinas enlarged this view. By connecting the sacraments with the grace of Christ's saving acts as instruments to principal cause (the stick held in one's hand), Aquinas made sacraments into contact with Christ. The scriptural references to "be born again of water and the spirit" (John 3:3) or to "eat of the flesh of the Son of Man and drink his Blood" (John 6:53) were explained as necessary tools to receive the divine grace won by Christ's Passion, Death, and Resurrection. Without the sacraments of Baptism and the Eucharist, one could not have eternal life, for these were the instruments by which Christ remained among believers and they were dispensed through his Church.

Aquinas successfully linked the sacraments to the fundamental Christian belief in both the material humanity and the spiritual divinity of Christ as "true God and true man," framing Christian sacramental theology by a Christological approach. The material components of sacraments like the water of Baptism or the bread and wine of the Eucharist are analogous to the incarnation of the Word made Flesh. To disparage the materiality of the sacraments is like denying the humanity of Christ. Thus, Christ is really present in the bread of the Eucharist and not merely in symbolic form, just as his risen body is a real physical body and not just a ghostly apparition (cf. John 20:27). At the same time, by attaching the Aristotelian concept of form and matter to the words and materials used in sacraments, Aquinas opened the door to the subjective factors of intention and understanding of ritual. The minister must grasp the meaning of the words in celebrating the sacrament and not treat the ritual as if it were magic.

In addition to speculative aspects of sacramental theology, Aquinas also addressed practical issues, some of which would arise again during the Reformation. Was a

---

BAUTIZO

Baptism or *bautizo* is a sacrament of the church, among both Catholics and Protestants. When Hispanics participate in this ritual, the sacrament incorporates traditional symbols different from Euro-Americans. For example, an important part of el bautizo is the fiesta following the religious ceremony, where families and friends gather to honor the one baptized. If the one being baptized is a child, the child is usually dressed in *el ropón*, a long white gown used during the ritual. It is traditional, especially among Mexicans and Cubans, for el ropón to be passed down from generation to generation. One tradition, *el bolo*, is based on a Mexican custom. The *padrino*, the godfather, as a sign of future abundance, throws coins into the air when leaving the church for children to gather. Probably the most important aspect of the bautizo is the selection of godparents, *los padrinos*. The padrinos form a spiritual bond with the child and the child's parents, becoming *compadrazgo*, co-parents. In the event the child's parents are no longer able to care for the child, the godparents assume the responsibility. In some economically deprived communities, parents have been known to ask those who are in a financially better position to serve as padrinos.

—MAD

---

sacrament invalid if the minister was in sin? No: the validity of the sacrament did not depend on the worthiness of the minister. Was it necessary to receive communion under both species of bread and wine? It was certainly preferable, but matters of health might intervene and communion with bread alone for the faithful was sufficient. How many of the sacraments derive from the Bible? All of them, but Christ gave his church the power to ritualize the sacraments, so that their form does not necessarily derive from the words of scripture. If Baptism confers the Holy Spirit, why is Confirmation needed? The adult confirmation strengthens the baptismal character received when an infant. Are the sacraments limited to those received by Jesus? He did not receive any, since neither did he need grace nor was grace possible until his Passion, Death, and Resurrection.

Application to Latino/a theology touches on this last point—namely, that sacraments were only possible after the winning of salvation manifest in the Resurrection. If grace was imparted through sacraments only after Christ's resurrection, then pious Jews of the Old Testament and good pagans who lived before Christ could not have received the Christian sacrament of Baptism, nor entered into Heaven. To resolve this dilemma, Aquinas developed the notion of "natural sacraments." He reasoned that if the subjective dispositions required for the Christian sacraments were present among Jews and pagans when they underwent similar rituals of initiation in their own religions, the salvific grace of redemption would be applied to them. These persons had Baptism of Desire, and rather than send them to Hell, a kind and merciful God allowed them to await Christ's Resurrection in limbo (i.e., "on the edge") before entering Heaven.

Formed by Thomistic reasoning within the Salamanca School, Bartolomé de Las Casas applied the natural sacraments and Baptism of Desire to the native people of the Americas. Las Casas was at pains to describe the rituals of native peoples by comparison with biblical practices such as first fruits. In his *Apologética*, the Dominican friar offers a wealth of description about native religions, suggesting that they served for these peoples the same sort of function of preparation for the Gospel as did the rituals of the Old Testament for Jews. In effect, Las Casas conceded Baptism of Desire to the native American religions.

Sacramental Theology in Baroque America after Trent

The Protestant Reformation presented serious challenges in Europe to sacramental theology. Luther and Calvin were inclined to decisively limit the role of the ordained clergy as sole dispensers of the sacraments. Moreover, focused more on a literal reading of the biblical texts than on traditional church practices, they accepted as sacraments only those rituals explicitly described in the New Testament. Finally, they placed the cause of grace exclusively on faith and God's inscrutable will. Calvin described the sacrament as "a testimony of divine grace toward us, confirmed by an outward sign, with mutual attestation of our piety toward him" (cited in Osborne, 49). In this and similar formulations, the efficacy of the sacrament depended upon the "invisible" characteristics of testimony and piety rather than on the joining of matter and form, understood as an automatic effect independent of faith. Calvin rejected the material sense of the Real Presence in the Eucharist by sarcastically repeating sophistry about a mouse nibbling at the host. Actually, Calvin agreed with St. Thomas about the need for a subjective understanding requisite for a sacrament (which a mouse could never have), even though the intent by the author of the *Institutes of the Christian Religion* was to distance Reformation theology from that of the Schoolmen. Moreover, there was no attention to the American natives in Calvin's Predestination theology.

In polemic response to Protestant objections, post-Tridentine theology in Europe emphasized the requisite disposition of matter, even in such an arcane issue as to whether the Mass constituted a "sacrifice" until and unless the host was destroyed. Because Luther and Calvin minimized the centrality of the clergy to the Christian life, the European Catholic theologians emphasized those roles, especially in conferring the sacraments.

Simple acceptance of these reforms would have reinforced the contention that the Church had been in error. In fact, Protestants had ridiculed the Middle Ages as an era of repression, ignorance, and superstition, claiming that the pure Christian message was set right by the Reformation. In rebuttal, Trent revisited the medieval period not as disaster but as a "golden age" of peace and social harmony. Christendom under one Church, it was suggested, was a more authentic reflection of Christ's will than the religious wars, dissension, and social dissolution occasioned by the Reformation.

Rather than examine doctrines and pronouncements, Trent can be evaluated by "material theology," the empirical testing of material effects. For example, indulgences were attached to prayers officially approved for their orthodoxy and were printed on the obverse side of "holy cards" carrying the images of Christ, Mary, and the saints. These holy cards were virtually everywhere, including private home altars, but the approved prayers ensured that the devotions would not repeat the exaggerated excesses of an uncontrolled syncretism. In a similar way, popular festivals of the saints would begin by taking the statue from the church, processing around the town, and returning to the church for the celebration of Mass. On the high altar, the crucifix was placed in the most prominent place, but the statues of the saints were put on side altars. Historian Henry Kamen (1993) calls these regulated practices the "machinery of Trent." They conjoined sacraments and sacramentals in a pastoral theology not always addressed in the polemic and speculative themes of formal theology, but more influential in shaping Catholicism.

The post-Tridentine Church in the Americas adapted European trends to American needs. In the Americas, there was no Protestantism to repel and no medieval past to extol in asserting Catholic hegemony. The challenge came instead from the vestiges of native religions in the precolonial past of the Americas. Moreover, whereas Protestants were a minority in European Catholic countries, by 1565 when Trent ended its sessions the majority American population was composed not of Europeans but rather of *criollos*, mestizos, ladinos, and natives. In fact, until the middle of the eighteenth century the chief languages in most of the Americas were the native tongues, not Spanish.

Incorporating rituals with signs and symbols into Latin American colonial religious culture faced two basic choices: repress the native past or syncretize with it. Although both approaches were used, the preference was for syncretism. Clearly, the precontact religions were not to be preserved in their entirety. But, as had been done in Europe with a Christian medieval past, Latin American theologians chose to recycle precontact religions. Given Trent's emphasis on religious practice, the effect was to find symbols and rituals that qualified as natural sacraments. The existence of certain religious practices before the arrival of Christian missionaries were cast as prefigurements of the sacraments and as providentially willed predispositions of the native peoples to be Christians. As had already been suggested in the writings of Las Casas, the American nations could be compared theologically to the pious Jews and good pagans of the Old Testament. Thus, the native religions were "recycled" in baroque fashion as anticipations of a Catholic fulfillment in Christ and the Church.

Consider, for instance, the *Symbolo catholico indiano* of the Peruvian-born Franciscan, Jerónimo Oré (1554–1630). In this treatise, Oré interprets Incan prayers to Pachacamac as an undeveloped monotheism. His book includes Christian hymns in the Quechua language, with a commentary in Castilian. Echoing ideas from the neoplatonism of Richard of St. Victor, Oré viewed Incan rites as anticipations of the Trinity and the Resurrection. Moreover, in a critical spirit to be echoed by other Peruvians such as the mestizo, Gracilaso de la Vega (1539–1616), and the ladino Felipe Guamán Poma de Ayala (c. 1538–c. 1620), Oré criticizes the established missionary Church as unresponsive to local needs and too overtly linked to imperial Spanish interests. By the end of the seventeenth century, Diego de Avedaño published a six-volume *Thesarus indicus* in Lima. His learned treatise examined the imperial conflicts with an evangelizing church, examined pastoral norms for imparting sacraments among natives, attacked Jansenists, and extolled the virtues of the recently beatified Dominican nun, Rose of Lima. His racial and cultural awareness also led him to call for the abolition

Portrait of nun and poet Sor Juana Inés de la Cruz. (Library of Congress)

of African slavery. Thus, Latin American theology during the baroque conjoined the aesthetic, syncretistic, cultural, and historical realities of Latin Catholicism with a strong sense of social justice. In Mexico, no less than in Peru, the same trends were to be found. The criollo priest Miguel Sánchez composed in 1630 a baroque theology extolling the local image of a mestiza Lady of Guadalupe. This image, as so many others, "confused" native religious symbols with Christian iconography, placing Mexican flowers and indigenous clothing on the Virgin but arrayed about her the moon and stars of the Woman in Revelations. The embrace of syncretistic symbolism celebrated as prefigurement of Christianity uniquely characterized post-Tridentine theology in the Americas.

It is difficult to separate these theological and religious currents from the emerging cultural identity. Latin American baroque theology placed scientific observation and historical speculation in its service. Since Pedro Álvares Cabral landed in Brazil when trying to tack eastward to round equatorial Africa, it was considered likely that the same thing happened in the voyage of St. Thomas the Apostle beyond the Mediterranean as described by Origen of Alexandria. It was postulated that the apostle had preached the Gospel in Brazil long before the arrival of the Europeans.

The Mexican priest, Carlos Singüenza y Góngora, made Mexico the apostle's destination, arguing that knowledge of how to build the Aztec pyramids had been filtered though the missionary preaching of the saint. For her part, Sor Juana Inés de la Cruz (1651–1695) argued in her auto-sacramental, *El Divino Narciso*, that the Aztec practice of human sacrifice was a contaminated memory of the Eucharist preached by St. Thomas in which the sacrifice of Christ's body and blood brought salvation. With these and other affirmations, theologians attributed to an apostolic origin certain symbols found in native religion that shared similarities with Christian signs and sacraments.

While the expansive post-Tridentine theology of baroque America differed from its polemicized European counterpart, there were constant exchanges, particularly on the level of popular religiosity. The holy cards, medals, and novenas of the period's religious expression fell into the category of "sacramentals" and were considered means of preparation for the sacraments. While such had been present throughout the medieval period, technical advances of printing and communication during the sixteenth and seventeenth centuries meant the same sacramentals were distributed around the world. Kamen reports, for instance, a *confradía* to the Peruvian madonna, Our Lady of Copacabana, in seventeenth-century Catalonia (Kamen 1993, 430–435). Rather than oppose their proliferation, the Vatican often encouraged and assisted the religious popularity of local American devotions. It was argued theologically that the miraculous apparition of Mary to people of color in Manila or Mexico City constituted proofs of the universality of Catholicism and its superiority to a missionary-less Protestantism. Ironically, while formal post-Tridentine sacramental theology conformed to centralized measures of orthodoxy, it promoted the informal material theology of culturally specific devotions. Thus, baroque Catholicism joined both centralization and diversification in a common message of superiority to Protestantism. Rather than rejection by the Church hierarchy, Latin American popular religiosity was extolled as evidence of "catholicity."

The technical proficiency of diffusion, the linkage with Church policy, and the global reach of these devotions were qualitatively superior to the resources of the medieval period. It can be suggested that the religious piety of the baroque deserves to be called "devotionalism" in order to distinguish it from the regionalized devotions of the Middle Ages. Devotionalism allowed the uniquely American popular religious expression to enter into the common cultural repertoire of the universal Church. For this reason, consideration of contemporary trends in sacramental theology requires understanding of the historical impact of Latin American devotionalism during the baroque as indeed is suggested by recent attention to "local theologies."

Post-Vatican II Trends in Sacramental Theology

The II Vatican Council produced new formulations for both sacraments and culture, particularly as reflected in the work of the Jesuit Karl Rahner and the Dominican Edward Schillebeeckx. Rahner called for a "Copernican revolution" in theology in which it was not that the Church waited for the world to recognize its message but that the Church reinterpreted its theology to reality in the modern world. Without divorcing his thinking from the broad outlines of Aquinas, Rahner introduced a Heideggerean notion of history into his description of how sacraments operate. In a sense, Rahner made the intelligibility of the Church in history a basis for sacramental efficacy, nudging aside the emphasis on the individual priest or the piety of the client.

A liberationist perspective to Rahner's thought was injected by Juan Luis Segundo. If Rahner was correct that the concept of "the church in history" must replace the "banking" concept of grace for each individual who receives the sacraments, argued Segundo, then the Church itself must become an instrument of liberation in history (*Artisans for a New Humanity* 1974, 4:97). The grace caused by the sacraments must be effective in real time and real history: it is not "stored up in heaven." Segundo criticized the II Vatican Council for neglecting the linkage of liberation to liturgy and the sacraments.

The title of his book, *Christ, the Sacrament of the Encounter with God*, is a straightforward statement of Schillebeeckx's perspective. Whereas the Schoolmen were preoccupied with static metaphysical issues about essence and act, Schillebeeckx was focused on process and interpersonal reaction. In his definition, the ritual of the

---

PRESENTATION OF CHILDREN

Presentation of Children is a practice that evokes the presentation of Jesus in the temple (Luke 2:22–40). Its liturgical observance dates back to fourth-century Jerusalem. Around the fifth century, the East focused on the Savior child's "encounter" with Simeon and Anna. Around the seventh century, Western churches meditated on Mary's "purification" in fulfillment of the law. Yet Simeon's confession of Christ as light to the Gentiles shapes the Western rite of the lighting and blessing of candles, known in Hispanic Catholicism as *La Candelaria*. Although the official feast is celebrated 40 days after Christmas (February 2), popular expressions are not always tied to this date or Christological themes. Emphasis falls on the unofficial custom of parents' presentation of children at the age of three, a church celebration (November 21) with origins in the apocryphal account of the presentation of Mary in the temple at the same age. Official Catholicism and classical Protestantism generally allow for presentations, but interpret them sacramentally as baptismal reaffirmations. Evangelicals and Pentecostals see them as reenactments of the presentation of children to receive Jesus' blessing (Matthew 19:13–15). The duty of parents and godparents to raise the child in the faith is promoted.

—*LAS*

---

sacrament was defined not by the pronouncement of words (form) coincidentally with material substances, but in the engagement of the person and Christ. Schillebeeckx's approach allows the instrumental causality in the Thomistic definition to better resonate with Protestant Reformation theology.

If the static approach is used to define the Eucharist, for instance, the "moment" of consecration when the priest pronounces the words "This is My Body" confects the sacrament. The Eucharistic moment "ends" when the host dissolves in the mouth or stomach of the recipient. In Schillebeeckx's new approach, the Eucharist as sacrament is celebrated in the entire liturgy and successfully completed in the continuing transformation of individual behavior to a Christlike model. In sum, while the static approach had identified the sacrament with consecrated bread and wine, the postconciliar stance made the sacrament into "sharing a meal with friends joined in Christ."

The most relevant effect of this new understanding of the sacraments has been the blurring of boundaries separating sacraments and sacramentals. The Council of Trent had followed the theology of the Schoolmen in distinguishing between the sacraments, which cause grace, and sacramentals (sacramentalia), which are "things set apart or blessed by the Catholic Church to manifest the respect due to the Sacraments, and so to excite good thoughts and to increase devotion, and through these movements of the heart to remit venial sin" (Session XXII, 15). Now, water is essential to the sacrament of Baptism, and traditionally, the holy water with which people bless themselves entering the church is only a sacramental. However, if the sacrament of Baptism is defined as an ongoing encounter with Christ renewed by the subject's embrace of the Christian life, then holy water is an extension of the Baptismal encounter. Baptism

QUINCEAÑERA

Quinceañera means 15 years old, but also refers to a rite of passage traditionally associated with girls that age. Both its history and value are controversial. Historical theories include Aztec roots, a connection to the Mozarabic rite, and the influence of the French invasion of Mexico. Critics charge it is too extravagant or mimics marriage (even invites sexual license). However, several denominations in many countries have official ceremonies for the rite, and families frequently also include receptions, meals, and dances as part of the fiesta. Likewise, some local churches have catechetical or other requirements. Several Hispanic scholars, however, dispute the critics and value the ritual as important to their culture and that it should be passed along to the next generation. Although variously interpreted, there is general agreement that it is a moment to give thanks for the girl, renew her Christian commitment, and receive a blessing. It strengthens family bonds, especially across generations, and helps the young lady start her own social network of compadres. As a rite of passage, it demonstrates to the newly pubescent how to negotiate her role as "jóvenes" (youth), and for the young lady so fêted, celebrates her contribution to the community's survival through her potential motherhood.

—KGD

may be limited to a once-only reception because it bestows what the Schoolmen called a "sacramental character," but the constant use of holy water is intended to recall this Baptism. Is grace bestowed not only in the one-time Baptism, but renewed with the pious use of the sacramental? This would mark an important distinction between merely cultural and profoundly religious practices.

Current Directions for Latina/o Sacramental Theology

The original impulse for contemporary Latino/a theology was the work of Virgilio Elizondo. Writing from a pastoral perspective as a theologian of Christian education, Elizondo developed his theology by exploring the pastoral experience of Mexican American devotion to Our Lady of Guadalupe. Without employing the name "material theology," he took stock of the icons, statues, and the like that characterized the religious practice of his Latina/o faithful. Elizondo uncannily infused an emerging Latino/a theology with the same perspectives that centuries before Latin American theology had developed in Baroque America: racial awareness and call to social justice. He also posited popular religious devotion as a constituent element of cultural identity, a theme present in the writings of the early twentieth century secular *pensador*, José Vasconcelos.

While none of Elizondo's major works constitute a sacramental theology, he has prepared the way for a "theology of sacramentals." He treats the devotion to Our Lady of Guadalupe—its history, its icons, its practices—as an occasion for enrichment of the Christian life. While he never has claimed that devotion to Guadalupe "causes grace" the way that sacraments do, he has reimagined this Marian devotion as an ongoing touchstone of religious encounter. Adapting the conciliar notions of religion and culture to the Mexican American circumstances, Elizondo has established the nexus between religious experience and cultural expression. I interpret him to mean that disposition for encounter with Christ on the part of many Mexican Americans often rests upon the use of sacramentals such as in Guadalupan devotion. Understood from the post-Vatican perspective of sacraments, Elizondo invites consideration of these sacramentals as initiating phases of encounter with Christ.

There is not space here to elaborate on the many theological explorations of Guadalupan devotion that have further developed the work of Elizondo. Significant development of other devotions and sacramentals are from Otto Maduro, *Mapas para la Fiesta*, and Roberto Goizueta's exploration of the Stations of the Cross. Most of these works consider popular religiosity to be at odds with the institutionalized church that dispenses the sacraments, echoing the dichotomy expounded by Orlando Espín in his interesting essay about popular religiosity as a theological source of *sensus fidelium*. However, the linkage of Latino/a theology to sacramental theology would require not dichotomy between popular religiosity and the sacraments, but continuity between them. The goal is expressed straightforwardly by Leonardo Boff:

> The sacraments are not the private property of the sacred hierarchy. They are basic constituents of human life. Faith sees grace present in the most elementary acts of life. So it ritualizes them and elevates them to the sacramental level. ... Today's Christians must be educated to see sacraments above and beyond the confines of the seven sacraments. As adults they should know how to enact rites that signify and celebrate the breakthrough of grace into their lives and communities. (Boff 1987, 7; 5)

Elizondo generally avoids dichotomizing the sacramentals of popular religiosity and reception of the sacraments. Indeed his unifying perspective is reflected in the volume edited by Ana María Díaz-Stevens, *Enduring Flame*, which brought an interdisciplinary light to bear on the Latino/a experiences.

If Latina/o theology still has a task in examining sacramental theology through the prism of the Latino/a experiences, there is an even greater need to address the meaning of syncretism with native religions and the African influences in so many Latino/a cultures. But most of the theological reflection on the role of non-Christian religions or natural sacraments examines them as separate from Christianity. Based on the premise that the Latino/a experience exhibits syncretism rather than "pure" native religion, the result has been little attention to Latina/os in the literature of Comparative Religion.

This premise may be changing as scholars become more aware of the syncretism of all religions with each other in a global age. For some, this is a reason not to consider sacraments and grace as substantially different from cultural expression and precontact rituals. The author of Mujerista Theology, for instance, places no importance on whether a person addresses in prayer the Aztec goddess Tonantzin or Mary, the Mother of Jesus Christ. However, as indicated in the complementary essays by Gustavo Benavides and Jaime Vidal in *Enigmatic Flame*, there seem to be grades and degrees in syncretism and syncretizing. The notion of syncretism may lead to a new line of questioning in sacramental theology in which the Latino/a experience will be central.

References and Further Reading

Boff, Leonardo. *Sacraments of Life, Life of the Sacraments* (Beltsville, MD: The Pastoral Press, 1987).

Díaz-Stevens, Ana María, and Anthony M. Stevens-Arroyo. *An Enduring Flame: Studies in Latino Popular Religiosity*, Volume I in the PARAL Series (New York: Bildner Center Books, 1994).

Garrigan, Siobhán. *Beyond Ritual: Sacramental Theology after Habermas* (Aldershot, Hampshire: Ashgate, 2004).

Kamen, Henry. *The Phoenix and the Flame: Catalonia and the Counter Reformation* (New Haven, CT: Yale University Press, 1993).

Osborne, Kenan B., OFM. *Lay Ministry in the Roman Catholic Church: Its History and Theology* (New York: Paulist Press, 1993).

Pérez y Mena, Andrés, and Anthony M. Stevens-Arroyo. *Enigmatic Powers: Syncretism with African and Indigenous Peoplés Religions Among Latinos*, Volume III in the PARAL Series (New York: Bildner Center Books, 1995).

Saranyana Saranya, Josep Ignasi, Carmen José Alejos-Grau, Elisaq Luque Alcaide, Luis Martínez Ferrer, Ana de Zaballa Beascoechea, and María Luisa Antonaya. *Teología en América Latina, vol. 1, Desde los orígenes a la Guerra de Sucesión (1493–1715)* (Madrid: Interamericana, 1999).

Stevens-Arroyo, Anthony. "The Evolution of Marian Devotionalism Within Christianity and the Ibero-Mediterranean Polity." *Journal for the Scientific Study of Religion* 37 (1998): 50–73.

Stevens-Arroyo, Anthony. "A Marriage Made in America: Trent and the Baroque." *From Trent to Vatican II: Historical and Theological Investigations*, ed. Raymond F. Bulman and Frederick J. Parrella (New York: Oxford University Press, 2006).

SOTERIOLOGY

Loida I. Martell-Otero

Soteriology is the area of theological inquiry that examines different doctrines of salvation. This entry examines the Latino/a understanding of salvation by discussing the soteriologies of Roman Catholic and *evangélico/a* scholars. Specifically, the entry begins with Orlando E. Costas and Virgilio P. Elizondo whose early works led to a renewed resurgence of Latino/a theologies. Throughout their writing careers they developed specific Christological themes from a Latino/a perspective that have soteriological implications. Then briefly discussed are the Christologies of Justo L. González and Ada María Isasi-Díaz whose later works on ancillary themes, including Trinitarian theology, pneumatology, and eschatology provide further insights about salvation. The brevity of this entry precludes an adequate presentation of the research of many other Latino/a scholars relevant to this topic. However, some of their findings that hold promise in the development of a clearer conceptualization of the doctrines of salvation that prevail in the Latina/o communities of faith are discussed. The entry concludes with a summary of the common soteriological themes that function as a basis for Latino/a views of salvation.

Orlando E. Costas

A Puerto Rican missiologist and pastor-scholar, Costas was the first Latino/a to serve as the academic dean of an accredited theological school in the United States. From the start of his career in the late 1970s until his untimely death in 1987, Costas's overriding passion was evangelization; that is, the communication of the "good news." This good news entailed God's work of grace to save humanity from the power of sin and death. For Costas, salvation means bringing life, particularly to the places where death and injustice reign. It is a holistic process that involves personal and structural transformation. Costas believed that salvation is represented by the biblical rubric of the Reign of God, a new kind of society that is life-giving. It is a way of life that offers justice, peace, and *shalom*, particularly to the oppressed and marginalized. While the Reign and salvation are gifts of God—an act of divine grace—Costas never implied that humankind was simply a passive recipient of salvation. He believed that humanity must play an active role. He perceived this role through the act of conversion. Conversion is the aspect of salvation that entails a process of personal and social transformation engendered by the Holy Spirit that leads people to struggle actively on behalf of the voiceless and powerless of society. One cannot claim to be saved and live indifferent to pain and death in the world. Thus for Costas an integral aspect of salvation is the God-given, Spirit-empowered ability to be agents of change and to struggle on behalf of those who cry out for justice.

Costas believed that Jesus Christ is God's means of salvation for the world. Jesus is saving as a marginalized poor man, a Galilean Jew who came to bring good news first and foremost to the "least of these"—the voiceless and powerless poor of the world. They are the "sinned against," described in the gospel as "the multitudes." Costas claimed that the multitudes are found today throughout the world. They are considered "nobodies" and live within a context of death as part of their everyday lives. According to Costas, Jesus' presence among them was an intentional salvific act of God: God resides in the margins. Through his ministry, Jesus brings life, healing, and humanization to their lives. He makes of the nobodies "somebodies." However, Costas was careful to note that while Jesus directs his primary focus to the multitudes, it is not his only focus. The people in the centers of power who are caught up in a matrix of death-dealing structural sin must also be given new life and humanized.

Costas believed that Jesus' death on the cross was the result of his ministry on behalf of the victims of injustice and his effort to confront sinful social structures. In this event, once again, one can perceive God's saving presence amid the suffering and forgotten of the world. Jesus could have walked away from the suffering, but instead "died outside the gate" where he remains, faithful to those who are outside the gates of justice and life (Hebrews 13:12–13). In so doing, he emptied the "powers and principalities" of their authority and overcame the power of sin and death. Costas interpreted Jesus' resurrection as God's rejection of hate, injustice, sin, and death. It was God's affirmation of Jesus' ministry of faithful love for the nobodies. Even here Costas understood that Jesus remains faithful to the marginalized. The resurrected Christ called the marginalized to Galilee, and issued there an invitation for them to become part of an eschatological community. It was at the margins of Galilee that they were empowered by the Spirit to go out as emissaries of the Reign. The nobodies have now become "somebodies" in God and for God. Thus God's new order of life, the Reign of God, entered human history through the ministry, death, and resurrection of Jesus.

The Holy Spirit also plays an important role in Costas's soteriology. The Spirit is the Spirit of Christ, and therefore the Spirit's mission is closely related to Jesus' ministry. In this sense, the Spirit is deeply incarnational: the Spirit is present in human history, acting in the lives of persons to humanize them and transform them. Furthermore, the Spirit acts in the world, saving creation from death and decay. Costas considered the Spirit to be the One who empowers believers, transforming them to become a proleptic community that begins to anticipate God's eschatological *telos* for all. They collaborate with the Spirit by becoming active agents for change, working on behalf of the marginalized and powerless and against oppressive social structures. Thus Costas's soteriology becomes a Trinitarian endeavor in light of the incorporation of this pneumatological (and eschatological) dimension.

Virgilio P. Elizondo

Elizondo is a Roman Catholic priest and theological scholar who contributed to the reinvigoration of Latina/o theologies with the publication of *Galilean Journey: The Mexican American Promise* in 1983, a distillation of his earlier doctoral work. He broke ground with two specific contributions in this book. The first was his particular theological method in which he reinterpreted the gospel through the lens of Mexican American culture, and the second was his use of *mestizaje* as a theological paradigm. This allowed Elizondo to reevaluate Christology and Guadalupana theology, through the lens of mestizaje.

For Elizondo, Jesus is a *mestizo* Galilean Jew, rejected by those in power who considered him both cultically impure and culturally compromised. As one so rejected by the ruling religious and political powers of his day, Jesus' very life and ministry express God's salvific intentions for humankind. According to Elizondo, God became flesh as a rejected one to demonstrate God's rejection of rejection. In Jesus Christ, God extends a call of fellowship to all who are marginalized because they are somehow perceived to be impure. Elizondo perceives in the Paschal events further evidence of God's love for the rejected and marginalized impure. Those deemed to be religiously pure and part of the cultural/political elite reject Jesus' call to change the structural injustices of his time and are instrumental in his death. In raising Jesus from the dead, God reveals that the pure are, in fact, impure. Elizondo views in these events a reaffirmation of God's acceptance of the marginalized impure, particularly of the rejected mestizos/as of the world. Thus Jesus is saving because he is God-incarnate-as-mestizo, a marginalized person who has come to bring a word of acceptance to the oppressed mestizas/os of his day and to confront the oppressive religious and political powers. For Elizondo, Jesus is also saving as God's resurrected One who brings a message of loving acceptance to the rejected while empowering them with a mission. They are called to be prophetic agents of change who confront the sinful social structures that marginalize those perceived to be impure.

These same themes are present in Elizondo's theology of *la Virgen de Guadalupe*/ the Virgen of Guadalupe. According to Mexican and Mexican American tradition, the Virgin appeared to the Amerindian, Juan Diego, on December 9, 1531—a decade after the final stages of the conquest of the Americas. Rather than appear in the guise of a white European, or as an Aztec deity, the Virgin appeared to Diego as a mestiza —a brown-complexioned woman with symbols in her dress that represented European Christian understanding of God, as well as Aztec religious beliefs. Elizondo sees in this important person the affirmation of a new mestiza people that have arisen from the ashes of the conquest. In la Virgen, God neither rejects totally the Christian beliefs of the conquistadores nor does God fully embrace them. Similarly, there is neither a total rejection of Aztec religiosity nor a total acceptance. Rather, for Elizondo, she embodies a divine acceptance and valuation of the mestizo realities that arise from the clash of these two worlds. Furthermore, Elizondo believes that God reaches out

Statue of the Virgin of Guadalupe appearing to Juan Diego, Indians, and Bishop. The statue is located at the Guadalupe Shrine in Mexico, where the Virgin Mary allegedly appeared to Juan Diego. (William Perry/Dreamstime)

through *la Morenita* (the Brown Virgin) to the marginalized Juan Diegos of the world who have been rejected by the political and religious powers of the day. Once again, in and through la Virgen, God asserts God's abiding presence in the midst of the rejected and oppressed, while confronting those in power with their complicity in supporting social sinful structures.

Through these two important mestizo/a persons, Elizondo asserts God's love for the mestizas/os of the world, who are often the poor, forgotten, and disempowered of the world. Furthermore, Elizondo sees in Christ and in la Virgen an important eschatological motif. As mestizos, they represent God's purpose to unite the cosmos into a diverse whole. Fragmentation and division are sinful realities that contradict this purpose. Elizondo claims that mestizos/as are also "eschatological" figures because in their very existence they represent a message of God to the world. In their very being, they are an announcement of "good news" (gospel) of holistic healing and salvation for the world, as well as a denouncement of human structures that divide, disempower, and dehumanize.

Justo L. González

González is a Cuban-born *evangélico* historian and theologian. In *Mañana: Christian Theology from a Hispanic Perspective* (1990), he discusses important theological themes interpreted through the lens of Latino/a experiences of *mestizaje*, marginality, and poverty. This allows him, for example, to reconsider the doctrine of the Trinity beyond traditional static formulas and to reflect upon its socioeconomic implications. According to González, just as God is three Persons who share equally the divine substance so that they are now One, as a society we are called to share our resources among all of creation. We are to live out the *imago Dei* by imitating God's "for-otherness" and loving spirit of sharing.

The incarnation is also of paramount importance for González's theology. The incarnation reveals to us that God is not a distant God of ontological formulation and intellectual reflection, but rather is the God of Jesus who is present before the cries of the suffering in human history. Jesus was a poor carpenter, and as such, demonstrates to us that God is not on the side of the powerful of the world, but has come to reside in the midst of the poor and the oppressed. For González, the incarnation demonstrates that God "speaks Spanish"—that is to say, that God is the God of those rejected as "other." He believes that this insight about God's identification with the rejected, the oppressed, and the poor was lost or distorted in the various Christological positions ultimately rejected by the early Church. Although rejected, González insists that these positions should be remembered because they continue to tempt the contemporary world. For example, the disempowered are often tempted to fall into the Gnostic error of seeking to escape the oppressive evils of an unjust world, rather than seek social change. The resolution of the Christological controversies led to the assertion of Jesus' full humanity *and* full divinity. González believes that to lose sight of either side of this dialectic is to lose sight of the fullness of God's salvation for all, particularly for the oppressed.

González continuously affirms two foundational principles: the theological importance of the incarnation, and God's active presence amid the oppressed. The incarnation reveals God to us. It is not a passing event, but is constitutive of the very identity of God. It is because of the incarnation that Christianity can affirm that God is present in human history. It is because of who Jesus was, and what Jesus did that Christianity can affirm that God is on the side of the poor and marginalized. This incarnational emphasis in conjunction with González's Trinitarian theology underscores the profound, but sometimes forgotten soteriological principle that it is *God* who saves through Jesus Christ.

González affirms that the incarnation not only reveals who God is for us, but also who we are intended to be for God and others. It reveals that we are called to be like God, to share, to love, and to be "for-others." Just as the Trinitarian God is relational, so we are called to be in loving relations, with God and with each other. One could say that for González, salvation is a process of humanization: to become more like God, we are called to be what God created us to be. We are called to be human beings in a world that seeks to take away our very humanity.

It is clear through González's discussion of Trinity and Christology that salvation is not a privatized or individualized event. This soteriological view is especially underscored in his understanding of the role of the Holy Spirit. The Spirit is the One who makes all things new, transforming sinful nature to make all of creation what it is not. González describes the Holy Spirit as the power of the future because the Spirit allows us to see the new order that God is bringing forth. This new order is the Reign of God, which González calls the Reign of love. It is not a spatial reality, but a temporal one; it is not a different place, but a different way of living. According to González, the Spirit not only empowers us to envision this new way of being, the Spirit also transforms us so that we begin to live this new reality today. When we live today in light of the promise of this different reality, we live as a *mañana* (tomorrow) people. While González does not explicitly state it in quite the same way, one could infer that for him, the oppressed are made human in an inhumane society through Jesus so that they can live as agents of change, empowered by the Spirit to be a mañana people who live a new reality and struggle on behalf of that new reality in the present.

Ada María Isasi-Díaz

One of the concerns for Latina scholars is that theologies articulated by their male colleagues at times fail to consider seriously the situations of oppression suffered by women. Latinas live under the quadruple oppression of race, culture, class, and gender. They are poor women who are treated often as if they had no intrinsic value. Latina *feministas* such as María Pilar Aquino and *mujeristas* such as Ada María Isasi-Díaz are concerned that theologies that emphasize "for-otherness" could only be more oppressive to women whose very cultures emphasize service to the other, often at the expense of their own well-being. Latina scholars often have argued that the questions of Latinas, particularly those of grassroots women, arise from the concerns about the well-being of their *familias* and communities, and out of their daily struggles (*la lucha*) for survival.

Isasi-Díaz is a Cuban Roman Catholic social ethicist who has dedicated her scholarly work to mujerista theology—which grants a privileged status to the experience of grassroots Latina women. Mujerista theology advocates for the liberation of oppressed Latina women and communities through the elaboration of a *proyecto histórico*/a historical project. In *La Lucha Continues: Mujerista Theology* (2004), she expounds on the socioethical themes related to this *proyecto* as well as to mujerista understandings of *lo cotidiano*, Christology, and reconciliation. For Isasi-Díaz, lo cotidiano is an essential component of how women do theology because it represents the space where the oppressed live and experience God. It is not a theological paradigm per se, but rather an epistemological tool. It represents a liminal space where macrostructures—religious, political, and socioeconomic—meet the material realities of grassroots women, and where one can determine if structural change has resulted in a liberative and just world for the marginalized.

According to Isasi-Díaz, salvation must be experienced as a historical reality at the level of lo cotidiano. Salvation is reconciliation. Reconciliation entails the healing of broken relations between humanity and God and among human beings. It is integrally related to justice. Isasi-Díaz defines injustice as all that separates us. Where there is injustice, there cannot be reconciliation, that is, the overcoming of broken relations. Therefore, injustice must be overcome so that God's presence can then be perceived in the midst of community and community formed. Isasi-Díaz believes that reconciliation is both a present task and future project, and therefore an intrinsic part of the proyecto histórico—the struggle for a just society and for humane living under oppressive conditions.

The fruit of reconciliation is embodied in what Isasi-Díaz has referred to as the "Kin-dom" of God. She rejects "kingdom" language as an inappropriate metaphor that only sustains patriarchal values. The term "kin-dom" underscores that God calls us to be in interdependent relations with one another and with God. It also underscores that God is a personal God, rather than a distant and indifferent one. For Isasi-Díaz, the Kin-dom is a metaphor that reminds us that liberation must take place at all dimensions of life. God's shalom must be experienced at the personal level (lo cotidiano) as well as the macrostructural level. Liberation must be spiritual as well as social, personal as well as political. Furthermore, Isasi-Díaz claims that the notion of Kin-dom supports the reconstitution of familia. The Kin-dom is a familia unlike the so-called nuclear family often celebrated in the United States and other First World countries. Rather, it is God's extended family, where everyone can experience "being at home."

While Isasi-Díaz considers Jesus Christ to be a mediator of the Kin-dom, she does not consider him its sole mediator. Noting that his name, *Jesucristo*, argues against facile dichotomies between his humanity (Jesus) and his divinity (Christ), Isasi-Díaz insists that a serious Christology needs to consider him as the full expression of what is human. This is what his life and ministry communicated, and therefore it is how he mediated the Kin-dom. However, precisely because his mediation is an expression of his full humanity and part of being fully human is being in community, she argues that Mary and the disciples are also mediators of the Kin-dom. They are mediators because they not only learned from Jesucristo, they were also the teachers of his religious and cultural traditions. The mediating role of Jesus' community allows Isasi-Díaz to conclude that they too are "Christs." Indeed, she asserts that anyone who lives and proclaims the Kin-dom is a mediator and therefore a Christ. In so doing, she does not consider that this diminishes Jesucristo's uniqueness, nor does it diffuse each "Christ's" essential role since each person carries within a seed of the divine, the *imago Dei*, which is necessary for the unfolding of the Kin-dom. The oppressed in particular become mediators of the Kin-dom when they refuse to lose hope in the face of overwhelming injustice, and when they demand that unjust social structures change rather than be complicit within such sinful systems. Others become mediators to the degree that they press on for justice and liberation and create structures in which everyone can live fully. For Isasi-Díaz, this encapsulates what salvation means.

Continuing the Dialogue

The four scholars discussed so far are not the only Latinas/os with important insights about salvation. While space does not allow a full discussion, it is important to note some key voices and their avenues of research that hold much promise in articulating Latina/o doctrines of salvation.

Any conversation about salvation must take into consideration the contributions of Latina scholars. In addition to the contributions of *mujerista* theology discussed in the previous section, mention must be made of such Latina Catholic *feministas* as María Pilar Aquino, Jeanette Rodríguez, Carmen Marie Nanko-Fernández, and others whose scholarly work is dedicated to the liberation of oppressed poor women and men. As such, their theologies are inherently soteriological in nature. Their contributions encompass areas such as cross-cultural dialogue to articulate a liberating paradigm for oppressed women, Guadalupana theology and its liberating motifs, and immigration issues and their impact on the Latino/a community. Latina *evangélica* scholars such as Daisy L. Machado, Nora O. Lozano-Díaz, Elizabeth Conde-Frazier, Zaida Maldonado-Pérez, and Loida I. Martell-Otero have offered constructive critiques of traditions that have proven to be oppressive for women and marginalized communities. They have reconceptualized notions of suffering, proposed new Trinitarian paradigms, and revisited the importance *testimonios*. Thus, these *evangélicas* have deepened the understanding of salvation for the Latino/a community of faith.

Catholic Latino scholars such as Orlando O. Espín and Roberto S. Goizueta have contributed to the soteriological dialogue with their proposals about the pneumatological role of Mary and the communal role of saints. *Evangélico* theologians such as Eldin Villafañe and Samuel Solitán have explored the liberating aspects of pneumatology in Pentecostal views of salvation, while others such as Luís G. Pedraja have provided a Christological analysis through the lens of Latina/o experience.

Summary and Conclusion: Latina/o Soteriology

Among the different discourses about salvation from a Latina/o perspective, one can perceive some consistent themes. To begin with, most or all of the theologians discussed above understand that salvation is from God. It is important to underscore this aspect given the tendency among some Christian communities to distort this theological insight, and caricature a wrathful God whom Christ has come to appease on our behalf. For Latinas/os, implicitly it is the Trinitarian God who is present as part of the divine *familia*. Therefore, it is God who seeks to protect those who are *desprovisto* (deprived) of societal protections.

Another common theme that is consistently raised is that the incarnation has *theological* as well as the soteriological implications. The affirmation that God would enter into human history through God's enfleshment as a poor, marginalized (*mestizo*) person, Jesus Christ, whose ministry is dedicated to those marginalized in his time is a statement about who God is and what God represents vis-à-vis the Latina/o community. It is incarnational not only in the sense of God's presence in and through this historical person, but also in the sense that God's salvation is actualized in human history in contextually specific ways. God is the One who stands on behalf of those abandoned by society in order to liberate them and transform the social structures that lead to their deaths. The insistence that there are real soteriological implications in the Christian affirmation of the enfleshment of the divine presence within a given sociohistorical locus allows Latina/o theologians to claim that God is also present in the ministry of the Holy Spirit, Mary, and the saints. Isasi-Díaz goes as far as to claim that this incarnate presence is manifest in each of us. Thus Latina/o scholars reaffirm God's communal nature, as well as God's real presence amid community, for the re-creation of a diversely holistic community.

This communal emphasis is critical for defining salvation from a Latino/o perspective. The Latina/o theologians discussed in this entry tend to understand sin in terms of oppressive social structures that have caused irreparable harm to the Latina/o community. The sinful realities of racism, cultural/ethnic discrimination, sexism, and political, economic, and social exploitation have led to the rupture of community. Since this is a people whose identity derives from being community, their very humanity is distorted and denied. They become invisible and peripheral, with no voice or power. Salvation therefore entails two crucial events: the humanization of the dehumanized and the re-formation of community.

Salvation is more than just a cosmic fix to a problem, however. While liberation from oppression is one dimension, it is not the only dimension that defines salvation. There is an aspect to salvation that is proactive: it entails becoming "somebody" with a vocation that inheres with God's eschatological vision. Latinos/as are transformed by God in order to go forth and be prophetic agents of change. We are called to proclaim the good news that God has broken the barriers that separate humanity from God, human beings from each other, and humankind from God's creation. We are called to become an intimate part of the divine familia and become a hospitable place of healing for those found homeless because of oppressive social structures. We are called to live out a new order of life, one that is defined by love, compassion, respect, and hope. We are saved to become a "light unto the world" and brothers and sisters in the Reign of God. Salvation is thus an act of loving grace from God for humanity, and a vocation of love from us to God and for all of God's creation.

References and Further Reading

Conde-Frazier, Elizabeth. "Hispanic Protestant Spirituality." *Teología en Conjunto: A Collaborative Hispanic Protestant Theology*, ed. José David Rodríguez and Loida I. Martell-Otero (Louisville, KY: Westminster John Knox Press, 1997).

Costas, Orlando E. *Liberating News: A Theology of Contextual Evangelization* (Grand Rapids, MI: William B. Eerdmans Publishing Co., 1989).

Elizondo, Virgilio. *Galilean Journey: The Mexican-American Promise* (Maryknoll, NY: Orbis Books, 2000).

González, Justo L. *Mañana: Christian Theology from a Hispanic Perspective* (Nashville: Abingdon Press, 1990).

Isasi-Díaz, Ada María. *La Lucha Continues: Mujerista Theology* (Maryknoll, NY: Orbis Books, 2004).

Martell-Otero, Loida I. "Of Satos and Saints: Salvation from the Periphery." *Perspectivas* 4 (Summer 2001): 7–38.

Martell-Otero, Loida I. *Liberating News: An Emerging U.S. Hispanic/Latina Soteriology of Crossroads* (PhD diss., Fordham University, 2005).

Pedraja, Luís G. *Jesus Is My Uncle: Christology from a Hispanic Perspective* (Nashville: Abingdon Press, 1999).

Villafañe, Eldin. *The Liberating Spirit: Toward an Hispanic American Pentecostal Social Ethic* (Grand Rapids, MI: William B. Eerdmans Publishing Co., 1993).

SPIRITUALITY

Gilberto Cavazos-González

Spirituality—the word conjures up many thoughts in our contemporary Western world. To some, spirituality is the essence of human existence; to others, it is a "New Age" encounter with the occult or a form of *curanderismo* (faith healing). Yet to others, spirituality is the traditional devotional practice of some ancient religion, and finally to some academics it is a field of theology, somewhat akin to psychology. This academic field facilitates distinguishing between various spiritualities and between different ways of understanding spirituality. This entry will consider the history of the field, the *corazón* (heart) and *arte* (art) of spirituality and lastly look at some characteristics of Latina/o spirituality(ies).

Historical Development

Many people claim to be spiritual, but what that means seems to vary from person to person. Sadly, spirituality is a much used and often misunderstood term. The English word "spirituality" has existed since the 1930s and became a part of the general parlance in the late 1950s. On the other hand, the Spanish equivalent *espiritualidad* has existed since the sixteenth century. It too has, however, only recently become a part of the general parlance. Very few Hispanic spiritual writers over the centuries have used the term "espiritualidad," preferring to speak instead of "union with God," the "life of perfection," justification, sanctification, piety, devotion, *mystica*, and even popular religiosity. The great Spanish mystics Teresa de Avila and Juan de la Cruz did not use the term. This is probably due to the long and convoluted history of the Latin term *spiritualitas* from which both the Spanish "espiritualidad" and the English "spirituality" take their origin.

As an academic science, spirituality is less than a century old and its initial manifestation as spiritual theology only dates back to the seventeenth century when scholars separated it from systematic theology. At that time spirituality as the lived expression of one's theological belief became generally studied as a part of moral theology. Its supernatural component was studied as mystical theology.

Carmen Quintero sings at a Spanish Easter service at the Primitive Christian Church in New York City. A growing number of Latino/as are turning to Protestant denominations, particularly Pentecostal and Evangelical, finding the worship styles and Hispanic pulpit leadership is a better fit for their spiritual needs. (AP Photo/Tina Fineberg)

The term "spirituality" is a Christian term that was invented in the fifth century when a Christian leader exhorted the newly baptized to behave in a manner consistent with their baptism. He told them that like all Christians they are expected to act and grow in spritualitas. It is uncertain as to who wrote the exhortation, but some believe it might have originated in heretical circles. Still, with this new term, the adjective *spiritualis* becomes the subject "spiritualitas" that one can act and grow in. Patristic writers slowly began to use this new concept and eventually began to write about ways in which one could progress spiritually in their *cotidiano* (day-to-day life). At the time, spirituality was theology, because theology was the pastoral care of the faithful.

"Until the Middle Ages all theology was spiritual theology, or the reflection of one's experience of faith, and it found expression in liturgy, scripture, private prayer, and pastoral experience" (Conde-Frazier 1997, 125). By the twelfth and thirteenth centuries, however, theology slowly became more scholastic and moved away from a pastoral focus. Scholastic theology preferred to study the relationship between faith and the critical understanding of faith and became considerably more dogmatic and doctrinal. In the thirteenth century Bonaventure, the mystical theologian, and other spiritual writers tried to reconcile the lived experience of faith with scholastic theology. However, by the fourteenth century, theology and spirituality became separate fields of interest. Theology was interested in objective doctrines that can be derived

MAL DE OJO

The Spanish term "Mal de Ojo" means "evil eye," an expression common in most cultures and ancient civilizations. A glance is believed to inflict harm on whom it falls, especially when the person casting it has intentions such as envy and jealousy. Children are considered particularly susceptible. The Greeks and the Romans had comparable expressions describing the same phenomenon, "baskania" and "fascinum," respectively. Various amulets were thought to ward off the evil eye, for example, the Eye of Horus among the Egyptians. The Bible encourages protection against people with the evil eye (Proverbs 23:6–8). Among Hispanics, the evil eye is commonly diagnosed by curanderos or folk healers, and symptoms may include distress, sleep disturbance, diarrhea, vomiting, and/or fever. Treatment is holistic, addressing physical, spiritual, and psychological components. It can include the use of herbal remedies, religious rituals, or ceremonial cleansing. For instance, the use of an egg and herbs on the body of the afflicted person is believed to extract the evil influences. Preventive measures to protect against evil eye may include prayers, the sign of the cross on vulnerable children, and the use of holy water, incantations, and/or amulets.

—FAO & KGD

and understood from divine revelation while spiritual writers turned instead to the subjective knowledge of faith as lived reality.

Until the Council of Trent during the sixteenth century theology had been one science, but the demands of the modern period led to its being separated into distinct disciplines of study. Dogmatic or systematic theology came to study the mystery of God's life and the economy of salvation. Moral theology studied how these theological beliefs could lead one to a moral life free of sin and pleasing to God.

The sixteenth century was a dynamic time for the development of Latino/a spirituality. Several things were happening concurrently that were bound to influence how Hispanics do spirituality. The Latin term "spiritualitas" was translated into Italian and Spanish in order to write treatises in the vernacular meant to help pastors and other spiritual leaders develop the laity's interest in the life of perfection and union with God. As European universities were dividing theology into various disciplines, the Spanish were setting up universities and schools in America to teach these varied disciplines. The Christian community was being divided by the Protestant and Catholic reformations, and the Spanish were running their infamous Inquisition. At the same time, Spain was in the midst of its Golden Age of Christian mysticism as a result of the Catholic reformation movements. This age gave birth to various schools of spirituality: the Franciscan Recollect movement, the Ignatian spiritual exercises, and the Carmelite way to union with God. These spiritual schools influenced how Latin Americans were being Christianized and how moral theology was developing.

In the seventeenth century moral theology developed the subscience of spiritual theology as a way of studying how Christians could avoid sin and live a just and holy life. While moral theology considered universal techniques for human action in view of

---

MAL AIRE

"Mal aire" literally means "bad or evil air." It can also be referred to as *mal viento,* "bad wind." Mal aire is a metaphysical disease caused by God, gods, or spirits. The term can either refer to a current of cold air that can carry and spread disease-causing germs or it can refer to bad spirit(s) that can invade the body and bring forth illness or bad fortune. Mal aire can be seen as the cause of anything from the common cold to cancer. It can occur due to excessive heat resulting from a fever or through heavy work or exercise. Mal aire can also be caused by excessive coldness, brought about by a draft or by water. For example, one way of getting mal aire is by too much outdoor walking either early in the cold morning or late at night. Another way of getting mal aire is by walking through a cemetery. Children are more susceptible to mal aire. Mal aire can be diagnosed by curandero/as or other folk healers who can then prescribe a healing. It can be treated by either an herbal remedy, a *limpieza* (ceremonial cleaning), and/or a ritual.

—MAD

---

morality and ethics, spiritual theology considered the via (way/path), practices, and orientations that influence spiritual growth. At this time the French school translated "spiritualitas" into *spiritualitè* in order to speak of faith, hope, charity, love, abandon, respect, devotion, worship, venerations, piety, etc., in the life of the believer seeking perfection.

The Spanish schools of spirituality (Franciscan Recollect, Ignatian Exercises, and Carmelite Reform) took seriously the psychological factor of the believer in his/her spiritual growth, and this led to spiritual theology's study of the subjective dimension of Christian life. The spiritual journey conditioned by the objective mysteries of divine revelation as put forth by Biblical, Dogmatic, and Moral theologies came to be seen as intimately bound to the individual dispositions of the believer. Supernatural grace/revelation impregnates the soul of the believer and develops in her/him as per his/her age, gender, psychological makeup, culture, and economic and social situation in life.

During the 1800s, spiritual theology was studied as ascetical and mystical theology, the theology of perfection, and the theology of the spiritual life. It was considered "the theological science that studies the progressive development of Christian life, which is to say the life of grace animated by the dynamic impulse to attain perfect sanctity, under the life-giving action of the Holy Spirit" (della Trinita, 464).

Like every academic discipline, spiritual theology has a subject of study that is (1) the life of grace (given to us in baptism) and (2) the spiritual life (the Holy Spirit in the believer). Spiritual theology is meant to study the agent of sanctification infused by God in the baptized and how it is meant to grow and develop personally and communally (cf. 1 Titus 4:1; Timothy 4:15; 1 Corinthians 9:24; Philippians 3:12–14; Ephesians 4:15–16). It studies the progressive and developmental stages of the spiritual life (of grace) as it is led by the Triune God, especially the Holy Spirit. It highlights the dogmatic principles involved, the laws that govern it, its successive stages, functions, and psychological conditions, its various aspects/manifestations, and its ultimate aspiration/goal (cf. della Trinita, 466).

Spiritual theology focused on studying the interior life or the life of perfection to discern methods of "normal" spiritual growth in comparison with the special "way" of the great mystics. This in turn led to the study of the need for ascetical practices and/or mystical experience in the Christian spiritual journey. In this latter development the life of the Christian as "life in the Spirit" became an object of study and theological discourse. This life was brought into conversation with the dogmatic discourse of theological anthropology and morality with a view of growth in virtue, especially charity (cf. Moioli 1597–1609).

Spiritual theology has a speculative-deductive methodology, which considers the principles of Christian life to be sanctifying grace, infused virtues, charism of the Spirit, relationships with supernatural entities, and relationship between spiritual growth and beatific vision. Contemporary Latina/o spirituality is still very much influenced by this look to the supernatural in the cotidiano. The speculative-deductive methodology of spiritual theology references history and experience as part of theological discourse as another way of studying the cotidiano of Christian spiritual experience. In this way a new method began that tied theological method to the methods of empirical sciences, especially that of psychology.

In the late nineteenth century, spiritual theology slowly grew to consider not only the theological sciences but also the social sciences as conversation partners in the study of the Christian spiritual life. This new development led to the writing of French manuals of spiritual theology in the 1920s. These led to the origin of a new theological discipline called Spirituality. With the translation of Pierre Pourrat's *La spiritualité Chrétienne* (1918–1928) and Adolphe Tanquerey's *La Vie Spirituelle* (1923–1931) "spiritualitas" was finally translated into the English word "spirituality."

After the promulgation of Pius IX's *Constitution Deus scientiarum Dominus* (1931), Catholic universities began to include spiritual theology or ascetics and mysticism not just as special or auxiliary disciplines but as a critical reflection on the lived experience of the faith that would then be brought into conversation with other theological disciplines, especially with moral theology. Iacobo Heerinckx published an important manual on spiritual theology entitled *Introductio in Theologiam Spiritualem* (Taurini-Romae 1931). This seminal work gathered the developments of this new theological discipline and focused on the content of the discipline: The spiritual itinerary and its three stages. Taking his cue from Pseudo-Dionysius, Bonaventure, and the Spanish mystics, he studied the Purgative Way, the Illuminative Way, and the Unitive Way. The Christian Spiritual Life, as the Spanish mystics had taught, is not so much a static reality as it is a journey or a pilgrimage with stages of development as one moves from sin to life. In this itinerary, the theologian can distinguish theologically valid criteria for the maturation process of Christian life.

Since the 1930s spiritual theology has reflected on a speculative reading of spiritual documents in conjunction with the lived experience of individual Christians confronting theory with praxis. As a result, it has individuated not only a general Christian spirituality but Christian spiritualities, particular ways in which individuals, movements, schools of thought, ethnic groups, and others integrate Christian values in a

LIMPIAS

Limpias are ceremonies of spiritual cleansing and "letting go" that have been part of indigenous tradition since before European contact, and are performed by a *curandera/o*, healer, who brushes off the person to be healed with herbs, feathers, flowers, or other medicine. The curandera/o knows the qualities of plants such as salvia, hierba de burro, Chiantzotzolli, hierba martina, and hierba negra. S/he prepares tinctures, incorporates ritual and prayer, and might even make referrals. Limpias may also include *platicas* in which the healer assists a person in talking through his or her needs or a *temezcal*, a traditional sweat lodge involving prayer and song and using hot stones or *Tatas and abuelita/os*, to generate heat when water is poured over them or sprinkled on them with herbs such as mint and rosemary. Limpias are often combined with Christian prayer as a legacy of syncretism that made possible the survival of a living tradition. Typical is the Otomi combination of crosses, St. Michael the Archangel, St. James, the four cardinal directions, and winds, sacrifice, military conquest, and the ancestors. Similarly, Conchero velaciones combine Christian saints and hymns with the four directions, copal, the building of altars to Aztec deities, culminating in flower limpias.

—MVS

lived manner according to their different circumstances in life. In this case it seems that the discipline Spirituality needs to continue studying how the traditional sources of Christian spirituality (Sacred Scripture, Liturgy, Christian Anthropology, Mysticism, the tension between Incarnation and Eschatology, etc.) are integrated or not by contemporary Christian spiritualities and how these traditional sources inform the lived Christian experience. This is done through a method of study that brings the discipline Spirituality into conversation with both theological disciplines and empirical sciences.

As previously mentioned, the English word "spirituality" became a popular word in the latter half of the twentieth century. At the same time Christians came to realize that all humans have spirituality and that just as there is a Christian spirituality, there are Muslim, Jewish, and Buddhist spiritualities (to name a few). This openness to the reality of non-Christian spiritualities has led Spiritualogians (theologians who specialize in the study of Spirituality) to be more serious about the reality of a variety of Christian spiritualities that stem from founders of spiritual schools, states of life, and even cultures. Spanish Catholicism was instrumental in the development of much of contemporary Christian Spirituality through is missionaries and mystics. These gave rise to much of the missionary spirituality that dominated the past five centuries of Christian evangelization. It also has led to Christian interest in prayer and mystical experience. However, it is only since spiritual theology gave way to Spirituality that we can speak of a Hispanic spirituality and a multiplicity of Latino/a spiritualities.

All of this history leads to the varied ways in which spirituality is understood in our contemporary societies. Spiritualogians have determined four ways in which spirituality is understood: (1) ontological: spirituality is the whole of the human experience

SUSTO

Susto is a spiritual imbalance or illness recognized by curanderos (some of whom describe it as "soul loss") and even contemporary psychiatrists (who label it a "culture-bound syndrome"). Susto is commonly recognized across all of Latin America where there is considerable agreement about causes and symptoms. Causes are fright or shock from an ambient source (e.g., witnessing a tragedy), and symptoms include trembling, crying, insomnia, and agitation. Although not a chronic illness, susto is acute and even fatal: it requires remedy. The best place for treatment is home or church, but although most healers agree on prayer, other kinds of cures differ especially by ethnicity (e.g., cleansings). Some believe susto is an ethnosomatic illness, that is, a culturally acceptable way for persons overwhelmed by circumstances to find a recognized respite (and recovery) that might otherwise be denied them due to the responsibilities of gender or social role. Certainly pastors can appreciate that a person's emotional, biomedical, and spiritual dimensions are neither unrelated nor unaffected by gender and social roles. And since prayer is virtually always part of the cure, openness to this experience and sensitivity to its cultural components is helpful to good ministry whenever a congregant complains of susto.

—FAO & KGD

because in various religious anthropologies human beings have a spirit and a soul as well as a body; (2) existential: spirituality is experienced in various ordinary and special ways, especially through relationships with others, particularly the transcendent or "divine Other"; (3) communal: spirituality is formulated in the traditions and/or tradition of a people's culture and/or religion; and finally (4) discipline: spirituality is a theological science or branch of learning that studies the phenomenon of a person's or community's spiritual reality and experience (cf. Downey 1997, 42–43).

In a similar vein, Gustavo Gutiérrez sees the development of Christian spirituality in three stages: (1) existential: life-changing experiences of certain saints and heroes; (2) communal: doctrines, devotions, art, schools of thought, and traditions that come from the community's assimilation of these experiences; and (3) formational: the development of new ways of being Christian (1983, 52–53).

Downey and Gutiérrez's understandings are not meant to be hierarchical, but rather descriptive of the way in which people speak of spirituality. Spiritualogians also understand that spirituality is a "self-implicating discipline" (cf. Frohlich 2001, 65–78), meaning that since the scholar participates in the field of study s/he cannot be completely separated from his/her subject of study.

Corazón: Spirituality

According to the *Real Academia Española* (RAE: Royal Academy of Spanish), *espiritualidad* (spirituality) is defined as that which is of a "spiritual" nature or condition and as the ideas, beliefs, attitudes, and/or inclinations related to the "spiritual life."

The key to understanding spirituality is to be found in the definition of *espiritual* (spiritual). Spiritual, from the Latin *spiritualis*, identifies those things related to the spirit. "Spiritual" people are seen as sensitive, religious, mystical, or idealistic people or persons not interested in material things.

In keeping with the RAE, spiritual people are those who prefer the *espíritu* (spirit) to matter. But, what is espíritu? In chemistry, spirit is the subtle vapors that come from wine and liquor or the purest and the most subtle substances that can be extracted from plants and other living things. In writing, spirit is a Greek symbol that indicates breathing or lack thereof in pronunciation. In Christianity "espiritual" refers to spirit, which the RAE defines as an immaterial and rational being, as a supernatural gift, and as the generating principle or intimate character (essence) of something. Spirit is the natural vigor that animates, enlivens, and strengthens the body. In Spanish thought, espíritu is the breath, stamina, brilliance, valor, vivacity, and/or genius of a person.

Although its root words (*ruah*, *pneuma*, *spiritus*) are found throughout the Scriptures of both Judaism and Christianity, the concept/term "spirituality" is not found in the Bible. In its place, Latina/os will notice that the Scriptures are about "relationship." Relationship seems to be the key to the Latino/a understanding of espiritualidad. Usually when Hispanics are asked to give definitions or descriptions of spirituality, they rarely if ever mention the spirit. Instead they speak of relationships, of being in harmony with God, others, and creation or about how important relationships like the one has with God and/or the Church can give purpose and meaning to life.

Many Latina/os will also describe the spiritual as being other than the material. Often this otherness can take on the European dualism of spirit versus matter but at the same time it has a touch of the Nahuatl concept of duality. Duality is not a conflictual philosophy like that of dualism. Rather, in duality there is complementarity; one reality needs the other. The spiritual and the material are two sides of the same coin. A human being cannot be spiritual without the material, and the material without the spiritual makes for a weak relationship. Spirituality is the *corazón* (heart) in which the soul nurtures and cares for both the spirit and the corporality that make it a person.

Gustavo Gutiérrez defines spirituality as "a walking in liberty according to the Spirit of love and of life" (Gutiérrez 1983, 49). Basically, he is affirming that *espiritualidad* is nothing less than "life in the spirit." For Christians "life in the spirit" is about the human spirit being in relationship or better *en conjunto* (union) with the Divine Spirit and other human spirits. This union is at the heart (*corazón*) of the mysticism of great Spanish mystics like Francisco de Osuna, Teresa de Avila, Pedro de Alcantara, and Juan de la Cruz. "Spirituality is all about relationship, for no one can live an authentic human life without relating to the 'other' who is God and neighbor. It is in relationship that we are formed and that we develop who we are" (Cavazos-González 2004, 49).

This sense of spirituality as the corazón of who we are in relationship is found in various stories from the book *Así Es: Stories of Hispanic Spirituality*. The editors describe spirituality "as a way of life that reveals, helps, and builds our relationship with God through the Good News of Jesus" (Asi Es 1994, 4–5).

In the stories that follow Bishop Ricardo Ramírez calls spirituality "the inner space that allows people to come in touch with themselves as believers. It is the area where 'the divine spirit touches the human spirit' " (Asi Es 1994, 5). Rosa María Icaza claims that spirituality "is translated into the love of God, which moves, strengthens and is manifested in love of neighbor and self" (Asi Es 1994, 5–6). Dominga Zapata claims that Hispanic spirituality "is rooted in life (it is) how I relate to the sacred, to others and to myself" (Asi Es 1994, 66).

These descriptions of spirituality touch on two types of relationships: an internal one where I relate to God and to myself and an external one in which I am in relationship to world and neighbor. Spirituality is both root and branches of who I am. It is the corazón that stirs us to action and the corazón that sustains us in hard times.

> Spirituality is that which helps us to relate to God and to each other . . . An individual's spirit relates to that of another and in that relating both spirits are touched and changed. As Hispanics meet and share faith with Latin Americans and Euro-Americans their spirits are growing and their *corazones* are being formed. A new Latino spirituality is being born through this process. (Cavazos-González 2004, 49–50)

Arte: Spirituality

In the latter half of the past century, the separation of spiritual theology and Spirituality became complete. Spiritual theology is a speculative theology. Spirituality, thanks to the work of Spiritualogians like Michael Downey and Mary Frohlich, is seen as discipline that focuses on method, instruction, and appropriation instead of speculative theory. But more than an academic discipline or science, Spirituality is an art that helps direct the praxis of the journey to spiritual growth.

Every art form has need for talent and study, grace and discipline, and so does spirituality. For Latino/as spirituality is first and foremost "life in the Spirit"; it comes from baptism and is lived as a gift from God. Still, it demands training and discipline. As the *Cursillo de Cristiandad* reminds its adherents, growth in Christian life demands prayer, study, and action. Those who would grow spiritually need to practice prayer, study the Word of God and the lives of the Saints, as well as act upon what they have heard in prayer and learned in study.

The Art of Spirituality is developed in the cotidiano. It is an art that needs to be practiced in the routine of life as well as in life's special moments. It is to be found in Latino/a popular religiosity, in popular culture, and in the joys and struggles of everyday life. It is an art that is

> an understanding that emerges as the result of the way the same basic gospel dimensions are combined in the daily life of Christians. The understanding, as I am calling it, must be clear enough to encourage a particular and distinctive way of Christian living and knowing, while at the same time broad or generic enough to allow for growth and individuality (personal and generational). (Espín 1997, 26–27)

Like every art form, spirituality has its master artists. The saints are the master artists whose charitable, just, and miraculous works are masterpieces that inspire awe and wonder. Of course, the only true master is Jesus, who is somehow present in his saints whom he has gifted and trained by his own example and continued inspiration.

Spirituality also has its manual, which is the Word of God, especially as found in the Gospel. Orlando Espín reminds us that popular Catholicism reads the Gospel literally and combines it with noncanonical traditions and "commonsensical wisdom" (Espín 1997, 27). Jean-Pierre Ruiz claims that Latino/as read the Scriptures (printed, painted, and narrated) through a "process of inculturation and actualization that yields productive encounters with biblical texts" (Ruiz 1998, 105). The ways Latina/os encounter the Gospel produce different forms of spiritualities based on how God is perceived in and through the "human experience of Jesus of Nazareth" who in his humanity and passion understands and sympathizes with the poor and the oppressed. In much of Jesus' mission he is reaching out to the marginalized. The most significant moments of Jesus' life are those in which he is being oppressed and made to suffer (Espín 1997, 27).

Latina/o Spirituality(ies)

Jesus' life also reveals his connection to the religiosity of his own people. He and his family practiced the rituals of Judaism, and he worshipped in both synagogue and Temple as well as at home and in the desert. Hispanic theologians like Orlando Espín, Virgilio Elizondo, and Anita de Luna pay particular attention to Latino/a popular religiosity and traditions as manifestations of a *mistica* or espiritualidad Latina. A reading of the book *Así Es* reveals that Latino/as "include the practices of popular religiosity as fundamental and expressive of Hispanic spirituality" (Asi Es, 7). These practices and devotions are steeped in history and tradition. They are handed on from one generation to the next, like a master artist teaches her/his trades to apprentices. Our traditions, devotions, customs, and struggles are the by-product of our spiritualities.

Eduardo C. Fernández points out that Hispanic Spirituality is really a variety of spiritualities because of the diversity of Hispanic cultures and religions that make up the U.S. Latino population (Fernandez 1983, 338–341). These varied spiritualities share several important characteristics. They are relational, emotional, festive, Christocentric, and transcendent. Latino/a spirituality(ies) is relational, especially in that it is nurtured by and helps build up the family. Because of this the matriarchal nature of many Hispanic cultures can be seen in the important role of mothers, grandmothers, and aunts in leading the religious and emotional life of the household and extended family. This relational aspect of Hispanic spirituality is seen in how Hispanics image the holy (God, María, and the Santos).

While many like to maintain that Latino/a spirituality is family oriented (Garcia 2000, 53–54), we need to contextualize that affirmation by saying that Latina/o spirituality is both popular and communal because of the sociocentered nature of many Hispanic cultures. "Popular" does not mean in the order of preference but rather that it comes from and belongs to the people. It is by being part of the people that the individual is formed and cultivated, "traditioned" if you will (Espín 2006, 10). Alvaro Dávila affirms that the "spiritual experience can only be recognized, reflected upon, and understood when we live in continuous dialogue with the memories of a people.

Trying to define the essence of life without this dialogue would result in an incomplete reality" (Asi Es, 87).

Many Latina/o spiritualities were born out of medieval affective spiritualities, and as a result Latino/a spirituality is an emotional spirituality. It focuses on the humanity of Christ and on the love that we can give to him. It comes from and touches the cor- azón of a person and a people. It is lived in the cotidiano with all of its emotional ups and downs. It is a festive spirituality built on *flor y canto* (flower and song, which is to say truth and beauty). Celebration is strong despite the reality of suffering and oppression found in the history and the present of many Hispanic cultures. This festive characteristic is nurtured by the Latino/a belief in Divine Providence or God's gener- ous presence and salvific action in the world. The festive spirit that is at the corazón of Hispanic spirituality turns Church feasts into communal celebrations with food, flowers, song, and dance in honor of Jesus, Mary, and patron saints.

The art of Latino/a Spirituality(ies) stresses Christocentrism, which accentuates relationships over doctrine, action over liturgy. This stress can be a temptation to reduce spirituality to that which makes one feel good, and for this reason we need to constantly evaluate our spirituality, "to measure and balance our orthodoxy and ortho- praxis" (Conde-Frazier 1997, 130). Relationships to God, neighbor, enemy, and self are where one shows her/his imitation of Christ. Jesus' relationship to his Abba extended itself to relationship with others. His life and teaching are interpreted as stressing the preeminence of compassion and solidarity with the poor and margin- alized. Knowledge of Scripture and participation in official liturgy are important, but they are nothing without the *sequela Christi* (walking in the footprints of Jesus). "Jesus will identify as his only those who have acted like him" (Espín 1997, 28). In recent times, the relational nature of Hispanic Spirituality has naturally moved it to the area of social justice. A Christian then is a person committed to the poor, margin- alized and oppressed through a life of solidarity, charity, and justice.

Finally Hispanic spirituality(ies) like all spiritualities is transcendent. It is a *mistica* or mystic in which people dwell, live, and have their being. Spirituality is "connecting to and being led by Christ through the Holy Spirit" (Conde-Frazier 1997, 144). The transcendent implications of this statement cannot be disregarded or ignored for the sake of the solidarity, charity, and justice spoken of above. The social implications of current Latino/a spirituality need to constantly be nourished by the transcendent roots of Christian Spirituality. The spiritual cannot simply be anthropocentric or even eco- centric; it must never forget that it is theocentric. *Si Dios quiere* (If God wills it), *Ojala* (Allah willing), and *Gracias a Dios* (Thanks be to God) are heard often in Latino/a conversations. These are constant reminders of God's presence in the cotidiano and of people's dependence on Divine Providence. The missionaries who taught us to say these things planted the seeds for a Latino/a Spirituality where the transcendent is here and now, already and not yet, where the duality of the sacred and the profane blend into one reality called life.

Conclusion

Christian spirituality is an art that helps direct the praxis of the faithful toward spiritual growth and union with God. This occurs because of the "interaction and weaving together of four dimensions: doctrine, discipline, liturgy, and personal action" (Conde-Frazier 1997, 125). A Mexican *dicho* (saying) claims that *Del dicho al hecho, hay mucho trecho* (from the word to action there is a deep ravine), and the above description of Latino/a spirituality(ies) can remain simply printed words in the lives of many Hispanics. If people are to be traditioned in authentic Christian spirituality, they need parents, relatives, and communities who will do the traditioning. The spiritualogian needs to be an important member of the traditioning community. For this reason Juan Sosa insists that the Latino/a theologian, liturgist, and pastoral minister has a responsibility to her/his people. We are to be messengers of hope and life "ready to walk with them these extra miles by reaching out to them at the deepest core, their 'circle of intangible,' and help them experience the liberating present of the Spirit-at-work within and among them" (Sosa 1998, 77).

References and Further Reading

Cavazos-González, Gilberto. "Cara y Corazón (Face and Heart): Toward a U.S. Latino Spirituality of Inculturation." *New Theology Review* 17 (2004): 46–55.

Conde-Frazier, Elizabeth. "Hispanic Protestant Spirituality." *Teologia en Conjunto: A Collaborative Protestant Theology*, ed. José David Rodriguez and Loida I. Martell-Otero (Louisville, KY: Westminster John Knox Press, 1997).

della Trinita, Beniamino. "Teología Espiritual." *Diccionario de espiritualidad III*, ed. Ermanno Ancilli (Barcelona: Herder, 1983).

Downey, Michael. *Understanding Christian Spirituality* (Mahwah, NJ: Paulist Press, 1997).

Espín, Orlando. *Faith of the People: Theological Reflections on Popular Catholicism* (Maryknoll, NY: Orbis, 1997).

———. "Traditioning: Culture, Daily Life and Popular Religion, and Their Impact on Christian Tradition." *Futuring Our Past: Explorations in the Theology of Tradition*, ed. Orlando O. Espín and Gary Macy (Maryknoll, NY: Orbis, 2006).

Fernández, Eduardo C. "Hispanic Spirituality." *The New Westminster Dictionary of Christian Spirituality*, ed. Philippe Sheldrake (Louisville, KY: Westminster John Knox Press, 1983).

Frohlich, Mary. "Spiritual Discipline, Discipline of Spirituality: Revisiting Questions of Definition and Method."*Spiritus: A Journal of Christian Spirituality* 1 (2001): 65–78.

Garcia, Alberto L. "Christian Spirituality in Light of the U.S. Hispanic Experience." *Word & World* XX (2000): 52–60.

Gutiérrez, Gustavo. *We Drink from Our Own Wells* (Maryknoll, NY: Orbis, 1983).

Moioli, Giovanni. "Teologia spirituale." *Nuovo Dizionario di spiritualità*, ed. Stefano De Fiores and Tullo Goffi (Milano: Edizioni San Paolo, 1985).

Pérez, Arturo, Consuelo Covarrubias, and Edward Foley, eds. *Así Es: Stories of Hispanic Spirituality* (Collegeville, MN: The Liturgical Press, 1994).

Ruiz, Jean-Pierre. "Biblical Interpretation from a U.S. Hispanic American Persepective." *El Cuerpo de Cristo: The Hispanic Presence in the U.S. Catholic Church*, ed. Peter Casarella and Raúl Gómez (New York: Crossroad Publishing Company, 1998).

Sosa, Juan. "Hispanic Liturgy and Popular Religiosity." *El Cuerpo de Cristo: The Hispanic Presence in the U.S. Catholic Church*, ed. Peter Casarella and Raúl Gómez (New York: Crossroad Publishing Company, 1998).

TEOLOGIA EN CONJUNTO

Daniel R. Rodríguez-Díaz

Teología en conjunto is a particular way of doing theology in a collaborative way. This method of doing theology relies on a polyphonic conversation where issues faced by the Latina/o diasporas, internally and in its relations with the larger American culture and the world, are addressed in light of the Christian faith. Through this method, Latino/a faith communities start by questioning the traditional way of doing theology, where modernity is assumed as normative and the standard narrative—beliefs and cultural trends—persists. It is a theology of and from the borderlands, one that mainly deals with the senses of life, where borderlands/diasporas become a discursive space to do theology. In this respect, the traditional ways of doing theology in the cultures of origin are also seen as suspect, particularly when the hermeneutics of dominance tend to prevail. This theological method requires a set of new lenses when "reading" Christian tradition, experience, and the cultures under consideration.

Historical Development

We can trace a long history of doing theology in conjunction with the Hispanic experience, especially during key moments of that history when the hermeneutics of dominance and cultural exclusion have threatened to silence the many voices of faith. Yet these voices contained distinctive tones and lyrics revealing their humanity and spiritual quest, even though these voices are not monolithic. Latina/o communities are diverse in many ways—history, religious traditions, countries of origin, generational lines—and while making it difficult to define these communities as a whole by using such names as Hispanic or Latina/o, they do share many things in common.

Two empires led the process—the Spanish was first, and in the nineteenth century the young "American Empire" took over. Centuries before the political formation of the United States, the first moment can be identified when members of religious orders and native people joined together their voices of faith. They sought to respond to the so-called "discovery," which soon turned into conquest and colonization. For instance, Antonio de Montesinos and Bartolomé de las Casas accused European

761

Christian colonizers of injustice for imposing slavery upon indigenous peoples. During the rule of the Spanish empire, the Regal Patronage served as the theological and legal foundation of the dominant ecclesiology. The church sought to safeguard its presence through the mediation of the state, and vice versa, the state gained legitimacy through the mediation of the church.

After independence in Latin America and the Caribbean to the present, a national oligarchy came to rule and plunder both human and natural resources. The European experience, assumed to be universally applicable, served to interpret Latin American/Caribbean history. The source of their hermeneutics, derived from a providential theory of history, generated an ideology of dominance wrapped in a theological/biblical language. The ecclesiology of Christendom—a particular way for church and civil society to relate to each other, where the state is the primary mediation—becomes the operating ecclesiology in this context.

The whole European experience was assumed to be applicable to Spanish and Portuguese domination in America; the medieval legal and theological system was transferred and used as the valid one. This reality would impact the way non-Europeans do their theology, mainly because they assume as normative both the European values and historical experience. This European methodology, where the epistemological conceptualization of Western culture is superimposed upon Catholic history, is found in the writings of theologians and interpreters of Scripture who championed the struggles for justice and freedom. With an inherently faulty epistemology to interpret colonial history, these voices are heard all over America and Europe. In spite of the limitations, they are able to offer alternatives to the realities of oppression during a period of approximately four centuries. A type of teologia en conjunto results from this experience, lacking a Latin American history of salvation identical to the theoretical thinking of the official theology of the church. For this integration to occur, we have to wait until the 1960s with the emergence of Third World liberation theologies, particularly in Latin America, assuming praxis as the source of theological thinking.

The Anglo-American Christendom

What occurs during the Anglo-American Christendom is "mainline" Protestantism playing a similar role and methodology in the task of doing theology. Instead of having just one single church or denomination mediating or legitimizing the state, we find many denominations, Protestant and Catholic. During the latter part of the twentieth century, evangelical Christianity is able to negotiate a new political/religious consensus with the present ruling elite intending to bring a modified version of cultural, political, and religious dominance.

For most of the twentieth century, the expressions for doing collaborative theology were limited by several factors. The first limiting factor was availability of sources, primary and secondary, and as a result the history of most churches found limited opportunities to be studied. Archival materials were scattered, often preserved in less than optimal conditions, and generally inaccessible. Hence the urgency to continue working in projects related to the preservation of oral histories and the rescue of archival material that is being destroyed through inadequate preservation. The second limiting factor was related to the dominance of a particular narrative—the Protestant-Puritan tradition—and its superimposition on Latina/o Church history. The third limiting factor was related to access to publishing houses.

All these began to change less than 20 years ago. Although we have to recognize many people who have collaborated for more than 20 years changing the theological map, two people need to be recognized as mentoring the whole process: Justo L. González, a Protestant historian, and Virgilio Elizondo, a Roman Catholic priest. With many others, women and men, a new school of collaborative theology was born. Always in conjunction with others, they helped in this process by their example—by trying to remain faithful to their vocation as theologians and pastors, and by leading in the organization and implementation of the most recent expression of doing collaborative Hispanic theology.

Since teologia en conjunto requires dialogue, it must be grounded in community. To be good theology it has to be practical; this means grounded in the people's senses of life up against the forces that seek to diminish or deny their humanity. In reality, what this represents is the recovery of the communal nature of Scripture, its principles, and its practices, where only a small portion of the Scriptures was intended for private reading. This represents a significant shift of the way theology was previously done. It is a theology from the people, by the people, and for the people, a theology of resistance, coming from the womb of an always reforming church, and by theologians who have discovered continuity with the origins of Christianity.

The 1960s left a strong legacy with the Black Civil Rights Movement, Black Power, the emergence of a Black theology, and the civil rights struggles in Latina/o communities coalesced to empower oppressed peoples around the world. The struggle to organize the community led by Latino/a women and men challenged the myth of docility held by Anglo-American church leaders. After years of relative silence, Latina/o communities across the United States raised their voices in protest; the actions were directed at both the institutional church and the larger society. A long fought issue among Hispanic church people was the lack of institutional representation. There were few Hispanic Catholic priests or Protestant pastors in the churches. Little effort was made to encourage and recruit Latino/as to church vocations. Theological education was so culturally specific that the only way to be considered ready for ministry was surrendering to total assimilation.

In the Catholic Church, the theology that resulted from Vatican II had a significant impact in Hispanic communities. Three basic theological principles were affirmed: (a) a church opened to the world with an evangelizing and humanizing mission; (b) the church present and "incarnated" in a culturally plural world that is also the world of the poor; (c) the church as the people of God where both laity and clergy work united in mission and ministry.

What Vatican II gave to the Latina/o community was a theology congruent with their praxis in a context of exclusion. The reaction of many church leaders was opposite to the reforms presented by the Council. This meant a long struggle within the church, one characterized by a traditional discourse trying to maintain the status quo led by Euro-Americans, while on the opposite side was the new theology led by Latino/a pastors and lay. Organizations like PADRES, an acronym for Priests Associated for Religious, Educational, and Social Rights, defined their mission to be "the voice of the voiceless" Hispanics. In 1971, a group of Latina religious women gathered in Houston and organized Las Hermanas to work in the fields of education, health, pastoral work, and sociology. The same year another important organization was born, the Mexican American Cultural Center (MACC), led by Father Elizondo. This effort represented the belief that Latino/as needed their own institutions. MACC's mission is to deal with issues of culture, pastoral service, preparation of missionaries, research and publications, media, and leadership development. This institution would become a center for promoting collaborative work in many fields, such as theology, Bible, Church History, Ethics, Pastoral Care, and Liturgy.

In 1988, the Academy of Catholic Hispanic Theologians of the United States (ACHTUS) was founded as a forum for sharing and discussing ideas and projects among U.S. Hispanic theologians. Their work is en conjunto; they understand that Latino/a theology cannot be anything but en conjunto. Nor can it be a copy or a "translation" of Latin American or Euro-American theologies. The theological method applied requires academic rigor and is not satisfied with merely seeking understanding, but how it impacts people's lives and histories.

From the beginning, ACHTUS's journal defined itself as a forum of and for Hispanic scholarship centered on "ideas that affect and/or enrich U.S. Latino theology." It has become a truly ecumenical journal where Protestant Latino/a theologians are important partners in an important project. Here both theologians and social scientists are continuously engaged in serious dialogue.

During the 1960s, Protestant participation in social issues was limited. Typically it was more based on the individual participation of Latino/a Protestants, lay and clergy, and few congregations. This was due in part to the internal struggles faced by the Hispanic churches in their denominations that showed little regard and commitment to a Latino/a church. The growth and vitality of the churches was dependent on their own resources and leadership imported from the countries of origin, more than on the connectional system of the denomination. The values and strategies of some denominations were more an obstacle than a help during this period.

The theological response to this situation came from people like Orlando Costas. His works were clearly written in the key of we-hermeneutics. Other collective voices were also heard during those years. For example, in 1981 the "Coalition of Hispanic Christian Leadership," a group of pastors, headed by Benjamin Alicea, which also included a laywoman, attended a conference at Riverside Church in New York City to protest the exclusion of Hispanics from the conference program. The group disrupted a panel on "Liberation Theology" by chanting ¡Basta ya. No nos pueden ignorar! (Enough. You cannot ignore us!). This was followed by the reading of a document the group called the "Riverside Manifesto."

The Manifesto included five complaints and demands: (1) social issues of the Hispanic community were not seriously addressed; (2) the contributions of Hispanic people were ignored; (3) the American religious establishment must assume its share of the responsibility; (4) Hispanic liturgy and theology had been denied its rightful place in the American religious community; and (5) theological seminaries and graduate schools of religion had discriminated against Hispanics.

LA COMUNIDAD

The organization La Comunidad (The Community) was founded on November 19, 1989, originally as La Comunidad of Hispanic American Scholars of Theology and Religion, and was reorganized and revitalized in 2000–2001. As an ecumenical association of Latina/o scholars of religion, La Comunidad proactively advances the interests and scholarship of Latinas and Latinos in biblical, theological, and religious studies. Membership in La Comunidad is open to Hispanics and non-Hispanics in sympathy with the stated mission and objectives of the organization and residing in the United States, Canada, and Puerto Rico. La Comunidad affirms the multilingual and multicultural scholarly expressions of its members; regularly hosts meetings and/or conferences of its members and interested parties; and seeks to be a supportive advocate for the employment, tenure, and promotion of Latina/os in biblical, theological, and religious studies. The majority of its members also hold membership in the American Academy of Religion, the Society of Biblical Literature, or both scholarly organizations. La Comunidad is Related Scholarly Organizations (RSO) of the American Academy of Religion and works in supportive collaboration with the Latino/a Religion, Culture and Society Group of the American Academy of Religion (formerly the Hispanic American Religion, Culture and Society Group).

—EDA

In the Southwest, the Mexican American Program at Perkins School of Theology represents another effort in building communities of collaboration. In 1975, Dr. Roy D. Barton started the Hispanic Instructors Program; its members meet at least once a year for formation and for sharing experiences from diverse teaching settings. Among the many accomplishments of this collaborative effort are the following: the journal *Apuntes*—a journal of Hispanic theology; a series of symposia under the title of "Redescubrimiento," planned around the theme of the Quincentennial of 1492; and programs for the training of laity in theology and in the practice of ministry.

In the spring of 1993, a national conference of Latina/o scholars and church leaders met at McCormick Theological Seminary in Chicago, under the leadership of Daniel R. Rodriguez, Professor of Church History at the Seminary. The purpose was to form a network of persons working on Latino/a Protestant Church History, to exchange information, to assess needs, and to begin planning future steps. As an outcome of the event, a book was published under the title *Hidden Stories: Unveiling the History of the Latino Church*. New initiatives were undertaken that included the organization of the Asociación para la Educación Teológica Hispana (AETH), the Hispanic Summer Program, La Comunidad, and the Hispanic Theological Initiative.

Another example of this collaboration was the event held early in the summer of 1995, when a group of Latina/os Protestant theologians, ethicists, pastors, and students gathered at Princeton Seminary with a very particular agenda: to discuss the distinctiveness of doing theology in a collaborative way. Two main characteristics were recognized during this event: First, that it is plural; it is as diverse as the communities

HISPANIC SUMMER PROGRAM

The Hispanic Summer Program, Inc. (HSP), also known as *el Programa Hispano de Verano*, is a graduate ecumenical program in theology and religion established in 1988. Noted historian and theologian Justo L. González with others created the HSP in response to a report he wrote on the state of Hispanic theological education, including the deplorably low numbers of Hispanic seminary graduates. While originally part of the Fund for Theological Education (FTE), in 1995 again, through the leadership of González, the HSP was relaunched as an independent consortium of sponsoring institutions including seminaries, university-related divinity schools, and graduate departments of religion. The HSP provides study and fellowship with Latino/a peers and non-Hispanics interested in Hispanic ministry through an intensive program of study, celebration, and cultural awareness. Approximately 100 students and eight Hispanic faculty gather at one of the sponsoring host sites, the location of which changes yearly. Typically, half of the courses are taught in Spanish and half in English. Additionally, the HSP offers another program for faculty of the sponsoring institutions, "Through Hispanic Eyes: A Seminar for Non-Hispanic Faculty," which provides an opportunity for non-Hispanic faculty to explore issues related to the teaching, contributions, recruitment, support, and participation of Latinos/as in academic programs, in churches, and in communities.

—EDA

where the method of doing theology is practiced. Second, that it is communal; as such it is inspired by a collaborative spirit. The themes discussed reflected their experiences as members of particular communities of faith. At the same time, the interactions during the encounter raised new questions and challenges to the participants, as well as a confirmation of the significance of doing theological work collaboratively.

The Theological Method

This theology has as its purpose to give both a foundation and an order to the faith of people from a plurality of cultures. It also enables them to interpret and project their lives, while engaging with the larger society where they find a particular cultural group that has assumed their way of doing theology as normative to the whole. The method defines a particular discursive space—borderlands/diaspora—to do theology. This means that theologians are located, side by side, with the oppressed and marginalized when doing theology. They take clues from a theology of the incarnate word (John 1:13)—"and lived among us." So it is a theology whose method seeks to be incarnational. For this reason, doing theology from your place also becomes autobiographical. It is not "talking" about "the oppressed" or "the people" (the objects of theology), it becomes more "we," thus requiring the use of we-hermeneutics in the shaping of a theological discourse.

People on the move with a plurality of cultures, traditions, and experiences require a portable method when doing theology. Any attempt to do theology runs into the

HISPANIC CHURCHES IN AMERICAN PUBLIC LIFE

The Pew Charitable Trusts funded $1.3 million for a research project to be conducted from 1999 through 2002. The project was named the Hispanic Churches in American Public Life (HCAPL). It brought together Jesse Miranda, a Pentecostal, and Virgilio Elizondo, a Roman Catholic. Gastón Espinosa was asked to develop and manage the study. The HCAPL project was the largest study ever conducted in the United States that specifically focused on Latino/a religions and politics. It surveyed and profiled the attitudes of 3,000 Latinos across the United States and in Puerto Rico and commissioned 16 original essays that explored the influence of Hispanic religions on political, civic, and social action. It was an ecumenical and nonsectarian study that sought to examine the impact of religion on political, civic, and social engagement among U.S. Latino/as. The Pew Charitable Trusts first approached Miranda about directing the study himself; however, in an effort to build bridges with the Latina/o Catholic community, he informed the Trusts that he would not accept the project unless they brought on a Latino Catholic leader like Elizondo to co-direct the project. The Trusts agreed. Miranda and Elizondo agreed to work together to address the social, political, and civic needs of the Latino/a community without having to set aside or "water-down" their deep theological convictions.

—GE

challenge presented by the wide variety within the Latina/o spectrum. When you consider the peoples of the southwestern region of the United States, you have to take into account centuries of constructing a narrative inspired by Spanish missions that were far away from the political centers of power of church life. Geography in great part required a portable method of doing theology. The isolation of many communities forced pastors to celebrate Mass in a community chapel only a few times a year. The major responsibility for evangelization rested in the families or a group of local laypersons. The daily life of the church was in the hands of lay leaders. They conducted burials, the ceremonies of Holy Week, including a reenactment of the events of Good Friday, as well as other religious activities of the Christian calendar. This kind of religious and social autonomy generated liturgies, hymns, and beliefs grounded in a communally inspired and constructed theological narrative.

As it was in the past, the same is today. Hispanic people are always on the move, always in search of jobs, better housing, schools, working conditions, safe neighborhoods, and places of worship. As in the past, religious institutions are not always prepared to offer the kind of hospitality and spiritual life for people who are already "walking with Jesus" or with "my virgencita." Many become "tent makers," releasing from their treasured memory the wealth of their spirituality, believed to come from the presence of God's Spirit in them. As in the past, today we find the laypeople carrying a major responsibility in the production of liturgies, hymns, and belief systems grounded in communally inspired theologies.

A Challenge to the Dominant Narrative

This theology is critical of both U.S. and Latin American/Caribbean historiography. It seeks to give a new meaning to the United States history—in particular it exposes the origins of the ideology of Manifest Destiny and sense of superiority characteristic of the dominant narrative. In American historiography the interpretative center of the dominant school has been the Protestant-Puritan tradition. It becomes primarily an emphasis on the religion transplanted by European immigrants, to the exclusion of the varying histories of Native Americans, African Americans, women, Latino/as, Catholics, Jews, Asian Americans, and ethnic Whites, whose identities have been obscured by the historical hegemony of the White Anglo-Saxon narrative. The resulting theologies tend to be shaped by the same ideology. The language used becomes the expression of a hermeneutics of conquest and suppression. It is a language that conceals domination and renders invisible all those who fail to participate in the same narrative and its underlying cultural experiences. It is the story centered on the telling and retelling of the mighty acts of the White conqueror.

The Euro-American religious history is still the center of interpretation for American Christianity in both Protestant and Catholic historiography. Catholic Church historians have given little attention to Latina/os, in spite of the fact that the church had been in the Southwest for more than 250 years when the United States seized the entire territory from Mexico in 1846. Most historians still imply that non-Hispanic clergy established the church. In their narratives, when Hispanics are mentioned, their stories are told with a functional "plot." The tendency is to make the selection that "best" represents the other stories.

Many contemporary historians work with a reformed version of the old canon where the religious values and vision of "America" as defined by the old paradigm are now extended to the other stories. Here the criterion is to identify the "contributions" of other traditions to the values defined by the standard narrative. The parts that do not fit into the scheme are treated as marginal.

The conquest and colonization of the Americas was also based on the same premise, a providential interpretation of the historical events with a theological-legal language that offered its rationality. The Protestant-Puritan tradition and the institution of the Regal Patronage were grounded in the premise of having God's favor. A sacred Mayan prayer from the Popul Vuh represents the voice of the majority of the conquered and colonized: "Remember us after we are gone. Don't forget us. Conjure up our faces and our words. Our image will be as a tear in the hearts of those who want to remember us."

The recovery of the historical memory is at the heart of doing theology en conjunto. It is an important tool for the critical dialogue with 500 years of colonial and neocolonial relations. Among the key elements in the process of recovery we find the resistance to submit to injustice and cultural annihilation. The present response and questioning of those who claim cultural and historical dominance with a corresponding theology becomes the next chapter in that long history to maintain the vitality of Hispanic culture and the dignity of those who are still forging it.

When doing theology in context the challenge is to be open to the possibility that cultures are also under judgment and that they are in need of transforming. The experience of recovery brings both dangerous memories as well as the joy of naming the fruits of our labor under duress. This experience goes both ways, remembering the struggles of our ancestors, and remembering the struggles and the history of resistance of the many who suffered slavery, discrimination, and exclusion in North America since the founding of Jamestown in 1607 in the territory of the Great Powhatan Confederacy.

This experience helps us connect with other people and their histories, allowing for the enlargement of the social space where life informs theological reflection. Through this process, new theologies of convergence keep emerging and the experience of living in community with a liberating vision expands beyond Latina/o communities. The method of doing theology en conjunto serves as a tool to respond to a major epistemological problem created by the cultural and social walls separating the many communities constituting the United States. This theology does not represent an attempt to add another theology to the mix, this way leaving the dominant narrative as normative, perhaps with a few modifications to give room to the "best" of what the "others" can contribute. The result of this effort is deceiving because the old standard prevails. The religious values and vision of the United States as defined by the old paradigm are now extended to other narratives, and the parts that do not fit into the scheme are treated as marginal.

What this method of doing theology intends to do is go beyond the issue of the hermeneutics of historical and theological inclusion or exclusion, and explore theologically the question of how the history of both the excluded and the included reveal the underlying contradictions of American society. This is why we need the kind of social analysis that offers critical insights into multiple religious histories of the American people. At the same time we need to examine the question of how far the traditional narrative has served to reinforce certain values, cognition, and symbols as a way to impose a particular worldview, social order, and values, while not ignoring the fruits of other cultures around the same national table, though many times in the same space but separate rooms.

This conversation forces one to address issues related to Hispanic tradition, theology, and culture. It becomes a conversation in which the community is confronted with the contradictions that are part of their particular pasts. These contradictions cut across denominational and confessional lines. Latina women speak of issues and experiences that Hispanic men, and members of the dominant culture, tend to ignore or misinterpret. Dominicans, Salvadorans, Puerto Ricans, Mexican Americans, Cubans, and many others bring their own agendas relevant to their communities.

While the conversation with the dominant culture continues, theologians, biblical scholars, historians, and people in the practice of ministry engage in conversations in/with their communities and they task themselves with taking a critical view of the community's theological legacy. They discover that traditional themes do not disappear or lose interest; it is only that they are presented differently in light of their reality. Since the point of departure for doing collaborative theology is marked by the concrete practices of Christians, questions related to issues of faith are raised about specific interpretations of revelation. Using this method, theology is concerned with and engaged in exploring transforming actions and social relations in light of the revelation. Simultaneously, theology asks the question on the impact that Hispanic reality has on the interpretation of revelation itself. Revelation interprets practice, while practice makes possible a new interpretation of revelation. Out of this communal effort emerges a new theological vein called Latina/o theology.

For some, Latino/a theology can only remain alive when it is narrated by members of the community. The crisis of the grand postmodern narrative as told in the United States opens the space for small theological narratives to be told and valued. In this regard, the work of Hispanic biblical scholars is essential. The significance of their effort lies in the fact that they listen attentively to the original story of the Jesus Christ event, and they tell it again to women, men, and children today. Telling and retelling the story requires an active memory in a community. By so doing, new generations will receive in an intelligible way God's saving events.

This kind of narrative, based on the incarnational model, demands a great deal from the reader or listener, in great part because it is based on life experiences. More than an intellectual exercise where the goal is the accumulation of information, it is more an opportunity to be open to the message of the narrative. On the side of the theologian, it is less demanding academically but more demanding existentially, since it assumes that the theologian must incarnate the narrative. Other theologians rely more on the identification of theological themes without too much regard for finding a unifying paradigm. We find such themes as the theology of la fiesta, the table, hymns/*coritos*, etc. There are still others more inclined to theologize novels, short stories, and other works of art.

Collaborative Theology and Mission

Collaborative theology is missional rather than definitional in its foundation. Among the challenges faced by theologians one finds the question of how to relate to the institutional church, which seems to be encapsulated in the worldview, values, and cognitions of the traditional American narrative. In this entry, we reviewed history with its contradictions, and how diasporic faith communities are claiming to possess new experiences of God's revelation in Jesus Christ. When considering that many Hispanic Catholics are not active in the church, and church growth in mainline Protestant denominations is less than significant, theologians are starting to explore clues to help identify the reasons.

One clue is found in the need to create community. Our faith proclaims that God is a communion of persons—different persons, but equal and living together in perfect communion. The present North American neoliberal context declares the value of the individual as supreme. The tendency of the individual is to isolate and seek her or his own welfare with limited or no concern for others. The end result is social fragmentation and a "survival of the fittest" attitude. Borderland/diasporic communities are always struggling with the forces of fragmentation. The experience of moving from their communities of origin entails a fragmentation from the core of their cultural systems; in their pilgrimage they depend on their memory and all the cultural objects accompanying them.

This is why the focus to mission includes the recovery of what is at the heart of Christianity. Beginning with the Hebrew Bible, the building of a just and affirming community is central; Jesus of Nazareth calls a group of disciples to a community and, through God's Spirit, promotes the formation of communities. In the midst of a religious culture that places high value on narrow satisfactions of individual needs or wants, borderlands/diaspora communities need to promote the well-being of the entire community. The temptation to deny it is also present, manifesting itself in ecclesiologies of isolation and churchism. For this reason, a collaborative theology promotes the creation of Christian communities congruent with the message and practice of Jesus. The promotion of this value becomes a high priority when defining mission in the North American context. Good theology ratifies the value of the community, and help breaks the power of subjective individualism that sacrifices the well-being of the community. Collaborative theology tries to balance the value of the individual and the collective. Living in community, persons should find space for their own subjectivity, as well as enough room for life in solidarity with others.

Another clue is found in the affirmation that cultural plurality is God's gift to humanity, followed by a critical analysis of human cultures, based on the assumption that the seeds of human brokenness grow and destroy community. A typical danger is to "see the speck in your neighbor's eye, but do not notice the log in your own eye." Borderland people are not exempt from just seeing the speck in their neighbor's eye; this "neighbor" could be the Anglo-American, a Latin American nation, gender, education, or religion. This limitation could lead to practices of exclusion, when in fact the idea of being critical is to enter into a creative dialogue in which both sides should expect renewal and the forging of an inclusive community. The reality is that these communities are all influenced by the enlightenment culture of modernity. This culture is based on the idea/power that human reason has unlimited power to guide and build an always better future, by means of a self-clarifying process of enlightenment.

In summary, teologia en conjunto is a theology of and from the borderlands, done in a collaborative way, working in unity and resistance with groups, sectors and leaders across gender, generations, racial-ethnic, nationalities, and denominational boundaries. This theology seeks to transform the church in order to become a church with a preferential option for the poor, seeking peace, justice, and reconciliation in the world. The method requires a critique of the interpretive lenses used when looking at Christian tradition, human experience, and culture.

References and Further Reading

Aponte, Edwin David, and Miguel A. De La Torre, eds. *Handbook of Latina/o Theologies* (St. Louis: Chalice Press, 2006).

Fernández, Eduardo C. *La Cosecha: Harvesting Contemporary United States Hispanic Theology (1972–1998)* (Collegeville, MN: The Liturgical Press, 2000).

Isasi-Díaz, Ada María, and Fernando Segovia, eds. *Hispanic/Latino Theology: Challenge and Promise* (Minneapolis: Fortress Press, 1996).

Padilla, Alvin, Roberto Goizueta, and Eldin Villafañe, eds. *Hispanic Christian Thought at the Dawn of the 21st Century: Apuntes in Honor of Justo L. González* (Nashville: Abingdon Press, 2005).

Rodriguez, Jose David, and Loida I. Martell-Otero, eds. *Teologia en Conjunto: A Collaborative Hispanic Protestant Theology* (Louisville, KY: Westminster John Knox Press, 1997).

About the Editor

Dr. Miguel A. De La Torre immigrated to the United States from Cuba with his family in 1959 and grew up as a practitioner of Catholicism and Santería. An ordained Southern Baptist minister, he holds a doctorate in social ethics and is associate professor for social ethics at the Iliff School of Theology in Denver, Colorado. He has also served as director of the Society of Christian Ethics and the American Academy of Religion. Dr. De La Torre has specialized in applying a social scientific approach to Latino/a religiosity within the United States, Liberation theologies in the Caribbean and Latin America, and postmodern/postcolonial social theory. He has written numerous articles and authored more than 17 books, including *Reading the Bible from the Margins*; *Santería: The Beliefs and Rituals of a Growing Religion in America*; and *Doing Christian Ethics from the Margins*.

List of Contributors

Anna Adams, Muhlenberg College (AA)

Efrain Agosto, Hartford Seminary (EA)

Alan Aja, Brooklyn College of the city University of New York (AAA)

Carmelo E. Álvarez, Christian Theological Seminary (CEA)

Edwin David Aponte, Lancaster Theological Seminary (EDA)

Hector Avalos, Iowa State University (HA)

Eric Daniel Barreto, Luther Seminary (EDB)

Luis E. Benavides, First United Methodist Church, Pittsfield, MA (LEB)

Fernando A. Cascante-Gómez, Union-PSCE (FCG)

Daniel Castelo, Seattle Pacific University (DC)

Gilberto Cavazos-González, Catholic Theological Union (GCG)

Elizabeth Conde-Frazier, Esperanza College of Eastern University (ECF)

Alejandro Crosthwaite, Pontifical University of St. Thomas Aquinas (AC)

Kenneth G. Davis, Saint Meinrad School of Theology (KGD)

Miguel A. De La Torre, Iliff School of Theology (MAD)

Neomi DeAnda, Loyola University, Chicago (NDA)

Miguel H. Díaz, College of Saint Benedict and Saint John's University (MHD)

Ana María Díaz-Stevens, Union Theological Seminary (ADS)

John-Charles Duffy, University of North Carolina, Chapel Hill (JCD)

Orlando O. Espin, University of San Diego (OOE)

Gastón Espinosa, Claremont McKenna College (GE)

Octavio Javier Esqueda, Southwestern Baptist Theological Seminary (OJE)

Eduardo C. Fernández, Jesuit School of Theology, Graduate Theological Union (ECF)

Arelis M. Figueroa, Union Theological Seminary, New York City (AMF)

Daniel F. Flores, Sociedad Wesleyana, (DFF)

Ismael Garciá, Austin Presbyterian Theological Seminary (IG)

Oscar García-Johnson, Fuller Theological Seminary (OGJ)

Roberto S. Goizueta, Boston College (RSG)

Raúl Gómez-Ruiz, Sacred Heart School of Theology (RG)

Rudy D. González, Southwestern Baptist Theological Seminary (RDG)

Juan Martinez Guerra, Fuller Seminary (JMG)

Andrés Quetzalcóatl Gonzalés Guerrero, Aims Community College (AQG)

Albert Hernández, Iliff School of Theology (AH)

Rodolfo J. Hernández-Díaz, University of Denver/Iliff School of Theology (RHD)

Anne Hoffman, Brooklyn College (ADH)

José Irizarry, Seminario Evangélico de Puerto Rico (JI)

Ada María Isasi-Díaz, Drew University (AMI)

David Manuel Lantigua, University of Notre Dame (DML)

Salvador A. Leavitt-Alcántara, Graduate Theological Union, Berkeley (SLA)

Luis D. León, University of Denver (LDL)

Virginia Loubriel-Chévere, Iglesia Cristiana (Discipulos de Cristo) en Puerto Rico (VLC)

Nora O. Lozano, Baptist University of the Americas, (NOL)

Rafael Luévano, Chapman University (RL)

Ramón Luzárraga, University of Dayton, Ohio (RL)

David Maldonado Jr., Perkins School of Theology (DMJ)

Loida I. Martell-Otero, Palmer Theological Seminary (LMO)

Juan Francisco Martinez, Fuller Theological Seminary (JFM)

Hjamil A. Martínez-Vázquez, Texas Christian University (HMV)

Timothy Matovina, University of Notre Dame (TM)

Lara Medina, California State University, Northridge (LM)

Néstor Medina, University of Toronto (NM)

David M. Mellott, Lancaster Theological Seminary (DMM)

José Daniel Montañez, Asociacion para la Educacion Teologica Hispana (JDM)

Nathaniel Samuel Murrells, University of North Carolina, Wilmington (NSM)

Carmen M. Nanko-Fernández, Catholic Theological Union (CMN)

Adriana Pilar Nieto, University of Denver/Iliff School of Theology (APN)

Oswald John Nira, Our Lady of the Lake University (OJN)

Eloy H. Nolivos, Regent University (EHN)

Elias Ortega-Aponte, Princeton Theological Seminary (EDA)

Fernando A. Ortiz, Gonzaga University (FAO)

Luis G. Pedraja, Middle States Commission on Higher Education (LGP)

Laura E. Pérez, University of California, Berkeley (LEP)

Leopoldo Perez, Oblate School of Theology (LP)

Ernesto Pichardo, Church of the Lukumi Babalu Aye, Hileah, FL (EP)

Santiago O. Piñón, University of Chicago (SOP)

Jose T. Poe, Casa Bautista de Publicaciones, El Paso, TX (JTP)

Rebeca M. Radillo, New York Theological Seminary (RMR)

Ricardo Hugo Rangel, University of California, San Diego (RHR)

Sarah J. Rangel-Sanchez, Washington State University, Pullman (SJR)

Elizabeth D. Rios, Center for Emerging Female Leadership and Save the Nations (EDR)

Luis Rivera-Rodriguez, McCormick Theological Seminary (LRR)

Daniel A. Rodriguez, Pepperdine University (DAR)

Joanne Rodríguez-Olmedo, Princeton Theological Seminary (JRO)

Daniel R. Rodríguez-Díaz, McCormick Theological Seminary (DRD)

Leopoldo A. Sánchez M., Concordia Seminary (LAS)

Ben Sanders III, University of Denver/Iliff School of Theology (BS)

Teresa Chávez Sauceda (TCS)

Anthony M. Stevens-Arroyo, Brooklyn College (ASA)

Adán Stevens-Díaz, Brooklyn College (ASD)

Christopher Tirres, DePaul University (CT)

Hector Luis Torres, The Chicago School of Psychology (HLT)

Larry Torres, University of New Mexico, Taos (LT)

Theresa L. Torres, University of Missouri, Kansas City (TLT)

Benjamin Valentin, Andover Newton Theological School (BV)

Alicia Vargas, Pacific Lutheran Theological Seminary, Berkeley (AV)

Manuel A. Vásquez, The University of Florida (MAV)

Marta Vides Saade, Ramapo College of New Jersey (MVS)

Philip Wingeier-Rayo, Pfeiffer University (PWR)

Index